a49102.

Presented

August 1993

THE FEMALE
POETS
OF GREAT BRITAIN

THE FEMALE
P⬢ETS
OF GREAT BRITAIN

CHRONOLOGICALLY ARRANGED

WITH COPIOUS SELECTIONS AND CRITICAL REMARKS

BY FREDERIC ROWTON

A FACSIMILE OF THE 1853 EDITION WITH A CRITICAL

INTRODUCTION AND BIBLIOGRAPHICAL APPENDICES

BY MARILYN L. WILLIAMSON

WAYNE STATE UNIVERSITY PRESS • DETROIT, 1981

Library of Congress Cataloging in Publication Data

Rowton, Frederic, 1818-1854.

The female poets of Great Britain.

1. English poetry—Women authors. I. Williamson, Marilyn L., 1927-   II. Title.

PR1177.R7 1980 821'.008'09287   80-22484

ISBN 0-8143-1664-6

ACKNOWLEDGMENTS

I wish to thank the following people who have helped in the preparation of the introduction and appendices to *Female Poets:* George Masterton of the Purdy Library, Wayne State University, for compiling the data used in Sources, Sherwyn Carr and Barbara Woodward at the Wayne State University Press for guidance in the early stages of the writing of the Introduction, and Wendy Lyon Wienner for valuable editorial assistance. *Female Poets* is, in several ways, Wendy's book.

M.L.W.

CONTENTS

A NOTE ON THE FACSIMILE EDITION

The text presented here in facsimile is from the second printing of one of the American editions. The book was published in several English and American editions: (1) *The female poets of Great Britain, chronologically arranged: with copious selections and critical remarks by Frederic Rowton.* London: Longman, Brown, Green, and Longmans, 1848. xxviii, 508 p.; another printing, 185?. (2) *The female poets of Great Britain, chronologically arranged . . . with additions of an American editor, and elegantly engraved illustrations by celebrated artists.* Philadelphia: Carey and Hart, 1849. xviii, 25-533 p.; another printing, Philadelphia: H. C. Baird, 1854 (Baird was successor to Carey and Hart); another printing, Philadelphia: H. C. Baird, 1856. (3) *Cyclopaedia of female poets; chronologically arranged with copious selections and critical remarks, with additions by an American editor.* Philadelphia: J. B. Lippincott, [185?]; another printing, [1874]; one copy, n.d. 533 p. (4) *Cyclopaedia. . . . Complete in one large royal octavo volume. Illustrated with numerous steel engravings.* Dayton, Ohio: Alvin Peabody, 1883. xviii, 25-533 p.

This publishing history suggests that an important audience for *Female Poets* existed in America. The Lippincott and Peabody *Cyclopaedias* were pirated editions, the Carey and Hart edition under a different title. Similarly, George Bethune's competing anthology, *The British Female Poets* (1848) also appeared as *Pearls from the British Female Poets*. Pirating each other's foreign books was a common practice among publishers in mid-century America,[1] and the piracy of these anthologies is some testimony to their popularity.

The copyright date of the anthology is a puzzle which might be explained by the American publisher's anticipation of piracy. The copyright date is 1848 for both the first American edition and the first British edition, yet all extant copies of the first American edition were published in 1849. It is possible that, as Matthew Carey and Thomas Longman had an agreement concerning exclusive sale of advance sheets, the American firm of Carey and Hart copyrighted the British edition in 1848 while preparing the American edition, with suitable additions, for their 1849 printing, doing so in a futile attempt to protect their rights in the United States. Before the advent of international copyright, when publication in both Britain and the United States was anticipated, a title page was first deposited in Washington and the book then published in Britain to establish copyright. The book was then officially published in America, copies being deposited in Washington within ten days.[2] The explanation above remains tentative, for the date on the text reproduced here is 1853, and the date entered for the second Baird edition, of which it is presumably a copy, is 1854. Publication late in the year for Christmas sales might account for some of these discrepancies.

Comparison of the original British edition of 1848 with American editions by Carey and Hart in 1849 and Baird in 1854 and 1856 reveals that the American editions were completely reset. The content of Rowton's Preface, Introductory Chapter, and paraphernalia for individual poets has been reproduced exactly by the American editor, with additions of the poets' work and appropriate commentary interspersed according to chronology.

The anonymous American editor of *Female Poets* was very possibly Rufus Griswold, who prepared for Carey and Hart several anthologies of American poetry, including *Female Poets of America* (1849). A glance at the poems the American editor added to *Female Poets of Great Britain* shows some selection for American taste, such as "The American Forest Girl" and "The Landing of the Pilgrim Fathers" by Charlotte Elizabeth Tonna, whose work would have been known to American readers from the edition of her works prepared by Harriet Beecher Stowe in 1844. The American editor added not only Tonna but Irwin, Steele, Ellis, Jewsbury, Hastings, Browne, Coleridge, and Lowe and further selections of Southey, Hemans, Norton, Landon, Cook, and Browning. These additions do not indicate a pattern of selection sharply different from Rowton's and are probably best explained by competition with George Bethune's *The British Female Poets*, as all the poets the American editor added to Rowton's collection are also in Bethune's.

In the 1849, 1854, and 1856 American editions there is a gap in pagination between the front matter and the selections from the poets, which begin with page 25. More front matter may have originally been planned for those editions—some words by the American editor, for example—and the text paginated accordingly.

NOTES

1. Aubert J. Clark, *The Movement for International Copyright in Nineteenth Century America* (Washington, D.C.: Catholic University of America Press, 1960), p. 37.

2. Simon Nowell-Smith, *International Copyright Law and the Publisher in the Reign of Queen Victoria* (Oxford: Clarendon Press, 1968), pp. 64-65.

INTRODUCTION

In the mid-nineteenth century, when Frederic Rowton edited *The Female Poets of Great Britain*, the text presented here in facsimile, he had three centuries of English women's poetry from which to draw his collection. Rowton organized the collection in chronological order, beginning with verse by Renaissance ladies like Mary Herbert, countess of Pembroke, or Lady Mary Wroth. These poets, and even lesser poets like Diana Primrose or Mary Fage, wrote poetry indistinguishable from that written by their male contemporaries. Their poetry is learned, polished, and often deeply religious; several writers also made translations, as did the men of this era. A few exceptional women transcended the limitations of their sexual role, produced work equal to that of their brothers, and wrote for the same, largely male audience; they inhabited a small world, however, one that disappeared with Elizabeth I.

Between 1550 and 1850, the evolving English middle classes gradually redefined sex roles, or "character."[1] Generally speaking, in the sixteenth and seventeenth centuries Protestantism encouraged the assumption that women are similar, if inferior, to men; previously accepted qualitative distinctions between the sexes gradually lost favor to quantitative ones. Human nature then was seen as the same in both men and women, although women were, theologically and theoretically, subservient to men. This view persisted. It was still held by Lady Mary Wortley Montagu, and was clearly expressed in Lady Anne Irwin's "Defense of Women." In the late eighteenth century, however, this assumption gradually gave way to such concepts of polarity and distinctness of sexual character as Rowton described in his introduction to *The Female Poets of Great Britain*. By Rowton's time, society had assigned each sex a qualitatively separate sphere, although the spheres were deemed complementary by many writers—even equal by some. These perceptions of sexual character had a powerful effect on the audience a woman envisioned for her poetry, on how she perceived herself as a poet, on the kind of career she could make as a writer, even on the kind of subjects about which she thought fit to write.

During these centuries, for example, women gradually stopped writing poetry about sexual love. In the seventeenth century it was a permissible theme for Philips, Killigrew, and Behn, but by the end of the eighteenth century the theme of sexual love had been replaced by mother love and domestic relationships. Most of the poems written about male-female relationships after that time celebrate a transcendence of the physical, as in Caroline Norton's "The Blind Man's Bride." In this context *Sonnets from the Portuguese,* a sequence addressed by a woman to a man, however it may idealize and sentimentalize the male-female relationship, seems an extraordinary work, even allowing that Elizabeth Barrett Browning wrote it for a private audience, and that it was apparently Robert Browning who decided to publish it.

The increase in prudishness during the centuries was doubtless also a question of class, as aristocrats tended to take more liberties with manners than other classes of English society; prudishness also increased in the poetry of middle-class men. But the change in class manners, as reflected in poetry, was an outer sign of a more important change, that of the class from which women poets came. In the Renaissance the aristocratic lady was the rule; in the seventeenth century a few merchant-class figures, like Philips and Behn, appeared.

The period of the revolution and the Restoration was a truly remarkable era for women poets. Between the 1630s and the end of the seventeenth century England produced a generation of women poets with distinctive spirit. Among them was Katherine Philips, the Matchless Orinda, the first women to write a book of poetry in English. Although she stylishly disdained publication, the collected edition of her plays and poems was edited and published by Sir Charles Cotterell in 1667, three years after her death. Aphra Behn was the first professional English woman of letters; she wrote not only poems but plays and novels. The duchess of Newcastle wrote plays, poems, essays, and a unique biography of her husband. Anne Killigrew, Anne Finch, countess of Winchelsea, and Lady Mary Lee Chudleigh all wrote of their experience with a woman's voice; if their names had been lost, one would still know that women wrote their poetry. Each was a feminist of sorts, and as the century progressed the feminist note became clearer: Lady Mary Chudleigh was an active controversialist, and the countess of Winchelsea threatened Pope with women's revenge for his poems against them. Such writers were conscious of their place in society and in the world of letters.

The impulse to speak out as women was new, and the feminine voice resonates in the writings of Mary Astell, in the attitudes of Lady Masham, and in the scholarship of Elizabeth Elstob. It would be hazardous to claim, however, that the existence of an unusual group of writers indicates especially favorable conditions for women in the seventeenth century.[2] While the disruptions of the Civil War ran deep, giving some women more responsibility than they had ever had, intellectual freedom and opportunities for women were hardly forthcoming in Milton's England. It seems likely that the women who did write in this period were the few very strong personalities with sufficient courage to speak out in their own voices.

In the Augustan period, Lady Mary Wortley Montagu, Susanna Centlivre, Catherine Cockburn, Elizabeth Thomas, Eliza Heywood, and Laetitia Pilkington were very much part of the London world of journalism and letters.[3] Gay included women writers among those honoring Pope for his translation of the *Iliad*,[4] and verse attacks and lampoons were freely exchanged among men and women. There was little of the unctuous chivalry of later ages, and the women of this time were tough scramblers. Laetitia Pilkington's 1748 memoirs record how

> humble hack writers, male and female, went about earning a livelihood in the first half of the eighteenth century—devilling for other men, writing by the yard, odd-jobbing for publishers and printers, or selling their souls to the producers of scurrilous scandal sheets. Scribbling away for dear life, with debtor's prison always just around the corner, Laetitia was fair game, as an unprotected woman, for any man who came along. Somehow she seems to have preserved her independence and her honour—spiritually, if not technically.[5]

The phenomenon of women writing for money, making an independent career of letters, was new in this era, and a general spirit of independence among the women was expressed in their art as well as their lives.[6]

By the Augustan period the majority of poets came from the middle classes. (The mid-eighteenth century saw poets like Mary Leapor, the gardener's daughter, and Ann Yearsley, the Bristol milkwoman, born from the lower classes, but they were sports of nature; the middle class spawned most poets through the nineteenth century.) With this change in class of origin came a corresponding change in the publication patterns of women poets. Aristocrats did not publish; their manuscripts were circulated by private hands. As a result, works of such aristocrats as the countess of Pembroke are still coming to light. While writers' class origin declined, the economic pressures on them to publish grew, and after Aphra Behn women occasionally—and then in increasing numbers—lived by publishing. Gradually, too, more and more women poets wrote for popular audiences, and writing professionally in a variety of genres became quite common.

If we look at the poems in *The Female Poets of Great Britain* from this time, we find Lady Mary, Mary Jones, Catherine Cockburn, and Jane Brereton all giving a feminine perspective on relations between the sexes; Lady Anne Irwin was distinctly a feminist. These poets did not portray women as always submissive to men or passive about their lives. Although they recognized women's subordinate role, they knew that in daily life women were often in control of men, and they rejoiced in these occasions, which frequently occur in what Jane Brereton called the "empire of love."

> Though born to rule, you must submit
> To my command with awe;
> Nor think your sex can you acquit,
> For Cupid's empire won't admit
> Nor own, a Salic Law.

In the pages of *The Female Poets of Great Britain* that follow Lady Anne Irwin's "Defense of Women," the independent feminine voice disappears, and in that the collection is representative, for after the 1739 Sophia Pamphlets,[7] no substantial feminist writing was done by English women until the extraordinary Mary Wollstonecraft. The poetry written by women in the second half of the eighteenth century already had begun to reflect the polarized values Rowton described in his introduction to *Female Poets*.

By the mid-eighteenth century women were a genuine reading public of which contemporary journalists were keenly aware. Magazines for women appeared, and in them many of the poets represented in *Female Poets* published poetry, both for income and to establish themselves. Inevitably, such compositions were shaped by the prospective audience—other women, who were beginning to be affected by the new conservative ideology. The number of women writing and the proportion of women in the reading audience continued to grow, so that by the late eighteenth century a significant number of women wrote for a living, and they wrote for an audience increasingly dominated by women, often women who lived in virtually enforced leisure. Because more and more journals were directed toward this audience, it became easier for women to publish, as contemporary anthologists observed.

As their class of origin declined, women writers had seen their lack of substantive formal education as a problem. Even aristocratic birth did not always assure a good education—Lady Mary thought hers disgraceful and Elizabeth Barrett Browning had special tutoring—yet the chances of being tutored and gaining access to a fine library were greater among the upper classes. In the Restoration and the earlier years of the eighteenth century there was a chorus of complaint about the education of women, which many of the poets joined.[8] By the end of the eighteenth century, however, two almost contradictory strains of thought about women's education had developed. One entailed a wide-scale rejection of the domestic and cultural "accomplishments" considered sufficient earlier, while the other expressed a growing fear of providing women an education comparable to that given men. Even relatively well-educated women like Hannah More and Laetitita Barbauld believed that too much learning would unfit women for their social role. This latter attitude anticipated the fear of learning and the sympathy with simple feeling which Rowton later expressed. By the nineteenth century, the earlier resentment at deprivation had turned into a powerful distrust of any substantial education for women. These doubts and fears quite naturally affected the kind of poetry women wrote and what kind of poetry was paid attention.

The goal to which women of the later eighteenth century were committed was the role of the lady whose destiny was to be wife, mother, and mistress of a household. Laetitia Barbauld's "To a Lady with Some Flowers" presents the quintessential spirit: "Nor blush, my fair, to own you copy these; / Your best, your sweetest empire is—to please." As the anthologist Eric Robertson suggested, Laetitia Barbauld and the Bluestockings were not really feminists. Despite the independent lives they themselves led, they accepted woman's social and theological subordination.[9]

The poetry of Hester Chapone, Elizabeth Carter, Anna Seward, and Hannah More, in the following pages, reveals the degree to which they reacted against the worldly voices of the earlier part of the century and the atheistic spirit of France. Hester Chapone's "Lines Written during a Storm," Elizabeth Carter's "Lines Written at Midnight," and Hannah More's "The Two Weavers" all show a solid, conservative faith in God and the world, but that faith did not preclude moral reform. Hannah More, Laetitia Barbauld, and Amelia Opie all used poetry to condemn slavery and other social ills, and from this time forward women frequently employed poetry as a means to galvanize public opinion about social wrongs. The Falconars, Mary Howitt, Charlotte Elizabeth Tonna, Caroline Norton, Eliza Cook, and Elizabeth Barrett Browning, for example, all wrote to urge the reform of society; indeed, poetry seemed a more potent weapon for social change then than it seems today. The list above makes clear that the tradition begun by the Bluestockings extended into the nineteenth century. The poetry of social change thus became one of the major expressions of the moral superiority of women, as taught by the prevailing sexual ideology. While the strong moral fervor common to the poetry of the Blue-stockings and the nineteenth-century poets precluded subjects like sexual love, poems filled with religious sentiment abounded. As a possible result of the narrowing intellectual confines of women's sphere, such poems contain no precise expositions of theology, but rather general expressions of simple faith.

Women's increasing concentration on the domestic sphere was expressed in the many poems with humble folk settings. *The Female Poets of Great Britain* illustrates this in the work of the Scottish poets Susanna Blamire and Anne Lindsay Barnard, who wrote effective lyrics and narratives in dialect; Anne Grant became well known for her writings on the Highlanders. This group of poets is among the most widely anthologized, in both the nineteenth and twentieth centuries, of any represented in *Female Poets*.

The emphasis on the domestic sphere also fostered in the women poets of this time an attraction to subjects involving children and the relations of children and parents. Not only children, but any helpless creature or victim—orphans, beggars, paupers, even a pet lamb— supplied a topic uniting the domestic and moral values in which women were supposed to excel. Another overwhelmingly important theme was death, which may well have surpassed children as the single most frequent subject. One is reminded, in reading Caroline Southey, Felicia Hemans, or Laetitia Elizabeth Landon, of the impor- tance of death to Emily Dickinson and to nineteenth-century American women in general; on both sides of the Atlantic the subject seems to have been a major preoccupation.[10] Melancholy, too, became a common topic; Rowton believed it a kind of Byronic indulgence on the part of certain poets like Laetitia Elizabeth Landon. Indulgence or not, the mood of melancholy is quite pervasive toward the end of the volume.[11]

The nineteenth century was the first age to define in structured terms the role and subjects of a woman poet. Up to this time a woman writer essentially invented herself, largely through male models to which she might react negatively or positively. She met obstacles, to be sure, and might have had limited personal resources because of restrictions on her education, but she had the freedom to define her subjects, her identity, and her relation to her audience. However, the nineteenth-century poets, and the earlier Bluestockings, often hardened the definitions of the woman writer's role into a code which should be followed. Laetitia Barbauld's poem, "On a Lady's Writing," for example, emphasized propriety as a goal in art as in life. Nineteenth-century women were the first to write according to a definite ideology formulated by society for their literary activity; this was a major change in the relation of women poets to their culture. Because these writers tended to conform to their "proper sphere" in subject and attitude, their poetry may appeal less to modern taste than that of earlier, less domestic eras. Rowton's introduction is valuable in allowing the modern reader to understand why his contemporaries wrote as they did.

In the nineteenth century, then, given this view of women, why publish a collection of women poets at all? *Female Poets of Great Britain* seems to have resulted in part from Frederic Rowton's respect for women's literary achievements and his awareness that there was no comparable anthology available to readers at the time, as he says in his preface. Rowton's sentiments were not unique; other editors, and publishers, were conscious of the considerable literary activity of the women of the century. Anthologist George Bethune thought "the manifestation of female talent . . . a striking characteristic" of his age, "and a very interesting proof of its moral advancement."[12] Caroline May was also impressed by "the number of female writers, especially in the department of belles-lettres," and noted that poetry, "the language of the affections," had been "freely employed among us to express the emotions of a woman's heart."[13] Rowton seems to have had in common with his contemporaries a high regard for both the moral and the emotional qualities of women's poetry, as well as a sense that the public for whom he was preparing the volume took pride that its civilization was demonstrated in the achievements of its women.

Another factor in the publication of *Female Poets* seems to have been anticipation of a large American audience. The size of that audience seems confirmed by the three printings of the Carey-Baird edition, the three printings of the Lippincott edition, and the willingness of the Ohio publisher to invest in steel engravings for the anthology thirty-five years after its appearance on the American scene. But how can one account for this audience? The feminist movement was far more important in nineteenth-century America than in England. For example, those women excluded from the World Anti-Slavery Convention in England led the 1848 Convention at Seneca Falls to formulate a declaration of women's rights, bringing the first wave of feminism to the American public's attention. Throughout the period in which *Female Poets* was circulated in America, women were convening to discuss their rights, and laws affecting women were changing far more rapidly in America than in England. Although such activity certainly did not guarantee the American public's sympathy with feminism, it may have spurred readers' interest in the poetry of women.

Thomas Longman, the English publisher of *Female Poets of Great Britain*, seems to have been especially sympathetic to the women's movement, if not to contemporary poetry; in the middle of the nineteenth century poetry apparently was not selling well. (When Eliza Action brought a book of poems to Longman, the head of the firm, he is reported to have said, "It is no good bringing me poetry; nobody wants poetry now. Bring me a cookery book, and we might come to terms."[14] Later she did just that, and both she and the firm made fortunes from it.) Longmans took

> a leading part in the development of what has come to be known as the women's movement. . . . they published in 1856 a book by Mrs. Jameson, who urged that a more enlarged sphere of social work ought to be allowed to women. Some years later, Longmans published a still more famous book on the same theme, namely, Mill's "Subjection of Women."[15]

If poetry was not selling, then, Rowton could appeal to the feminist bias of his publisher. Rowton's introduction is moderate, and the tone might well have attracted Victorians on both sides of the Atlantic who thought poetry a natural means by which women could have a civilizing effect on their society. The combination of Rowton's desire to extend the influence of women and the possibility of displaying their historical progress in poetry as an ornament of Victorian civilization— these, and a supportive publisher and a good potential American market—would seem to account for the publication of *Female Poets of Great Britain*. To account for its format, the presentation of solely women poets, one must look to the ideas Rowton presented in his introduction.

Most of what we know about Frederic Rowton (1818–1854) is contained in his obituary, which notes that he was "one of the Directors of the National Freehold Land Society"; he also "held for some years the position of one of the secretaries of the Society for the Abolition of Capital Punishment, and was the author of an essay, entitled 'Capital Punishment Reviewed.'" Rowton's obituary lists, in addition to *Female Poets of Great Britain*, yet another publication, *The Debater; a new theory of the Art of Speaking* . . . (1846), and mentions that "in the title-page of the 'The Debater' he styled himself a 'lecturer on general literature.'"[16]

Not much to go on, but then he died at thirty-six. Still, one can deduce from his work with the National Freehold Land Society (the freehold land societies bought land which was then divided into small parcels for purchase by working-class people) and his opposition to capital punishment that Rowton was a humanitarian. In that context one may understand his sympathy with the peaceful and civilizing influence women then represented in society. As he made clear in this introduction to *Female Poets*, Rowton was repelled by "War, Passion, Glory, and Sensual Pleasures" in poetry as in life, and believed that more public attention to women's poetry would allow "the gentler glow of woman's unobtrusive spirit" to mitigate the male impulse to use force and glorify violence. He respected the female intellect, and saw his anthology as giving proper recognition to women poets whose achievements had been neglected and despised, observing that "even the present day, with all its boasted gallantry, has done much to repulse and retard women's advancement."

But Rowton was not a radical feminist, or even a feminist, as one discovers on reading his introductory chapter. The essay is a valuable document, for it contains a concise statement of the prevailing sexual ideology of Victorian England, especially as it applied to poetry. Rowton praised women for having many admirable qualitites and hoped for their greater influence on society, but he did not question the basic social roles and character assigned to Victorian women. His vision of men and women striving together for a better world is a credit to his humane impulses, but it is narrowed by commonplaces about male and female character.

In this vision of society, the woman created at home a haven of purity, gentleness, and peace in which the man could take refuge from his economic or political struggles. Woman here represented Christian values; she was passive and sexually passionless, but superior to man in spiritual and moral matters. She maintained this superiority, moreover, by not venturing into a world which would defile her. While man governed the world with his head, woman ruled its heart. Rowton's statement of the credo is eloquent and moderate; he emphasized the positive aspects of women's sphere, but he did not question, as the American feminists did, the fundamental assumptions of this ideology. In fact, few in mid-Victorian England took issue with this concept of the separate spheres. In this period English feminism was largely directed at particular injustices, and "unlike the contemporary protest of French feminists such as Flora Tristan and Pauline Roland, the essentially pragmatic reformism of the first half of the Victorian era hardly questioned the woman's vocation in the family, nor her special aptitudes."[17] Rowton thus is representative of the prevailing social codes.

The belief in distinct male and female spheres was widely accepted in the Victorian era, and its origins are not obscure. Rousseau first defined for modern times those sexual characters on which it was based, stressing the complementarity of man and woman and celebrating the divergence of the sexes: "A perfect man and a perfect woman should no more be alike in mind than in face. . . . The man should be strong and active; the woman should be weak and passive."[18] Man is, indeed, dependent on woman, but she needs him more than he needs her, for "Nature herself has decreed that woman, both for herself and her children, should be at the mercy of man's judgment."[19] With only necessary modifications, Rousseau's paradigm of the interdependence of opposites and of sexual polarity worked its way into everyday thought in England and America. A few confirmed feminists protested it; one of them, Elizabeth Cady Stanton, said, "If God had assigned a sphere to man and one to woman, we claim the right to judge ourselves of His Design in reference to *us,* and we accord to man the same privilege."[20] Along with the majority, Rowton accepted the social model of the spheres, although he ascribed far more intellectual excellence to women than Rousseau would have accepted, and feared the consequences of the male aggression Rousseau praised.

In the nineteenth century, the notion of separate male and female spheres had profound implications for critical assessments and audience expectations of writing by women: in literature, the doctrine of the spheres created a double standard. In this view, women's domestic sphere of sentiment predicated the kind of poetry they would write and determined the appropriate judgment to make about their poetry. For example, in her introduction to *The American Female Poets* (1853), Caroline May pointed out that

> not many ladies in this country are permitted sufficient leisure from the cares and duties of home to devote themselves, either from choice, or as a means of living, to literary pursuits. Hence, the themes which have suggested the greater part of the following poems have been derived from the incidents and associations of every-day life. And home, with its quiet joys, its deep pure sympathies, and its secret sorrows, with which a stranger must not intermeddle, is a sphere by no means limited for woman, whose inspiration lies more in her heart than her head.[21]

For Caroline May and others, the expected themes of women's poetry were those found in their sphere, the home and the heart.

The notion of separate spheres also affected critical judgments of fiction written by women. In examining the ideas of M. A. Stodart, who wrote *Female Writers: Thoughts on Their Proper Sphere* (1842), Inga-Stina Ewbank finds her atypical of the period in believing fiction to be evil, but typical in attributing special qualities to the female mind: delicacy, sensitivity, intuition, morality, quickness of sympathy and polish—but not imaginative daring. Stodart also assumed that as women had a smaller sphere of observation, there would be a closer relationship between their writing and their lives than was the case with men. Women would, nevertheless, always maintain high moral idealism and a ladylike decorum in their subject matter; these ideas echo those held at the turn of the century by the Bluestockings, Hannah More, Laetitia Barbauld, and Hester Chapone. Ewbank shows how these beliefs operate in the reviews of the Brontë novels and how they are violated by the works themselves, so that the Brontës emerge "each in her own way as an unwomanly writer."[22]

Similarly, Elaine Showalter demonstrates that pervailing Victorian stereotypes of women effected in reviewers an unfortunate tendency to treat women fiction writers as part of a class rather than as autonomous individuals; the writers consequently tended to be conservative about the woman question, or to conceal their identities, or both. Reviewers often condemned women writers for using coarse language or describing experiences deemed only suitable for men, so that "women were either implicitly or explicitly denied the freedom to explore and describe their own experience."[23] Victorian prudery did not exempt males, to be sure, but it was more oppressive for women because of the limiting assumptions made about their sexual character.

In his essay "The Lady Novelists,"[24] George Henry Lewes revealed attitudes similar to Rowton's. Lewes assumed that women had a significant place in literature; as they were fundamentally different from men, they had different experiences of life, which it was the virtue of their literature to present. Like Rowton, Lewes believed that the masculine mind is primarily intellectual and rational, the feminine emotional and intuitive, and he acknowledged the need for both. While Lewes was more daring than Rowton in his call for women to write from their own experience, he shared with Rowton moderate assumptions and a sympathetic tone. Rowton's introduction to *Female Poets of Great Britain* allows us to see how these commonplace assumptions about women applied to their poetry, both as it was written and as it was received.

Indeed, Rowton's selections of nineteenth-century verse justify Caroline May's characterization of the woman poet as limiting her poetic subjects to her sexual sphere in the natural course of things, and supply the literary context for Bethune's remark that

> in all pertaining to the affections, which constitute the best part of human nature, we readily confess her superiority; it is, therefore, consistent with her character that the genius of woman should yield peculiar delight when its themes are love, childhood, the softer beauties of creation, the joys or sorrows of the heart, domestic life, mercy, religion, and the instincts of justice. Hence her excellence in the poetry of sensibilities. There are instances of her boldly entering the sphere of man, and asserting strong claims to share the honours of his sterner engagements; but the *Daciers*, *De Staels*, and *Hannah More's*, are variations from the rule prescribed by wise Providence.[25]

With several notable exceptions, Bethune's is an accurate description of the poems of the nineteenth century. But, as *Female Poets of Great Britain* amply demonstrates, this narrowing of themes to what we now think of as "women's verse" was mostly accomplished by women of minor talent whose poetry conformed to conventional expectations like those expressed by Rowton, May, or Bethune. Such poetry confirmed readers' and writers' sense of the separateness of the poetry of men and women, so that anthologies that presented the poetry of only one sex would seem a matter of course to both poets and readers. To know that women's poetry was not always "women's verse" one need only look through the poems in *Female Poets*; the poetry of women from the seventeenth and eighteenth centuries has a different character and different relation to the work of men.

In a critical work somewhat later than *Female Poets,* a similar but even more conservative framework obtained. In his 1883 *English Poetesses,* Eric Robertson was far less supportive of women's achievements than Rowton or Lewes. Robertson believed that women had not, and probably would not, equal men in poetry because their creativity is expressed in reproduction—children are women's poems. Robertson's opinions about what kind of poetry women should write. are very like those of Bethune, May, or Rowton. He criticized the seventeenth-century and Augustan writers for their unladylike subjects, masculine tone, or lack of refinement, but he praised the Bluestockings because their example "raised the tone of English thought with regard to the value of their sex," and because "they never lost sight of domesticity as the basis of their sociology."[26] As he moved closer to his own time Robertson became less moral and more aesthetic. Still, Robertson believed that even the women of his own time should be compared to one another because they could not be compared to men: "the more women write poetry, the more carefully are we able to compare their poetical powers with men's powers, and the more completely is the case made out against them."[27]

Robertson's evaluations of individual poets, moreover, resulted from a distinct biographical bias which he freely admitted, and which was characteristic of nineteenth-century criticism of writing by women. This critical consideration of women's lives and their poetry together may account for the renown of certain poets, such as Elizabeth Barrett Browning, in the authors' own time and their critical obscurity after their death. Most nineteenth-century critics of women's writing treated a woman's life and her art as one text, and reasoned back and forth between them.

That nineteenth-century women writers were aware, as they always have been, of the condescending implications of this double standard is evident in Elizabeth Barrett Browning's caution that

> You never can be satisfied with praise
> Which men give women when they judge a book
> Not as mere work, but as mere woman's work,
> Expressing the comparative respect,
> Which means the absolute scorn.[28]

Although other women, like Charlotte Brontë,[29] lamented the double standard, many more accepted it, especially later in the nineteenth century, for in a society that distinguished between the sexes as strongly as did Victorian England, it would have been difficult not to use a double standard in literary judgments, as in all others.

Against this background, Rowton's selections of early writers seem rather independent; his selections of his contemporaries more conventional. He excluded very few of the earlier poets represented in Alexander Dyce's *Specimens of English Poetesses* (1825), on which he depended rather heavily for poets before the late eighteenth century, but Rowton and the American editor added substantially to Dyce's selections of individual eighteenth- and nineteenth-century poems. Although Rowton's choices and comments usually reinforce the moral, "domestic" bias of his introduction, he was quite willing to include Aphra Behn and to like her poetry, though he printed fewer of her poems than Dyce. He also included (but did not approve of) Lady Mary Chudleigh's "To the Ladies." Unlike other anthologists, he was willing to represent that with which he could not agree; the only exception to this seems to be De la Rivière Manley, omitted, probably, on moral grounds. Rowton's conventionality also is evident in his acceptance of Dyce's selections from the work of Katherine Philips, which accent "domestic duties"; one could hardly guess at the contents of the 1667 edition of her poems from those appearing in *Female Poets of Great Britain*.

Rowton also depended on Dyce for the Augustan age, and then collected beyond him for the later eighteenth century. The poems by Elizabeth Thomas and Eliza Haywood included here give only a partial impression of the whole poetic activity of these women, but at least they are in the collection. They illustrate quite well Rowton's notion of female genius, as he articulated it in relation to the poems of Laetitia Barbauld: "The quick intuitive perception, the chaste tenderness, the delicate, *musical* flow of thought . . . distinguish the female mind."

As is evident in the following pages, Rowton feared advanced learning in women, and his bias against it emerges more strongly as he nears his own time. Men and women of Rowton's era, and back to the

Bluestockings, believed that "the spheres of the sexes are different and require different faculties, and different education." These fixed beliefs affected Rowton's assessments of the quality of poetry written by women, so that poems of simple feeling were to his mind better poems than those written out of what he termed the "intellectual" knowledge of "erudite ladies." In this Rowton is certainly representative; if the prevailing nineteenth-century English anti-intellectual bias affected the appraisal of Robert Browning's poetry by his contemporaries, the bias was even more severe with regard to his wife's poetry, because of her sex.

Rowton did not altogether abandon the customary biographical approach to women's writing, but he is quite modern in preferring to concentrate on the poetry before him, and he could arrive at independent judgments, as he did concerning Hannah More. Possibly he was encouraged in this by Dyce, who had a scholar's interest in the text, but if one reads Robertson's criticism along with Rowton's, Rowton's independent attitude seems remarkable. Although his biases were the moral, anti-intellectual ones by which his age judged the work of women writers, he tolerated a wider range of work than any of his contemporaries, printed what he did not like, judged poems for himself, and gave poetry precedence over biography. Rowton may not have approved of Elizabeth Barrett Browning's education, but he wrote of her poetry, rather than of her romantic life.

Unlike his fellow anthologists Rowton was not systematic in announcing his sources, although he acknowledged his debt to Dyce. Rowton and the American editor added twenty-eight figures to those in Dyce, and Rowton also selected different poems from Dyce for many figures, among them Newcastle, Killigrew, Monk, Winchelsea, Brereton, Leapor, Montagu, Jones, Robinson, Chapone, Carter, and Smith. This suggests that Rowton had recourse to the published works of these poets (see Selected Bibliography: Individual Authors). There does not seem to be a pattern to these changes, except for the necessary reduction in the number of selections in order to make room for a third again as many poets from the later periods. All of the Victorian anthologists included more examples from the work of poets of their own time, and Rowton seems to have gathered the work of living poets through correspondence with them.

The central section of the volume, where Rowton was no longer guided by Dyce and therefore collected independently, is most revealing of his practice as an anthologist; here he included Caroline

Symonds, Miss Scott, Maria and Harriet Falconar, Isabella Howard, the countess of Carlisle, Mrs. Leicester, Helen Maria Williams, Susanna Blamire, Mrs. Henry Rolls, Lady Sophia Burrell, Lucy Aiken, Margaret Hodson, Mary Howitt, Caroline Southey, Lady Caroline Norton, Maria Abdy, Eliza Cook, Fanny Kemble, Elizabeth Barrett Browning, and Charlotte Young. This list is a tribute to Rowton's range of taste. Although several poets seem to fit his model of femininity, Margaret Hodson and Eliza Cook wrote on "masculine" subjects, and Lady Burrell's verse is sometimes coarse. Moreover, Rowton had to search a good deal for some of his material. He found Miss Scott's work in Ellis' *Specimens of Early English Poets*, Mrs. Henry Rolls's poems in a commonplace book, and Caroline Symonds' and Mrs. Leicester's in unpublished manuscripts. Thus Rowton's efforts to collect for this portion of *Female Poets of Great Britain* seem to have been substantial, and if his critical assessments often seem somewhat conventional to the modern reader, his commitment to making available three centuries of the poetry of women is impressive.

The achievements and history of women are now subjects of serious inquiry; historical texts are being rescued from obscurity and scattered materials gathered and published so that students and professional scholars alike will have access to them.[30] The publication of *The Female Poets of Great Britain* is another step in this recovery of the heritage of women. Although criticism of women's prose has come of age, poetry by women, and especially by English women, has been given relatively little attention.[31] Women have written far more, and more important, prose than poetry, and scholars have naturally followed the writers' lead. Even so, more critical work has been done on American than British women poets; there is now one survey of that field,[32] and two anthologies of American women poets, edited by Caroline May and by Rufus Griswold, have now been reprinted. That there is a similar need to make available English women's poetry is demonstrated by the recent statement—in a book about women's poetry—that "until the twentieth century, there was no body of poetry by women in English."[33] As the following pages show, the poetry is there and we have only to read it.

A distinct pattern, the "transience of female literary fame,"[34] has contributed to the neglect of this heritage; as noted earlier, the work that earned many women literary fame in their lifetimes disappeared from sight in subsequent years. This was unfortunately true for many of the writers in *Female Poets;* when Rowton prepared his volume in 1848, he recognized several Bluestockings, like Hannah More, whose fame was already beginning to wane, although they had been powerful figures at the turn of his century. This pattern of transience is related to the intermittent progress of feminism, in which each successive wave in the struggle toward equity brought with it new writings, which only faded from sight when feminist ideals lost their hold on society's consciousness. "Thus each generation of women writers has found itself, in a sense, without a history, forced to rediscover the past anew."[35]

Female Poets of Great Britain helps rectify this loss and provides a delightful opportunity to look at three centuries of English women's poetry. While the works of most of the writers represented here are available in American libraries (see Selected Bibliography: Individual Authors), it is the special value of the anthology to assemble them in a way that gives the reader a sense of continuities and relationships. Indeed, *Female Poets of Great Britain* contains more examples of English women poets than any available anthology from either the nineteenth or the twentieth century. Bethune's anthology, for example, does not include many of the earlier poets represented here because Bethune clearly assumed there had been historical progress in female talent, which he demonstrated by "taking as he passed along, only those of real merit or accidental distinction . . . and reserving the bulk of the book for more copious extracts from those whose writings are most highly appreciated for moral and poetical excellence."[36] Although Bethune sometimes gives the reader a better sense than Rowton of an individual poet's range and characteristics, his notion of moral excellence led him to omit Aphra Behn and a host of eighteenth-century figures whom Rowton included. Still, Bethune is worth consulting for his generous examples of individual poets, especially poets of the nineteenth century. Also worth consulting in any survey of the poetic tradition of English women is the anthology to which Rowton was much indebted for his material, Alexander Dyce's *Specimens of British Poetesses.* Dyce's collection is the opposite of Bethune's in that it is strong in the early works, many of which Bethune omitted. Because it was published earlier, however, it does not include many of the nineteenth-century poets Bethune emphasized. *Female Poets of Great Britain* thus has the virtues of both Dyce and Bethune, and seems in fact to identify almost all the notable figures before Elizabeth Barrett Browning. It is therefore a worthy candidate for reissue, particularly because of its especially valuable introduction, and because in one version or another the collection is available at only twenty-eight libraries in North America.

A reading of *Female Poets* may raise issues that have not been touched on in this short essay. The quality of a poet's work, for example, is difficult to judge from Rowton's selections because he frequently did not include her best work, or even her most representative poems. Although certain poets represented in the anthology are of only historical interest, Mary Herbert, countess of Pembroke, Katherine Philips, Anne Killigrew, Aphra Behn, Anne Finch, countess of Winchelsea, Mary Tighe, Joanna Baillie, Anna Laetitia Barbauld, and Elizabeth Barrett Browning have earned a permanent place in English letters, even though this place is not necessarily secured by the poems Rowton selected for *Female Poets*. Moreover, critical evaluation of the poetry of many of the writers in *Female Poets* is undergoing substantial change as their work is read more extensively and their already recognized work is more seriously appraised. The countess of Pembroke, for example, has been known primarily as Sir Philip Sidney's sister and as the editor of his *Arcadia,* as the translator of Garnier's *Antonie* and other works, and as the patron-friend of Daniel, Donne, Nash, Jonson, and others. Recent study of her work demonstrates, however, that her translations of the Psalms surpass the quality of her brother's, and that she may have used the Spenserian stanza before Spenser.[37]

Aphra Behn has long been recognized for her novels and plays, but not for her poetry—possibly because it "reveals a frank delight in sex that conflicts with the popular Restoration image of the passive woman."[38] Critics are only now discovering the high quality of her poetry. The stature of several writers whose poetry appears in *Female Poets* rests largely on their work in other genres—drama, fiction, letters, or biography. Susannah Centlivre, Margaret Cavendish, duchess of Newcastle, Eliza Haywood (Heywood, in Rowton's text), Lady Mary Wortley Montagu, Hannah More, and Anna Seward have all written better prose or drama than poetry. What appears in Rowton's collection is but a lesser phase of their work.

Recent studies of women's poetry have brought about not only reevaluations of various poets' work but greater awareness of their importance to literary history. For example, Mary Tighe taught John Keats important lessons about the Spenserian stanza,[39] and Joanna Baillie's romantic dramas inspired Byron's admiration and imitation. Baillie's early plays contained "the best dramatic blank verse of the age"; [40] they also influenced Wordsworth, whose work reflects the psychological ideas on which she based dramatic characterization. [41] Any listing of such literary influences would also include Elizabeth Barrett Browning's powerful influence on the work of Emily Dickinson. [42] Some women poets were important within a particular literary milieu. Lady Mary Wortley Montagu has always been accounted significant for her time, and the impact on their age of lesser figures like Susannah Centlivre or Eliza Haywood is just now being explored. [43] Felicia Hemans' poetry was admired by Wordsworth and castigated by Byron, but there is ample evidence that both read her work with great interest. [44] Scholars are beginning to study the work of women who heretofore have been known because of their relationships to famous male writers, and in doing so have discovered that Esther Vanhomrigh's epistolary style may have influenced Swift's. [45] Hester Thrale Piozzi's writings on marriage now have interest for students of eighteenth-century culture which is quite apart from her relationship with Dr. Johnson. [46]

A great deal recently has been learned about women's poetry, and much is left to discover. The process is not simply one of filling gaps. Scholars and critics now genuinely value the special insights of women poets into their lives and their societies, and appreciate such work as the feminist writings of Lady Mary Chudleigh, or the poetry in which the countess of Winchelsea speaks about being a woman poet, as significant to both literary and cultural history. Recent critical and historical studies also show that an understanding and knowledge of the poetry of women will enhance an understanding of the poetry of men as well, by placing it in the larger context in which it was written. The more seriously we study women's poetry, the more sensitive our judgments about all poetry will become.

Before leaving them, I cannot resist adding a final note about these women who have become friends and examples as I have read their poems and discovered their lives. When considered as a group, they would have made an impressive difference in history even if none had ever written a line. Aphra Behn served as a spy in the Netherlands. Lady Mary introduced smallpox inoculation into England. Hannah More's Sunday school and reform tracts had a significant effect on her society. Helen Maria Williams' *Letters from France* was powerful enough to get her imprisoned by Robespierre. Still other women writers were central to the anti-slavery campaign, and raised their voices against conditions in factories and the exploitation of children. Caroline

Norton helped to change English law; she was a reluctant reformer, but she made history in her struggle to see her sons, of whom her estranged husband had complete control, and to keep the money she had earned, to which her husband had legal claim.[47] *Eliza Cook's Journal* and the *Christian Lady's Magazine,* edited by Charlotte Elizabeth Tonna, both dealt with serious social issues and are but two of many examples of women's contributions to serious journalism from the eighteenth century on. Against this background of social activity, Lincoln's reference to Harriet Beecher Stowe as the little lady who started the big war might be a description, differing in scale but not in kind, of many women writers. And those who have occasional doubts about the impact of poetry on life may remember that Susan B. Anthony carried Elizabeth Barrett Browning's *Aurora Leigh* across the American continent in her trunk.

NOTES

1. See Ruth H. Bloch, "Untangling the Roots of Modern Sex Roles: A Survey of Four Centuries of Change," *Signs* 4 (Winter, 1978):237-52.

2. Roger Thompson accents the limitations set on English women in *Women in Stuart England and America: A Comparative Study* (London: Routledge and Kegan Paul, 1974), pp. 12-13. Myra Reynolds emphasizes a change in spirit after the Restoration in *The Learned Lady in England, 1650–1760* (Boston: Houghton, Mifflin, 1920), p. 428; Lawrence Stone gives a similar interpretation of the effects of the Civil War in *The Family, Sex and Marriage in England, 1500–1800* (New York: Harper and Row, 1977), pp. 336-41.

3. Alison Adburgham, *Women in Print: Writing Women and Women's Magazines from the Restoration to the Accession of Victoria* (London: Allen and Unwin, 1972), chaps. 3-6.

4. "Mr Popes Welcome from Greece a Copy of Verses wrote by Mr Gay upon Mr Popes having finisht his Translation of Homers Ilias," in John Gay, *Poetry and Prose,* ed. V. A. Dearing with C. E. Beckwith (Oxford: Clarendon Press, 1974), 1:256-57.

5. Adburgham, *Women in Print,* p. 94.

6. See Miriam J. Benkovitz, "Some Observations on Women's Concept of Self in the Eighteenth Century," *Women in the Eighteenth Century and Other Essays,* ed. Paul Fritz and Richard Morton (Toronto: Hakkert, 1976), pp. 37-54.

7. In 1739 "a person of Quality" using the pseudonym "Sophia" published a pamphlet titled *Woman not inferior to Man.* "Sophia" was answered in *The Natural Right of Men to Sovereignty over the other Sex. The Natural Right,* a reply to it, and the first tract were all published together in *Beauty's Triumph or the Superiority of the Fair Sex invincibly proved* (1751). Myra Reynolds summarizes speculation

about "Sophia" 's identity (*Learned Lady in England*, pp. 313-15); Doris M. Stenton, *The English Woman in History* (London: Allen and Unwin, 1957; rpt. Schocken Books, 1977), p. 293, suspects all three pamphlets were written by a male journalist.

8. See Reynolds, *Learned Lady in England*, chap. 3.

9. Eric S. Robertson, *English Poetesses: A Series of Critical Biographies with Illustrative Extracts* (London: Cassell, 1883), p. 77. See also Stenton, *English Woman in History*, p. 295; Reynolds, *Learned Lady in England*, p. 429.

10. See Ann Douglas, *The Feminization of American Culture* (New York: McGraw Hill, Avon Books, 1977), chap. 6, "The Domestication of Death: The Posthumous Congregation."

11. Douglas' work is helpful in understanding the roots of sentimentality; the circumstances of Victorian women's lives—primarily excessive dependence and powerlessness—would have made them prone to depression. Their sentimentality allowed them to savor the emotion that the countess of Winchelsea called in "Ardelia to Melancholy" her "old inveterate foe."

12. George W. Bethune, ed., *The British Female Poets with Biographical and Critical Notices* (Philadelphia: Lindsay and Blakiston, 1848), p. iii.

13. Caroline May, ed., *The American Female Poets* (Philadelphia: Lindsay and Blakiston, 1853), p. v.

14. Frank A. Mumby, *Publishing and Bookselling: A History from the Earliest Times to the Present Day*, rev. ed. (London: Jonathan Cape, 1954), p. 229.

15. Harold Cox and John E. Chandler, *The House of Longman with a Record of their Bicentenary Celebrations* (London: Longmans, Green, 1925), p. 28.

16. *Gentleman's Magazine*, June, 1855, p. 654.

17. Françoise Basch, *Relative Creatures: Victorian Women in Society and the Novel* (New York: Schocken Books, 1974), p. 10.

18. Jean Jacques Rousseau, *Emile*, trans. Barbara Foxley (London: J. M. Dent, Everyman's Library, 1966), p. 322.

19. *Ibid.*, p. 328.

20. Elizabeth Cady Stanton, "There Is No Such Thing as a Sphere for a Sex," in *Voices from Women's Liberation*, ed. Leslie B. Tanner (New York: Harcourt Brace, New American Library, 1970), p. 41. Stanton's statement was first made in Rochester, New York, in 1848, the year *Female Poets of Great Britain* first appeared.

21. May, *American Poets*, p. vi.

22. Inga-Stina Ewbank, *Their Proper Sphere: A Study of the Bronte Sisters as Early Victorian Female Novelists* (Cambridge, Mass.: Harvard University Press, 1966), p. 48.

23. Elaine Showalter, "Women Writers and the Double Standard," in *Women in Sexist Society*, ed. Vivian Gornick and Barbara K. Moran (New York: Mentor, New American Library, 1971), p. 478.

24. George Henry Lewes, "The Lady Novelists," in *Women's Liberation and Literature*, ed. Elaine Showalter (New York: Harcourt Brace Jovanovich, 1971), pp. 171-83.

25. Bethune, *British Poets*, pp. iii-iv.

26. Robertson, *English Poetesses*, p. 77.

27. *Ibid.*, p. xv.

28. Elizabeth Barrett Browning, "Aurora Leigh," *Complete Poetical Works*, ed. H. W. Preston (Boston: Houghton Mifflin, 1900), p. 273.

29. See Ewbank, *Their Proper Sphere*, pp. 1-2.

30. Jo Ann Delores Een and Marie B. Rosenberg-Dishman, eds., *Women and Society: An Annotated Bibliography* (Beverly Hills and London: Sage Publications, 1978), list reprints of the works of Anna Seward; the 1850 edition of Caroline May's *The American Female Poets;* Black's *Notable Women Writers* (1893); the 1873 edition of Rufus Griswold's *Female Poets of America;* and Robertson's *English Poetesses.* In Garland's Romantic Context Series of Significant Minor Poetry, 1789–1830, various works of Joanne Baillie and Felicia Hemans have been reprinted.

31. See Sidney Janet Kaplan, "Review Essay: Literary Criticism," *Signs* 4 (1979):514. Cf. Gloria Bowles, "Criticism of Women's Poetry," *Signs* 3 (1978):712-18, who quotes Elaine Showalter (1975) and Annette Kolodny (1976) on the lack of critical work on poetry.

32. Emily S. Watts, *The Poetry of American Women from 1632 to 1945* (Austin: University of Texas Press, 1977).

33. Suzanne Juhasz, *Naked and Fiery Forms: Modern American Poetry by Women, A New Tradition* (New York: Harper and Row, 1976), p. 1.

34. Germaine Greer, in Elaine Showalter, *A Literature of Their Own: British Women Novelists from Brontë to Lessing* (Princeton: Princeton University Press, 1977), p. 11.

35. *Ibid.*, pp. 11-12.

36. Bethune, *British Poets*, p. ix.

37. See Mary R. Mahl and Helene Koon, eds., *The Female Spectator: English Women Writers before 1800* (Bloomington: Indiana University Press, 1977), pp. 62-65; J. C. A. Rathmell, ed., *The Psalms of Sir Philip Sidney and the Countess of Pembroke* (New York: New York University Press, 1963).

38. Mahl and Koon, *The Female Spectator*, p. 166.

39. See Earle Vonard Weller, ed., *Keats and Mary Tighe* (New York: Modern Language Association of America, 1928).

40. Donald H. Reiman, ed., *The Family Legend and Metrical Legends of Exalted Characters,* by Joanne Baillie (New York: Garland, 1976), p. vii.

41. *Ibid.*

42. Ellen Moers, *Literary Women: The Great Writers* (New York: Doubleday, 1976), pp. 55-62.

43. See Patricia M. Spacks, "Ev'ry Woman Is at Heart a Rake," *Eighteenth-Century Studies* 8 (1974) :27-64; F. P. Lock, *Susanna Centlivre* (Boston: Twayne, 1979).

44. Donald H. Reiman, ed., *Poems: England and Spain, Modern Greece,* by Felicia Hemans (New York: Garland, 1978).

45. Irwin Ehrenpreis, "Letters of Advice to Young Spinsters," in *The Lady of Letters in the Eighteenth Century* (Los Angeles: William Andrews Clark Memorial Library of UCLA, 1969).

46. Patricia M. Spacks, *The Female Imagination* (New York: Avon Books, 1972).

47. Katherine Moore, *Victorian Wives* (New York: St. Martin's Press, 1974), chap. 3.

THE

FEMALE POETS

OF

GREAT BRITAIN,

CHRONOLOGICALLY ARRANGED:

WITH

COPIOUS SELECTIONS AND CRITICAL REMARKS.

BY

FREDERIC ROWTON

WITH ADDITIONS BY AN AMERICAN EDITOR,

AND ELEGANTLY ENGRAVED ILLUSTRATIONS
BY CELEBRATED ARTISTS.

PHILADELPHIA:
HENRY C. BAIRD,
(SUCCESSOR TO E. L. CAREY,)
No. 7 HART'S BUILDINGS, SIXTH STREET ABOVE CHESTNUT.
1853.

Printed by T. K. & P. G. Collins.

PREFACE.

THE design of the Author, in writing the following pages, is to supply a want which must have been frequently experienced by every student of our literary annals; — the want of a History of our Female Poets. Of our *male* Poets there are (to say the least of it) histories enough. Johnson, Campbell, Aiken, Anderson, Southey, and others, have done due honour to the genius of the rougher sex; and have left us — so far as they have gone — nothing to be desired.

But where are the memorials of the Female mind? In the records above alluded to, the Poetesses of Britain are either left unnoticed altogether, or mentioned with a flippant carelessness which is even more contemptuous than total silence. One or two small works (among which Mr. Dyce's *Specimens of British Poetesses* is the only one of merit and research) have been devoted to the subject, it is true; but even the worthiest of these productions is at best but, incomplete. It cannot surely be pretended that this neglect of our Female Poets is attributable to any lack of genius in the sex. In these enlightened days it may certainly be taken for granted that women have souls : and further, that their souls have no small influence upon the world of thought and action. This admission made, it will follow that the mental efforts of woman have as good a claim as man's to be recorded; and that we should be deeply ashamed of ourselves for so long withholding from them that prominent place in the world's esteem which is so undoubtedly their due.

To tell the truth, we have already suffered severely for our folly in this matter. Had the soul of woman been allowed to operate more widely in the world, it cannot be doubted that humanity would have been far wiser, and better, and happier than it is.

Man's coarser spirit has preponderated in the universe of life, and has made us much too gross, material, sensual, and violent. Our passions, sentiments, and beliefs, have all been too strong, too rough, too vehement ; and we have gone through much strife and sorrow on this account. They should have been tempered, harmonised, smoothed down, softened by contact with the mind of woman. Our mental atmosphere has contained too large a proportion of *one* of its elements ; and hence, it has neither been so pure nor so wholesome as it might have been. Only *one-half* of the human soul has yet had a fair scope for development, — and that the coarser half ; the other has been circumscribed in its operations, and thus has been left to run to waste.

The Author confidently hopes that the work which he here presents to the reader will justify the position which he has assumed, and at least prove that the Poetical Faculty is not confined to one of the sexes. If it should only serve to direct critical attention to the subject, he will be fully satisfied ; for he will know, that in such case our Female Poets will soon be as honourably appreciated as they unquestionably deserve to be.

The Author takes this opportunity to return his grateful thanks to those of our living Poetesses whose names occur in this volume, for the permission which they have so readily given him to make extracts from their works, and for the kind interest which they have, without exception, manifested in his undertaking.

London, 1848.

** The publishers have had this work revised, and the present edition contains many important additions, which are distinguished by being marked in the table of contents with an asterisk [*].

Philadelphia, June, 1848.

is satisfied with that; he distrusts first appearances, and inquires into their essential qualities.

The Poetical Selections which form the bulk of this work will, I think, amply illustrate and fully prove the distinctions which I have attempted to draw in the preceding paragraphs. They will show, if I mistake not, that while Man's intellect is meant to make the world stronger and wiser, Woman's is intended to make it purer and better. The reader will not fail to notice how rarely our Female Poets have addressed themselves to the mere understanding, and on the other hand how constantly they have sought to impress the feelings of the race; how little they have endeavoured to increase our wisdom, and how much they have laboured to promote our virtue. It is for man to ameliorate our condition; it is for woman to amend our character. Man's Poetry teaches us Politics; Woman's, Morality. In all the Poems contained in this Volume, it would be difficult to find a passage written to accelerate man's political advancement: whilst every page will display some effort to stimulate his moral progress. In one place we shall see a Katherine Philips exhibiting the deceitfulness of Pleasure; in another, a Mary Chandler proclaiming the blessings of Temperance; in a third, a Lady Carew enjoining the duty of Forgiveness; in a fourth, an Amelia Opie teaching the sinfulness of War; in a fifth, a Mary Howitt sweetly sympathising with the wants and sufferings of the Poor; in all, we shall find a cheerful love for Humanity, a noble trust in Virtue, and a hoping, clinging, earnest Piety. Woman's mind not equal in strength to man's! Can we venture to say that man's mind is equal in value to woman's?

It is not, however, to promote a rivalry between the sexes that these pages are written. They aim, not at separating the two half minds of the world, but at making them act in concert and unison. Single, they are incomplete; but together they are powerful for every kind of good.

Man without woman is strong, but unenduring; courageous, but impatient; enterprising, but incautious. He is self-relying, but easily deceived; confident, but soon cast down; undertakes much, but is soon wearied. Left to itself, his hope fails almost

3

at its birth; his faith speedily turns to doubt; his mind preys upon itself; he becomes gloomy, suspicious, and misanthropical. On the other hand, woman without man is timid, feeble, apprehensive, and defenceless. The first shock of doubt or affliction overcomes her; and afterwards she hopes beyond reason. Evil preys upon her unresisted; she confides to be deceived: her affections become idolatrous; her sympathies, weaknesses; and her religion grows into superstition.

Thus the perfect mental character is only formed by the union of the two incomplete parts. United, there is strength with endurance, enterprise with caution, courage with patience. Self-reliance is moderated by dependence. Thought is aided by feeling. Reason is confirmed by sympathy. Reliance links itself with belief, ambition with love, faith with piety; despondency meets with cheerfulness, affliction with consolation, and despair with hope.

It is our policy, therefore, no less than our duty, to admit and develop, in their fullest extent, the noble intellectual gifts which nature has bestowed on woman. Urged by a blinding pride, or a ridiculous envy, we have for ages denied her right to share with us the throne of intellect; and, as has before been urged, we have paid a heavy penalty for our folly. Let us amend our fault for the future. Let us give woman's mind that free scope for its exertions which we have so long refused it. And let us gratefully recognise in woman, a partner, not a rival, in the mental race; a fellow worker, and that a pure and courageous one, in the great task of enlightening and elevating the whole family of man!

FREDERICK ROWTON.

CONTENTS.

xli

CONTENTS.

B

CONTENTS.

INTRODUCTORY CHAPTER.

In presenting to the reader a History of the Female Poets of Great Britain, the author feels called upon to make a few general remarks upon the subject.

First, he would express his profound conviction that the Poetesses of our country have displayed a richness and depth of genius which may challenge the admiration, and demand the serious attention, of the world. The following pages offer, in the humble opinion of their Compiler, undeniable evidence in support of this belief; and further show that the female soul contains inexhaustible mines of precious jewels, the existence of which has as yet been scarcely recognised. The fact that this is almost the first book expressly devoted to the poetical productions of the British Female mind, tends strongly to prove that woman's intellect has been overlooked, if not despised, by us hitherto ; and that it is high time we should awake to a sense of our folly and injustice. We have practically, if not professedly, avowed our belief that the thoughts of the feminine soul are not worth preserving : with how little reason we have done so, this work aims to show.

It may be true that woman's verse is less exciting than man's ; and less " interesting" to the mass of readers: but I am inclined to think that this is so only because the mind of the world has been hitherto unduly stimulated, and therefore can only relish highly-seasoned food. War, Passion, Glory, and Sensual Pleasures have been the chief subjects of verse down to a comparatively recent period ; and not until this false excitement has altogether passed away, can the gentler glow of woman's unobtrusive spirit be fairly felt. The qualities of woman's mind are the *stars* of the mental hemisphere : and during the time that is past, they have been outblazed by fiercer fires; but the heaven is now clearing, and the soft starlight is becoming visible.

I would go on to observe that other influences have tended to repress the poetical faculty of woman, and to keep it in the background of the universe. Our system of educating females has narrowed their sphere of observation, contracted their experience, and done its best to chain their intellects to the mere frivolities of life. Further, their poetical attempts have met with discouragements. I do not mean to say that they have not been flattered and applauded,— every Poetess has found her little coterie of admirers, who have fed her to surfeit with their unwholesome adulation; but I mean that the world has on the whole disregarded the mental efforts of woman, or else has looked upon them as something out of the proper sphere of the sex, and therefore to be petted and *protegéed* and lionized, rather than honestly welcomed and carefully cultivated. If I am asked for proof of this assertion, I point to the fact that our female versifiers, though always applauded highly by cotemporaries, have never yet been included in the list of our national Poets.

I know that of late this fault of neglect has been, in part, amended. During the last half-century our Poetesses have received a far healthier kind of regard: indeed their claim to distinction has been so far admitted as to make our wise men ask one another whether they should any longer permit such a word as Poet*ess* at all? But this in no degree disproves the assertion which I have made,— that, on the whole, woman's intellectual efforts have been in effect discouraged. Nay, even the present day, with all its boasted gallantry, has done much to repulse and retard woman's advancement. Have we not seen that when young Female Poets have by their genius placed themselves prominently before the public, they have been met with shameful malice and slander, and bidden back, wounded in heart, into privacy and retirement? Critics who could not deny their talents, have belied their characters; and a gossiping world has only been too ready to believe the calumniators.

Indeed, considering the hindrances in woman's way, the wonder is, not that she has done so little, but that she has done so much. To me there could not be a clearer proof of the strength and excellence of the female intellect, than is found in the fact that woman has persevered so long, and accomplished such great things, in spite of the difficulties she has had to encounter : and I cannot but think that the superior place which woman now holds in the world's esteem, as compared with her relative position in past ages, is due, not to man's justice, but to her own determination.

But, not to speculate further upon what woman's literary efforts might have been under more favourable circumstances, let us now speak of her works as we find them exemplified in the pages before us.

It may be at once admitted that woman has not soared so high as man has done in the realm of Poetry. We certainly have no female Shakspere. We have Poetesses who resemble him : Joanna Baillie is often like him ; so is Miss Holford ; so is Miss Mitford ; so are many others who could be named ; but the similarity is in single features, not in the whole character. We have no female Milton, either. Many of our lady Poets are sublime, many devotional : Mrs. Barbauld has Milton's solemn sense of adoration ; Mrs. Rowe has his meditative calmness ; Mrs. Hemans has his gentle, confiding humility : — but where is the female imagination that has mounted such stupendous heights, or penetrated such awful depths ? We must remember, however, that there is but one Shakspere, but one Milton ; and that men seem as little likely as women to furnish their counterparts.

But what other great British Poets are there with whom we have not Poetesses to compare ? Have we not a Byron in Miss Landon, a Cowper in the Countess of Winchelsea, a Spenser in Mrs. Tighe, a Goldsmith in Mrs. Grant, a Johnson in Hannah More, a Wycherly in Mrs. Centlivre, a Collins in Mrs. Radcliffe, a Coleridge in Mrs. Browning, a Wordsworth in Mary Howitt, a Scott (and more) in Joanna Baillie ? Or if it will still be maintained that some, or even all, of these ladies fail to reach the full height of the Poets they resemble, where is to be found the dogmatist daring enough to say that the difference is sufficiently great to be set up as a mark of distinction between the one sex and the other ? I cannot doubt that if woman had been permitted the enjoyment of the same opportunities as man, she would have presented to the world works as lofty in imagination and as noble in sublimity as any that have proceeded from the greatest of the other sex.

The doctrine of woman's intellectual inferiority is one which I cannot think upon without an impatience bordering on indignation. That our mothers, wives, sisters — that one half of the human race — should be deemed to be endowed with an inferior kind, or degree, of intelligence to that which animates the remaining portion of the species, is a theory so monstrous, that I can only wonder at even a savage age believing it. Woman intellectually inferior to man ! Woman, who is man's helpmeet; woman, who has the care of the infant mind, and can impress it as she will ; woman, who from the cradle to the grave has power to command, to enslave, to direct, man's intellect at her pleasure ! Is it credible that a belief so absurd should have gained footing in the world at all ? It may be. But it is incredible that it should form a subject for debate in this, the nineteenth century. It is at least a satisfaction to think that, in addition to the immense amount of testimony which the records of all arts and sciences bear to woman's mental equality, the present volume furnishes a further overpowering proof to the same effect.

I am quite prepared to grant that the mental constitutions of the sexes are *different ;* but I am not at all prepared to say that " difference" means " inferiority." It is easy enough to understand that the sphere of woman's duty requires powers altogether dissimilar from those which are needed by man ; but that this is any proof of a smaller development of mind, I beg leave emphatically to deny. Woman's qualities may be less conspicuous, but they are quite as important ; they may be less apparent, but they are quite as influential. Man has to bear outward, tangible, rule ; and his faculties are necessarily of an authoritative, evident, external, commanding order. Woman has to bear invisible sway over the hidden mechanism of the heart ; and her endowments are of a meek, persuasive, quiet, and subjective kind : seen rather in result than in action. Man rules the mind of the world : woman its heart.

To man belongs the sway of FORCE. To direct and use actual strength, whether it be of the intellect or of the body, is his province. It is his to tame barbarism, to establish law, to control thought, to develope energy : and the senate, the platform, the mart, the pulpit, and the battle-field, are his scenes of action. It is his to explore, to analyse, to judge, to arrange, to provide. It is his to inquire, to test, to determine. Exertion, enterprise, action, and deliberation, are his duties. Reason is his weapon : and the establishment of Truth is the great task he has to perform.

To woman belongs the sway of INFLUENCE. Her province is to soften, round off, smooth down, the angularities of life and conduct : to act (gently, but unceasingly) upon the swift-beating heart of the world, soothing it into calmness when violent; mildly stimulating it into action when torpid; and refining, purifying and exalting its passions and aspirations when excited. Home is her empire, and affection her sceptre. It is hers to endure, to watch, to suggest, to inspirit, to reinvigorate, to sustain. It is hers to colour and perfume and beautify the way of life; to adorn existence, and to make it musical. It is hers to resist and counteract the deadening influences of the world. Man goes forth to his labour day after day; he performs day after day the same cramping round of duties : it is woman's office to preserve him from becoming a mere machine. He comes in contact with villany and selfishness : it is hers to keep alive in his bosom the generous flame of virtue. He falls in with the degraded and deceiving: it is hers to prevent their evil influence upon him, and to keep up a proper estimate of humanity. It is hers, when the world has disgusted him with its hollowness, to restore him by the tranquil delights of home. It is hers, when misfortune overtakes him, to cheer him with hope, and support his sinking spirit. It is hers to preserve in their purity the moral sentiments of his nature. It is hers, while intellectual knowledge makes him wise, by moral persuasion to render him good. It is hers at all seasons to inspire him with a purifying love for the Beautiful, and to anchor his soul firmly in the everlasting rock of Religion.

I repeat, then, that woman's sphere requires a *different* mental constitution from that of man, not an *inferior* one : and very different we find the intellectual faculties of the sexes to be. It is worth our while to note a few of these peculiarities.

Looking at the whole spiritual character, we see some such broad distinctions as the following.— Man is bold, enterprising, and strong; woman cautious, prudent, and steadfast. Man is self-relying and self-possessed; woman timid, clinging, and dependent. Man is suspicious and secret; woman confiding. Man is fearless; woman apprehensive. Man arrives at truth by long and tedious study; woman by intuition. He thinks; she feels. He reasons; she sympathises. He has courage; she patience. He soon despairs; she always hopes. The strong passions are his; ambition, love of conquest, love of fame. The mild affections are hers; love of home, love of virtue, love of friends. Intellect is his; heart is hers. In the religious sentiments they are equally unlike. His is the religion of the understanding; hers the religion of faith. Man must have a creed; woman's piety is independent of all rubrics.

Or taking the mere intellectual faculties of the female mind, apart from the whole spiritual organization, we find a marked difference from those of man. The qualities of the Female Intellect seem to be rather negative than positive : they appear to be fitted more for passive endurance than for aggressive exertion. They can grasp less; but they can hold longer. Just as woman's physical frame is formed for smaller but more continuous labour than man's, so her mental constitution seems less competent to violent than to sustained action. She appears to have inferior force, but greater evenness : not so much energy, but more equability, of character.

Woman's intellectual perceptions are infinitely quicker than man's. She sees in a moment. Incongruities, resemblances, differences, characteristics, are intuitively and instantly perceived by her. The whole range of her mental faculties appears to be apter, readier, quicker, than man's. She has a finer perception of colour; a more correct ear for tune; a truer taste; a readier sensibility to beauty in form; a more sensitive appreciation of melody. Man's intellectual perceptions are comparatively slow. He sees farther, but his vision is not so instantaneous. I think his insight into essences is truer than her's; but I believe that she has a better appreciation of surfaces. She sees at once, and

FEMALE POETS

OF

GREAT BRITAIN.

JULIANA BERNERS.

1460.

THE first British Poetess of whom we have any record is the lady whose name is mentioned above; Juliana, daughter of Sir James Berners, or Barnes, of Roding, in Essex, Knight; and sister of Richard, first Lord Berners. She flourished in the middle of the fifteenth century; about fifty years after Chaucer and Gower. She received what at that time was considered a learned education; and eventually became Prioress of Sopwell Nunnery, near St. Albans. Her literary productions consist of three tracts, one on Hunting, another on Hawking, and the third on Armory, or Heraldry: they are to be found in *The Book of St. Albans, printed at Westminster, by Wynkyn de Worde,* 1496.

Her style is excessively coarse and unfeminine, and wholly inconsistent with her sacred calling; but the barbarism of the times is a sufficient, if not a complete excuse for her. From the era of Richard the Third much refinement cannot be expected.

The tract on *Hunting*, which is the only one in rhyme, furnishes the following short extract: quite long enough, I am sure, in the opinion of the reader.

4   c   25

OPENING OF THE POEM.

Mi dere sones, where ye fare, be frith, or by fell,
Take good hede in his tyme how Tristrem wol tell;
How many maner bestes of venery there were,
Listenes now to oure Dame, and ye shullen here.
Ffowre maner of bestes of venery there are,
The first of hem is a hert, the second is an hare;
The boor is one of tho,
The wolff, and no mo.
And whereso ye comen in play or in place,
Now shal I tel you which ben bestes of chace;
One of tho a buk, another a doo,
The ffox and the marteryn, and the wilde roo;
And ye shall, my dere sones, other bestes all,
Where so ye hem finde, rascall hem call,
In frith or in fell,
Or in fforest, y yow tell.
And to speke of the hert, if ye wil hit lere,
Ye shall cal him a calfe at the first yere;
The seconde yere a broket, so shal he be,
The third yere a spayard, lerneth this at me;
The iiii yere calles hem a stagge, be eny way
The fift yere a grete stagge, my dame bade you say.

The *Epilogue* to this book of Hunting is not without merit.

TO HAVE A FAITHFUL FRIEND.

A faithful friend would I fain find,
    To find him there he might be found;
But now is the world wext so unkind,
    That friendship is fall to the ground.
Now a friend I have found,
    That I will neither ban ne curse:
But of all friends in field or town,
    Ever gramercy mine own purse.

My purse it is my privy wife:
(This song I dare both sing and say :)
It parteth men of muche strife,
    When every man for himself shall pay.
As I ride in rich array,
    For gold and silver men will me flourish;
By this matter I dare well say,
    Ever gramercy mine own purse.

As I ride with gold so rede,
    And have to do with landys law,
Men for my money will make me speed,
    And for my goods they will me knowe:
More and less to me will draw
    Both the better and the worse;
By this matter I say *in sawe* *
    Ever gramercy mine own purse.

It fell by me upon a time,
    As it hath done by many one mo,
My horse, my neat, my sheep, my swine,
    And all my goods, they tell me fro:
I went to my friends and told them so.
    And home again they bade me truss:
I said again when I was wo,
    Ever gramercy mine own purse.

Therefore I rede you, sires all,
    To assay your friends or you have need;
For an ye come down, and have a fall,
    Full few of them for you will grede.
Therefore assay them every one,
    Both the better and the worse.—
Our Lord, that shope that both sun and moon,
    Send us spending in our purse !

* Proverbially.

QUEEN ANNE BOLEYN.

1507—1536.

THE following pathetic and womanly verses have been ascribed to this ill-fated lady. Sir John Hawkins, in his *History of Music*, vol. iii. p. 30, says that they were communicated to him by "a very judicious antiquary, lately deceased." Whether this statement is sufficient, however, to establish Anne Boleyn's claim to the authorship of the production, the reader must decide. I believe that the verses have never been attributed to any other person.

> Defiled is my name full sore,
>   Through cruel spite and false report,
> That I may say, for evermore,
>   Farewell, my joy! adieu, comfort!
> For wrongfully ye judge of me,
>   Unto my fame a mortal wound;
> Say what ye list, it will not be,
>   Ye seek for that cannot be found.
>
> O Death! rock me on sleep!
>   Bring me a quiet rest:
> Let pass my very guiltless ghost
>   Out of my careful breast:
> Toll on the passing bell,
> Ring out the doleful knell,
> Let the sound my death tell,
>   For I must die,
>   There is no remedy,
>   For now I die.

My paines who can express?
  Alas! they are so strong,
My dolour will not suffer strength
  My life for to prolong:
Toll on the passing bell, &c.

Alone, in prison strong,
  I wail my destiny;
Wo worth this cruel hap that I
  Should taste this misery.
Toll on the passing bell, &c.

Farewell my pleasures past,
  Welcome my present pain;
I feel my torments so increase,
  That life cannot remain.
Cease now the passing bell,
Rung is my doleful knell,
For the sound my death doth tell:
  Death doth draw nigh,
  Sound my end dolefully,
  For now I die.

It is as well, perhaps, to say that in the above Lines, the spelling is modernised; and that the same course is followed, as far as possible, in all the extracts from the older writers.

c*

ANNE ASKEWE.

1520—1546.

ANNE ASKEWE was the daughter of William Askewe, or Ayscough, of Kelsey, in the county of Lincoln; and was born in the year 1520. Her natural talents were great, and she received a learned education. Her family followed the Roman Catholic faith, and by her father's desire (although against her own inclination) she married a Roman Catholic gentleman, named Ryme. Her mind, always of a deeply religious cast, after much thought became deeply impressed with the belief that the Roman Catholic religion was not the true one, and she abjured it in favour of Protestantism. Upon this, her husband drove her from his house, and she found refuge with some friends in London. While in that city, she sought to interest the King (Henry the Eighth) in her behalf, through Queen Katherine (Parr); but in vain. Gardiner, Bishop of Winchester, caused her to be seized and committed to prison on a charge of heresy. After a short detention, however, she was liberated. But in a little while she was again arrested, thrown into the Tower, found guilty of heresy, and condemned to die at the stake.

Her demeanour, throughout the whole proceedings, was in the highest degree heroic; and affords a striking proof of the strength of the religious sentiment in woman. A contemporary writer (Mr. Loud, of Lincoln's Inn) says of her—"I must needs confess of Mrs. Askewe, now departed to the Lord, that the day afore her execution, and the same day also, she had an angel's countenance and a smiling face; though when the hour of darkness came, she was so racked, that she could not stand, but was holden up between two serjeants." On being fastened to the stake, she was asked for the last time to recant; the royal pardon being offered her if she would do so. Her reply was, "I do not come here to deny my Lord and Master." The faggots were thereupon lighted, and she was burnt to ashes. This was in 1546, in the twenty-sixth year of her age.

After her last examination in Newgate, she composed the following lines : the true martyr spirit is visible in every word of them :—

Like as the armëd knight
  Appointed to the field,
With this world will I fight,
  And faith shall be my shield.

Faith is that weapon strong
  Which will not fail at need ;
My foes therefore among
  Therewith will I proceed.

As it is had in strength
  And force of Christës way,
It will prevail at length,
  Though all the devils say nay.

Faith in the fathers old
  Obtained righteousness,
Which make me very bold
  To fear no world's distress.

I now rejoice in heart,
  And hope bid me do so,
For Christ will take my part
  And ease me of my woe.

Thou say'st, Lord, whoso kncck,
  To them wilt thou attend ;
Undo therefore the lock,
  And thy strong power send.

More enemies now I have
  Than hairs upon my head;
Let them not me deprave,
  But fight thou in my stead.

On thee my care I cast,
  For all their cruel spite,
I set not by their hast,
  For thou art my delight.

I am not she that list
  My anchor to let fall;
For every drizzling mist,
  My ship substantial.

Not oft I use to write
  In prose nor yet in rhyme,
Yet will I show one sight
  That I saw in my time.

I saw a royal throne
  Where Justice should have sit,
But in her stead was one
  Of moody cruel wit.

Absorb'd was righteousness
  As of the raging flood:
Satan in his excess
  Suck'd up the guiltless blood.

Then thought I, Jesus, Lord,
  When thou shalt judge us all,
Hard is it to record
  On these men what will fall.

Yet Lord, I thee desire,
  For that they do to me,
Let them not taste the hire
  Of their iniquity!

It would be difficult, I think, to find a more illustrious instance of consistent Christian faith than is displayed in these Lines. They present a noble evidence of woman's exalted courage in the hour of trial, and of the pure and forgiving spirit with which she can endure persecution.

5

QUEEN ELIZABETH.

1533—1603.

AMONG the vanities of this royal lady, the most innocent, perhaps, was her desire of shining as a Poet: whether she *does* shine
or not, the present writer will not undertake to determine. That
she gained very extravagant praises from contemporary critics is
not perhaps surprising : Royalty enters into the lists of Literature
so rarely, that a few extra-sweet plaudits may be pardoned when
it makes its appearance there.

I transcribe first the Lines written by the Royal Poet when a
Prisoner at Woodstock.

> Oh, Fortune ! how thy restless wavering state
>   Hath fraught with cares my troubled wit !
> Witness this present prison, whither fate
>   Could bear me, and the joys I quit :
> Thou causedest the guilty to be loos'd
> From bands, wherein are innocents inclos'd :
>   Causing the guiltless to be strait reserv'd,
>   And freeing those that death had well deserv'd.
> But by her envy can be nothing wrought,
> So God send to my foes all they have thought.

Puttenham, in his *Art of English Poesy*, speaking of the
rhetorical figure Exargasia, or the Gorgeous, says, " I find none
example in English metre so well maintaining this figure as this
ditty of her Majesty's own making, passing sweet and harmoni-
cal : which figure being, as his very original name purporteth,
the most beautiful and gorgeous of all others, it asketh in reason
to be reserved for a last compliment, and decyphered by a lady's

pen, herself being the most beautiful, or rather beauty of queens."
It is to be feared that Mr. Puttenham's loyalty sent to sleep his
taste.

The poem relates to the plotters in favour of Mary, Queen of
Scots.

> The doubt of future foes
>   Exiles my present joy,
> And wit me warns to shun such snares
>   As threaten mine annoy.
> For falsehood now doth flow,
>   And subject faith doth ebb ;
> Which would not be if reason ruled,
>   Or wisdom weav'd the web.
> But clouds of toys untried
>   Do cloak aspiring minds ;
> Which turn to rain of late repent,
>   By course of changed winds.
> The top of hope suppos'd
>   The root of ruth will be ;
> And fruitless all their graffed guiles,
>   As shortly ye shall see.
> Then dazzled eyes with pride,
>   Which great ambition blinds,
> Shall be unseal'd by worthy wights,
>   Whose foresight falsehood finds.
> The Daughter of Debate,*
>   That eke discord doth sow,
> Shall reap no gain where former rule
>   Hath taught still peace to grow.
> No foreign banish'd wight
>   Shall anchor in this port ;
> Our realm it brooks no strangers' force,
>   Let them elsewhere resort.

* Mary, Queen of Scots.

Our rusty sword with rest
  Shall first his edge employ,
Shall poll their tops that seek
  Such change, and gape for joy.

It would seem that her majesty—
       " Whose *realm* would brook no stranger force,"
had a *heart* of more yielding materials. Tyrant as she was, Queen Elizabeth did homage to a greater tyrant still,—the name of him—LOVE. The candid critic must confess that " the beauty of queens" *whines* somewhat under the influence of *la belle passion.* The following woe-begone stanzas were written on the departure of some favourite from court :—

I grieve and dare not show my discontent ;
  I love, and yet am forced to seem to hate ;
I do, yet dare not say I ever meant ;
  I seem stark mute, but inwardly do prate :
I am, and not ; I freeze, and yet am burn'd,
Since from myself, my other self I turn'd.

My care is like my shadow in the sun,
  Follows me flying, flies when I pursue it ;
Stands and lies by me, does what I have done ;
  This too familiar care does make me rue it :
No means I find to rid him from my breast,
Till by the end of things it be supprest.

Some gentler passions slide into my mind,
  For I am soft and made of melting snow ;
Or be more cruel, Love, and so be kind,
  Let me or float or sink, be high or low :
Or let me live with some more sweet content,
Or die, and so forget what love e'er meant.

Signed, " *Finis, Eliza. Regina,* upon
Moun . . . . . . 's departure."

One cannot read this passage without feeling that whatever may have been Queen Elizabeth's poetical powers, she at least had not the faculty of self-portraiture. For when she says of herself —

"That she is *soft*, and made of *melting snow*,"

one cannot, with all the charity in the world, coincide with her. Had the royal Limner compared herself to *ice* instead of snow, she might have won our assent to her proposition : but "melting snow"—— no, no! that is not by any means the verdict of History!

D

MARY, COUNTESS OF PEMBROKE.

1560—1621.

THIS lady was a sister of Sir Philip Sidney, and appears to have been a most excellent and accomplished person. Spenser mentions her as

> —— "most resembling, both in shape and spirit,
> Her brother dear:"

and Sir Philip dedicated his *Arcadia* to her.

She wrote largely, both in prose and verse, and was a most generous patron of literature.

Her poems display no inconsiderable amount of learning, and are characterised by much elegance and grace. She assisted her brother in a translation of the Psalms, which was first printed so recently as 1823.

A DIALOGUE

Between two Shepherds, Thenot and Piers, in praise of Astræa.

THENOT.

I sing divine Astræa's praise,
O Muses! help my wits to raise,
And heave my verses higher.

PIERS.

Thou need'st the truth but plainly tell,
Which much I doubt thou can'st not well,
Thou art so oft a liar.

THENOT.

If in my song no more I show,
Than heaven and earth and sea do know,
   Then truly I have spoken.

PIERS.

Sufficeth not no more to name ;
But being no less, the like, the same,
   Else laws of truth be broken.

THENOT.

Then say she is so good, so fair,
With all the earth she may compare,
   Not Momus' self denying.

PIERS.

Compare may think where likeness holds,
Nought like to her the earth enfolds,
   I look'd to find you lying.

THENOT.

Astræa sees with Wisdom's sight,
Astræa works by Virtue's might,
   And jointly both do stay in her.

PIERS.

Nay, take from them, her hand, her mind,
The one is lame, the other blind ;
   Shall still your lying stain her ?

THENOT.

Soon as Astræa shows her face,
Straight every ill avoids the place,
   And every good aboundeth.

PIERS.

Nay, long before her face doth show,
The last doth come, the first doth go ;
   How loud this lie resoundeth.

THENOT.

Astræa is our chiefest joy,
Our chiefest guard against annoy,
Our chiefest wealth, our treasure.

PIERS.

Where chiefest are, there others be,
To us none else but only she ;
When wilt thou speak in measure ?

THENOT.

Astræa may be justly said,
A field in flowery robe array'd,
In season freshly springing.

PIERS.

That spring endures but shortest time,
This never leaves Astræa's clime;
Thou liest instead of singing.

THENOT.

As heavenly light that guides the day,
Right so doth shine each lovely ray,
That from Astræa flieth.

PIERS.

Nay, darkness oft that light inclouds,
Astræa's beams no darkness shrouds ;
How loudly Thenot lieth !

THENOT.

Astræa rightly term I may,
A manly palm, a maiden bay,
Her verdure never dying.

PIERS.

Palm oft is crooked, bay is low ;
She still upright, still high doth grow ;
Good Thenot, leave thy lying !

THENOT.

Then, Piers, of friendship tell me why,
My meaning true, my words should lie,
And strive in vain to raise her?

PIERS.

Words from conceit do only rise,
Above conceit her honour flies;
But silence, nought can praise her.

CHORUS FROM THE TRAGEDY OF ANTONY.

1595.

The boiling tempest still
Makes not sea-waters foam,
Nor still the northern blast
Disquiets quiet streams,
Nor who, his chest to fill,
Sails to the morning beams,
On waves wind tosseth fast,
Still keeps his ship from home.

Nor Jove still down doth cast,
Inflamed with bloody ire,
On man, on tree, on hill,
His darts of thundering fire:
Nor still the heat doth last
On face of parched plain,
Nor wrinkled cold doth still
On frozen furrows reign.

6   D*

But still as long as we
In this low world remain,
Mishaps, our daily mates,
Our lives do entertain ;
And woes which bear no dates,
Still perch upon our heads ;
None go, but straight will be
Some greater in their steads.

Nature made us not free,
When first she made us live ;
When we began to be,
To be began our woe ;
Which growing evermore,
As dying life doth grow,
Do more and more us grieve,
And tire us more and more.

O blest who never breath'd,
Or whom, with pity moved,
Death from his cradle 'reav'd,
And swaddled in his grave.
And blessed also he
(As curse may blessing have),
Who low, and living free,
No prince's charge hath prov'd.

By stealing sacred fire,
Prometheus, then unwise,
Provoking gods to ire,
The heap of ills did stir ;
And sickness, pale and cold,
Our end which onward spur
To plague our hands, too bold,
To filch the wealth of skies.

In heaven's hate since then,
Of ill with ill enchain'd,

We race of mortal men
Full fraught our breasts have borne;
And thousand, thousand woes
Our heavenly souls now thorn,
Which free before from those,
No earthly passion pain'd.

War and war's bitter cheer
Now long time with us stay,
And fear of hated foe
Still, still increaseth sore.
Our harms worse daily grow :
Less yesterday they were
Than now, and will be more
To-morrow than to-day.

That this lady was much esteemed in her own day, we may
fairly infer from her Epitaph : written by Ben Jonson :

EPITAPH.

Underneath this sable hearse
Lies the subject of all verse,
Sidney's sister, Pembroke's mother;
Death ! ere thou hast slain another
Learn'd, and fair, and good as she,
Time shall throw a dart at thee.

ELIZABETH MELVILL,

1603,

WAS daughter of Sir James Melvill of Halhill, and wife of Colvill of Culross. She wrote *Ane Godlie Dreame, compiled in Scottish metre*, the first edition of which appeared at Edinburgh in 1603. In the following quotation, the language has been Anglicised.

FROM ANE GODLIE DREAME.

I lookëd down, and saw a pit most black,
Most full of smoke, and flaming fire most fell;
That ugly sight made me to fly aback,
I fear'd to hear so many shout and yell:
I him besought that he the truth would tell—
Is this, said I, the Papists' purging place,
Where they affirm that silly souls do dwell,
To purge their sin, before they rest in peace?

The brain of man most surely did invent
That purging place, he answer'd me again:
For greediness together they consent
To say that souls in torment may remain,
Till gold and goods relieve them of their pain.
O spiteful sprites that did the same begin!
O blindëd beasts, your thoughts are all in vain,
My blood alone did save thy soul from sin.

This pit is Hell, where through thou now must go,
There is thy way that leads thee to the land:
Now play the man, thou need'st not tremble so,
For I shall help and hold thee by the hand.
Alas! said I, I have no force to stand,
For fear I faint to see that ugly sight;
How can I come among that baleful band?
Oh, help me now, I have no force nor might!

Oft have I heard that they that enter there
In this great gulf, shall never come again:
Courage, said he, have I not bought thee dear?
My precious blood it was not shed in vain.
I saw this place, my soul did taste this pain,
Or ere I went into my Father's gloire;
Through must thou go, but thou shalt not remain;
Thou needs't not fear, for I shall go before.

I am content to do thy whole command,
Said I again, and did him fast embrace:
Then lovingly he held me by the hand,
And in we went into that fearful place.
Hold fast thy grip, said he, in any case
Let me not slip, whatever thou shalt see;
Dread not the death, but stoutly forward press
For Death nor Hell shall never vanquish thee.

His words so sweet did cheer my heavy heart,
Incontinent I cast my care aside;
Courage, said he, play not a coward's part,
Though thou be weak, yet in my strength confide.
I thought me blest to have so good a guide,
Though I was weak I knew that he was strong;
Under his wings I thought me for to hide,
If any there should press to do me wrong.

Into that Pit, when I did enter in,
I saw a sight which made my heart aghast;

Poor damnëd souls, tormented sore for sin,
In flaming fire were burning fierce and fast :
And ugly sprites, and as we thought them past,
My heart grew faint and I began to tire ;
Ere I perceived, one seizëd me at last
And held me high above a flaming fire.

The fire was great, the heat did pierce me sore,
My faith was weak, my grip was wondrous small,
I trembled fast, my fear grew more and more,
My hands did shake that I him held withal.
At length they loos'd, then they began to fall,
I cried, O Lord! and caught him fast again ;
Lord Jesus, come! and take me out of thrall :
Courage, said he, now thou art past the pain.

With this great fear, I staggerëd and woke,
Crying, O Lord! Lord Jesus come again!
But after this no kind of rest I took,
I press'd to sleep, but that was all in vain.
I would have dream'd of pleasure after pain,
Because I know I shall it find at last :
God grant my guide may still with me remain,
It is to come that I believed was past.

LADY ELIZABETH CAREW.

1613.

WHO this lady was is not altogether certain. She is generally understood to have been the wife of Sir Henry Carew, or Cary. She was a lady of great accomplishments, and was called, by John Davis, of Hereford, in the dedication prefixed to his *Muses' Sacrifice*, or *Divine Meditations*, "a darling, as well as patroness, of the muses."

The chief, indeed the only, work attributed to her is *The Tragedy of Mariam, the Fair Queen of Jewry, written by that learned, virtuous, and truly noble lady*, E. C., 1613; a play abounding in fine womanly touches of feeling and sentiment. I extract the

CHORUS TO THE FOURTH ACT.

The fairest action of our human life
Is scorning to revenge an injury:
For who forgives without a further strife,
His adversary's heart doth to him tie.
And 'tis a firmer conquest, truly said,
To win the heart, than overthrow the head.

If we a worthy enemy do find,
To yield to worth it must be nobly done;
But if of baser metal be his mind,
In base revenge there is no honour won.
Who would a worthy courage overthrow,
And who would wrestle with a worthless foe?

We say our hearts are great and cannot yield;
　　Because they cannot yield it proves them poor;
Great hearts are task'd beyond their power, but seld*
　　The weakest lion will the loudest roar.
Truth's school for certain doth this same allow,
High-heartedness doth sometimes teach to bow.

A noble heart doth teach a virtuous scorn,
　　To scorn to owe a duty overlong;
To scorn to be for benefits, forborne,
　　To scorn a lie, to scorn to do a wrong.
To scorn to bear an injury in mind,
To scorn a free-born heart slave-like to bind.

But if for wrongs we needs revenge must have,
　　Then be our vengeance of the noblest kind;
Do we his body from our fury save,
　　And let our hate prevail against our mind?
What can 'gainst him a greater vengeance be,
Than make his foe more worthy far than he?

Had Mariam scorn'd to leave a due unpaid,
　　She would to Herod then have paid her love;
And not have been by sullen passion sway'd.
　　To fix her thoughts all injury above
Is virtuous pride.　Had Mariam thus been proud,
Long famous life to her had been allow'd.

* Seldom.

LADY MARY WROTH,

1621,

Was the daughter of Robert, Earl of Leicester, (a younger brother of Sir Philip Sidney), and the wife of Sir Robert Wroth. In 1621 she published a romance, called *Urania*, interspersed with poetry. It was to Lady Wroth that Ben Jonson dedicated *The Alchymist*.

From the romance to which I have alluded, I make the following selections.—

SONG.

Who can blame me if I love,
Since Love before the world did move?
When I lov'd not, I despair'd,
Scarce for handsomeness I car'd;
Since so much I am refined,
As new-framed of state and mind,
   Who can blame me if I love,
    Since Love before the world did move?

Some in truth of Love beguil'd,
Have him blind and childish styl'd;
But let none in these persist,
Since so judging judgment miss'd.
    Who can blame me?

Love in chaos did appear;
When nothing was, yet he seem'd clear:
Nor when light could be descried,
To his crown a light was tied.
    Who can blame me?

Love is truth and doth delight,
Whereas Honour shines most bright:
Reason's self doth Love approve,
Which makes us ourselves to love.
          Who can blame me?

Could I my past time begin,
I would not commit such sin,
To live an hour, and not to love;
Since Love makes us perfect prove,
          Who can blame me?

SONG.

Love, a child, is ever crying;
Please him, and he straight is flying;
Give him, he the more is craving,
Never satisfied with having.

His desires have no measure;
Endless folly is his treasure;
What he promiseth he breaketh,
Trust not one word that he speaketh.

He vows nothing but false matter;
And to cozen you will flatter;
Let him gain the hand, he'll leave you,
And still glory to deceive you.

He will triumph in your wailing;
And yet cause be of your failing:
These his virtues are, and slighter
Are his gifts, his favors lighter.

Fathers are as firm in staying,
Wolves no fiercer in their preying;
As a child, then, leave him crying,
Nor seek him so given to flying.

The reader will not fail to notice the remarkably contradictory sentiments which these two poems present upon that important subject, the character of Cupid. Like the lawyer in Cowper's *Eyes and Nose*, the fair author pleads upon both sides of the question. In the one song we are told that

"Love, *a child*, is ever crying,"—

and that we are to

"Trust not *one* word that he speaketh :"

in the other we are informed that Love is *truth*, and that those who call him childish

"Have, so judging, judgment miss'd."

Which doctrine are we to believe?

ANNE, COUNTESS OF ARUNDEL.

1630.

THIS lady was sister of Thomas, Lord Dacre, and the wife of Philip, Earl of Arundel, who died in the Tower of London, in 1595. The following verses, written by her on the cover of a letter, have been preserved by Mr. Lodge (Illustrations of British History, vol. iii.), who is of opinion that they were called forth by the death of her husband.

> In sad and ashy weeds I sigh,
>   I groan, I pine, I mourn ;
> My oaten yellow reeds I all
>   To jet and ebon turn.
> My watery eyes, like winter's skies,
>   My furrow'd cheeks o'erflow :
> All heavens know why, men mourn as I,
>   And who can blame my woe ?
>
> In sable robes of night my days
>   Of joy consumed be ;
> My sorrow sees no light ; my lights
>   Through sorrow nothing see :
> For now my sun his course has run,
>   And from his sphere doth go
> To endless bed of folded lead,
>   And who can blame my woe ?
>
> My flocks I now forsake, that so
>   My sheep my grief may know ;
> The lilies loth to take, that since
>   His death presum'd to grow.

I envy air, because it dare
Still breathe and he not so ;
Hate earth that doth entomb his youth,
And who can blame my woe ?

Not I, poor I alone — (alone
How can this sorrow be ?)
Not only men make moan, but more
Than men make moan with me :
The gods of greens, the mountain queens,
The fairy circled row,
The Muses nine, and Powers divine,
Do all condole my woe.

I have not been able to discover any other poems attributed to
this lady, and therefore I conclude that her writings were few.
The verses quoted do not look like the production of a practised
writer, certainly, for the thoughts are obscure, and the style
laboured. The last stanza seems to me particularly unhappy.
The expression "gods of greens" is almost laughable ; and the idea
of the " Muses nine," *et cetera*, condoling her woe, is ludicrously
ridiculous. What could Terpsichore, for instance, have to mourn
for in the loss of Lord Arundel? And why should " the mountain queens" make moan with his widowed lady? The woe
seems very forced and unnatural throughout.

E*

DIANA PRIMROSE,

1630,

WROTE an insufferably prosy tract of twelve pages, called *A Chain of Pearl, or a Memorial of the peerless Graces and heroic Virtues of Queen Elizabeth, of glorious memory, composed by the noble lady, Diana Primrose.* The pearls which form this chain are the *Religion, Chastity, Prudence, Temperance, Clemency, Justice, Fortitude, Science, Patience,* and *Bounty* of her Majesty : all of which are described at length.

I give, as a sample of this fulsome panegyric,

THE EIGHTH PEARL—SCIENCE.

Among the virtues intellectual,
The van is led by that we Science call ;
A pearl more precious than the Egyptian queen
Quaff'd off to Antony : of more esteem
Than Indian gold, or most resplendent gems,
Which ravish us with their translucent beams.
How many arts and sciences did deck
This Heroina ! who still had at beck
The Muses and the Graces, when that she
Gave audience in state and majesty :
Then did the goddess Eloquence inspire
Her royal breast : Apollo with his lyre
Ne'er made such music ; on her sacred lips
Angels enthroned, most heavenly manna sips.
Then might you see her nectar-flowing vein
Surround the hearers ; in which sugar'd stream
She able was to drown a world of men,

And drown'd with sweetness to revive again.
Alasco, the ambassador Polonian,
Who perorated like a mere Slavonian,
And in rude rambling Rhetoric did roll,
She did with Attic eloquence control.
Her speeches to our Academians,
Well shew'd she knew among Athenians
How to deliver such well-tuned words
As with such places punctually accords.
But with what Oratory-ravishments
Did she imparadise her Parliaments!
Her last most princely speech doth verify,
How highly she did England dignify.
Her loyal Commons how did she embrace,
And entertain with a most royal grace!

In justice to Mrs. Primrose, we should call to mind that many contemporary writers of the other sex far surpassed her in their adulations of Royalty. Indeed, she follows some of them at a very humble distance. And I think that flattery is at all times far less chargeable upon the female than upon the male sex. Woman keeps much closer to truth than man does. Whether it be that her natural timidity leads her to keep always in sight of land, or that she has a more honest and consistent regard for verity, it might seem like flattery to determine ; but certain it is, that she very rarely sails out boldly into the sea of falsehood, or trusts herself to any considerable distance upon its treacherous waters.

MARY FAGE.

1637.

THIS lady deserves mention, if only for her ingenuity. In a volume published by her in 1637, and entitled *Fame's Roule*, she presents no fewer than four hundred and twenty anagrams and acrostics upon the names of the Royal Family and the nobility ! Such instances of patient labour are (happily) rare.

To the Right Hon. JOHN, *Earl of* CLARE, *Lord* HOUGHTON, *of Houghton.*

JOHN HOLLIS.

Anagramma,

Oh! on hy hills.

In virtue when I see you make such speed,
Oh! it doth then no admiration breed,
Hy, on hy hills of honor that you stand :
Nature commandeth virtue such a band.
Honor on virtue ever should attend :
Oh, on hy hills you may forever wend :
Loving of virtue which doth shine so clear,
Likely it is, you Earl of *Clare* appear.
Insue then well, what you have well begun,
So *on hy hills* to stand you well have won.

To the Right Hon. JOHN, *Earl of* WEYMES, *Lord* WEYMES.

JOHN WEYMES.

Anagramma,

Shew men joy.

In your great honour free from all alloy,
O truly noble *Weymes*, you *shew men joy ;*
Having your virtues in their clearer sight,
Nothing there is can breed them more delight.
With *joy* your wisdom so doth men content :
Ever we pray it might be permanent :
Your virtuous life doth breed so great delight,
Men wish you endless *joy*, you to requite ;
Eternal *joy* may unto you succeed,
Shewing men joy, who do our comfort breed.

It is due to our Female Poets to observe, that as a body they are singularly free from such acrostical and alliterative fancies. Not more than two or three of the Sisterhood have manifested in any degree that cruelty of disposition which consists in subjecting the words they employ to the torture-drill of ingenuity : — and the majority of them disdain any use of language but a simple and sensible one. I cannot call to mind a punster among them.

8

ANNA HUME,

1644,

WAS the daughter of David Hume, of Godscroft. In 1644 she published, at Edinburgh, *The Triumphs of Love, Chastity, Death: translated out of Petrarch;* from which Book the following selection is made.

TO THE READER.

Reader, I have oft been told,
Verse that speak not Love are cold.
I would gladly please thine ear,
But am loth to buy 't too dear.
And 'tis easier far to borrow
Lovers' tears than feel their sorrow.
Therefore he hath furnisht me
Who had enough to serve all three.

FROM THE TRIUMPH OF DEATH. — (CHAP. 1.)

Lauretta meeting cruel Death,
Mildly resigns her noble breath.

The fatal hour of her short life drew near,
That doubtful passage which the world doth fear;
Another company, who had not been
Freed from their earthly burden, there were seen,

To try if prayers could appease the wrath,
Or stay the inexorable hand of death.
That beauteous crowd conven'd to see the end
Which all must taste ; each neighbour, every friend
Stood by, when grim death with her hand took hold
And pull'd away one only hair of gold.
Thus from the world this fairest flower is ta'en
To make her shrine more bright, not out of spleen.
How many moaning plaints, what store of cries
Were utter'd there, when fate shut those fair eyes
For which so oft I sung ; whose beauties burn'd
My tortur'd heart so long : whiles others mourn'd
She pleas'd, and quiet did the fruit enjoy
Of her blest life ; farewell, without annoy,
True saint on earth, said they : so might she be
Esteem'd, but nothing 'bates death's cruelty.

     *   *   *   *

Now at what rate I should the sorrow prize,
I know not ; nor have art that can suffice
The sad affliction to relate in verse
Of these fair Dames that wept about her hearse :
Courtesy, Virtue, Beauty, all are lost.
What shall become of us ? none else can boast
Such high perfection, no more we shall
Hear her wise words, nor the angelical
Sweet music of her voice ; whiles thus they cried,
The parting spirit doth itself divide
With every virtue from the noble breast,
As some grave hermit seeks a lonely rest ;
The heavens were clear, and all the ambient air
Without a threatening cloud ; no adversaire
Durst once appear, or her calm mind affright :
Death singly did herself conclude the fight ;
After, when fear and the extremest plaint
Were ceased, the attentive eyes of all were bent
On that fair face, and by despair became
Secure ; she who was spent, not like a flame
By force extinguish'd, but as lights decay,—

And undiscernëd waste themselves away :
Thus went the soul in peace, so lamps are spent,
As the oil fails which gives them nourishment :
In sum, her countenance you still might know
The same it was, not pale, but white as snow
Which on the tops of hills in gentle flakes
Falls in a calm, or as a man that takes
Desired rest, as if her lovely sight
Were clos'd with sweetest sleep, after the sprite
Was gone. If this be that fools call to die,
Death seem'd in her exceeding fair to be.

For the foregoing passage I am indebted to the Rev. Mr.
Dyce's *Specimens of British Poetesses*, a work of much research
and merit.   I take this opportunity to acknowledge very considerable obligations to that production.

MRS. ANNE BRADSTREET.

[Mrs. Anne Bradstreet, though born in England, lived nearly
all her life in America, where she died about the middle of the
seventeenth century.   She was the daughter of one and the wife
of another Governor of Massachusetts, and she was celebrated
by the Puritan Fathers as the " glory of her sex," as the " tenth
muse," &c., &c.   Her name and history appear more appropri-
ately in " The Female Poets of America." — *Editor.*]

ANN COLLINS.

1653,

WROTE a book called *Divine Songs and Meditations*, from which I extract the following

SONG.

The Winter being over,
In order comes the Spring,
Which doth green herbs discover,
And cause the birds to sing.
The night also expired,
Then comes the morning bright,
Which is so much desired
By all that love the light.
This may learn
Them that mourn,
To put their grief to flight:
The Spring succeedeth Winter,
And day must follow night.

He therefore that sustaineth
Affliction or distress,
Which every member paineth
And findeth no release:
Let such therefore despair not,
But on firm hope depend,
Whose griefs immortal are not,
And therefore must have end
They that faint

F

With complaint
Therefore are to blame :
They add to their afflictions,
And amplify the same.

For if they could with patience
Awhile possess the mind,
By inward consolations
They might refreshing find,
To sweeten all their crosses,
That little time they 'dure:
So might they gain by losses,
And sharp would sweet procure.
But if the mind
Be inclined
To unquietness,
That only may be called
The worst of all distress.

He that is melancholy,
Detesting all delight,
His wits by sottish folly
Are ruinated quite.
Sad discontent and murmurs
To him are incident:
Were he possessed of honors,
He could not be content.
Sparks of joy
Fly away,
Floods of care arise;
And all delightful motion
In the conception dies.

But those that are contented,
However things do fall,
Much anguish is prevented,
And they soon freed from all.
They finish all their labours

With much felicity,
Their joy in trouble savours
Of perfect piety.
Cheerfulness
Doth express
A settled pious mind ;
Which is not prone to grudging,
From murmuring refin'd.

The calm, pious cheerfulness of sentiment displayed in the
above lines will not fail to yield a warm sensation of pleasure to
the reader. I make especial reference to it, because I think it
characteristic of the female spirit generally, as this volume will
prove almost in every page ; and because I think that a critic is
bound to take every possible opportunity to pay honour to those
writers who address the better feelings of humanity.

MARY MORPETH,

1656,

"A Scotch poetess, and a friend of the poet Drummond, of whom, besides many other things in poetry, she had a large *Encomium* in verse."—*Theatrum Poetarum.*

TO WILLIAM DRUMMOND, OF HAWTHORNDEN.

(Prefixed to his Poems, 1656.)

I never rested on the Muses' bed,
Nor dipt my quill in the Thessalian fountain,
My rustic muse was rudely fosterëd,
And flies too low to reach the double mountain.

Then do not sparks with your bright suns compare,
Perfection in a woman's work is rare;
From an untroubled mind should verses flow;
My discontent makes mine too muddy show;
And hoarse encumbrances of household care,
Where these remain, the Muses ne'er repair.

If thou dost extol her hair,
Or her ivory forehead fair,
Or those stars whose bright reflection
Thralls thy heart in sweet subjection.
Or when to display thou seeks
The snow-mixt roses on her cheeks,
Or those rubies soft and sweet

Over those pretty rows that meet:
The Chian painter as asham'd
Hides his picture so far fam'd;
And the queen he carv'd it by
With a blush her face doth dye,
Since those lines do limn a creature,
That so far surpass'd her feature.
When thou show'st how fairest Flora
Prankt with pride the banks of Ora,
So thy verse her streams doth honour,
Strangers grow enamour'd on her;
All the swans that swim in Po
Would their native brooks forego,
And, as loathing Phœbus' beams,
Long to bathe in cooler streams.
Tree-turned Daphne would be seen
In her groves to flourish green;
And her boughs would gladly spare
To frame a garland for thy hair,
That fairest nymphs, with finest fingers
May thee crown the best of singers.
But when thy Muse, dissolv'd in showers,
Wails that peerless prince of ours,
Cropt by too untimely fate,
Her mourning doth exasperate
Senseless things to see thee mourn,
Stones do weep, and trees do groan,
Birds in air, fishes in flood,
Beasts in field forsake their food;
The Nymphs foregoing all their bowers
Tear the chaplets deckt with flowers;
Sol himself with misty vapour
Hides from earth his glorious taper,
And, as moved to hear thee 'plain,
Shows his grief in showers of rain.

MARY MORPETH, *of Oxlie.*

Mary Morpeth was the author of several Poetical Epistles, with titles like the following:—*To the most Illustrious John, Earl of Lauderdale; a congratulatory welcome of an heart-well-wishing quill:* but I find nothing in those poems that is worth extracting.   Should the reader be disposed, however, from the style of the passage above quoted, to entertain a higher opinion of our fair author's merits than I do, I may refer him to a volume of Scottish Fugitive Poetry, which was published at Edinburgh in 1823, and which contains several of the letters in verse to which I have alluded. . They will be found under the signature of "M. M."

KATHERINE PHILIPS,

1631—1664,

WAS the daughter of John Fowles, of Bucklersbury, a London merchant, and was born in 1631. She was married in 1647 to Mr. James Philips, of the Priory, Cardigan, and died of small-pox in 1664.

Mrs. Philips has always seemed to me to be one of the best of our Female Poets. Her versification, though often careless, is chaste and harmonious, and her sentiments extremely pure and excellent. She appears to have enjoyed considerable fame, for Cowley and Dryden celebrated her genius, and Jeremy Taylor dedicated to her his *Discourse on Friendship*.

That must have been a noble spirit which in such a licentious and gaudy era as the reign of Charles the Second could conceive and embody the following

ODE AGAINST PLEASURE.

There's no such thing as pleasure here,
　'Tis all a perfect cheat,
Which does but shine and disappear,
　Whose charm is but deceit:
The empty bribe of yielding souls,
Which first betrays, and then controls.

'Tis true, it looks at distance fair,
　But if we do approach,
The fruit of Sodom will impair,
　And perish at a touch;
It being than in fancy less,
And we expect more than possess.

For by our pleasures we are cloy'd
And so desire is done ;
Or else, like rivers, they make wide
The channels where they run ;
And either way true bliss destroys,
Making us narrow, or our joys.

We covet pleasure easily,
But ne'er true bliss possess ;
For many things must make it be,
But one may make it less.
Nay, were our state as we would choose it,
'Twould be consumed by fear to lose it.

What art thou, then, thou wingëd air,
More weak and swift than fame ?
Whose next successor is despair,
And its attendant shame.
The' experienced prince then reason had
Who said of Pleasure, — " It is mad."

It is from passages like this that we gain a true idea of the
power and mission of the female mind.   To refine, to exalt, and
to purify the soul of the world, is woman's noble office : to keep
chaste its sentiments, to spiritualise its affections, and to detach
it from the too-material pleasures and engagements of life, is her
lofty duty : and the poem above quoted is one proof among
many in this work, how earnestly and ably, even under the most
discouraging circumstances, she applies herself to her allotted
task.   Great indeed is the debt that morality owes to her !

The pure and chaste sentiments which Katherine Philips
urged may further be seen in this fine poem, called

A COUNTRY LIFE.

How sacred and how innocent
A country life appears ;
How free from tumult, discontent,
From flattery or fears !

This was the first and happiest life,
　　When man enjoy'd himself;
Till pride exchangëd peace for strife,
　　And happiness for pelf.

'Twas here the poets were inspired,
　　Here taught the multitude;
The brave they here with honour fir'd,
　　And civilised the rude.

That golden age did entertain
　　No passion but of love ;
The thoughts of ruling and of gain
　　Did ne'er their fancies move.

None then did envy neighbour's wealth
　　Nor plot to wrong his bed ;
Happy in friendship and in health,
　　On roots, not beasts, they fed.

They knew no law nor physic then,
　　Nature was all their wit :
And if there yet remain to men
　　Content, sure this is it.

What blessings doth this world afford
　　To tempt or bribe desire !
Her courtship is all fire and sword,
　　Who would not then retire ?

Then welcome dearest solitude,
　　My great felicity ;
Though some are pleas'd to call thee rude,
　　Thou art not so, but we.

Them that do covet only rest,
　　A cottage will suffice:
It is not brave to be possest
　　Of earth,. but to despise.

Opinion is the rate of things,
 From hence our peace doth flow ;
I have a better fate than kings,
 Because I think it so.

When all the stormy world doth roar,
 How unconcern'd am I !
I cannot fear to tumble lower
 Who never could be high.

Secure in these unenvy'd walls,
 I think not on the state,
And pity no man's case that falls
 From his ambitious height.

Silence and innocence are safe ;
 A heart that's nobly true
At all these little arts can laugh
 That do the world subdue.

While others revel it in state,
 Here I'll contented sit,
And think I have as good a fate
 As wealth and pomp admit.

Let some in courtship take delight,
 And to the' Exchange resort ;
Then revel out a winter's night,
 Not making love, but sport.

These never knew a noble flame,
 'Tis lust, scorn or design :
While vanity plays all their game,
 Let peace and honour mine.

When the inviting spring appears,
 To Hyde Park let them go,
And hasting thence be full of fears
 To lose Spring-Garden show.

Let others (nobler) seek to gain
    In knowledge happy fate,
And others busy them in vain
    To study ways of state.

But I resolvëd from within,
    Confirmëd from without,
In privacy intend to spin
    My future minutes out.

And from this hermitage of mine,
    I banish all wild toys,
And nothing that is not divine
    Shall dare to tempt my joys.

There are below but two things good,
    Friendship and Honesty;
And only those of all I would
    Ask for felicity.

In this retir'd and humble seat,
    Free from both war and strife,
I am not forc'd to make retreat,
    But choose to spend my life.

The subjoined lines seem to me to contain some sound philosophy, most pointedly expressed.

TO MY ANTENOR, MARCH 16, 1660–1.

My dear Antenor, now give o'er,
For my sake talk of graves no more;
Death is not in our power to gain,
And is both wish'd and fear'd in vain.
Let 's be as angry as we will,
Grief sooner may distract than kill;
And the unhappy often prove
Death is as coy a thing as love.

Those whose own sword their death did give,
Afraid were, or asham'd, to live ;
And by an act so desperate,
Did poorly run away from fate ;
'Tis braver much t' outride the storm,
Endure its rage, and shun its harm ;
Affliction nobly undergone,
More greatness shows than having none.
But yet the wheel in turning round,
At last may lift us from the ground ;
And when our fortune 's most severe,
The less we have, the less we fear.
And why should we that grief permit,
Which cannot mend nor shorten it ?
Let 's wait for a succeeding good,
Woes have their ebb as well as flood ;
And since the parliament have rescued you,
Believe that Providence will do so too.

Mrs. Philips was known, as a poetess, by the name of Orinda ;
and was as exemplary in the discharge of her domestic duties as
she was celebrated for her poetical abilities.

PRINCESS ELIZABETH.

1597—1662.

THIS lady was the amiable daughter of King James the First; and she became the Queen of Bohemia. The following verses were given by her to Lord Harrington of Exton, her preceptor; they are, as will be seen, full of devout feeling, very gracefully and eloquently expressed.

This is joy, this is true pleasure,
If we best things make our treasure,
And enjoy them at full leisure,
Evermore in richest measure.

God is only excellent,
Let up to Him our love be sent:
Whose desires are set or bent
On aught else, shall much repent.

Theirs is a most wretched case,
Who themselves so far disgrace,
That they their affections place
Upon things nam'd vile and base.

Let us love of heaven receive,
These are joys our hearts will heave
Higher than we can conceive,
And shall us not fail nor leave.

Earthly things do fade, decay.
Constant to us not one day:
Suddenly they pass away,
And we can not make them stay.

All the vast world doth contain,
To content man's heart, are vain,
That still justly will complain,
And unsatisfied remain.

God most holy, high and great,
Our delight doth make complete :
When in us he takes his seat,
Only then are we replete.

Why should vain joys us transport?
Earthly pleasures are but short,
And are mingled in such sort,
Griefs are greater than the sport.

And regard of this yet have,
Nothing can from death us save,
Then we must into our grave,
When we most are pleasure's slave.

By long use our souls will cleave
To the earth ; then it we leave ;
Then will cruel death bereave,
All the joys that we receive.

Thence they go to hellish flame,
Ever tortur'd in the same,
With perpetual blot of name,
Flout, reproach, and endless shame ,

Torment not to be exprest,
But O then ! how greatly blest,
Whose desires are whole addrest
To the heavenly things and best.

Thy affections shall increase
Growing forward without cease,
Even until thou diest in peace,
And enjoyest eternal ease.

When thy heart is fullest fraught
With heaven's love, it shall be caught
To the place it lov'd and sought,
Which Christ's precious blood hath bought.

Joys of those which there shall dwell,
No heart can think, no tongue can tell ;
Wonderfully they excel,
Those thy soul will fully swell.

Are these things indeed even so ?
Do I certainly them know,
And am I so much my foe,
To remain yet dull and slow ?

Doth not that surpassing joy,
Ever freed from all annoy,
Me inflame ? and quite destroy
Love of every earthly toy ?

Oh, how frozen is my heart !
Oh, my soul ! how dead thou art !
Thou, O God ! we may impart,
Vain is human strength and art.

O my God ! for Christ his sake,
Quite from me this dulness take ;
Cause me earth's love to forsake,
And of heaven my realm to make.

If early thanks I render thee,
That thou hast enlightened me,
With such knowledge that I see
What things must behoveful be :

That I hereon meditate,
That desire, I find (though late)
To prize heaven at higher rate,
And these pleasures vain to hate.

O, enlighten more my sight,
And dispel my darksome night,
Good Lord, by thy heavenly light,
And thy beams most pure and bright.

Since in me such thoughts are scant,
Of thy grace impair my want,
Often meditations grant,
And in me more deeply plant.

Work of wisdom more desire,
Grant I may with holy ire
Slight the world, and me inspire
With thy love to be on fire.

What care I for lofty place,
If the Lord grant me his grace,
Shewing me his pleasant face,
And with joy I end my race.

This is only my desire,
This doth set my heart on fire,
That I might receive my hire,
With the saints' and angels' quire

O my soul of heavenly birth,
Do thou scorn this basest earth,
Place not here thy joy and mirth.
Where of bliss is greatest dearth.

From below thy mind remove,
And affect the things above :
Set thy heart and fix thy love
Where thou truest joys shalt prove.

If I do love things on high,
Doubtless them enjoy shall I,
Earthly pleasures if I try
They pursuëd faster fly.

O Lord! glorious, yet most kind,
Thou hast these thoughts put in my mind;
Let me grace increasing find,
Me to thee more firmly bind.

To God glory, thanks and praise,
I will render all my days,
Who has blest me many ways,
Shedding on me gracious rays.

To me grace, O Father! send,
On thee wholly to depend,
That all may to thy glory tend;
So let me live, so let me end.

Now to the true Eternal King,
Not seen with human eye,
The' immortal, only wise, true God,
Be praise perpetually!

The foregoing extract is taken from the *Nugæ Antiquæ*. I
am not aware that the Princess wrote any other poems; but that
her powers and acquirements were well appreciated, there is
plenty of evidence to show. Like many of the noble ladies of
her time, the Princess Elizabeth was well taught in classical and
polite learning. It will be observed that most of the Female Poets
of the sixteenth and seventeenth centuries were highly-educated
women of rank: and the ease and grace with which they bore their
scholastic attainments will not fail to be remarked by the reader.

G*

FRANCES BOOTHBY,

1670,

Lived in the reign of Charles the Second, and was related to
Lady Yate, of Harvington in Worcestershire, as we learn from
the dedication of the only piece she has written, a play called
Marcelia.

SONG.

You powerful Gods ! if I must be
An injur'd offering to Love's deity,
Grant my revenge, this plague on men,
That woman ne'er may love again.
Then I'll with joy submit unto my fate,
Which by your justice gives their empire date.

Depose that proud insulting boy,
Who most is pleas'd when he can most destroy ;
O let the world no longer govern'd be
By such a blind and childish Deity !
For if you gods be in your power severe,
We shall adore you, not from love, but fear.

But if you'll his divinity maintain,
O'er men, false men, confine his torturing reign ;
And when their hearts love's greatest torments prove,
Let that not pity, but our laughter move.
Thus scorn'd and lost to all their wishes aim,
Let Rage, Despair, and Death, then end their flame.

MARGARET, DUCHESS OF NEWCASTLE.

1673.

THIS very voluminous and indefatigable authoress was born at St. John's, near Colchester, about the end of the reign of James the First: her father was Sir Charles Lucas. She became one of the Maids of Honour to Queen Henrietta Maria, whom she accompanied to France. She there was married to the Marquis of Newcastle, who assisted her in her literary labours. The noble pair produced between them nearly twelve folio volumes of plays, poems, orations, and essays; most of them sufficiently ambitious in their aim, but none of them at all remarkable for wit or genius.

The Duchess is not without force, and that, too, often of a picturesque and effective sort, as the following extracts will show: but the bulk of her works are insufferably tame, commonplace, and prosy.

OF THE THEME OF LOVE.

O Love, how thou art tired out with rhyme!
Thou art a tree whereon all poets climb;
And from thy branches every one takes some
Of thy sweet fruit, which Fancy feeds upon.
But now thy tree is left so bare and poor,
That they can hardly gather one plum more.

DESCRIPTION OF THE ELFIN QUEEN.

She on a dewy leaf doth bathe,
And as she sits the leaf doth wave :

There, like a new fall'n flake of snow
Doth her white limbs in beauty show.
Her garments fair her maids put on,
Made of the pure light from the sun.

PERSONIFICATION OF MELANCHOLY.

Her voice is low, and gives a hollow sound;
She hates the light, and is in darkness found;
Or sits with blinking lamps, or tapers small,
Which various shadows make against the wall.
She loves nought else but noise which discord makes,
As croaking frogs, whose dwelling is in lakes;
The raven's hoarse, the mandrake's hollow groan,
And shrieking owls, which fly i' the night alone :
The tolling bell which for the dead rings out;
A mill where rushing waters run about;
The roaring winds, which shake the cedars tall,
Plough up the seas, and beat the rocks withal.
She loves to walk in the still moonshine night,
And in a thick dark grove she takes delight;
In hollow caves, thatch'd houses, and low cells,
She loves to live, and there alone she dwells.

The account which Melancholy gives of herself scarcely agrees
with the foregoing portrait of her by her rival, Mirth.

MELANCHOLY'S DESCRIPTION OF HER DWELLING.

I dwell in groves that gilt are with the sun;
Sit on the banks by which clear waters run;
In summers hot down in a shade I lie;
My music is the buzzing of a fly;
I walk in meadows, where grows fresh green grass;
In fields where corn is high, I often pass;

Walk up the hills, where round I prospects see,
Some brushy woods, and some all champaigns be ;
Returning back, I in fresh pastures go,
To hear how sheep do bleat, and cows do low ;
In winter cold, when nipping frosts come on,
Then I do live in a small house alone ;
Although 'tis plain, yet cleanly 'tis within,
Like to a soul that's pure and clear from sin ;
And there I dwell in quiet and still peace,
Not fill'd with cares how riches do increase ;
I wish nor seek for vain and fruitless pleasures ;
No riches are, but what the mind intreasures.
Thus am I solitary, live alone,
Yet better lov'd the more that I am known ;
And though my face ill-favour'd at first sight,
After acquaintance, it will give delight.
Refuse me not, for I shall constant be ;
Maintain your credit and your dignity.

THE FUNERAL OF CALAMITY.

Calamity was laid on sorrow's hearse,
And coverings had of melancholy verse ;
Compassion, a kind friend, did mourning go,
And tears about the corpse, as flowers, strow ;
A garland of deep sighs by Pity made
Upon Calamity's sad corpse was laid ;
Bells of complaint did ring it to the grave,
Poets a monument of fame it gave.

QUEEN MAB'S DINNER-TABLE.

Upon a mushroom there is spread
A cover fine, of spider's web ;

11

And for her stool a thistle-down,
And for her cup an acorn's crown,
Wherein strong nectar there is fill'd
That from sweet flowers is distill'd.
Flies of all sorts, both fat and good,
Partridge, snipes, quails and poult, her food,
Pheasants, larks, cocks, or any kind,
Both wild and tame, you there might find.
But for her guard serves grosser meat,
On stall-fed dormouse they do eat.

ANNE KILLEGREW,

1685,

Was the daughter of Dr. Henry Killegrew, Master of the Savoy, and one of the Prebendaries of Westminster. She was born shortly before the restoration of Charles the Second, and died in 1685. She appears to have been highly accomplished, and to have gained a high reputation amongst her contemporaries. Dryden says of her, —

> "Art she had none, yet wanted none;
> For nature did that want supply,
> So rich in treasures of her own,
> She might our boasted stores defy :
> Such noble vigour did her verse adorn,
> That it seem'd borrow'd where 'twas only born."

The following poem is a pleasing specimen of her verse : —

THE COMPLAINT OF A LOVER.

See'st thou yonder craggy rock,
  Whose head o'erlooks the swelling main,
Where never shepherd fed his flock,
  Or careful peasant sow'd his grain?

No wholesome herb grows on the same,
  Or bird of day will on it rest;
'Tis barren as the hopeless flame,
  That scorches my tormented breast.

Deep underneath a cave doth lie,
　　The entrance hid with dismal yew,
Where Phœbus never show'd his eye,
　　Or cheerful day yet piercëd through.

In that dark melancholy cell,
　　(Retreat and solace to my woe,)
Love, sad despair, and I, do dwell,
　　The springs from whence my griefs do flow.

Treacherous love that did appear,
　　(When he at first approached my heart,)
Drest in a garb far from severe,
　　Or threatening aught of future smart.

So innocent those charms then seem'd,
　　When Rosalinda first I spy'd,
Ah! who would them have deadly deem'd?
　　But flowers do often serpents hide.

Beneath those sweets concealëd lay,
　　To love that cruel foe, Disdain,
With which, alas! she does repay
　　My constant and deserving pain.

When I in tears have spent the night,
　　With sighs I usher in the sun,
Who never saw a sadder sight
　　In all the courses he has run.

Sleep, which to others ease does prove,
　　Comes unto me, alas! in vain;
For in my dreams I am in love,
　　And in them, too, she does disdain.

Sometimes t' amuse my sorrow, I
　　Unto the hollow rocks repair,
And loudly to the echo cry,
　　Ah! gentle nymph, come ease my care.

Thou, who times past a lover wert,
   Ah, pity me, who now am so;
And by a sense of thine own smart
   Alleviate my mighty woe.

Come flatter, then, or chide my grief;
   Catch my last words and call me fool;
Or say she loves for my relief,
   My passion either soothe, or school.

The following is her

EPITAPH, WRITTEN BY HERSELF.

When I am dead, few friends attend my hearse,
And for a monument, I leave — my verse.

HERODIA'S DAUGHTER

Presenting St. John's head in a charger.

Behold, dear mother, who was late our fear,
Disarm'd and harmless, I present you here;
The tongue tied up that made all Jewry quake,
And which so often did our greatness shake :
No terror sits upon his awful brow,
Where fierceness reign'd, there calmness triumphs now.
As lovers use he gazes on my face,
With eyes that languish as they sued for grace ;
Wholly subdued by my victorious charms,
See how his head reposes in my arms.
Come join then with me in my just transport,
Who thus have brought the hermit to the court.

H

It seems that our author was accused of plagiarism by her
contemporaries; or that at least, in Dryden's phrase, her vigour
" seemed borrowed." The following is her notice of the
charge :—

> The envious age, only to me alone,
> Will not allow what I do write my own;
> But let them rage, and 'gainst a maid conspire,
> So deathless numbers from my tuneful lyre
> Do ever flow ; so Phœbus, I by thee
> Inspired divinely, and possest may be ;
> I willingly accept Cassandra's fate,
> To speak the truth, although believed too late.

ANNE, MARCHIONESS OF WHARTON,

1685,

Was the daughter of Sir Henry Lee, of Ditchley, in Oxfordshire, and first wife of Thomas Wharton, Esq., afterwards Marquis of Wharton. She wrote Paraphrases on *The Lamentations of Jeremiah* and on *The Lord's Prayer; Verses to Mr. Waller,* an *Elegy on Lord Rochester,* the Poems quoted below, and some other effusions, but not many. She was highly esteemed in her own day, and was complimented by Waller and Dryden. She died in 1685.

The following poem appears in Dryden's *Miscellany:*

VERSES

On the Snuff of a Candle: made in Sickness.

See there the taper's dim and doleful light,
   In gloomy waves rolls silently about,
And represents to my dim weary sight,
   My light of life almost as near burnt out.

Ah, health! best part and substance of our joy,
   (For without thee 'tis nothing but a shade,)
Why dost thou partially thyself employ,
   Whilst thy proud foes as partially invade?

What we, who ne'er enjoy, so fondly seek,
   Those who possess thee still, almost despise;
To gain immortal glory, raise the weak,
   Taught by their former want thy worth to prize.

Dear, melancholy Muse! my constant guide,
    Charm this coy health back to my fainting heart,
Or I'll accuse thee of vainglorious pride,
    And swear thou dost but feign the moving art.

But why do I upbraid thee, gentle Muse,
    Who for all sorrows mak'st me some amends?
Alas! our sickly minds sometimes abuse
    Our best physicians and our dearest friends.

SONG.

How hardly I conceal'd my tears?
    How oft did I complain?
When, many tedious days, my fears
    Told me I lov'd in vain.

But now my joys as wild are grown,
    And hard to be concealed;
Sorrow may make a silent moan,
    But joy will be reveal'd.

I tell it to the bleating flocks,
    To every stream and tree,
And bless the hollow murm'ring rocks
    For echoing back to me.

Thus you may see with how much joy
    We want, we wish, believe;
'Tis hard such passion to destroy,
    But easy to deceive.

The Marchioness of Wharton's paraphrase of the 53d chapter
of Isaiah suggested Waller's *Cantos of Divine Poesy*, and led

that writer to address to her several complimentary verses. Lady Wharton's poems are distinguished by a fine sweetness of sentiment, and her thoughts are always very gracefully and delicately expressed. Her productions are widely scattered, and are to be found in different miscellaneous collections of contemporary verse.

12   II.*

MRS. TAYLOR.

1685.

In a *Miscellany, being a Collection of Poems by several Hands*, published by Aphara Behn, in 1685, are the three following Pieces, "made by Mrs. Taylor," of whom there is no account.

SONG.

Ye virgin powers, defend my heart
From amorous looks and smiles,
From saucy Love, or nicer Art,
Which most our sex beguiles:

From sighs and vows, from awful fears
That do to Pity move,
From speaking silence, and from tears,
Those springs that water Love.

But if through Passion I grow blind,
Let Honour be my guide,
And where frail nature seems inclin'd,
There fix a guard of Pride.

A heart whose flames are seen though pure,
Needs every virtue's aid,
And those who think themselves secure,
The soonest are betray'd.

TO MERTILL,

Who desired her to speak to Clorinda of his love.

Mertill, though my heart should break
   In granting thy desire,
To cold Clorinda I will speak,
   And warm her with my fire.

To save thee from approaching harm.
   My death I will obey ;
To save thee sinking in the storm,
   I'll cast myself away.

May her charms equal those of thine,
   No words can e'er express,
And let her love be great as mine ;
   Which thee would only bless !

May you still prove her faithful slave,
   And she so kind and true ;
She nothing may desire to have,
   Or fear to lose—but you.

SONG.

Strephon has fashion, wit, and youth.
   With all things else that please :
He nothing wants but love and truth,
   To ruin me with ease.

But he is flint, and bears the art
   To kindle stray desire ;
His power inflames another's heart,
   Yet he ne'er feels the fire.

Alas! it does my soul perplex,
    When I his charms recall,
To think he should despise the sex,
    Or what's worse, love them all.

My wearied heart, like Noah's dove,
    In vain may seek for rest,
Finding no hope to fix my love,
    Returns into my breast.

The smoothness, grace, and lively fancy displayed in the three poems which I have above quoted lead us to imagine that Mrs. Taylor was a practised writer : but I can find no further trace of her than that which is here presented. There is something in the nice rounding off of the sentences, and in the soft, semi-voluptuous sentiment, which makes me almost suspect that "Mrs. Taylor" was no other than Mrs. Aphara Behn herself. To say the least of it, she was evidently brought up in the same school of taste as that which produced the clever but meretricious writer just named.

APHARA BEHN,

1645—1689,

Is one of the most prominent, but one of the least estimable, of the British Female Poets. She has been called "a Female Wycherley," and there could not well be a more characteristic description of her. To a fine and subtle humour she joins great grossness of thought; and to a lively and laughing imagination she unites an essential coarseness of passion which disfigures and depraves nearly all she writes. Allowances are of course to be made for the wicked era in which she flourished (the reign of the second Charles); but still it must be confessed that the licentiousness complained of is not (as in some other writers of the same period) a mere adjunct, which can be lopped off, but an integral part of the composition, which cannot be removed from the rest.

Aphara Johnson was born in 1645, of a good family, her father being Lieutenant-Governor of Surinam. At her father's death the family returned to London, where she married a Dutch merchant, named Behn. She became a favourite at court, and displayed so much ability, that Charles the Second entrusted her with several political affairs of importance, in which she did the state some service. She was even sent out to the Netherlands on a secret mission, and was enabled to give some valuable information to the Government. On finding, however, that her services were not sufficiently recognised, she quitted the stormy arena of politics, and devoted herself entirely to literary pursuits.

Her chief works are *Oronooko*, a novel, on which Southern's tragedy of the same name is founded ; a volume of Miscellaneous Poems, and a number of Plays, which are amongst the grossest productions ever given to the world. Mrs. Behn died in 1689.

This lady's muse has been likened to Moore's, and not, I think, without some reason. She exhibits the same liveliness and pointedness of fancy, and writes with an aptness and happy expressiveness which might easily be mistaken for the similar characteristics of Ireland's bard. The following lyric has quite the expression of Moore, although it is deficient in the *point* which always distinguishes that writer.

Love in fantastic triumph sat,
    Whilst bleeding hearts around him flow'd ;
For whom fresh pains he did create,
    And strange tyrannic power he show'd.
From thy bright eyes he took his fires
    Which round about in sport he hurl'd ;
But 'twas from mine he took desires
    Enough t' undo the amorous world.

From me he took his sighs and tears,
    From thee his pride and cruelty ;
From me his languishment and fears,
    And every killing dart from thee ;
Thus thou and I the god have arm'd,
    And set him up a deity ;
But my poor heart alone is harm'd ;
    Whilst thine the victor is, and free.

I quote, next, a poem, entitled,

THE DIFFERENCE BETWEEN HYMEN AND CUPID— MARRIAGE AND LOVE.

In vain does Hymen with religious vows
    Oblige his slaves to wear his chains with ease,
A privilege alone that *Love* allows :—
    'Tis Love alone can make our fetters please.

The angry tyrant lays his yoke on all,
   Yet in his fiercest rage is charming still;
Officious Hymen comes whene'er we call,
   But haughty Love comes only when he will.

For fluency and harmony of style, Mrs. Behn has scarcely a
superior in our language. I do not know a poem that flows
more smoothly and musically than the following : —

THE RETURN.

Amyntas! whilst you
Have an art to subdue,
And can conquer a heart with a look or a smile :
You pitiless grow,
And no faith will allow ;
'Tis the glory you seek when you rifle the spoil.

Your soft warring eyes,
When prepared for the prize,
Can laugh at the aids of my feeble disdain :
You can humble the foe,
And soon make her to know,
Though she arms her with pride, that her efforts are vain.

But, shepherd! beware,
Though a victor you are,
A tyrant was never secure on his throne ;
Whilst proudly you aim
New conquests to gain,
Some hard-hearted nymph may return you your own !

IN IMITATION OF HORACE.

What mean those amorous curls of jet?
　For what heart-ravish'd maid
Dost thou thy hair in order set,
　Thy wanton tresses braid?
And thy vast stores of beauties open lay,
That the deluded fancy leads astray?

For pity hide thy starry eyes,
　Whose languishments destroy;
And look not on the slave that dies
　With an excess of joy.
Defend thy coral lips, thy amber breath;
To taste these sweets, alas! is certain death.

LADY MARY CHUDLEIGH,

1656—1710,

Was the author of a book entitled *Poems on several Occasions*, and published in London in the year 1703. She was the daughter of Richard Lee, Esquire, of Winsloder, in Devonshire, and wife of Sir George Chudleigh, Baronet, of Ashton, in the same county. She was born in 1656, and died in 1710. Besides her poems, she was the author of a volume of Essays, which was published in 1710.

THE RESOLVE.

For what the world admires I'll wish no more,
    Nor court that airy nothing of a Name ;
Such fleeting shadows let the proud adore,
    Let them be suppliants for an empty fame.

If Reason rules within and keeps the throne,
    While the inferior faculties obey,
And all her laws without reluctance own,
    Accounting none more fit, more just than they ;

If Virtue my free soul unsullied keeps,
    Exempting it from passion and from stain ;
If no black guilty thoughts disturb my sleeps,
    And no past crimes my vext remembrance pain :—

If though I pleasure find in living here,
    I yet can look on death without surprise ;
If I've a soul above the reach of fear,
    And which will nothing mean or sordid prize :

13   I

A soul which cannot be depress'd by grief,
   Nor too much rais'd by the sublimest joy ;
Which can, when troubled, give itself relief,
   And to advantage all its thoughts employ ; —

Then am I happy in my humble state,
   Although not crown'd with glory nor with bays ;
A mind that triumphs over vice and fate
   Esteems it mean to court the world for *praise*.

Lady Chudleigh distinguished herself by her clever champion-
ship of her sex at a time when the female mind was far too little
esteemed.   There is a noble assertion and defence of Woman's
mental powers in her Poem entitled *The Ladies' Defence ; or
the Bride-woman's Counsellor answered.   A Poem in a Dia-
logue between Sir John Brute, Sir William Loveall, Melissa,
and a Parson.*   The poor parson is admirably put down.   I regret that I cannot find an extractable passage which will give a
good idea of the genius and good sense displayed in this production.
   I think, however, that Lady Chudleigh could *defend* her sex
much more wisely than she could *advise* them.   Let the following lines bear witness : —

TO THE LADIES.

Wife and servant are the same,
But only differ in the name :
For when that fatal knot is tied,
Which nothing, nothing, can divide,
When she the word *obey* has said,
And man by law supreme has made,
Then all that's kind is laid aside,
And nothing left but state and pride :
Fierce as an Eastern prince he grows,
And all his innate rigour shows :

Then but to look, to laugh, or speak,
Will the nuptial contract break.
Like mutes, she signs alone must make,
And never any freedom take ;
But still be govern'd by a nod,
And fear her husband as her god ;
Him still must serve, him still obey,
And nothing act and nothing say,
But what her haughty lord thinks fit,
Who with the power has all the wit.
Then shun, oh ! shun that wretched state,
And all the fawning flatterers hate :
Value yourselves, and men despise :
You must be proud, if you'll be wise.

THE HONOURABLE MARY MONK,

1715,

Was the daughter of Lord Molesworth, of Ireland, and the wife of George Monk, Esq. In 1715 was published, after her death, a volume entitled *Marinda: Poems and Translations.* In the Dedication to the Princess of Wales, written by her father, we are told " Most of them are the product of the leisure hours of a young gentlewoman, lately deceased ; who, in a remote country retirement, without omitting the daily care due to a large family, not only perfectly acquired several languages, but the good morals and principles contained in those books, so as to put them in practice, as well during her life and languishing sickness as the hour of death : in short, she died not only like a Christian, but like a Roman lady; and so became at once the object of the grief and comfort of her relations."

The following are extracted from the book referred to : —

I. FROM THE EPISTLE TO MARINDA.

A just applause and an immortal name
Is the true object of the Poet's aim ;
In quest of this they boldly quit the shore,
And dangerous seas and unknown lands explore.
In the whole plan their interest has no share,
The goods of fortune are beneath their care :
They on the smoke of public incense live,
Look down on wealth, and think it mean to thrive.

II. ON PROVIDENCE.

As a kind mother with indulgent eye
Views her fair charge, and melts with sympathy,
And one's dear face imprints with kisses sweet,
One to her bosom clasps, one on her knee
Softly sustains in pleasing dignity,
And one permits to cling about her feet;
And reads their various wants, and each request
In look or action or in sigh express'd:
This little supplicant in gracious style
She answers; that she blesses with a smile;
Or if she blames their suit, or if approves,
And whether pleas'd or griev'd, yet still she loves:
    With like regard high Providence divine
Watches affectionate o'er human race,
    One feeds, one comforts, does to all incline,
    And each assists with kind parental care;
Or, once denying us some needful grace,
    Only denies to move an ardent prayer;
Or, courted for imaginary wants,
Seems to deny, but in denying grants.

III. VERSES

Written on her Deathbed, at Bath, to her Husband in London.

Thou who dost all my worldly thoughts employ,
Thou pleasing source of all my earthly joy,
Thou tenderest husband and thou dearest friend,
To thee this first, this last adieu I send!
At length the conqueror Death asserts his right,
And will for ever veil me from thy sight;

I*

He woos me to him with a cheerful grace,
And not one terror clouds his meagre face ;
He promises a lasting rest from pain,
And shews that all life's fleeting joys are vain ;
The' eternal scenes of heaven he sets in view,
And tells me that no other joys are true.
But love, fond love, would yet resist his power,
Would fain awhile defer the parting hour:
He brings thy mourning image to my eyes,
And would obstruct my journey to the skies.
But say, thou dearest, thou unwearied friend !
Say, shouldst thou grieve to see my sorrows end ?
Thou know'st a painful pilgrimage I've past ;
And shouldst thou grieve that rest is come at last ?
Rather rejoice to see me shake off life,
And die as I have liv'd, thy faithful wife.

ANNE, COUNTESS OF WINCHELSEA,

1720,

WAS the daughter of Sir William Kingsmill, of Sidmonton, in the county of Southampton. She was Maid of Honour to the Duchess of York, second wife of James the Second, and married Heneage, Earl of Winchelsea. She died in 1720.

Her poems have been highly admired for their simplicity and naturalness. She seems to have been the precursor of the school of Cowper. "It is remarkable," says Wordsworth, "that excepting *The Nocturnal Reverie* (one of Lady Winchelsea's poems), and the *Windsor Forest* of Pope, the poetry of the period intervening between the publications of *Paradise Lost* and *The Seasons* does not contain a single new image of external nature."

A NOCTURNAL REVERIE.

In such a night, when every louder wind
Is to its distant cavern safe confin'd,
And only gentle Zephyr fans his wings,
And lonely Philomel, still waking, sings;
Or from some tree, fam'd for the owl's delight,
She, hollowing clear, directs the wanderer right:
In such a night, when passing clouds give place,
Or thinly veil the heavens' mysterious face;
When in some river, overhung with green,
The waving moon and trembling leaves are seen;
When freshen'd grass now bears itself upright,
And makes cool banks to pleasing rest invite,

Whence springs the woodbine and the bramble-rose,
And where the sleepy cowslip shelter'd grows;
Whilst now a paler hue the foxglove takes,
Yet chequers still with red the dusky brakes;
When scatter'd glow-worms, but in twilight fine,
Show trivial beauties watch their hour to shine;
Whilst Sal'sbury stands the test of every light,
In perfect charms and perfect virtue bright:
When odours which declin'd repelling day,
Through temperate air uninterrupted stray;
When darken'd groves their softest shadows wear,
And falling waters we distinctly hear;
When through the gloom more venerable shows
Some ancient fabric, awful in repose;
While sun-burnt hills their swarthy looks conceal,
And swelling hay-cocks thicken up the vale:
When the loos'd horse now, as his pasture leads,
Comes slowly grazing through the' adjoining meads,
Whose stealing pace, and lengthen'd shade we fear,
Till torn up forage in his teeth we hear;
When nibbling sheep at large pursue their food,
And unmolested kine rechew the cud;
When curlews cry beneath the village walls,
And to her straggling brood the partridge calls;
Their short-lived jubilee the creatures keep,
Which but endures whilst tyrant man does sleep;
When a sedate content the spirit feels,
And no fierce light disturbs, whilst it reveals;
But silent musings urge the mind to seek
Something too high for syllables to speak;
Till the free soul to a composedness charm'd,
Finding the elements of rage disarm'd,
O'er all below a solemn quiet grown,
Joys in the' inferior world, and thinks it like her own:
In such a night let me abroad remain,
Till morning breaks, and all 's confus'd again;
Our cares, our toils, our clamours are renewed,
Or pleasures, seldom reached, again pursued.

In reply to some lines of Pope's addressed to her concerning *The Rape of the Lock,* the Countess writes thus playfully to her clever antagonist ; —

Disarm'd with so genteel an air,
  The contest I give o'er ;
Yet, Alexander, have a care,
  And shock the sex no more.

We rule the world our whole life's space ;
  Men but assume that right ;
First slaves to every tempting face,
  Then martyrs to our spite.

You of one Orpheus sure have read,
  Who would like you have writ,
Had he in London town been bred,
  And polish'd, too, his wit.

But he, poor soul ! thought all was well,
  And great should be his fame,
When he had left his wife in hell,
  And birds and beasts could tame.

Yet venturing then with scoffing rhymes,
  The women to incense,
Resenting heroines of those times
  Soon punish'd his offence.

And as the Hebrews roll'd his scull,
  And harp besmear'd with blood,
They clashing as the waves grew full,
  Still harmonis'd the flood.

But you our follies gently treat,
  And spin so fine the thread,
You need not fear his awkward fate,
  The Lock won't cost the Head.

14

Our admiration you command,
　　For all that's gone before ;
What next we look for at your hand
　　Can only raise it more.

Yet, sooth, the ladies I advise
　　(As me to pride has wrought),
We're born to wit, but to be wise
　　By admonitions taught.

The following, for aptness and point, might have come from
the pen of Cowper : —

THE ATHEIST AND THE ACORN.

Methinks the world is oddly made,
　　And every thing 's amiss,
A dull, presuming Atheist said,
As stretch'd he lay beneath a shade,
　　And instanc'd it in this :

Behold, quoth he, that mighty thing,
　　A pumpkin large and round,
Is held but by a little string,
Which upwards cannot make it spring,
　　Or bear it from the ground.

While on this oak an acorn small,
　　So disproportion'd grows ;
That who with sense surveys this all,
This universal casual ball,
　　Its ill contrivance knows.

My better judgment would have hung
　　The pumpkin on the tree,
And left the acorn, lightly strung,
'Mongst things which on the surface sprung,
　　And small and feeble be.

No more the caviller could say,
 Nor farther faults descry ;
For as he upwards gazing lay,
An acorn, loosen'd from its stay,
 Fell down upon his eye.

The wounded part with tears ran o'er,
 As punish'd for the sin ;
Fool ! had that bough a pumpkin bore,
Thy whimsies would have work'd no more,
 Nor scull have kept them in.

In the ensuing extract, too, there is much well-expressed thought and harmonious versification.

LIFE'S PROGRESS.

How gaily is at first begun
 Our life's uncertain race !
Whilst yet that sprightly morning sun,
With which we just set out to run,
 Enlightens all the place.

How smiling the world's prospect lies,
 How tempting to go through !
Not Canaan to the prophet's eyes,
From Pisgah, with a sweet surprise,
 Did more inviting shew.

How soft the first ideas prove,
 Which wander through our minds !
How full the joys, how free the love,
Which does that early season move,
 As flow'rs the western winds !

Our sighs are then but vernal air,
　　But April drops our tears,
Which swiftly passing, all grows fair,
Whilst beauty compensates our care,
　　And youth each vapour clears.

But oh ! too soon, alas ! we climb,
　　Scarce feeling, we ascend
The gently rising hill of Time,
From whence with grief we see that prime,
　　And all its sweetness end.

The die now cast, our station known,
　　Fond expectation past ;
The thorns which former days had sown
To crops of late repentance grown,
　　Through which we toil at last.

Whilst every care 's a driving harm,
　　That helps to bear us down ;
Which faded smiles no more can charm
But every tear 's a winter-storm,
　　And every look 's a frown.

SONG.

Would we attain the happiest state
　　That is design'd us here ;
No joy a rapture must create,
　　No grief beget despair

No injury fierce anger raise,
　　No honour tempt to pride ;
No vain desires of empty praise
　　Must in the soul abide :

No charms of youth or beauty move
The constant settled breast :
Who leaves a passage free to love,
Shall let in all the rest.

In such a heart soft peace will live,
Where none of these abound ;
The greatest blessing Heav'n does give,
Or can on earth be found.

One of Lady Winchelsea's most powerful productions is her
poem called *The Spleen.* I extract a few lines from this fine
apostrophe :

Patron thou art to every gross abuse,
The sullen husband's feign'd excuse,
When the ill humour with his wife he spends,
And bears recruited wit and spirits to his friends.
The son of Bacchus pleads thy power,
As to the glass he still repairs
Pretends but to remove thy cares,
Snatch from thy shades one gay and smiling hour,
And drown thy kingdom in a purple shower.
    *   *   *   *
By thee, Religion, all we know
That should enlighten here below,
Is veil'd in darkness, and perplext
With anxious doubts, with endless scruples vext,
And some restraint implied from each perverted text :
Whilst Touch not, Taste not, what is freely given,
Is but thy niggard voice, disgracing bounteous Heaven.

K

ESTHER VANHOMRIGH.

1691—1721.

THE " Vanessa" of Swift; to whom the following lines refer.

ODE TO SPRING.

Hail, blushing goddess, beauteous Spring!
Who in thy jocund train doth bring
Loves and graces, smiling hours,
Balmy breezes, fragrant flowers ;
Come, with tints of roseate hue,
Nature's faded charms renew.

Yet why should I thy presence hail ?
To me no more the breathing gale
Comes fraught with sweets, no more the rose
With such transcendent beauty blows,
As when Cadenus blest the scene,
And shared with me those joys serene.
When, unperceiv'd, the lambent fire
Of friendship kindled new desire ;
Still listening to his tuneful tongue,
The truths which angels might have sung
Divine imprest their gentle sway,
And sweetly stole my soul away.

My guide, instructor, lover, friend,
Dear names, in one idea blend ;
Oh! still conjoin'd, your incense rise,
And waft sweet odours to the skies.

SUSANNA CENTLIVRE,

1660—1723,

WAS born about 1660. Her maiden name was Freeman. Her third husband, Joseph Centlivre, was one of Queen Anne's cooks. He fell in love with her at Windsor, where she performed the part of Alexander the Great, in Lee's play of that name. She will long be remembered as the authoress of *The Wonder, The Busy Body*, and other clever but gross comedies.

The following is the Prologue to her Play of *A Bold Stroke for a Wife:* —

> To-night we come upon a bold design,
> To try to please without one borrowed line:
> Our plot is new and regularly clear,
> And not one single tittle from Molière.
> O'er buried poets we with caution tread,
> And parish sextons leave to rob the dead.
> For you, bright British fair, in hopes to charm ye,
> We bring to-night a lover from the army.
> You know the soldiers have the strangest arts,
> Such a proportion of prevailing parts,
> You 'd think that they rid post to women's hearts.
> I wonder whence they draw their bold pretence ;
> We do not choose them sure for our defence :
> That plea is both impolitic and wrong,
> And only suits such dames as want a tongue.
> Is it their eloquence and fine address ?
> The softness of their language ? — Nothing less.
> Is it their courage, that they bravely dare
> To storm the sex at once ? — Egad ! 'tis there :

They act by us as in the rough campaign ;
Unmindful of repulses, charge again :
They mine and countermine, resolv'd to win,
And if a breach is made, they will come in.
You 'll think by what we have of soldiers said,
Our female wit was in the service bred :
But she is to the hardy toil a stranger ;
She loves the cloth, indeed, but hates the danger :
Yet to this circle of the brave and gay
She bids one, for her good intentions, say
She hopes you 'll not reduce her to half-pay.
As for our Play, 'tis English humour all ;
Then will you let our manufacture fall ?
Would you the honour of our nation raise,
Keep English credit up, and English plays.

MRS. CATHERINE COCKBURN.

1679—1749.

This lady was the daughter of Captain David Trotter, a Scottish gentleman, who lived in the reign of Charles the Second, to whom he was well known, and who called him "honest David." Our authoress was born in 1679, and gave early marks of genius. At fourteen she wrote very excellent verses; and at seventeen produced a tragedy, called *Agnes de Castro*, which was acted with great success at the Royal Theatre. In 1700, when twenty-one years of age, we find her to be one of nine ladies who wrote a joint work, entitled *The Nine Muses, or Poems written by so many Ladies upon the Death of the late famous John Dryden, Esquire*. About this time she married Mr. Cockburn, a clergyman, who falling into a scruple about the oath of abjuration, was obliged to give up his curacy. Notwithstanding the difficulties and privations she had to endure under these circumstances, Mrs. Cockburn appears to have followed her literary pursuits with even greater ardour; and she wrote, besides her plays and poems, some remarkably clever and acute treatises in defence of the philosophy of Locke. Her *Vindication of Locke's Christian Principles* is an extremely powerful piece of reasoning.

After suffering some considerable changes of fortune, Mrs. Cockburn died on the 11th of May, 1749, in the seventieth year of her age.

Her poetry has a compression of thought and an ease of style which greatly distinguished it from the verse of most female writers in her time.

15　　　　　　K*

THE CAUTION.

Soft kisses may be innocent,
  But ah! too easy maid, beware ;
Though that is all thy kindness meant,
  'Tis love's delusive fatal snare.

No virgin e'er at first design'd
  Through all the maze of love to stray ;
But each new path allures her mind,
  Till, wandering on, she lose her way.

'Tis easy ere set out to stay ;
  But who the useful art can teach,
When sliding down a steepy way,
  To stop, before the end we reach?

Keep ever something in thy power
  Beyond what would thy honour stain ;
He will not dare to aim at more,
  Who for small favours sighs in vain.

THE VAIN ADVICE.

Ah, gaze not on those eyes! forbear
That soft enchanting voice to hear :
Not looks of basilisks give surer death
Nor Syrens sing with more destructive breath.

Fly, if thy freedom thou 'dst maintain :
Alas! I feel the advice is vain !
A heart whose safety but in flight does lie,
Is too far lost to have the power to fly.

ELIZABETH THOMAS.

1675—1730.

THE following poem from the pen of this lady had a singular origin. Mrs. Thomas became much disturbed in her mind respecting the doctrine of predestination, and, after studying the cnief writers on that subject, found herself, as many besides her have done, more and more perplexed. Upon this she retired (as is related in her Memoirs) to her closet, where, after a most serious discussion of this point with herself, she formed the following poem ; which she often read to confirm her in her sentiments. It is a fine burst of womanly faith.

PREDESTINATION ; OR THE RESOLUTION.

Ah ! strive no more to know what fate
　　Is pre-ordain'd for thee :
'Tis vain in this my mortal state,
　　For Heaven's inscrutable decree
Will only be reveal'd in vast Eternity.
　　Then, O my soul !
Remember thy celestial birth,
And live to Heaven while here on earth :
　　Thy God is infinitely true —
　　All Justice, yet all Mercy, too :
To him, then, through thy Saviour pray
For grace, to guide thee on thy way,
　　And give thee Will to do.
But humbly, for the rest, my soul !
Let Hope, and Faith, the limits be
Of thy presumptuous curiosity !

In the *Life of Mrs. Thomas,* prefixed to *Pylades and Corinna* (2d edit. 1736), the authoress relates the history of this poem, as given above.   She goes on to say that " she languished for some time in perplexity upon the awful subject of Fate and Freewill ; and hearing that Bishop Burnet's *Exposition of the Thirty-nine Articles* was in the press, she waited the publication with the utmost impatience.   But alas ! she was never the nearer : for the Bishop stated the different opinions of each sect with such candour, that it was impossible to find out which he most leaned to himself."

Mrs. Thomas received from Dryden the poetical name of Corinna ; and she figures in *The Dunciad.*

MARY BARBER.

1734.

OF this lady I have been able to learn but little. All that I can say of her is that she was the wife of a tradesman in Dublin, and that, in 1734, she published a volume of poems, prefaced by a letter from Dean Swift to John, Earl of Orrery. I have never been able to meet with this book, although I have diligently searched for it. For the following extract I am indebted to the Reverend Mr. Dyce's *Specimens of British Poetesses.*

ON SENDING MY SON AS A PRESENT TO DR. SWIFT, DEAN OF ST. PATRICK'S, ON HIS BIRTHDAY.

A curious statue, we are told,
Is priz'd above its weight in gold;
If the fair form the hand confess
Of Phidias, or Praxiteles:
But if the artist could inspire
The smallest spark of heavenly fire,
Though but enough to make it walk,
Salute the company, or talk,
This would advance the prize so high,
What prince were rich enough to buy?
Such if Hibernia could obtain,
She sure would give it to the Dean:
So to her patriot should she pay
Her thanks upon his natal day.

A richer present I design,
A finished form, of work divine,
Surpassing all the power of art ;
A thinking head, a grateful heart :
A heart that hopes, one day, to show
How much we to the Drapier owe.
Kings could not send a nobler gift,
A meaner were unworthy Swift

MRS. ELIZABETH ROWE,

1736,

WAS the daughter of Mr. Walter Singer, a gentleman of good family in London. In her twenty-second year she published a volume of poems, which met with much success. In 1710 she married Mr. Thomas Rowe, a literary gentleman, who died a few years after their marriage. Mrs. Rowe died in 1736. She is well known as the writer of a work entitled *Letters from the Dead to the Living.*

HYMN.

The glorious armies of the sky
To Thee, Almighty King,
Triumphant anthems consecrate,
And hallelujahs sing.

But still their most exalted flights
Fall vastly short of Thee :
How distant then must human praise
From Thy perfection be !

Yet how, my God, shall I refrain,
When to my ravish'd sense
Each creature every where around
Displays thy excellence?

The active lights that shine above,
In their eternal dance,
Reveal their skilful Maker's praise
With silent elegance.

The blushes of the morn confess
That thou art still more fair,
When in the East its beams revive,
To gild the fields of air.

The fragrant, the refreshing breeze,
Of every flowery bloom,
In balmy whispers own from Thee
Their pleasing odours come.

The singing birds, the warbling winds,
And water's murmuring fall ;
To praise the First Almighty Cause
With different voices call.

Thy numerous Works exalt Thee thus,
And shall I silent be ?
No ; rather let me cease to breathe,
Than cease from praising Thee !

DESPAIR.

Oh ! lead me to some solitary gloom,
Where no enlivening beams nor cheerful echoes come ;
But silent all, and dusky let it be,
Remote and unfrequented but by me ;
Mysterious, close, and sullen as that grief
Which leads me to its covert for relief.
Far from the busy world's detested noise,
Its wretched pleasures, and distracted joys ;
Far from the jolly fools, who laugh and play,
And dance, and sing, impertinently gay,
Their short inestimable hours away ;
Far from the studious follies of the great,
The tiresome farce of ceremonious state.
There, in a melting, solemn, dying strain,

Let me all day upon my lyre complain,
And wind up all its soft harmonious strings
To noble, serious, melancholy things.
And let no human foot but mine e'er trace
The close recesses of the sacred place :
Nor let a bird of cheerful note come near,
To whisper out his airy raptures here.
Only the pensive songstress of the grove —
Let her, by mine, her mournful notes improve ;
While drooping winds among the branches sigh,
And sluggish waters heavily roll by.
Here to my fatal sorrows let me give
The short remaining hours I have to live.
Then with a sullen, deep-fetched groan expire,
And to the grave's dark solitude retire.

Among Prior's Poems will be found " An Answer to Mrs.
Singer's Pastoral on Love and Friendship."

16   L

JANE BRERETON.

1685—1740.

THIS clever writer, who was very popular in her own day, was the daughter of Mr. Thomas Hughes, a gentleman of good family, in Flintshire, where she was born in 1685. In 1711 she married Mr. Thomas Brereton, of Oxford University; with whom, however, she lived so unhappily, that a separation took place a few years after their union. In 1721 she retired into Wales; and she died in 1740.

It was the custom of literary ladies in the seventeenth century to assume some fanciful name, and to write under that appellation. Mrs. Brereton signed herself "Melissa," and under that *nom de guerre* acquired some celebrity in the pages of the *Gentleman's Magazine*. She particularly distinguished herself in some poetical controversies which were carried on in that work. For readiness, tact, and good, strong, witty satire she has not many superiors among lady-writers.

Mrs. Brereton's productions are by no means remarkable for the delicacy and gracefulness that usually distinguish the writings of the female sex : on the contrary, there is a roughness, a vigour, a breadth in them, which might lead the reader to fancy that the productions of Melissa proceeded from the pen of a gentleman, rather than from that of a lady.

There is something very charming in the disdain with which she addresses one of her lovers :

TO DAMON.

Cease, Damon, cease, I 'll hear no more ;
Your fulsome flattery give o'er ;

I scorn this mean fallacious art
By which you'd steal, not win, my heart:
In me it never can compassion move,
And sooner will aversion raise than love.

If you to love would me incline,
Assert the man, forbear to whine;
Let time and plain sincerity
And faithful love your pleaders be;
For trust me, Damon, if those fail,
These servile wheedling tricks will ne'er prevail.

Poor Damon must have looked rather sheepish, one fancies, at such a rebuke as this from his mistress; and the gentleman named below—Philotinus—must equally have felt that he got, in sporting phrase, "decidedly the worst of it."

TO PHILOTINUS.

Philotinus! if you'd approve
Yourself a faithful lover,—
You must no more my anger move,
But in the mildest terms of love
Your passion still discover.

Though born to rule, you must submit
To my command with awe;
Nor think your sex can you acquit,
For Cupid's empire won't admit
Nor own, a Salic Law.

Mrs. Brereton's satire is of an equally bold, strong, and stinging sort. The following lines have been generally, but erroneously attributed to Lord Chesterfield:

ON BEAU NASH'S PICTURE AT FULL LENGTH, BETWEEN THE BUSTS
OF SIR ISAAC NEWTON AND MR. POPE.

The old Egyptians hid their wit
    In hieroglyphic dress,
To give men pains to search for it,
    And please themselves with guess.

Moderns, to tread the self-same path,
    And exercise our parts,
Place figures in a room at Bath,—
    Forgive them, God of Arts !

Newton, if I can judge aright,
    All wisdom doth express ;
His knowledge gives mankind new light.
    And swells their happiness.

Pope is the emblem of true wit,
    The sunshine of the mind ;
Read o'er his works for proof of it,
    You 'll endless pleasure find.

Nash represents man in the mass,
    Made up of wrong and right ;
Sometimes a knave, sometimes an ass,
    Now blunt, and now polite.

The picture, placed the busts between,
    Adds to the thought much strength ;
Wisdom and Wit are little seen,
    But Folly 's at full length.

MARY CHANDLER,

1687—1745,

Was the daughter of a dissenting minister at Bath. Pope commended her poetry. Sound sense and harmonious versification characterise her works.

TEMPERANCE.

Fatal effects of luxury and ease!
We drink our poison and we eat disease;
Indulge our senses at our reason's cost,
Till sense is pain, and reason hurt or lost.
Not so, O Temperance bland! when rul'd by thee,
The brute 's obedient, and the man is free.
Soft are his slumbers, balmy is his rest,
His veins not boiling from the midnight feast.
Touch'd by Aurora's rosy hand, he wakes
Peaceful and calm, and with the world partakes
The joyful dawnings of returning day,
For which their grateful thanks the whole creation pay;—
All but the human brute: 'tis he alone,
Whose works of darkness fly the rising sun.
'Tis to thy rules, O Temperance! that we owe
All pleasures, which from health and strength can flow;
Vigour of body, purity of mind,
Unclouded reason, sentiments refin'd,
Unmixt, untainted joys without remorse,
The intemperate sinner's never failing curse.

L*

ELIZA HAYWOOD,

1693—1756,

Was the daughter of a London tradesman, and was born in the year 1693. She wrote several books, chiefly novels, one of which, *Betsy Thoughtless*, is said to have suggested Miss Burney's *Evelina*. She died in 1756.

EXTRACT FROM THE TEA TABLE.

Ximene, fearing to be forsaken by Palemon, desires he would kill her.

If by my words my soul could be exprest,
You will not wonder at my fond request:
But in compassion with my wish partake,
'Tis kinder far to kill than to forsake.
'Tis not long life, but glorious death, renowns
The hero's honours, and the martyr crowns;
Laurels acquired in youth, in age decay,
Or by superior force are torn away,
To deck some new-made, hated, favourite's brow,
Who in the noble ruin great does grow.
A happy end is still the wise man's prayer,
Death is a safe, a sure retreat from care.
Should I live longer, I may lose your love,
And all the hells of desperation prove.
But now to die — now, in my joy's high noon,
Ere the cold evening of contempt comes on,
Were to die blest; and baffle cruel fate,
Which, envious, watches close to change my state.
Nay, more, to die *for thee!* and *by thee*, too!
Would all my rival's happiness outdo:

My love would live forever in thy mind,
And I should pity those I left behind.
To have those eyes, dear heaven-drest orbs of light,
Convey soft pity to expiring sight,
That voice, whose every melting note inspires
Dissolving languishments, and warm desires,
Tun'd to kind, mournful, murmurings at my pain,
Would give a pride which life could never gain!
Haste then, the joys of passion to refine,
Let through my breast thy glittering weapon shine,
Dispel my fears, and keep me ever thine!

Miss Haywood was, for some reason or other, included in Pope's *Dunciad;* but, says a writer on the subject, " it is probable that Pope was as much actuated by some provocation of a personal nature, as by indignation at the immorality of her early writings, for which, however, her later works greatly atoned."

ELIZABETH TOLLET,

1694—1754,

WAS the author of a volume of *Poems*, and *Susanna*, a sacred drama.

WINTER SONG.

Ask me no more my truth to prove,
What I would suffer for my love ;
With thee I would in exile go
To regions of eternal snow ;
O'er floods by solid ice confin'd,
Through forest bare, with northern wind ;
While all around my eyes I cast,
Where all is wild, and all is waste.
If there the timorous stag you chase,
Or rouse to fight a fiercer race,
Undaunted, I thy arms would bear,
And give thy hand the hunter's spear.
When the low sun withdraws his light,
And menaces an half-year's night,
The conscious moon and stars above
Shall guide me with my wandering love.
Beneath the mountain's hollow brow,
Or in its rocky cells below,
Thy rural feast I would provide,
Nor envy palaces their pride ;
The softest moss should dress thy bed,
With savage spoils about thee spread ;
Whilst faithful love the watch should keep,
To banish danger from thy sleep.

ON A DEATH'S HEAD.

On this resemblance, where we find
A portrait drawn from all mankind,
Fond lover! gaze awhile, to see
What beauty's idol charms shall be!
Where are the balls that once could dart
Quick lightning through the wounded heart?
The skin, whose tint could once unite
The glowing red and polished white?
The lip in brighter ruby drest?
The cheek with dimpled smiles opprest?
The rising front, where beauty sate,
Thron'd in her residence of state;
Which, half disclos'd, and half conceal'd,
The hair in flowing ringlets veil'd?
'Tis vanished all! remains alone
The eyeless scalp of naked bone;
The vacant orbits sunk within;
The jaw that offers at a grin.
Is this the object, then, that claims
The tribute of our youthful flames?
Must amorous hopes and fancied bliss,
Too dear delusions, end in this?
How high does Melancholy swell!
Which sighs can more than language tell;
Till Love can only grieve or fear;
Reflect a while, then drop a tear
For all that's beautiful or dear.

17

LÆTITIA PILKINGTON.

1712—1750.

THIS lady, the daughter of Dr. Van Lewen, of Dublin, and wife of the Reverend Mr. Pilkington, was born in 1712, and manifested her poetical genius at an early age. She acquired much fame by her writings, which, however, are not quite so chaste and moral as they might be. She died in 1750.

One of the best and purest of her productions is the following

ODE, IN IMITATION OF HORACE.

I envy not the proud their wealth,
    Their equipage and state ;
Give me but innocence and health,
    I ask not to be great.

I in this sweet retirement find
    A joy unknown to kings ;
For sceptres to a virtuous mind
    Seem vain and empty things.

Great Cincinnatus at his plough
    With brighter lustre shone,
Than guilty Cæsar e'er could show,
    Though seated on a throne.

Tumultuous days, and restless nights,
    Ambition ever knows,
A stranger to the calm delights
    Of study and repose.

Then free from envy, care, and strife,
Keep me, ye powers divine !
And pleas'd, when ye demand my life,
May I that life resign !

Mrs. Pilkington's sharp, clever style, is well seen in the succeeding

SONG.

Lying is an occupation
Us'd by all who mean to rise ;
Politicians owe their station
But to well concerted lies.

These to lovers give assistance
To ensnare the fair one's heart,
And the virgin's best resistance
Yields to this commanding art.

Study this superior science,
Would you rise in church or state,
Bid to truth a bold defiance,
'Tis the practice of the great.

MARY LEAPOR,

1722—1746,

WAS the daughter of the gardener of Judge Blencowe, of Marston
St. Lawrence, in Northamptonshire ; and it is said that she was
herself in service. Her writings, of which two volumes have
appeared, display very considerable genius.

THE TEMPLE OF LOVE — A DREAM.

When lonely night composed the drowsy mind,
And hush'd the bosom of the weary hind,
Pleas'd with plain nature, and with simple life,
I read the scenes of Shore's deluded wife,
Till my faint spirits sought the silent bed,
And on its pillow dropt my aching head ;
Then fancy, ever to her Mira kind,
Prepar'd her phantoms for the roving mind.

Behold a fabric rising from the ground,
To the soft timbrel and the cittern's sound ;
Corinthian pillars the vast building hold,
Of polished silver, and Peruvian gold ;
In four broad arches spread the shining doors,
The blazing roofs enlighten all the floors :
Beneath a sparkling canopy, that shone
With Persian jewels, like a morning sun,
Wrapp'd in a robe of purest Tyrian dye,
Cytherea's image met the ravish'd eye ;
Whose glowing features would in point beguile,
So well the artist drew her mimic smile.

Her shining eyes confess'd a sprightly joy,
Upon her knees reclined her wanton boy ;
On the bright walls around her and above,
Were drawn the statutes and the arts of love :
These taught the silent language of the eye,
The broken whisper, and amusing lie ;
The careless glance peculiar to the fair,
And vows of lovers that dissolve in air ;
The graceful anger, and the rolling eyes,
The practis'd blush, and counterfeit surprise,
The language proper for pretending swains,
And fine description for imagin'd pains ;
The friendly caution, and designing ease,
And all the arts that ruin while they please.

Now enter'd, follow'd by a splendid train,
A blooming damsel and a wealthy swain ;
The gaudy youth in shining robes array'd ;
Behind him follow'd the unthinking maid :
Youth in her cheek like opening roses sprung,
Her careless tresses on her shoulders hung.
Her smiles were cheerful as enlivening May ;
Her dress was careless, and her eyes were gay.
Then to soft voices and melodious sound
The board was spread, the sparkling glasses crown'd ;
The sprightly virgin in a moment shines
In the gay product of the eastern mines ;
Then Pride comes in with patches for the fair,
And spicy odours for her curling hair ;
Rude Riot, in a crimson vest array'd,
With smooth-faced Flattery like a chambermaid ;
Soft Pomp and Pleasure at her elbow stand,
And Folly shakes the rattles in her hand.

But now her feeble structure seem'd to shake ;
Its bases trembled, and its pillars quake ;
Then rush'd Suspicion through the lofty gate,
With heart-sick Loathing, led by ghastly Hate ;

M

And foaming Rage, to close the horrid band,
With a drawn poniard in her trembling hand.
Now like an earthquake shook the reeling frame,
The lamps extinguish in a purple flame ;
One universal groan was heard, and then
The cries of women, and the voice of men:
Some roar out vengeance, some for mercy call,
And shrieks and tumult fill the dreadful hall ;

At length the spectres vanish'd from my sight;
Again the lamps resum'd a feeble light,
But chang'd the place : no splendour there was shown,
But gloomy walls, that mirth had never known ;
For the gay dome where pleasure us'd to dwell
Appear'd an abbey, and a doleful cell ;
And here the sad, the ruin'd nymph was found,
Her robe disorder'd and her locks unbound ;
While from her eyes the pearly drops of woe
Wash'd her pale cheek, where roses us'd to blow :
Her blue and trembling lips prepar'd to breathe
The sighs that made her swelling bosom heave ;
Thus, stupid with her grief, she sat and prest
Her lily hands across her pensive breast:
A group of ghastly phantoms stood behind,
Whose task it is to rack the guilty mind ;
Wide-mouth'd Reproach with visage rude and thin,
And hissing Scandal, made a hideous din ;
Remorse, that darted from her deadly wings
Invenom'd arrows and a thousand stings ;
Then with pale cheeks, and with a ghastly stare,
Peep'd o'er her shoulder hollow-eyed Despair,
Whose hand extended bore a bleeding heart,
And Death behind her shook his threatening dart:
These forms with horror fill'd my aching breast,
And from my eyelids drove the balm of rest:
I woke, and found old night her course had run,
And left her empire to the rising sun.

HENRIETTA, LADY LUXBOROUGH,

1756,

Was half sister to the famous Lord Bolingbroke. In Dodsley's Collection, some pieces of poetry, ascribed to a *Lady of Quality*, proceeded from her pen ; one of them is given here. A volume of her Letters to Shenstone was printed in 1775. She died in 1756.

THE BULLFINCH IN TOWN.

Hark to the blackbird's pleasing note,
  Sweet usher of the vocal throng !
Nature directs his warbling throat,
  And all that hear, admire the song.

Yon bullfinch, with unvaried tone,
  Of cadence harsh, and accent shrill,
Has brighter plumage to atone
  For want of harmony and skill.

Yet discontent with nature's boon,
  Like man, to mimic art he flies ;
On Opera-pinions hoping soon
  Unrivall'd he shall mount the skies.

And while to please some courtly fair,
  He one dull tune with labour learns,
A well-gilt cage remote from air
  And faded plumes, is all he earns !

Go, hapless captive ! still repeat
  The sounds which nature never taught ;
Go, listening fair ! and call them sweet,
  Because you know them dearly bought.

Unenvied both ! go hear and sing
  Your studied music o'er and o'er ;
Whilst I attend th' inviting spring,
  In fields where birds unfetter'd soar.

MRS. PENNINGTON,

1734—1759,

WAS the author of a poem called *The Copper Farthing*, an imitation of *The Splendid Shilling*, and some miscellaneous verses, one of which productions is subjoined. She died in 1759, aged 25.

ODE TO MORNING.

Hail, roseate Morn! returning light!
To thee the sable queen of night
 Reluctant yields her sway ;
And, as she quits the dappled skies,
On glories greater glories rise,
 To greet the dawning day.

O'er tufted meads gay Flora trips ;
Arabia's spices scent her lips,
 Her head with rose-buds crown'd ;
Mild Zephyr hastes to snatch a kiss,
And, fluttering with the transient bliss,
 Wafts fragrance all around.

The dew-drops, daughters of the Morn,
With spangles every bush adorn,
 And all the broider'd vales ;
Their voice to thee the linnets raise,
The lark, soft trilling in thy praise,
 Aurora, rising, hails !

18   M *

While nature, now in lively vest
Of glory green, has gaily drest
    Each tributary plain;
While blooming flowers, and blossom'd trees,
Soft waving with the vernal breeze,
    Exult beneath thy reign ;

Shall I with drowsy poppies crown'd
By sleep in silken fetters bound,
    The downy god obey ?
Ah no ! through yon embowering grove,
Or winding valley let me rove,
    And own thy cheerful sway !

For short-lived are thy pleasing powers :
Pass but a few uncertain hours,
    And we no more shall trace
Thy dimpled cheek, and brow serene ;
Or clouds may gloom the smiling scene,
    And frowns deform thy face.

So in life's youthful bloomy prime,
We sport away the fleeting time,
    Regardless of our fate ;
But by some unexpected blow
Our giddy follies we shall know,
    And mourn them when too late !

MARY MASTERS,

1750,

PUBLISHED poems, which, as Boswell informs us, were corrected by Dr. Johnson. I extract as a specimen the subjoined verses.

TO LUCINDA.

Lucinda, you in vain dissuade
    Two hearts from mutual love;
What amorous youth, or tender maid,
    Could e'er their flames remove?

What if the charms in him I see
    Only exist in thought;
Yet Cupid, like the Mede's decree,
    Is firm, and changeth not.

Seek not to know my passion's spring,
    The reason to discover;
For reason is an useless thing,
    When we've commenc'd the lover.

Should lovers quarrel with their fate,
    And ask the reason why
They are condemn'd to dote on that,
    Or for this object die?

They must not hope for a reply,
    And this is all they know;
They sigh, and weep, and rave, and die,
    Because it must be so.

Love is a mighty god, you know,
    That rules with potent sway ;
And when he draws his awful bow,
    We mortals must obey.

Since you the fatal strife endur'd,
    And yielded to his dart;
How can I hope to be secur'd,
    And guard a weaker heart ?

MRS. MADAN.

About 1750.

ONE of the Cowper family, and the wife of Colonel Madan.

VERSES

Written in her brother's Coke upon Littleton.

O thou, who labour'st in this rugged mine,
Mayst thou to gold th' unpolish'd ore refine!
May each dark page unfold its haggard brow!
Doubt not to reap, if thou canst bear to plough.
To tempt thy care, may, each revolving night,
Purses and maces swim before thy sight!
From hence in times to come, adventurous deed!
Mayst thou essay to look and speak like Mead!
When the black bag and rose no more shall shade
With martial air the honours of thy head;
When the full wig thy visage shall enclose,
And only leave to view thy learned nose;
Safely mayst thou defy beaux, wits, and scoffers,
While tenants, in fee simple, stuff thy coffers!

Our author's brother appears to have followed this advice very
closely, for he became Lord Chancellor of England.

LADY ANNE IRWIN.

ANNE HOWARD, whose father was Earl of Carlisle, was twice married. Her husbands were Viscount Irwin and Colonel Douglass. She is chiefly celebrated as a poet for the defence of her sex against Pope's "*Characters of Women*," which Duncombe says "entitles her to a grateful tribute from all female hands."— Died, 1760.

By custom doomed to folly, sloth and ease,
No wonder Pope such female triflers sees ;
Nor would the satirist confess the truth,
Nothing so like as male and female youth ;
Nothing so like as man and woman old,
Their joys, their woes, their hates, if truly told ;
Though different acts seem different sexes' growth,
'T is the same principle impels them both.
— View daring man, strong with ambition's fire ;
The conq'ring hero or the youthful squire,
By different deeds aspire to deathless fame,
One numbers man, the other numbers game.
— View a fair nymph, blessed with superior charms,
Whose tempting form the coldest bosom warms ;
No eastern monarch more despotic reigns
Than this fair tyrant of the Cyprian plains.
Whether a crown or bauble we desire,
Whether to learning or to dress aspire,
Whether we wait with joy the trumpet's call,
Or wish to shine the fairest at a ball ;
In either sex the appetite 's the same,
For love of power is still the love of fame.

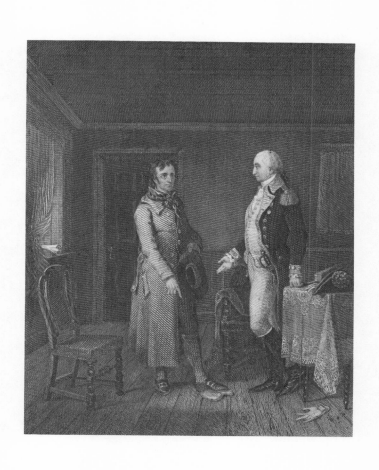

— Woman must in a narrow orbit move,
But power alike both males and females love.
What makes the difference then, you may inquire,
Between the hero and the rural squire ?
Between the maid bred up with courtly care,
Or she who earns by toil her daily fare ?
Their power is stinted, but not so their will,
Ambitious thoughts the humblest cottage fill;
For as they can they push their little fame,
And try to leave behind a deathless name.
In education all the difference lies;
Woman, if taught, would be as learned and wise
As haughty man, inspired by arts and rules;
Where God makes one, nature makes many fools;
And though nugatixes are daily found,
Flattering nugators equally abound.
Such heads are toy-shops filled with trifling ware,
And can each folly with each female share.
A female mind like a rude fallow lies,
No seeds are sown, but weeds spontaneous rise.
As well might we expect in winter spring,
As land untilled a fruitful crop should bring.
As well we might expect Peruvian ore
We should possess, yet dig not for the store.
Culture improves all fruits, all sorts we find,
Wit, judgment, sense, fruits of the human mind.
Can female youth, left to weak woman's care,
Misled by custom, Folly's fruitful heir ;
Told that their charms a monarch may enslave ;
That beauty, like the gods, can kill or save ;
Taught the arcana, the mysterious arts,
By ambush, dress to catch unwary hearts ;
Or, wealthy born, taught to lisp French or dance,
Their morals left, Lucretius-like, to chance ;
Unused to books, nor virtue taught to prize,
Whose mind a savage waste, unpeopled lies,
Which to supply, trifles fill up the void,
And idly busy to no end employed ;

Can these resist, when soothing pleasure woos?
Preserve their virtue, when their fame they lose?
Can they on other themes converse or write,
Than what they hear all day, or dream all night?

LADY MARY WORTLEY MONTAGU.

1690—1762.

THE celebrated daughter of the Duke of Kingston. She was born in 1690. Her fame chiefly rests upon her *Letters*. Her poetry is of rather a coarse, masculine, sensuous order, and is quite destitute of imagination. It has, however, some good sensible touches that go far to redeem it from the charge of mediocrity. She died in 1762.

THE LADY'S RESOLVE.

Whilst thirst of praise and vain desire of fame
In every age is every woman's aim ;
With courtship pleas'd, of silly toasters pioud,
Fond of a train, and happy in a crowd ;
On each proud fop bestowing some kind glance,
Each conquest owing to some loose advance :
While vain coquettes affect to be pursued,
And think they 're virtuous if not grossly lewd :
Let this great maxim be my virtue's guide ;
In part she is to blame that has been tried :
He comes too near that comes to be denied.

HYMN TO THE MOON.

Thou silver deity of secret night,
    Direct my footsteps through the woodland shade ;
Thou conscious witness of unknown delight,
    The lover's guardian, and the muse's aid !

19   N

By thy pale beams I solitary rove,
  To thee my tender grief confide,
Serenely sweet you gild the silent grove,
  My friend, my goddess, and my guide !

Even thee, fair queen, from thy amazing height,
  The charms of young Endymion drew ;
Veil'd with the mantle of concealing night ;
  With all thy greatness, and thy coldness, too.

ADVICE.

Good madam, when ladies are willing,
  A man must needs look like a fool ;
For me I would not give a shilling
  For one who would love out of rule.

You should leave us to guess by your blushing,
  And not speak the matter so plain ;
'T is ours to write and be pushing,
  'T is yours to affect a disdain.

That you are in a terrible taking,
  By all these sweet oglings I see ;
But the fruit that can fall without shaking
  Indeed is too mellow for me.

AN ANSWER TO A LADY WHO ADVISED LADY M. TO RETIRE.

You little know the heart that you advise ;
I view this various scene with equal eyes ;
In crowded court I find myself alone,
And pay my worship to a nobler throne.

Long since the value of this world I knew;
Pitied the folly and despised the shew:
Well as I can, my tedious part I bear,
And wait dismissal without pain or fear.

Seldom I mark mankind's detested ways,
Not hearing censure, nor affecting praise;
And unconcern'd, my future fate I trust
To that sole Being merciful and just.

FRANCES SHERIDAN,

1724—1776,

THE mother of Richard Brinsley Sheridan, was born in 1724. Her maiden name was Chamberlaine. She is chiefly known by her novels of *Sidney Biddulph* and *Nourjahad*. She died in 1767.

ODE TO PATIENCE.

Unaw'd by threats, unmov'd by force,
My steady soul pursues her course,
  Collected, calm, resign'd;
Say, you who search with curious eyes
The source whence human actions rise,
  Say, whence this turn of mind?

'T is Patience! lenient goddess, hail!
O let thy votary's vows prevail,
  Thy threaten'd flight to stay;
Long hast thou been a welcome guest,
Long reign'd an inmate in this breast,
  And rul'd with gentle sway.

Through all the various turns of fate,
Ordain'd me in each several state,
  My wayward lot has known;
What taught me silently to bear,
To curb the sigh, to check the tear,
  When sorrow weigh'd me down?

'T was Patience ! temperate goddess, stay !
For still thy dictates I obey,
    Nor yield to passion's power ;
Though by injurious foes borne down,
My fame, my toil, my hopes o'erthrown,
    In one ill-fated hour.

When robb'd of what I held most dear,
My hands adorn'd the mournful bier
    Of her I lov'd so well ;
What, when mute sorrow chain'd my tongue,
As o'er the sable hearse I hung
    Forbade the tide to swell ?

'T was Patience ! goddess ever calm !
O pour into my breast thy balm,
    That antidote to pain ;
Which flowing from thy nectar'd urn,
By chemistry divine can turn
    Our losses into gain.

When sick and languishing in bed,
Sleep from my restless couch had fled,
    (Sleep which e'en pain beguiles,)
What taught me calmly to sustain
A feverish being, rack'd with pain,
    And dress'd my looks in smiles ?

'T was Patience ! Heaven-descended maid
Implored, flew swiftly to my aid,
    And lent her fostering breast ;
Watch'd my sad hours with parent care,
Repell'd the approaches of despair,
    And sooth'd my soul to rest.

Say, when dissevered from his side,
My friend, protector, and my guide —
    When my prophetic soul,
                N*

Anticipating all the storm,
Saw danger in its direst form,
　What could my fears control ?

'T was Patience ! gentle goddess, hear !
Be ever to thy suppliant near,
　Nor let one murmur rise ;
Since still some mighty joys are given,
Dear to her soul, the gifts of heaven,
　The sweet domestic ties.

MARY JONES.

1750.

" Miss Jones lived at Oxford, and was often of our parties. She was a very ingenious poetess, and published a volume of poems ; and, on the whole, was a most sensible, agreeable, and amiable woman. She was a sister to the Reverend River Jones, chanter of Christ-church Cathedral at Oxford, and Johnson used to call her *The Chantress.* I have heard him often address her in this passage from *Il Penseroso,* ' Thee, chantress of the woods among, I woo,' &c. Note on a letter from Johnson to T. Warton, in 1757."— *Boswell's Life of Johnson,* vol. i.

In the preface to her volume, Miss Jones calls her poems "the produce of pure nature only, and most of them wrote at a very early age." Our author seems to have enjoyed considerable celebrity, for the names of a vast number of subscribers appear prefixed to the work alluded to,—*Miscellanies in Prose and Verse,* 1750.

I subjoin two specimens of Miss Jones's powers ; by which it will be seen that she excelled in lively strains, and possessed a quaint and humorous genius.

I. EXTRACT FROM AN EPISTLE TO LADY BOWYER.

How much of paper's spoil'd ! what floods of ink !
And yet how few, how very few, can think !
The knack of writing is an easy trade ;
But to think well requires — at least a head.
Once in an age one genius may arise,
With wit well cultured, and with learning wise :
Like some tall oak, behold his branches shoot,
No tender scions springing from the root.

Whilst lofty Pope erects his laurell'd head,
No lays like mine can live beneath his shade:
Nothing but weeds, and moss, and herbs, are found: —
Cut, cut them down; why cumber they the ground?

And yet you 'd have me write? — For what? To whom?
To curl a favourite in a dressing-room?
To mend a candle when the snuff 's too short?
Or save rappee for chambermaids at court?
Glorious ambition! — noble thirst of fame!
No! but you 'd have me write — to get a name!
Alas! I 'd live unknown, unenvy'd too;
'T is more than Pope with all his wit can do.
'T is more than you with wit and beauty join'd,
A pleasing form, and a discerning mind.
The world and I are no such cordial friends:
I have my purpose, they their various ends.
I say my prayers, and lead a sober life,
Nor laugh at Cornus, or at Cornus' wife.
What 's fame to me, who pray and pay my rent?
If my friends know me honest, I 'm content.

II.   TO STELLA, AFTER THE SMALL-POX.

When skilful traders first set up,
To draw the people to their shop,
They straight hang out some gaudy sign,
Expressive of the goods within.
The Vintner has his boy and grapes,
The Haberdasher thread and tapes,
The Shoemaker exposes boots,
And Monmouth Street old tatter'd suits.

So fares it with the nymph divine;
For what is beauty but a sign?

A face hung out, through which is seen
The nature of the goods within.
Thus the coquette her beau ensnares
With studied smile and forward airs;
The graver prude hangs out a frown
To strike the audacious gazer down;
But she alone whose temperate wit
Each nicer medium can hit,
Is still adorn'd with every grace,
And wears a sample in her face.

What though some envious folks have said
That Stella now must hide her head,
That all her stock of beauty 's gone,
And e'en the very sign took down;
Yet grieve not at the fatal blow,
For if you break awhile, we know
'T is bankrupt like, more rich to grow.
A fairer sign you 'll soon hang up,
And with fresh credit open shop;
For nature's pencil soon shall trace,
And once more finish off your face:
Which all your neighbours shall outshine,
And of your *Mind* remain the sign!

MRS. ANNE STEELE.

Mrs. Steele was the daughter of a Baptist clergyman, and was born in Hampshire. She may be said to claim a place by the side of Dr. Watts as a writer of sacred songs. Died, **1779.**

TO MY WATCH.

Little monitor, by thee
Let me learn what I should be;
Learn the round of life to fill,
Useful and progressive still.
Thou canst gentle hints impart
How to regulate the heart;
When I wind thee up at night,
Mark each fault and set thee right,
Let me search my bosom too,
And my daily thoughts review;
Mark the movements of my mind,
Nor be easy till I find
Latent errors brought to view,
Till all be regular and true.

FRANCES BROOKE,

1745—1789,

WAS the daughter of a clergyman named Moore, residing in Devonshire, and wife of the Reverend J. Brooke. She was born in 1745, and died in 1789. Mrs. Brooke was the author of the operettas entitled *Rosina* and *Marian ;* both of which are very elegant and pleasing productions. Besides these she wrote some novels, plays, and poems, which are now forgotten.

Mrs. Brooke's verses have a spirit, a clear, sparkling, living style, which is very delightful. The following song from *Marian* sounds like the shout of a clear merry voice ringing in the open morning air.

To the chase, to the chase ! on the brow of the hill
    Let the hounds meet the sweet-breathing morn ;
Whilst full to the welkin, their notes clear and shrill,
    Join the sound of the heart-cheering horn.
What music celestial ! when urging the race
Sweet Echo repeats — " To the chase, to the chase !"

Our pleasure transports us, how gay flies the hour !
    Sweet health and quick spirits attend ;
Not sweeter when evening convenes to the bower,
    And we meet the loved smile of a friend.
See the stag just before us ! He starts at the cry : —
He stops—his strength fails—speak, my friends—must he die ?

His innocent aspect while standing at bay,
    His expression of anguish and pain,
All plead for compassion,—your looks seem to say
    Let him bound o'er his forests again.
Quick, release him to dart o'er the neighbouring plain,
Let him live, let him bound o'er his forests again !

This last stanza is " pure womanly." No male writer would have let the stag loose again, or even have debated about his death. The conception is in my idea most beautifully feminine, and embodies one of the most exquisite touches of pity I know of.

The following little song, too, from the same opera, has something very plaintive in it.

> By the osiers so dank,
> As we sat on the bank,
> And look'd at the swell of the billow,
> This chaplet he wove
> As a token of love;
> Alas ! 't was the branch of the willow.

> How sad all the day
> Through the meadows I stray,
> And rest flies at night from my pillow!
> The garland I wore
> From my ringlets I tore,
> Alas ! must I wear the green willow ?

Here is another little sparkling piece ; extracted from *Rosina.*

> Her mouth, which a smile
> Devoid of all guile
> Half opens to view,
> Is the bud of the rose
> In the morning that blows,
> Impearl'd with the dew.

> More fragrant her breath
> Than the flow'r-scented heath
> At the dawning of day ;
> The hawthorn in bloom,
> The lily's perfume,
> Or the blossoms of May.

Her *Ode to Health*, too, is a very graceful and harmonious composition.

ODE TO HEALTH.

The Lesbian lute no more can charm,
Nor my once panting bosom warm ;
   No more I breathe the tender sigh ;
Nor when my beauteous swain appears
With downcast look and starting tears,
   Confess the lustre of his eye.

With Freedom blest, at early dawn,
I wander o'er the verdant lawn,
   And hail the sweet returning Spring ;
The fragrant breeze, the feather'd choir
To raise my vernal joys conspire,
   While Peace and Health their treasures bring.

Come, lovely Health ! divinest maid !
And lead me through the rural shade,
   To thee the rural shades belong :
T is thine to bless the simple swain,
And, while he tries the tuneful strain,
   To raise the raptur'd poet's song.

Behold the patient village hind !
No cares disturb his tranquil mind ;
   By thee, and sweet Contentment blest,
All day he turns the stubborn plain,
And meets at eve his infant train,
   While guiltless pleasure fills his breast.

O ever good and bounteous ! still
By fountain fresh, or murmuring rill,
   Let me thy blissful presence find !
Thee, Goddess ! thee my steps pursue,
When, careless of the morning dew,
   I leave the lessening vales behind.

o

MRS. GREVILLE.

Of this lady, whose *Prayer for Indifference* has been so
much admired, I can give no account.

PRAYER FOR INDIFFERENCE.

Oft I 've implor'd the gods in vain,
    And pray'd till I 've been weary ;
For once I 'll seek my wish to gain
    Of Oberon, the Fairy.

Sweet airy being, wanton sprite,
    Who lurk'st in woods unseen,
And oft by Cynthia's silver light,
    Trip'st gaily o'er the green :

If e'er thy pitying heart was mov'd,
    As ancient stories tell,
And for the Athenian maid* who lov'd,
    Thou sought'st a wondrous spell ;

O deign once more t' exert thy power !
    Haply some herb or tree,
Sovereign as juice of western flower,
    Conceals a balm for me.

I ask no kind return of love,
    No tempting charm to please ;
Far from the heart those gifts remove,
    That sighs for peace and ease ;

* See " Midsummer Night's Dream."

Nor peace, nor ease, the heart can know,
    That, like the needle true,
Turns at the touch of joy or woe,
    But, turning, trembles too.

Far as distress the soul can wound,
    'T is pain in each degree;
'T is bliss but to a certain bound,
    Beyond, is agony.

Then take this treacherous sense of mine,
    Which dooms me still to smart;
Which pleasure can to pain refine,
    To pain new pangs impart.

O haste to shed the sovereign balm,
    My shatter'd nerves new string;
And for my guest, serenely calm,
    The nymph Indifference bring!

At her approach, see Hope, see Fear,
    See Expectation fly!
And Disappointment in the rear,
    That blasts the promis'd joy!

The tear which Pity taught to flow
    The eye shall then disown;
The heart that melts for others' woe
    Shall then scarce feel its own.

The wounds which now each moment bleed,
    Each moment then shall close;
And tranquil days shall still succeed
    To nights of calm repose.

O Fairy Elf! but grant me this,
    This one kind comfort send,
And so may never-fading bliss
    Thy flowery paths attend!

So may the glow-worm's glimmering light
  Thy tiny footsteps lead
To some new region of delight,
  Unknown to mortal tread!

And be thy acorn goblet filled
  With heaven's ambrosial dew,
From sweetest, freshest flowers distill'd,
  That shed fresh sweets for you!

And what of life remains for me
  I 'll pass in sober ease;
Half pleased, contented will I be,
  Content but half to please.

For the answer to this Poem, by the Countess of Carlisle, **see** page 218.

CONSTANTIA GRIERSON,

1706—1733,

WAS an Irish poetess, of extraordinary erudition. She was born
in 1706. "She died," says Mrs. Mary Barber (with whose
poems her own were published), "at the age of 27, and was
allowed, long before, to be an excellent scholar, not only in Greek
and Roman literature, but in history, divinity, philosophy, and
mathematics. She gave a proof of her knowledge in the Latin
tongue, by her dedication of the Dublin edition of Tacitus to the
Lord Carteret, and by that of Terence to his son, to whom she
likewise wrote a Greek epigram." Mrs. Pilkington informs us
that she was also mistress of Hebrew ; that her parents were
poor, illiterate country people ; and that when questioned how
she had acquired such learning, she said " she had received som
little instruction from the minister of the parish, when she could
spare time from her needle-work, to which she was closely kept
by her mother."

The following lines are addressed *To Miss Lætitia Van
Lewen (afterwards Mrs. Pilkington) at a Country Assize.*

> The fleeting birds may soon in ocean swim,
> And northern whales through liquid azure skim ;
> The Dublin ladies their intrigues forsake,
> To dress and scandal an aversion take ;
> When you can in the lonely forest walk,
> And with some serious matron gravely talk
> Of possets, poultices, and waters 'still'd,
> And monstrous casks with mead and cider fill'd ;
> How many hives of bees she has in store,
> And how much fruit her trees this summer bore ;
> Or, home returning, in the yard can stand,
> And feed the chickens from your bounteous hand :

21   o*

Of each one's top-knot tell, and hatching pry,
Like Tully, waiting for an augury.

When night approaches, down to table sit
With a great crowd, choice meat, and little wit;
What horse won the last race, how mighty Tray,
At the last famous hunting, caught the prey;
Surely you can't but such discourse despise,
Methinks I see displeasure in your eyes:
O my Lætitia! stay no longer there,
You 'll soon forget that you yourself are fair;
Why will you keep from us, from all that 's gay,
There in a lonely solitude to stay?
Where not a mortal through the year you view,
But bob-wigged hunters, who their game pursue
With so much ardour, they 'd a cock or hare
To thee in all thy pleasing charms prefer.

You write of belles and beaux that there appear,
And gilded coaches, such as glitter here;
For gilded coaches, each estated clown
That gravely slumbers on the bench has one;
But beaux! they 're young attorneys sure you mean,
Who thus appear to your romantic brain.
Alas! no mortal there can talk to you,
That love, or wit, or softness ever knew;
All they can speak of 's *capias* and law,
And writs to keep the country fools in awe.
And if to wit or courtship they pretend,
'T is the same way that they a cause defend;
In which they give of lungs a vast expense,
But little passion, thought, or eloquence:
Bad as they are, they 'd soon abandon you,
And gain and clamour in the town pursue.
So haste to town, if even such fools you prize,
O haste to town! and bless the longing eyes
                                    Of your CONSTANTIA.

HENRIETTA O'NEIL,

1758—1793,

WAS the only daughter of Charles, Viscount Dungarvon, and wife of John O'Neil, Esquire, of Slanes Castle, in the county of Antrim, who was created an Irish Peer about two months after the death of his wife.   Lady O'Neil was born in 1758, and died in 1793.

The two poems here quoted have been preserved in the works of her friend, Charlotte Smith.

ODE TO THE POPPY.

Not for the promise of the labour'd field,
Not for the good the yellow harvests yield,
   I bend at Ceres' shrine;
For dull to humid eyes appear
The golden glories of the year;
   Alas! a melancholy worship's mine:

I hail the goddess for her scarlet flower!
   Thou brilliant weed,
   That dost so far exceed
The richest gifts gay Flora can bestow,
Heedless I pass'd thee in life's morning hour,
   Thou comforter of woe,
Till sorrow taught me to confess thy power.

   In early days, when Fancy cheats,
    A varied wreath I wove,
   Of laughing Spring's luxuriant sweets,
    To deck ungrateful Love:

The rose, or thorn, my labours crown'd,
As Venus smil'd, or Venus frown'd,
But Love and Joy and all their train are flown ;
E'en languid Hope no more is mine,
And I will sing of thee alone :
Unless perchance the attributes of Grief,
The cypress bud and willow leaf
Their pale funereal foliage blend with thine.

Hail, lovely blossom ! thou canst ease
The wretched victims of Disease ;
Canst close those weary eyes in gentle sleep,
Which never open but to weep ;
For oh ! thy potent charm
Can agonizing Pain disarm ;
Expel imperious Memory from her seat,
And bid the throbbing heart forget to beat.

Soul-soothing plant, that can such blessings give,
By thee the mourner bears to live !
By thee the hopeless die !
Oh, ever friendly to despair,
Might Sorrow's pallid votary dare,
Without a crime that remedy implore,
Which bids the spirit from its bondage fly,
I'd court thy palliative aid no more.

No more I'd sue that thou shouldst spread
Thy spell around my aching head ;
But would conjure thee to impart
Thy balsam for a broken heart !
And by thy soft Lethean power,
Inestimable flower !
Burst these terrestial bonds, and other regions try !

VERSES WRITTEN ON SEEING HER TWO SONS AT PLAY.

Sweet age of blest delusion ! blooming boys,
Ah ! revel long in childhood's thoughtless joys,
With light and pliant spirits, that can stoop
To follow sportively the rolling hoop :
To watch the sleeping top with gay delight,
Or mark with raptur'd gaze the sailing kite,
Or eagerly pursuing Pleasure's call,
Can find it centred in the bounding ball !
Alas ! the day *will* come, when sports like these
Must lose their magic and their power to please ;
Too swiftly fled, the rosy hours of youth
Shall yield their fairy charms to mournful Truth ;
Even now, a mother's fond prophetic fear
Sees the dark train of human ills appear ;
Views various fortune for each lovely child,
Storms for the bold, and anguish for the mild ;
Beholds already those expressive eyes
Beam a sad certainty of future sighs ;
And dreads each suffering those dear breasts may know
In their long passage through a world of woe ;
Perchance predestin'd every pang to prove,
That treacherous friends inflict, or faithless love ;
For ah ! how few have found existence sweet,
Where grief is sure, but happiness deceit !

The first of the two beautiful poems above quoted will be found
in Charlotte Smith's *Desmond ;* the last in the same writer's
second Volume of Poems : but I have met with both of them
frequently in books containing poetical selections. I am not
aware that Lady O'Neil wrote any other verses.

MARY ROBINSON,

1758—1800,

Was a native of Bristol, where she was born in 1758. Her father, whose name was Darby, was a merchant there. At the age of fifteen she married a young lawyer, Mr. Robinson, but the union was not a happy one. Profligacy and extravagance soon reduced his circumstances, and Mrs. Robinson, whose beauty and talents were remarkable, turned for subsistence to the stage. Her character suffered by her connection with the theatre; and she became, unfortunately, notorious for her gallantries. As an authoress, she displays very considerable powers, but, being one of the Della Cruscan school, she was mercilessly attacked by Gifford. She died in 1800.

I extract two of her poems.

I. SONNET.

High on a rock, coeval with the skies,
   A temple stands, rear'd by immortal powers
   To Chastity divine ! ambrosial flowers
Twining round icicles, in columns rise,
Mingling with pendent gems of orient dyes !
   Piercing the air, a golden crescent towers,
Veil'd by transparent clouds ; while smiling hours
Shake from their varying wings celestial joys !
   The steps of spotless marble scatter'd o'er
With deathless roses, arm'd with many a thorn,
   Lead to the altar. On the frozen floor,
Studded with tear-drops, petrified by scorn,
   Pale vestals kneel, the goddess to adore,
While Love, his arrows broke, retires forlorn.

THE SNOW-DROP.

The Snow-drop, Winter's timid child,
   Awakes to life, bedew'd with tears ;
And flings around its fragrance mild,
And where no rival flow'rets bloom,
Amid the bare and chilling gloom,
   A beauteous gem appears !

All weak and wan, with head inclin'd,
   Its parent breast the drifted snow ;
It trembles while the ruthless wind
Bends its slim form ; the tempest lowers,
Its emerald eye drops crystal showers
   On its cold bed below.

Poor flower ! on thee the sunny beam
   No touch of genial warmth bestows ;
Except to thaw the icy stream
Whose little current purls along
Thy fair and glossy charms among,
   And whelms thee as it flows.

The night breeze tears thy silken dress,
   Which deck'd with silvery lustre shone ;
The morn returns not thee to bless,
The gaudy crocus flaunts its pride,
And triumphs where its rival died,
   Unshelter'd and unknown !

No sunny beam shall gild thy grave,
   No bird of pity thee deplore ;
There shall no spreading branches wave,
For Spring shall all her gems unfold,
And revel mid her buds of gold,
   When thou art seen no more !

Where'er I find thee, gentle flower,
  Thou still art sweet and dear to me !
For I have known the cheerless hour,
Have seen the sunbeams cold and pale,
Have felt the chilling wintry gale,
  And wept and shrunk like thee

MRS. HESTER CHAPONE.

1727—1801.

MRS. CHAPONE, well known for her admirable *Letters on the Improvement of the Mind*, was the daughter of Mr. Mulso, of Twywell, in Northamptonshire, and was born in 1727. She married in 1760, but her husband died within the first year of their union, leaving her in very straitened circumstances. Her first poetical work, a Volume of Miscellanies, appeared in 1775, and attracted much attention. It is to her prose writings, however, that she chiefly owes her fame. She died in 1801.

WRITTEN DURING A STORM AT MIDNIGHT, 1749.

In gloomy pomp whilst awful midnight reigns,
   And wide o'er earth her mournful mantle spreads,
   Whilst deep-voiced thunders threaten guilty heads,
And rushing torrents drown the frighted plains,
And quick-glanc'd lightnings to my dazzled sight
Betray the double horrors of the night;

A solemn stillness creeps upon my soul,
   And all its powers in deep attention die;
   My heart forgets to beat; my steadfast eye
Catches the flying gleam; the distant roll,
Advancing gradual, swells upon my ear
With louder peals, more dreadful as more near.

Awake, my soul, from thy forgetful trance!
   The storm calls loud, and Meditation wakes,
   How at the sound pale Superstition shakes,
22   P

Whilst all her train of frantic Fears advance!
Children of Darkness, hence ! fly far from me!
And dwell with Guilt and Infidelity!

But come, with look composed and sober pace,
  Calm Contemplation, come ! and hither lead
  Devotion, that on earth disdains to tread;
Her inward flame illumes her glowing face,
Her upcast eye and spreading wings prepare
Her flight for Heaven, to find her treasure there.

She sees enraptured, through the thickest gloom,
  Celestial beauty beam, and midst the howl
  Of warring winds, sweet music charms her soul;
She sees, while rifted oaks in flame consume,
A Father-God, that o'er the storm presides,
Threatens, to save — and loves when most he chides!

ODE TO SOLITUDE.

Thou gentle nurse of pleasing woe,
To thee from crowds, and noise, and show,
  With eager haste I fly ;
Thrice welcome, friendly Solitude,
O let no busy foot intrude,
  Nor listening ear be nigh!

Soft, silent, melancholy maid,
With thee to yon sequester'd shade
  My pensive steps I bend ;
Still at the mild approach of night,
When Cynthia lends her sober light,
  Do thou my walk attend!

To thee alone, my conscious heart
Its tender sorrow dares impart,
    And ease my lab'ring breast;
To thee I trust the rising sigh
And bid the tear that swells my eye
    No longer be supprest.

With thee among the haunted groves,
The lovely sorceress, Fancy, roves;
    O let me find her here !
For she can time and space control,
And swift transport my fleeting soul
    To all it holds most dear.

Ah ! no—ye vain delusions, hence !
No more the hallow'd innocence
    Of Solitude pervert !
Shall Fancy cheat the precious hour,
Sacred to Wisdom's awful power,
    And calm Reflection's part ?

O Wisdom ! from the sea-beat shore
Where, listening to the solemn roar,
    Thy loved Eliza * strays,
Vouchsafe to visit my retreat,
And teach my erring, trembling feet
    Thy heaven-protected ways !

O guide me to the humble cell
Where Resignation loves to dwell,
    Contentment's bower in view !
Nor pining grief with absence drear,
Nor sick suspense, nor anxious fear,
    Shall there my steps pursue.

* Eliza Carter.

There, let my soul to Him aspire,
Whom none e'er sought with vain desire,
   Nor lov'd in sad despair;
There, to his gracious will divine,
My dearest, fondest hope resign,
   And all my tenderest care.

Then peace shall heal this wounded breast,
That pants to see another blest,
   From selfish passion pure;
Peace, which when human wishes rise,
Intense, for aught beneath the skies,
   Can never be secure.

GEORGIANA, DUCHESS OF DEVONSHIRE,

1757—1806,

WAS the daughter of John, Earl Spencer, and was born in 1757. " This beautiful woman, who shone a brilliant star in the fashionable world, cultivated and liberally patronised literature and the fine arts.   Gibbon says, ' She was made for something better than a duchess.'   The following poem has been translated into French by the Abbé De Lille."   The duchess died in 1806.

THE PASSAGE OF THE MOUNT ST. GOTHARD.

To my Children.

Ye plains, where threefold harvests press the ground,
    Ye climes, where genial gales incessant swell,
Where Art and Nature shed profusely round
    Their rival wonders — Italy, farewell !

Still may thy year in fullest splendour shine !
    Its icy darts in vain may Winter throw !
To thee a parent, sister, I consign,
    And wing'd with health, I woo thy gales to blow.

Yet pleas'd Helvetia's rugged brows I see,
    And through their craggy steeps delighted roam ;
Pleas'd with a people, honest, brave, and free,
    Whilst every step conducts me nearer home.

I wander where Tesino madly flows,
    From cliff to cliff in foaming eddies tost ;
On the rude mountain's barren breast he rose,
    In Po's broad wave now hurries to be lost.

P*

His shores neat huts and verdant pastures fill,
  And hills where woods of pine the storm defy;
While, scorning vegetation, higher still
  Rise the bare rocks, coeval with the sky.

Upon his banks a favour'd spot I found,
  Where shade and beauty tempted to repose :
Within a grove, by mountains circled round,
  By rocks o'erhung, my rustic seat I chose.

Advancing thence, by gentle pace and slow,
  Unconscious of the way my footsteps prest,
Sudden, supported by the hills below,
  St. Gothard's summits rose above the rest.

Midst towering cliffs, and tracts of endless cold,
  The' industrious path pervades the rugged stone,
And seems — Helvetia ! let thy toils be told —
  A granite girdle o'er the mountain thrown.

No haunt of man the weary traveller greets,
  No vegetation smiles upon the moor,
Save where the floweret breathes uncultur'd sweets,
  Save where the patient monk receives the poor.

Yet let not these rude paths be coldly traced,
  Let not these wilds with listless steps be trod ;
Here fragrance scorns not to perfume the waste,
  Here charity uplifts the mind to God.

His humble board the holy man prepares,
  And simple food and wholesome lore bestows;
Extols the treasures that his mountain bears,
  And paints the perils of impending snows.

For whilst bleak Winter numbs with chilling hand,
  Where frequent crosses mark the traveller's fate,
In slow procession moves the merchant band,
  And silent treads where tottering ruins wait.

Yet, midst those ridges, midst that drifted snow,
　　Can Nature deign her wonders to display ;
Here Adularia shines with vivid glow,
　　And gems of crystal sparkle to the day.

Here, too, the hoary mountain's brow to grace,
　　Five silver lakes in tranquil state are seen ;
While from their waters many a stream we trace,
　　That, scap'd from bondage, rolls the rocks between.

Hence flows the Reuss to seek her wedded love,
　　And, with the Rhine, Germanic climes explore ;
Her stream I mark'd, and saw her wildly move
　　Down the bleak mountain, through her craggy shore.

My weary footsteps hop'd for rest in vain,
　　For steep on steep in rude confusion rose :
At length I paus'd above a fertile plain,
　　That promis'd shelter, and foretold repose.

Fair runs the streamlet o'er the pasture green,
　　Its margin gay, with flocks and cattle spread ;
Embowering trees the peaceful village screen,
　　And guard from snow each dwelling's jutting shed.

Sweet vale ! whose bosom wastes and cliffs surround,
　　Let me awhile thy friendly shelter share !
Emblem of life ! where some bright hours are found
　　Amidst the darkest, dreariest years of care.

Delv'd through the rock, the secret passage bends ;
　　And beauteous horror strikes the dazzled sight ;
Beneath the pendent bridge the stream descends
　　Calm — till it tumbles o'er the frowning height.

We view the fearful pass — we wind along
　　The path that marks the terrors of our way —
Midst beetling rocks, and hanging woods among,
　　The torrent pours, and breathes its glittering spray

Weary at length, serener scenes we hail —
  More cultur'd groves o'ershade the grassy meads ;
The neat though wooden hamlets deck the vale,
  And Altorf's spires recall heroic deeds.

But though no more amidst those scenes I roam,
  My fancy long each image shall retain —
The flock returning to its welcome home,
  And the wild carol of the cow-herd's strain.

Lucernia's lake its glassy surface shows,
  Whilst Nature's varied beauties deck its side ;
Here rocks and woods its narrow waves enclose,
  And there its spreading bosom opens wide.

And hail the chapel ! hail the platform wild !
  Where Tell directed the avenging dart,
With well-strung arm, that first preserv'd his child,
  Then wing'd the arrow to the tyrant's heart.

Across the lake, and deep embower'd in wood,
  Behold another hallow'd chapel stand,
Where three Swiss heroes lawless force withstood,
  And stamp'd the freedom of their native land.

Their liberty required no rites uncouth,
  No blood demanded, and no slaves enchained ;
Her rule was gentle, and her voice was truth,
  By social order form'd, by laws restrain'd.

We quit the lake — and cultivation's toil,
  With Nature's charms combin'd, adorns the way ;
And well-earn'd wealth improves the ready soil,
  And simple manners still maintain their sway.

Farewell, Helvetia ! from whose lofty breast
  Proud Alps arise, and copious rivers flow ;
Where, source of streams, eternal glaciers rest,
  And peaceful Science gilds the plain below.

Oft on thy rocks the wondering eye shall gaze,
Thy valleys oft the raptur'd bosom seek —
There, Nature's hand her boldest work displays,
Here, bliss domestic beams on every cheek.

Hope of my life! dear children of my heart!
That anxious heart, to each fond feeling true,
To you still pants each pleasure to impart,
And more — O transport! — reach its home and you.

23

MISS ELIZABETH CARTER,

1717—1806,

ONE of the most learned of the British poetesses, was the daughter of Dr. Nicholas Carter of Deal, in Kent, where she was born in the year 1717. Her father appears to have taken the greatest possible pains with her education; and, although at first slow and inapt at study, she eventually became remarkably distinguished for her extensive and varied acquirements. She was well acquainted with the Greek, Latin, Hebrew, French, Italian, Spanish, and German languages; and, in later life, attained considerable knowledge of Portuguese and Arabic. Miss Carter acquired great celebrity by her translation of Epictetus, and was intimately acquainted with Dr. Johnson and the other chief literary characters of the day.

She never married. She had consented to an union with a gentleman whose name has not transpired; but she eventually refused him in consequence of his having written some verses which she did not approve! It is satisfactory to add, that the gentleman subsequently found a less squeamish partner.

Miss Carter died in London in 1806, being 89 years of age.

This lady's poetical writings display but little passion or imagination, and have none of those strong thoughts and sublime ideas which betoken lofty genius: but her verses exhibit great classical purity, and are remarkable for an unusual sweetness of versification. They embody, too, a cheerful serenity very highly calculated to improve the reader's mind; for although Miss Carter translated Epictetus, she by no means followed his philosophy.

The following *Ode to Wisdom* (which originally appeared in Richardson's Clarissa), is a fair average sample of her powers.

ODE TO WISDOM.

The solitary bird of night
Through the thick shades now wings his flight,
   And quits this time-shook tower ;
Where shelter'd from the blaze of day,
In philosophic gloom he lay,
   Beneath his ivy bower.

With joy I hear the solemn sound,
Which midnight echoes waft around,
   And sighing gales repeat :
Favourite of Pallas ! I attend,
And faithful to thy summons, bend
   At Wisdom's awful seat.

She loves the cool, the silent eve,
Where no false shows of life deceive,
   Beneath the lunar ray.
Here Folly drops each vain disguise,
Nor sports her gaily-colour'd dyes,
   As in the glare of day.

O Pallas ! queen of ev'ry art,
That glads the sense and mends the heart,
   Blest source of purer joys :
In ev'ry form of beauty bright,
That captivates the mental sight,
   With pleasure and surprise :

To thy unspotted shrine I bow :
Attend thy modest suppliant's vow,
   That breathes no wild desires :
But, taught by thy unerring rules,
To shun the fruitless wish of fools,
   To nobler views aspires.

Not Fortune's gem, Ambition's plume,
Nor Cytheræa's fading bloom,
    Be objects of my prayer :
Let Avarice, Vanity, and Pride,
Those envied, glittering toys, divide,
    The dull rewards of care.

To me thy better gifts impart,
Each moral beauty of the heart,
    By studious thoughts refined ;
For Wealth, the smiles of glad content,
For Power, its amplest, best extent,
    An empire o'er the mind.

When Fortune drops her gay parade,
When Pleasure's transient roses fade,
    And wither in the tomb ;
Unchang'd is thy immortal prize,
Thy ever-verdant laurels rise
    In undecaying bloom.

By thee protected, I defy
The coxcomb's sneer, the stupid lie
    Of ignorance and spite :
Alike contemn the leaden fool,
And all the pointed ridicule
    Of undiscerning wit.

From envy, hurry, noise, and strife,
The dull impertinence of life,
    In thy retreat I rest :
Pursue thee to the peaceful groves,
Where Plato's sacred spirit roves,
    In all thy beauties drest.

He bade Ilissus' tuneful stream
Convey thy philosophic theme,
    Of perfect fair and good :

Attentive Athens caught the sound,
And all her listening sons around
     In awful silence stood :

Reclaim'd, her wild licentious youth,
Confess'd the potent voice of truth,
     And felt its just control :
The passions ceas'd their loud alarms,
And Virtue's soft persuasive charms
     O'er all their senses stole.

Thy breath inspires the poet's song,
The patriot's free unbiass'd tongue,
     The hero's generous strife :
Thine are retirement's silent joys,
And all the sweet engaging ties
     Of still, domestic life.

No more to fabled names confined,
To thee, supreme, all perfect Mind,
     My thoughts direct their flight;
Wisdom's thy gift, and all her force
From Thee derived, eternal source
     Of Intellectual light !

O send her sure, her steady ray,
To regulate my doubtful way,
     Through life's perplexing road;
The mists of error to control,
And through its gloom direct my soul
     To happiness and good !

Beneath her clear discerning eye,
The visionary shadows fly
     Of Folly's painted show :
She sees, through every fair disguise,
That all but Virtue's solid joys
     Is vanity and woe.

Q

LINES WRITTEN AT MIDNIGHT DURING A THUNDER-STORM.

Let coward Guilt, with pallid Fear,
　To sheltering caverns fly,
And justly dread the vengeful fate
　That thunders through the sky.

Protected by that Hand, whose law
　The threatening storms obey,
Intrepid Virtue smiles secure
　As in the blaze of day.

In the thick cloud's tremendous gloom,
　The lightning's lurid glare,
It views the same all gracious Power
　That breathes the vernal air.

Through Nature's every varying scene,
　By different ways pursued,
The one eternal end of Heaven
　Is universal good.

With like beneficent effect,
　O'er flaming ether glows,
As when it tunes the linnet's voice,
　Or blushes in the rose.

By reason taught to scorn those fears
　That vulgar minds molest,
Let no fantastic terrors break
　My dear Narcissus' rest.

Thy life may all the tenderest care
　Of Providence defend;
And delegated angels round
　Their guardian wings extend!

When through Creation's vast expanse
    The last dread thunders roll,
Untune the concord of the spheres,
    And shake the rising soul;

Unmov'd, may'st thou the final storm
    Of jarring worlds survey,
That ushers in the glad serene
    Of everlasting day!

ANN YEARSLEY,

1760—1806,

A NATIVE of Bristol, where she lived until maturity, in very humble circumstances. She was lifted from obscurity by Mrs. Hannah More, who published her poems ; and prefaced them by a letter to Mrs. Montagu.

Mrs. Yearsley's poems, although often laboured and artificial, frequently display great force and felicity of expression ; but they contain nothing striking in thought or sentiment.

FROM CLIFTON HILL.

Ye silent, solemn, strong, stupendous heights,
Whose terror-striking frown the schoolboy frights
From the young daw ; whilst in your rugged breast
The chattering brood, secur'd by Horror, rest :
Say, Muse, what arm the lowering brothers cleft,
And the calm stream in this low cradle left?
Coeval with Creation they look down,
And, sunder'd, still retain their native frown.
Beneath those heights, lo ! balmy springs arise,
To which pale Beauty's faded image flies ;
Their kindly powers life's genial heat restore,
The tardy pulse, whose throbs were almost o'er,
Here beats a livelier tune. The breezy air,
To the wild hills invites the languid fair ;
Fear not the western gale, thou timorous maid,
Nor dread its blast shall thy soft form invade ;
Though cool and strong the quickening breezes blow,
And meet thy panting breath, 't will quickly grow

More strong: then drink the odoriferous draught,
With unseen particles of health 't is fraught
Sit not within the threshold of Despair,
Nor plead a weakness fatal to the fair;
Soft term for Indolence, politely given,
By which we win no joy from earth or heaven.
Foul fiend! thou bane of health, fair virtue's bane,
Death of true pleasure, source of real pain!
Keen exercise shall brace the fainting soul,
And bid her slacken'd powers more vigorous roll.

  *   *   *   *   *

How thickly cloth'd, yon rock of scanty soil,
Its lovely verdure scorns the hand of toil.
Here the deep green, and here the lively plays,
The russet beech, and ever blooming bays;
The vengeful black-thorn, of wild beauties proud,
Blooms beauteous in the gloomy chequer'd crowd:
The barren elm, the useful feeding oak,
Whose Hamadryad ne'er should feel the stroke
Of axe relentless, till twice fifty years
Have crown'd her woodland joys and fruitful cares.

The poisonous reptiles here their mischiefs bring,
And through the helpless sleeper dart the sting;
The toad envenom'd, hating human eyes,
Here springs to light, lives long, and aged dies.
The harmless snail, slow journeying, creeps away,
Sucks the young dew, but shuns the bolder day.
The long-nosed mouse, the woodland rat is here,
The sightless mole, with nicely pointed ear:
The timid rabbit hails the impervious gloom,
Eludes the dog's keen scent, and shuns her doom.

Various the tenants of this tangled wood,
Who skulk all day, all night review the flood,
Chew the wash'd weed driven by the beating wave,
Or feast on dreadful food, which hop'd a milder grave.

24   Q*

Hail, useful Channel ! Commerce spreads her wings,
From either pole her various treasure brings ;
Wafted by thee, the mariner, long stray'd,
Clasps the fond parent and the sighing maid ;
Joy tunes the cry ; the rocks rebound the roar :
The deep vibration quivers 'long the shore :
The merchant hears, and hails the peeping mast,
The wave-drench'd sailor scorns all peril past :
Now love and joy the noisy crew invite,
And clumsy music crowns the rough delight.

FROM A POEM ON MRS. MONTAGU.

Oft as I trod my native wilds alone,
Strong gusts of thought would rise, but rise to die ;
The portals of the swelling soul ne'er oped
By liberal converse, rude ideas strove
Awhile for vent, but found it not, and died.
Thus rust the mind's best powers.   Yon starry orbs,
Majestic ocean, flowery vales, gay groves,
Eye-wasting lawns, and heaven-attempting hills,
Which bound the horizon, and which curb the view ;
All those, with beauteous imagery, awaked
My ravish'd soul to extacy untaught,
To all the transport the rapt sense can bear ;
But all expired, for want of powers to speak ;
All perish'd in the mind as soon as born,
Eras'd more quick than ciphers on the shore,
O'er which the cruel waves unheedful roll.

CAROLINE SYMONDS,

1792—1803,

THE most precocious of our female poets, was the daughter of the Rev. Charles Symonds, and was born in 1792. She died at the age of eleven years, and it may be safely said that none of our poetesses have exhibited any thing like the same genius at the same age.

I subjoin a variety of specimens.

THE HAREBELL.

In Spring's green lap there blooms a flower,
Whose cup imbibes each vernal shower;
That sips fresh nature's balmy dew,
Clad in her sweetest, purest blue;
Yet shuns the ruddy eye of morning,
The shaggy wood's brown shades adorning.
Simple flow'ret! child of May!
Though hid from the broad gaze of day,
Doom'd in the shade thy sweets to shed,
Unnotic'd droops thy languid head;
Still nature's darling thou'lt remain,
She feeds thee with her softest rain;
Fills each sweet bud with honied tears,
With genial gales thy bosom cheers.
Ah, then unfold thy simple charms,
In yon deep thicket's circling arms,
Far from the fierce and sultry glare,
No heedless hand shall harm thee there;

Still, then, avoid the gaudy scene,
The flaunting sun, th' embroider'd green,
And bloom, and fade, with chaste reserve, unseen.

THE FADED ROSE,

Which grew on the tomb of Zelida.

I gaz'd on the rose-bud, I heav'd a deep sigh,
   And mine eyelid was gemm'd with a tear;
O let me, I cried, by my Zelida lie,
   For all that I value sleeps here!

Her sweetness, simplicity, virtue, and charms,
   Could with naught but a seraph compare;
Ah! now since my Zelida's torn from my arms,
   There is nothing I love, but despair.

This rose-tree once flourish'd, and sweeten'd the air,
   Like its blossom, all lovely, she grew!
The scent of her breath, as its fragrance was rare,
   And her cheeks were more fresh than its hue.

She planted, she lov'd it, she water'd its head,
   And its bloom every rival defied;
But alas! what was beauty or virtue, soon fled,
   In Spring they both blossom'd and died.

And now for my bosom this life has no charms,
   I feel all its troubles and care;
And since my dear Zelida's torn from my arms,
   There is nothing I love, but despair.

The subjoined lines display great delicacy of feeling, and exhibit a sweetness and simplicity of fancy, very remarkable in so young a writer.

SONNET.

To Lady Lucy Foley, on her birthday, February, 1803.

No morn now blushes on the enamour'd sight,
  No genial sun now warms the torpid day ;
  Since February sternly check'd his ray,
When Lucy's eyes first beam'd their azure light.
What though no vernal flowers my hand invite
  To crop their fragrance on your natal day ;
  Lucy, for you the snow-drop and the bay,
Shall blend the unfading green and modest white.
Though on this festive hour with aspect bleak,
  Stern Winter frowns, in icy garments drest ;
Still may the rosy Summer robe your cheek,
  And the green Spring still bud within your breast ;
Till the world fading on your closing eyes,
You find a golden Autumn in the skies.

The following sonnet, singularly applicable to herself, was made ner Epitaph :

THE BLIGHTED ROSEBUD.

(Inscribed on the Writer's Tomb.)

Scarce had thy velvet lips imbib'd the dew,
  And nature hail'd thee, infant queen of May ;
  Scarce saw thy opening bloom the sun's broad ray,
And on the air its tender fragrance threw ;
When the north wind enamour'd of thee grew,
And from his chilling kiss, thy charms decay ;

Now droops thine head, and fades thy blushing hue
    No more the queen of flowers, no longer gay.
So blooms a maid, her guardian's health and joy,
    Her mind array'd in innocency's vest;
When suddenly, impatient to destroy,
    Death clasps the victim to his iron breast:
She fades—the parent, sister, friend, deplore
The charms and budding virtues now no more.

MRS. CHARLOTTE SMITH,

1749—1806,

ONE of the most admired of our female poets, is also a noble specimen of womanly excellence. She was the daughter of Nicholas Turner, Esq., of Stoke House in Surrey, where she was born in 1479. Deprived of her mother at an early age, she was induced in her fifteenth year to marry Mr. Smith, the son of a rich merchant: the bridegroom's age being only twenty-one. Carelessness and extravagance on Mr. Smith's part, and the death of his father, whose will was so complicated that all the property was swallowed up in lawsuits, reduced the unhappy pair to great embarrassments. The husband was thrown into prison, which the wife shared with him : and it was while labouring under these difficulties that Mrs. Smith turned her literary talents to account. In 1782 she published a volume of Sonnets, which was favourably received by the public, and passed through no fewer than eleven editions. The domestic life of Mr. and Mrs. Smith becoming more and more unhappy, a separation at length took place; and Mrs. Smith retired to a cottage near Chichester, where she applied herself assiduously and cheerfully to literary pursuits. She here produced her well-known novels of *Emmeline, Ethelinde*, and *Celestina*, and various other works in prose and verse. She died at Tilford, near Farnham, in 1806.

Mrs. Smith's poetry is at once forcible and elegant : her descriptions of nature are peculiarly true and pleasing: and her sentiments, although somewhat sombre in their tone, are marked by great purity of thought, and clearness of expression. Her love of flowers is exquisitely developed.

SONNET.

Written at the close of Spring.

The garlands fade that Spring so lately wove,
    Each simple flower, which she had nurs'd in dew,
Anemonies, that spangled every grove,
    The primrose wan, and harebell mildly blue.
No more shall violets linger in the dell,
    Or purple orchis variegate the plain,
Till Spring again shall call forth every bell,
    And dress with humid hands her wreaths again.
Ah, poor humanity! so frail, so fair,
    Are the fond visions of thy early day,
Till tyrant passion and corrosive care,
    Bid all thy fairy colours fade away!
Another May new buds and flowers shall bring;
Ah! why has *Happiness* no second Spring?

SONNET.

Sighing, I see yon little troop at play,
    By sorrow yet untouch'd, unhurt by care,
While free and sportive they enjoy to-day,
    Content, and careless of to-morrow's fare.
O happy age! when Hope's unclouded ray
    Lights their green path, and prompts their simple mirth,
Ere yet they feel the thorns that lurking lay
    To wound the wretched pilgrims of the earth,
    Making them rue the hour that gave them birth,
And threw them on a world so full of pain,
    Where prosperous folly treads on patient worth,
And to deaf pride misfortune pleads in vain!
Ah! for their future fate how many fears
Oppress my heart, and fill mine eyes with tears!

SONNET,

The Glow-worm.

When, on some balmy-breathing night of Spring,
 The happy child, to whom the world is new,
Pursues the evening moth of mealy wing,
 Or from the heathbell beats the sparkling dew ;
He sees before his inexperienc'd eyes
 The brilliant Glow-worm, like a meteor, shine
On the turf bank ; — amaz'd and pleas'd he cries,
 " Star of the dewy grass, I make thee mine !"
Then, ere he sleep, collects the moisten'd flower,
 And bids soft leaves his glittering prize enfold,
And dreams that fairy lamps illume his bower ;
 Yet with the morning shudders to behold
His lucid treasure, rayless as the dust : —
So turn the World's bright joys to cold and blank disgust.

SONNET.

To the Moon.

Queen of the silver bow ! by thy pale beam
 Alone and pensive, I delight to stray,
And watch thy shadow trembling in the stream,
 Or mark the floating clouds that cross thy way.
And while I gaze, thy mild and placid light
 Sheds a soft calm upon my troubled breast ;
And oft I think, fair planet of the night,
 That in thy orb the wretched may have rest :
The sufferers of the earth perhaps may go,
 Releas'd by death, to thy benignant sphere,
And the sad children of despair and woe
 Forget in thee their cup of sorrow here.
Oh, that I soon may reach thy world serene,
Poor wearied pilgrim in this toiling scene !

25   R

SONNET.

On the Departure of the Nightingale.

Sweet poet of the woods, a long adieu!
 Farewell, soft minstrel of the early year!
Ah! 'twill be long ere thou shalt sing anew,
 And pour thy music on the night's dull ear.
Whether on Spring thy wandering flights await,
 Or whether silent in our groves you dwell,
The pensive muse shall own thee for her mate,
 And still protect the song she loves so well.
With cautious step the love-lorn youth shall glide
 Through the lone brake that shades thy mossy nest;
And shepherd girls from eyes profane shall hide
 The gentle bird, who sings of pity best;
For still thy voice shall soft affections move,
And still be dear to sorrow, and to love!

SONNET.

Should the lone wanderer, fainting on his way,
 Rest for a moment of the sultry hours,
And, though his path through thorns and roughness lay,
 Pluck the wild rose, or woodbine's gadding flowers,
Weaving gay wreaths beneath some sheltering tree,
 The sense of sorrow he awhile may lose.
So have I sought thy flowers, fair Poesy!
 So charm'd my way with Friendship and the Muse.
But darker now grows life's unhappy day,
 Dark with new clouds of evil yet to come,
Her pencil sickening Fancy throws away,
 And weary Hope reclines upon the tomb,
And points my wishes to that tranquil shore,
Where the pale spectre Care pursues no more.

ANNA SEWARD,

1747—1809,

THE daughter of the Reverend Thomas Seward, Canon Residentiary of Lichfield, was born in 1747. She early manifested a remarkable taste for poetry, and before she was nine years old, she could repeat the three first books of Paradise Lost. Her father, although himself a poet, endeavoured to repress her passion for the muse : but when she became of an age to choose her own studies, she devoted herself to poetical composition. In spite of a somewhat inflated and turgid style, Miss Seward gained a large share of public favour; we find that the was called "The Swan of Lichfield :" but she has few admirers in the present day. Sir Walter Scott, to whom she bequeathed three volumes of poetry for publication, pronounced her verses " execrable."

I subjoin some varied specimens of Miss Seward's powers.

SONNET.

December Morning, 1782.

I love to rise ere gleams the tardy light,
  Winter's pale dawn ; and as warm fires illume
  And cheerful tapers shine around the room,
Through misty windows bend thy musing sight,
Where round the dusky lawn, the mansions white,
  With shutters clos'd, peer faintly through the gloom,
  That slow recedes ; while yon grey spires assume,
Rising from their dark pile, an added height
By indistinctness given.   Then to decree

The grateful thoughts to God, ere they unfold
To Friendship or the Muse, or seek with glee
   Wisdom's rich page : O hours ! more worth than gold,
By whose blest use we lengthen life, and free
   From drear decays of age, outlive the old !

TIME PAST.

Written, January, 1773.

Return, blest years ! when not the jocund Spring,
   Luxuriant Summer, nor the amber hours
Calm Autumn gives, my heart invok'd, to bring
   Joys, whose rich balm o'er all the bosom pours ;
When ne'er I wished might grace the closing day,
   One tint purpureal, or one golden ray ;
When the loud storms, that desolate the bowers,
   Found dearer welcome than Favonian gales,
And Winter's bare, bleak fields, than Summer's flowery vales.

Yet not to deck pale hours with vain parade,
   Beneath the blaze of wide-illumin'd dome ;
Not for the bounding dance ; not to pervade
   And charm the sense with music ; nor as roam
The mimic passions o'er theatric scene,
   To laugh, or weep ; O ! not for these, I ween,
But for delights that made the heart their home,
   Was the grey night-frost on the sounding plain
More than the sun invok'd, that gilds the grassy lane.

Yes, for the joys that trivial joys excel,
   My lov'd Honora, did we hail the gloom
Of dim November's eve ; and, as it fell,
   And the bright fire shone cheerful round the room,
Dropt the warm curtains with no tardy hand,

And felt our spirits and our hearts expand ;
Listening their steps, who still, where'er they come,
Make the keen stars, that glaze the settled snows,
More than the sun invok'd, when first he tints the rose.

Affection — Friendship — Sympathy,— your throne
Is Winter's glowing hearth ; — and ye were ours,
Thy smile, Honora, made them all our own.
Where are they now ? — alas ! their choicest powers
Faded at thy retreat ; — for thou art gone,
And many a dark, long eve I sigh alone,
In thrill'd remembrance of the vanish'd hours,
When storms were dearer than the balmy gales,
And the grey barren fields than green luxuriant vales.

SONG.

From thy waves, stormy Lannow, I fly ;
  From the rocks that are lash'd by their tide ;
From the maid whose cold bosom, relentless as they,
  Has wreck'd my warm hopes by her pride !
Yet lonely and rude as the scene,
  Her smile to that scene could impart
A charm that might rival the bloom of the vale —
  But away, thou fond dream of my heart !
    From thy rocks, stormy Lannow, I fly !

Now the blasts of the winter come on !
  And the waters grow dark as they rise !
But 't is well ! — they resemble the sullen disdain
  That has lour'd in those insolent eyes.
Sincere were the sighs they represt,
  But they rose in the days that are flown !
Ah, nymph ! unrelenting and cold as thou art,
  My spirit is proud as thine own !
    From thy rocks, stormy Lannow, I fly !
      R*

Lo ! the wings of the sea-fowl are spread
　To escape the loud storm by their flight ;
And these caves will afford them a gloomy retreat
　From the winds and the billows of night:
Like them, to the home of my youth,
　Like them, to its shades I retire ;
Receive me, and shield my vext spirit, ye groves,
　From the pangs of insulted desire !
　　To thy rocks, stormy Lannow, adieu !

THE GRAVE OF YOUTH.

When life is hurried to untimely close,
In the years of crystal eyes and burnish'd hair,
Dire are the thoughts of death ; eternal parting
From all the precious soul's yet known delights,
All she had clung to here ; from youth and hope,
And the year's blossom'd April ; bounding strength,
Which had outleap'd the rose, when morning suns
Yellow'd their forest glade ; from reaper's shout
And cheerful swarm of populous towns ; from Time,
Which tells of joys forepast, and promises
The dear return of seasons, and the bliss
Crowning a fruitful marriage ; from the stores
Of well-engrafted knowledge ; from all utterance,
Since in the silent grave, no talk ! no music !
No gay surprise, by unexpected good,
Social, or individual ! — no glad step
Of welcome friend, with more intenseness listen'd
Than warbled melody ! no father's counsel !
No mother's smile ! no lover's whisper'd vow !
There nothing breathes save the insatiate worm,
And nothing is, but the drear altering corse,
Resolving silently to shapeless dust,
In unpierc'd darkness and in black oblivion.

MISS SCOTT (OF ANCRAM).

IN the third volume of Ellis's *Specimens of the Early English Poets*, are two poems by Miss Scott, of Ancram. The following is one of them.

THE OWL.

While the Moon, with sudden gleam,
 Through the clouds that cover her,
Darts her light upon the stream,
 And the poplars gently stir,
  Pleas'd I hear thy boding cry !
  Owl, that lov'st the cloudy sky,
  Sure, thy notes are harmony !

While the maiden, pale with care,
 Wanders to the lonely shade,
Sighs her sorrows to the air,
 While the flowerets round her fade,
  Shrinks to hear thy boding cry !
  Owl, that lov'st the cloudy sky,
  To her it is not harmony !

While the wretch, with mournful dole,
 Wrings his hands in agony,
Praying for his brother's soul,
 Whom he piercëd suddenly,
  Shrinks to hear thy boding cry,
  Owl that lov'st the cloudy sky,
  To him it is not harmony.

MRS. MARY TIGHE.

1773—1810.

THIS highly gifted lady was the daughter of the Rev. William Blachford, of the county of Wicklow, where she was born in or about the year 1773. She is chiefly known by her splendid poem of *Psyche*, which for gorgeousness of colouring and refinement of imagination, is scarcely behind the best verses of Moore, while it is certainly more chaste and spiritual in its sentiment. Mrs. Tighe died in 1810.

FROM PSYCHE.

(Canto II.)

Psyche's return to the Palace of Love.— Her disobedience.— Love asleep.— Psyche's amazement.— The flight of Love.— Sudden banishment of Psyche from the Island of Pleasure.

Illumin'd bright now shines the splendid dome,
Melodious accents her arrival hail :
But not the torch's blaze can chase the gloom,
And all the soothing powers of music fail ;
Trembling she seeks her couch with horror pale,
But first a lamp conceals in secret shade,
While unknown terrors all her soul assail.
Thus half their treacherous counsel is obey'd,
For still her gentle soul abhors the murderous blade.

And now with softest whispers of delight,
Love welcomes Psyche still more fondly dear ;
Not unobserv'd, though hid in deepest night,
The silent anguish of her secret fear.

He thinks that tenderness excites the tear
By the late image of her parent's grief,
And half-offended seeks in vain to cheer:
Yet while he speaks, her sorrows feel relief,
Too soon more keen to sting from this suspension brief!

Allow'd to settle on celestial eyes,
Soft Sleep exulting now exerts his sway,
From Psyche's anxious pillow gladly flies
To veil those orbs, whose fierce and lambent ray
The powers of heaven submissively obey.
Trembling and breathless then she softly rose,
And seiz'd the lamp, where it obscurely lay,
With hand too rashly daring to disclose
The sacred veil which hung mysterious o'er her woes.

Twice, as with agitated step she went,
The lamp expiring shone with doubtful gleam,
As though it warn'd her from her rash intent:
And twice she paus'd, and on its trembling beam
Gaz'd with suspended breath, while voices seem
With murmuring sound along the roof to sigh ;
As one just waking from a troublous dream,
With palpitating heart and straining eye,
Still fix'd with fear remains, still thinks the danger nigh.

O daring Muse! wilt thou indeed essay
To paint the wonders which that lamp could shew?
And canst thou hope in living words to say
The dazzling glories of that heavenly view?
Ah! well I ween, that if with pencil true
That splendid vision could be well exprest,
The fearful awe imprudent Psyche knew
Would seize with rapture every wondering breast,
When Love's all-potent charms divinely stood confest.

All imperceptible to human touch,
His wings display celestial essence light,
26

The clear effulgence of the blaze is such,
The brilliant plumage shines so heavenly bright,
That mortal eyes turn dazzled from the sight :
A youth he seems in manhood's freshest years ;
Round his fair neck, as clinging with delight,
Each golden curl resplendently appears,
Or shades his darker brow, which grace majestic wears .

Or o'er his guileless front the ringlets bright
Their rays of sunny lustre seem to throw,
That front than polish'd ivory more white !
His blooming cheeks with deeper blushes glow
Than roses scatter'd o'er a bed of snow :
While on his lips, distill'd in balmy dews,
(Those lips divine, that even in silence know
The heart to touch,) persuasion to infuse,
Still hangs a rosy charm that never vainly sues.

The friendly curtain of indulgent sleep,
Disclos'd not yet his eyes' resistless sway,
But from their silky veil there seemed to peep
Some brilliant glances with a soften'd ray,
Which o'er his features exquisitely play,
And all his polish'd limbs suffuse with light.
Thus through some narrow space the azure day
Sudden its cheerful rays diffusing bright,
Wide darts its lucid beams, to gild the brow of night.

His fatal arrows, and celestial bow
Beside the couch were negligently thrown,
Nor needs the god his dazzling arms to show
His glorious birth, such beauty round him shone
As sure could spring from Beauty's self alone ;
The gloom which glow'd o'er all of soft desire
Could well proclaim him Beauty's cherish'd son :
And Beauty's self will oft these charms admire,
And steal his witching smile, his glance's living fire.

Speechless with awe, in transport strangely lost,
Long Psyche stood with fix'd adoring eye :
Her limbs immovable, her senses tost
Between amazement, fear and ecstasy,
She hangs enamour'd o'er the deity.
Till from her trembling hand extinguish'd falls
The fatal lamp — he starts — and suddenly
Tremendous thunders echo through the halls,
While ruin's hideous crash bursts o'er the affrighted walls.

Dread horror seizes on her sinking heart,
A mortal chillness shudders at her breast,
Her soul sinks fainting from death's icy dart,
The groan scarce utter'd dies but half exprest,
And down she sinks in deadly swoon opprest :
But when at length awaking from her trance,
The terrors of her fate stand all confest,
In vain she casts around her timid glance,
The rudely frowning scenes her former joys enhance.

No traces of those joys, alas, remain !
A desert solitude alone appears :
No verdant shade relieves the sandy plain,
The wide-spread waste no gentle fountain cheers,
One barren face the dreary prospect wears ;
Nought through the vast horizon meets her eye
To calm the dismal tumult of her fears,
No trace of human habitation nigh,
A sandy wild beneath, above a threatening sky.

Beautiful, however, as is this poem of *Psyche*, I am not sure
that Mrs. Tighe is not more successful when she is less ambitious. The following verses give a good specimen of her more
simple style :

THE LILY.

How wither'd, perish'd, seems the form
    Of yon obscure unsightly root !

Yet from the blight of wintry storm,
  It hides secure the precious fruit.

The careless eye can find no grace,
  No beauty in the scaly folds,
Nor see within the dark embrace
  What latent loveliness it holds.

Yet in that bulb, those sapless scales,
  The lily wraps her silver vest,
Till vernal suns and vernal gales
  Shall kiss once more her fragrant breast.

Yes, hide beneath the mouldering heap
  The undelighting slighted thing;
There in the cold earth buried deep,
  In silence let it wait the Spring.

Oh! many a stormy night shall close
  In gloom upon the barren earth,
While still in undisturb'd repose,
  Uninjur'd lies the future birth;

And Ignorance, with sceptic eye,
  Hope's patient smile shall wondering view;
Or mock her fond credulity,
  As her soft tears the spot bedew.

Sweet smile of hope, delicious tear,
  The sun, the shower indeed shall come;
The promis'd verdant shoot appear,
  And nature bid her blossoms bloom.

And thou, O virgin Queen of Spring!
  Shalt from thy dark and lowly bed,
Bursting thy green sheath's silken string,
  Unveil thy charms, and perfume shed;

Unfold thy robes of purest white,
　Unsullied from their darksome grave,
And thy soft petals' flowery light
　In the mild breeze unfetter'd wave.

So Faith shall seek the lowly dust,
　Where humble Sorrow loves to lie,
And bid her thus her hopes entrust,
　And watch with patient cheerful eye ;

And bear the long, cold, wintry night,
　And bear her own degraded doom,
And wait till Heaven's reviving light,
　Eternal Spring ! shall burst the gloom.

s

MISSES MARIA AND HARRIET FALCONAR.

1788.

THESE two ladies are remarkable specimens of precocious genius. Maria Falconar was but seventeen years of age, and Harriet but fourteen, when (in 1788) they gave to the world their *Poems on Slavery.* The works are very pleasing and characteristic specimens of female talent, and are written with a strength of moral tone which is surprising in such youthful minds.

FROM MARIA FALCONAR'S POEM.

Once Superstition, in a fatal hour,
O'er Europe rais'd the sceptre of her power;
She reign'd triumphant minister of death,
And Peace and Pleasure faded in her breath;
Deep in monastic solitude entomb'd,
The bud of beauty wither'd ere it bloom'd;
The brilliant eye where love had sought to dwell,
Shed all its lustre o'er the cloister'd cell;
The smiling lip, of bright vermillion dye,
Grew pale, and quiver'd with the passing sigh;
The music floating from each tuneful tongue,
With midnight hymns the Gothic arches rung.
Here, through Reflection's eye, the pensive mind
Sought with regret for objects far behind;
And found Remembrance, as she heav'd a sigh,
Drew back the soul just soaring to the sky;
Save where misguided zeal in peace withdrew,
From each bright pleasure, each enchanting view.

The still retreat pale Melancholy sought,
And found each object suited to her thought;
Soft Sensibility might here deplore,
And feel the shaft of falsehood wound no more;
The sport of fortune, long to comfort lost,
With hope far banish'd, expectation cross'd;
Explor'd these scenes to weep for anguish past,
Where the swell'd throbbing heart has burst at last.
The Eternal from the throne of grace survey'd,
With eye averse, the sacrifice they made;
No forc'd devotion found acceptance there,
No grateful incense issu'd from her prayer.
Thus Superstition could not fix her sway
In heaven, but look'd on earth to seize her prey;
And yet, unsated with domestic pain,
Sought to extend the terrors of her reign.
She saw, as on the fatal height she stood,
Her impious altars drench'd in guiltless blood;
Where Fortitude with candid virtue join'd,
And sought by sacred truths to save mankind;
There she bestow'd her persecutions dire,
And close pursu'd with unrelenting ire;
Nor ceas'd to scourge them with her vengeful rod,
Till each, a martyr saint, embrac'd his god.

The younger of the two sisters displays, I think, the superior
genius. Her feeling is stronger; her declamation more warm
and eloquent. The following is an extraordinary passage for a
girl of fourteen : —

The British youth, torn from his much lov'd home,
O'er foreign seas and foreign coasts to roam,
Amid the fury of the piercing blast,
The swell'd wave circling round the shiver'd mast,
While bursting peals of thunder rend the skies,
And o'er the deck, the foaming billows rise,
Awhile in terror views the lightning glare
With streaming horror, through the midnight air :

— The storm once past, he gains the friendly ray
Of Hope, to guide him through the dangerous way ;
Smiling, she bids each future prospect rise,
Through Fancy's varied mirror, to his eyes.
Not so the slave: oppress'd with secret care,
He sinks the hapless victim of despair ;
Or doom'd to torments that might even move
The steely heart, and melt it into love ;
Till, worn with anguish, withering in his bloom,
He falls, an early tenant of the tomb!

Shall Britain view, unmov'd, sad Afric's shore
Delug'd so oft in streams of purple gore !
Britain, where science, peace, and plenty smile,
Virtue's bright seat, and freedom's favour'd isle !
Rich are her plains and fruitful is her clime,
The scourge of tyrants, and the boast of time ;
Of every virtue, every worth possest,
That fires the hero's or the patriot's breast :
There, nobly warm'd with animating fire,
Our Shakspere struck his soul-commanding lyre ;
There scenes of bliss immortal Milton sung,
And notes harmonious issued from his tongue :
And bards like these shall boast in every age,
While native genius glows in Hayley's page ;
While genius bids, to our enchanted eyes,
In Swift's own strains, a second Pope arise.
When Truth, perplex'd in error's thorny maze,
Threw o'er the world obscur'd and darken'd rays,
Then Newton rose, unveil'd the beauteous maid :
He spoke, and nature stood at once display'd.
These were the souls that Britain once possess'd,
When genuine virtue fir'd the patriot's breast ;
And still shall she protect fair freedom's cause,
And vindicate her violated laws ;
Waft peace and freedom to a wretched land,
And scatter blessings with a liberal hand.

ELIZABETH TREFUSIS,

1808,

SISTER of the late Lord Clinton, published in 1808 two volumes of *Poems and Tales*, from which the following verses are extracted.

THE BOY AND BUTTERFLY.

Proud of its little day, enjoying
  The lavish sweets kind nature yields,
In harmless sports each hour employing,
  Ranging the gardens, woods, and fields,
A lovely butterfly extending
  Its grateful wing to Sol's warm beams,
No dreaded danger saw impending,
  But basked secure in peaceful dreams.
A wandering urchin view'd this treasure
  Of gaudy colours fine and gay;
Thoughtless, consulting but his pleasure,
  He chas'd it through the livelong day.
At last the young but sly dissembler
  Appear'd to follow other flies,
Then turning, seiz'd the little trembler,
  Who, crush'd beneath his fingers, dies!
Surpris'd, he sees the hasty ruin
  His reckless cruelty had wrought;
The victim (which, so long pursuing,
  Scarce raised a wish or claimed a thought,)
Now bids the tears of genuine sorrow
  O'er his repentant bosom flow!

27   s*

Yet — he 'll forget it ere the morrow,
  And deal to others equal woe ! —
Thus the vain man, with subtle feigning,
  Pursues, o'ertakes poor woman's heart ;
But soon his hapless prize disdaining,
  She dies ! — the victim of his art.

  In a novel which the authoress destroyed, occurs the Poem now
about to be quoted ; the following is the explanation which Miss
Trefusis prefixes to the verses : —

[At the death of her child, and fifteen months after her marriage with
Edmond, the unfortunate Eudora discovers that he is still tenderly attached
to her rival Enna, and that she is herself the only obstacle to their happiness. Full of love and grief, she determines to remove that obstacle by sui-
cide.]

EUDORA'S LAMENTATION OVER HER DEAD CHILD.

I.

Make it wide, make it deep, and with moss be it lin'd,
  His delicate limbs no rude pebbles shall wound ;
My babe with its mother in death shall be join'd !
Then the lord of my wishes, no longer unkind,
  May shed a fond tear on the grief-hallow'd ground.
    Lay it close by my side,
    Lay it close by my side,
'T is the child of my Edmond ? and I — was his bride.

II.

Who says that I murder'd the peace of my love,
  That his heart was another's, his hand only mine ?
Hush, hush ! 't is not true ! — her affection to prove,
His Eudora each obstacle soon will remove ;
  Content for his sake every bliss to resign.
    With my babe on my breast,
    With my babe on my breast,
My heart's lord shall be happy ! and I — be at rest !

III.

Then if, hand lock'd in hand, o'er my grave they should stray,
   And vanity smile o'er the ruins of love,
Yet let justice and pity instruct them to say,
" She merited better, but fate had its way :
   And now her pure spirit is soaring above !
     With her babe on her breast.
     With her babe on her breast,
Now earth shrinks from her view, and the mourner 's at rest."

MISS JANE ELLIOT,

SISTER to Sir Gilbert Elliot, of Minto, was the author of the much-admired ballad which is subjoined: "in which," says Sir Walter Scott, in the *Minstrelsy of the Scottish Border,* "the manner of the ancient minstrels is so happily imitated, that it required the most positive evidence to convince me that the song was of modern date."

THE FLOWERS OF THE FOREST.

I 've heard the lilting at our yowe-milking,
    Lasses a' lilting before the dawn of day ;
But now they are moaning on ilka green loaning —
    The Flowers of the Forest are a' wede away.

At buchts, in the morning, nae blythe lads are scorning,
    The lasses are lonely and dowie and wae ;
Nae daffin', nae gabbin', but sighing and sabbing,
    Ilk ane lifts her leglen and hies her away.

In hairst, at the shearing, nae youths now are jeering,
    The bandsters are lyart, and runkled, and gray ;
At fair, or at preaching, nae wooing, nae fleeching —
    The Flowers of the Forest are a' wede away.

At e'en, at the gloaming, nae swankies are roaming,
    'Bout stacks wi' the lasses at bogle to play,
But ilk ane sits drearie, lamenting her dearie —
    The Flowers of the Forest are a' wede away

Dule and wae for the order, sent our lads to the Border!
The English, for ance, by guile wan the day ;
The Flowers of the Forest, that foucht aye the foremost,
The prime o' our land, are cauld in the clay.

We hear nae mair lilting at our yowe-milking,
Women and bairns are heartless and wae ;
Sighing and moaning on ilka green loaning,—
The Flowers of the Forest are a' wede away.

MRS. ALICIA COCKBURN.

1794.

Alicia Rutherford of Fernilie, North Britain, who became the wife of Mr. Patrick Cockburn, advocate, belonging to the Scotch bar, was the author of the following ballad, called *The Flowers of the Forest — Part Second*. I am not aware what else she wrote. She died in Edinburgh, in 1794.

THE FLOWERS OF THE FOREST.

I 've seen the smiling
Of Fortune beguiling;
I've felt all its favours, and found its decay:
Sweet was its blessing,
Kind its caressing;
But now it is fled — it is fled far away.

I 've seen the Forest
Adornëd the foremost
With flowers of the fairest most pleasant and gay;
Sae bonnie was their blooming!
Their scent the air perfuming!
But now they are wither'd and weded away.

I 've seen the morning
With gold the hills adorning,
And loud tempest storming before the mid-day.
I 've seen Tweed's silver streams
Shining in the sunny beams,
Grow drumly and dark as he rowed on his way.

Oh, fickle Fortune,
Why this cruel sporting?
Oh, why still perplex us, poor sons of a day?
Nae mair your smiles can cheer me,
Nae mair your frowns can fear me;
For the Flowers of the Forest are a' wede away.

It is generally understood that this pleasing ballad refers to the
battle of Flodden Field.   Another copy of verses on this subject
was written by Miss Jane Elliot, sister to Sir Gilbert Elliot of
Minto, whose composition will be found at page 212.

HANNAH COWLEY,

1743—1809,

WAS born at Tiverton, in Devonshire, in the year 1743. She was the daughter of Mr. Philip Parkhouse, a bookseller of eminence in that town; and, being well instructed, gave early signs of genius. She is chiefly known as the author of some very clever plays, among which is the extremely amusing and effective comedy of *The Belle's Stratagem*. She wrote, however, some miscellaneous poems which met with very considerable success at the time of their publication, and are even yet much esteemed. Amongst them may be named *The Maid of Arragon*, a poem in blank verse; *The Siege of Acre;* and *Edwina, the Huntress*. She was married in 1768 to Mr. Cowley, an officer in the service of the East India Company, between whom and herself the warmest attachment ever subsisted. She died in 1809.

The following poem will give a good idea of her powers : —

ON THE DEATH OF CHATTERTON.

Ill-fated Chatterton ! for thee I raise
A mingled ray of censure and of praise !
Bright star of Genius ! torn from life and fame,
My tears, my verse, shall consecrate thy name !
Ye Muses ! who around his natal bed
Bestowed your gifts, and all your influence shed ;
Apollo ! that didst fire his infant breast,
And in his genuine numbers shine confest,
Ah, why on him such sensate nerves bestow
To heighten torture to the child of woe !

Thou haggard Poverty ! whose cheerless eye
Makes note of Rapture change to deepest sigh,
Subdued by thee his pen no more obeys,
No more revives the song of ancient days,
Check'd in his flight, his lofty genius cowers,
Locks her faint wings, and yields to thee her powers !

Behold him, Muses ! see your favourite son,
The prey of want ere manhood is begun ;
The heart which you inspired by anguish torn,
The mind you cherish'd, drooping and forlorn !
See now ! Despair her sable form extends,
Creeps to his couch, and o'er his pillow bends !
Ah, see ! a deadly bowl, till now conceal'd,
Before his eyes is gradually reveal'd ;
Some spirit seize it ! seize the liquid snare,
Cast it to earth, or dissipate in air —
Stay, hapless youth ! refrain, abhor the draught,
With racking pangs, with deep Repentance fraught !
Oh, hold ! the cup with woe eternal flows,
More, more than Death ! the poisonous juice bestows.

In vain ! — he drinks ! see how the scorching fires
Rush through his veins ! see, writhing, he expires !
No sorrowing friend, no sister, parent nigh,
To soothe his pangs, or catch his parting sigh,
Alone, unknown, the Muses' favourite dies,
And with the vulgar dead, unnoted lies !

Bright star of Genius ! torn from Life and Fame,
My tears, my verse, shall consecrate thy name !

28

ISABELLA, COUNTESS OF CARLISLE,

1795,

WAS the author of the following lines.   She died in 1795.

THE FAIRY'S ANSWER.

*To Mrs. Greville's Prayer for Indifference.**

Without preamble, to my friend
These hasty lines I 'm bid to send,
    Or give, if I am able :
I dare not hesitate to say,
Though I have trembled all the day —
    It looks so like a fable.

Last night's adventure is my theme ;
And should it strike you as a dream,
    Yet soon its high import
Must make you own the matter such,
So delicate, it were too much
    To be composed in sport.

The moon did shine serenely bright,
And every star did deck the night,
    While zephyr fann'd the trees ;
No more assail'd my mind's repose,
Save that yon stream, which murmuring flows,
    Did echo to the breeze.

* Vide p. 158.

Enwrapt in solemn thoughts I sate,
Resolving o'er the turns of fate,
    Yet void of hope or fear ;
When lo ! behold an airy throng,
With lightest steps and jocund song,
    Surprised my eye and ear.

A form superior to the rest
His little voice to me address'd,
    And gently thus began :
" I 've heard strange things from one of you,
" Pray tell me if you think 't is true ;
    " Explain it, if you can.

" Such incense has perfum'd my throne !
" Such eloquence my heart has won!
    " I think I guess the hand :
" I know her wit and beauty too,
" But why she sends a prayer so new,
    " I cannot understand.

" To light some flames, and some revive,
" To keep some other just alive,
    " Full oft I am implor'd ;
" But with peculiar power to please,
" To supplicate for nought but ease !
    " 'T is odd, upon my word !

" Tell her, with fruitless care I 've sought:
" And though my realms, with wonders fraught;
    " In remedies abound,
" No grain of cold Indifference
" Was ever yet allied to sense
    " In all my fairy round.

" The regions of the sky I 'd trace,
" I 'd ransack every earthly place,
    " Each leaf, each herb, each flower,

" To mitigate the pangs of fear,
" Dispel the clouds of black despair,
  " Or lull the restless hour.

" I would be generous as I 'm just ;
" But I obey, as others must,
  " Those laws which fate has made.
" My tiny kingdom how defend,
" And what might be the horrid end,
  "Should man my state invade ?

" 'T would put your mind into a rage,
" And such unequal war to wage,
  " Suits not my royal duty !
" I dare not change a first decree ;
" She 's doom'd to please, nor can be free,
  "Such is the lot of Beauty ! "

This said, he darted o'er the plain,
And after follow'd all his train ;
  No glimpse of him I find :
But sure I am, the little sprite
These words, before he took his flight,
  Imprinted on my mind.

DON QUIXOTE.

MRS. LEICESTER.

About 1800.

OF this lady I know no more than this : — that I occasionally meet with her name attached to little lively productions like the following. The female muse seems particularly happy in the invention of stories to illustrate a sentiment or to point a moral: and the subjoined lines appear to me to be a good specimen of this facility.

THE MOCK HERO.

Horatio, of idle courage vain,
Was flourishing in air his father's cane :
And as the fumes of valour swell'd his pate,
Now thought himself this hero, and now that :
" And now," he cried, " I will Achilles be ;
My sword I 'll brandish ; — mark ! the Trojans flee !
Now I 'll be Hector, when his angry blade
A lane through heaps of slaughter'd Grecians made !
And now my deeds still braver, I' ll evince,
I am no less than — Edward the Black Prince!
Give way, ye coward French ! " ———
                                    As thus he spoke
And aim'd in fancy a sufficient stroke
To fix the fate of Cressy or Poictiers,
Heroically spurning trivial fears,
His milk-white hand he strikes against a nail,
Sees his own blood, and feels his courage fail ;
Ah, where is now that boasted valour flown,
That in the tented field so late was shown ?
Achilles weeps, great Hector hangs his head,
And the Black Prince goes whimpering to bed !
                    T*

MRS. HANNAH MORE.

1745—1833.

THIS excellent and accomplished lady was a daughter of Jacob More, a village schoolmaster, at Stapleton, in Gloucestershire, where she was born in the year 1745. Her literary talents were developed early, for in her seventeenth year she published a Pastoral Drama, called *The Search after Happiness,* and for nearly seventy years she continued to write in various shapes for the public. She died in 1833.

Mrs. More's chief poetical productions are her Tragedies of *The Inflexible Captive, Percy,* and *The Fatal Falsehood:* her *Sacred Dramas: Florio: The Bas Bleu: Sensibility:* and *Sir Eldred of the Bower.* Dr. Johnson considered Hannah More the best of the female versifiers of her day ; but the memory of her poetic fame cannot be said to have survived her. She is now generally considered to have been a melodious and sensible versifier, but not possessed of much true poetic fire.

For myself, I venture to think that Hannah More has scarcely received her merited share of fame as a poet. For, notwithstanding her didactic style, and somewhat mechanical mode of thought, I think I can often detect in her writings the real poetry of inspiration. Here are two little proverbs which show, I think, a genuine poetic wit.

> " In men this blunder still you find,
> All think their little set, mankind."—

> " Small habits well pursued betimes,
> May reach the dignity of crimes."

There is something more than measured prose, too, in the following extract from *Sensibility*:

Since trifles make the sum of human things,
And half our misery from our foibles springs;
Since life's best joys consist in peace and ease,
And though but few can serve, yet all may please;
O let the ungentle spirit learn from hence,
A small unkindness is a great offence.
To spread large bounties, though we wish in vain,
Yet all may shun the guilt of giving pain.
To bless mankind with tides of flowing wealth,
With rank to grace them, or to crown with health,
Our little lot denies; yet liberal still,
God gives its counterpoise to every ill;
Nor let us murmur at our stinted powers,
When kindness, love, and concord may be ours.
The gift of minist'ring to others' ease,
To all her sons impartial Heaven decrees;
The gentle offices of patient love,
Beyond all flattery, and all price above;
The mild forbearance at a brother's fault,
The angry word suppress'd, the taunting thought:
Subduing and subdued the petty strife,
Which clouds the colour of domestic life;
The sober comfort, all the peace which springs
From the large aggregate of little things;
On these small cares of daughter, wife, and friend,
The almost sacred joys of *Home* depend:
There, Sensibility, thou best may'st reign,
Home is thy true legitimate domain.

A good characteristic specimen of Hannah More's lively, good humoured, moralising style of verse is contained in her story called

THE TWO WEAVERS.

As at their work two weavers sat,
Beguiling time with friendly chat,
They touch'd upon the price of meat,
So high a weaver scarce could eat.

What with my babes and sickly wife,
Quoth Dick, I 'm almost tir'd of life ;
So hard we work, so poor we fare,
'T is more than mortal man can bear.

How glorious is the rich man's state,
His house so fine, his wealth so great ;
Heaven is unjust, you must agree,
Why all to him, and none to me ?

In spite of what the Scripture teaches,
In spite of all the pulpit preaches,
The world, indeed I 've thought so long,
Is rul'd, methinks, extremely wrong.

Where'er I look, howe'er I range,
'T is all confus'd, and hard, and strange ;
The good are troubled and opprest,
And all the wicked are the blest.

Quoth John, our ignorance is the cause
Why thus we blame our Maker's laws ;
Parts of his ways alone we know,
'T is all that man can see below.

Seest thou that carpet, not half done,
Which thou, dear Dick, hast well begun ?
Behold the wild confusion there !
So rude the mass, it makes one stare.

A stranger, ignorant of the trade,
Would say no meaning 's there convey'd ;
For where 's the middle, where 's the border ?
The carpet now is all disorder.

Quoth Dick, my work is yet in bits,
But still in every part it fits ;
Besides, you reason like a lout,
Why man, that carpet 's inside out !

Says John,—Thou say'st the thing I mean,
And now I hope to cure thy spleen :
This world, which clouds thy soul with doubt,
Is but a carpet inside out.

As when we view these shreds and ends,
We know not what the whole intends ;
So when on earth things look but odd,
They 're working still some scheme of God.

No plan, no pattern can we trace,
All wants proportion, truth, and grace ;
The motley mixture we deride,
Nor see the beauteous upper side.

But when we reach the world of light,
And view these works of God aright ;
Then shall we see the whole design,
And own the workman is divine.

What now seem random strokes will there
All order and design appear ;
Then shall we praise what here we spurn'd,
For then, the carpet will be turn'd.

Thou 'rt right, quoth Dick, no more I 'll grumble
That this world is so strange a jumble ;
My impious doubts are put to flight,
For my own carpet sets me right.

29

As a sample of Mrs. More's dramatic poetry, I select the following passage from *Daniel*, one of her *Sacred Dramas*. It is the speech of Daniel on being condemned to death :

> And what is death, my friend, that I should fear it ?
> To die ! why 't is to triumph : 't is to join
> The great assembly of the good and just :
> Immortal worthies, heroes, prophets, saints !
> Oh, 't is to join the band of holy men,
> Made perfect by their sufferings ! 'T is to meet
> My great progenitors ; 't is to behold
> The illustrious patriarchs : they with whom the Lord
> Deign'd hold familiar converse ! 'T is to see
> Bless'd Noah and his children : once a world.
> 'T is to behold (O rapture to conceive !)
> Those we have known, and lov'd, and lost below :
> Behold Azariah and the band of brothers
> Who sought in bloom of youth the scorching flames !
> Nor shall we see heroic men alone,
> Champions who fought the fight of faith on earth ;
> But heavenly conquerors, angelic hosts,
> Michael and his bright legions who subdued
> The foes of Truth ! To join their blest employ
> Of love and praise ! To the high melodies
> Of choirs celestial to attune my voice,
> Accordant to the golden harps of saints !
> To join in blest hosannahs to their king !
> Whose face to see, whose glory to behold,
> Alone were heaven, though saint or seraph none
> Should meet our sight, and only God were there !
> This is to die ! Who would not die for this ?
> Who would not die that he might live for ever ?

There is a well expressed truth in the following : —

PASSION THE SOURCE OF MISERY.

> Yet Heaven's decrees are just and wise,
> And man is born to bear ;

Joy is the portion of the skies,
Beneath them all is care.

Yet blame not Heav'n ; 't is erring man
Who mars his own best joys ;
Whose passion uncontroll'd the plan
Of promis'd bliss destroys.

The deadliest wounds with which we bleed,
Our crimes inflict alone :
Man's mercies from God's hand proceed.
His miseries from his own.

MISS HELEN MARIA WILLIAMS,

1780—1823,

WAS the author, amongst other verses, of some of the most musical and expressive sonnets in our language. The first of these here printed is a great favourite of Wordsworth's.

SONNET TO HOPE.

O ever skill'd to wear the form we love!
To bid the shapes of fear and grief depart;
Come, gentle Hope! with one gay smile remove
The lasting sadness of an aching heart.
Thy voice, benign enchantress! let me hear;
Say that for me some pleasures yet shall bloom,
That Fancy's radiance, Friendship's precious tear,
Shall soften, or shall chase, misfortune's gloom.
But come not glowing in the dazzling ray,
Which once with dear illusions charm'd the eye;
O! strew no more, sweet flatterer! on my way
The flowers I fondly thought too bright to die;
Visions less fair will soothe my pensive breast,
That asks not happiness, but longs for rest!

PARAPHRASE.

Psalm LXXIV. 16, 17.

My God! all nature owns thy sway,
Thou giv'st the night and thou the day!
When all thy lov'd creation wakes,
When morning, rich in lustre, breaks,

And bathes in dew the opening flower,
To Thee we owe her fragrant hour ;
And when she pours her choral song,
Her melodies to Thee belong !
Or when, in paler tints array'd,
The evening slowly spreads her shade,
That soothing shade, that grateful gloom,
Can more than day's enlivening bloom
Still every fond and vain desire,
And calmer, purer thoughts inspire ;
From earth the pensive spirit free,
And lead the soften'd heart to Thee.
In every scene thy hands have dress'd,
In every form by thee impress'd,
Upon the mountain's awful head,
Or where the sheltering woods are spread ;
In every note that swells the gale,
Or tuneful stream that cheers the vale,
The cavern's depth or echoing grove,
A voice is heard of praise and love.
As o'er thy work the seasons roll,
And soothe, with change of bliss, the soul,
Oh, never may their smiling train
Pass o'er the human scene in vain !
But oft as on the charm we gaze,
Attune the wondering soul to praise ;
And be the joys that most we prize
The joys that from thy favour rise !

SONNET.

To Twilight.

Meek twilight ! haste to shroud the solar ray,
   And bring the hour my pensive spirit loves ;
When o'er the hill is shed a paler day,
   That gives to stillness, and to night, the groves.

U

Ah, let the gay, the roseate morning hail,
    When in the various blooms of light array'd,
She bids fresh beauty live along the vale,
    And rapture tremble in the vocal shade :
Sweet is the lucid morning's opening flower,
    Her choral melodies benignly rise :
Yet dearer to my soul the shadowy hour,
    At which her blossoms close, her music dies :
For then mild Nature, while she droops her head,
Wakes the soft tear 't is luxury to shed.

SONG.

Ah, Evan, by thy winding stream
    How once I lov'd to stray,
And view the morning's reddening beam,
    Or charm of closing day !

To yon dear grot by Evan's side,
    How oft my steps were led,
Where far beneath the waters glide,
    And thick the woods are spread !

But I no more a charm can see
    In Evan's lovely glades ;
And drear and desolate to me
    Are those enchanting shades.

While far — how far from Evan's bowers,
    My wandering lover flies ;
Where dark the angry tempest lowers,
    And high the billows rise !

And O, where'er the wanderer goes,
    Is that poor mourner dear,
Who gives, while soft the Evan flows,
    Each passing wave a tear !

And does he now that grotto view ?
  On those steep banks still gaze ?
In fancy does he still pursue
  The Evan's lovely maze ?

O come ! repass the stormy wave,
  O toil for gold no more !
Our love a dearer pleasure gave
  On Evan's peaceful shore.

Leave not my breaking heart to mourn
  The joys so long denied ;
Ah, soon to those green banks return,
  Where Evan meets the Clyde !

SONNET.

To the Moon.

The glittering colours of the day are fled —
  Come, melancholy orb ! that dwell'st with night,
Come, and o'er earth thy wandering lustre shed,
  Thy deepest shadow, and thy softest light.
To me congenial is the gloomy grove,
  When with faint rays the sloping uplands shine;
That gloom, those pensive rays, alike I love,
  Whose sadness seems in sympathy with mine.
But most for this, pale orb ! thy light is dear,
  For this, benignant orb ! I hail thee most,
That while I pour the unavailing tear,
  And mourn that hope to me in youth is lost —
Thy light can visionary thoughts impart,
And lead the Muse to soothe a suffering heart.

HABITUAL DEVOTION.

While Thee I seek, protecting Power!
　Be my vain wishes still'd;
And may this consecrated hour
　With better hopes be fill'd!

Thy love the powers of thought bestow'd:
　To Thee my thoughts would soar;
Thy mercy o'er my life has flow'd; —
　That mercy I adore!

In each event of life, how clear
　Thy ruling hand I see!
Each blessing to my soul more dear,
　Because conferr'd by Thee!

In every joy that crowns my days,
　In every pain I bear,
My heart shall find delight in praise,
　Or seek relief in prayer.

When gladness wings my favour'd hour,
　Thy love my thoughts shall fill;
Resign'd, when storms of sorrow lour,
　My soul shall meet thy will.

My lifted eye, without a tear,
　The louring storm shall see;
My stedfast heart shall know no fear;
　That heart will rest on Thee!

ELEANOR ANNE FRANKLIN.

1790—1825,

WAS the daughter of Mr. Porden, an architect, and wife of the enterprising Captain Franklin. She wrote *The Veils, or the Triumph of Constancy ; Cœur de Lion, or the Third Crusade ;* and *The Arctic Expedition.* She died in 1825.

The following extract is from *Cœur de Lion.* Queen Berengaria, in the garb of a minstrel, has arrived at the castle of Trivallis, where Richard is confined.

> She left her steed beneath the beechen shade,
> " And art thou there? my best belov'd !" she said ;
> " Upbraiding all that to thy help should fly,
> " Nor think'st what fond, what anxious heart is nigh."
>
> Eve's last soft flushes fade, and all is still,
> While veil'd in gloom, she climbs the arduous hill.
> Rude was the path, nor oft by pilgrim worn,
> O'er-grown with briars, long, wildering and forlorn :
>
> Scarce might the horseman trace that dangerous way,
> Through brakes, impervious to the summer day,
> Now wrapt in night : while onward as she hies,
> Scar'd at her step, the birds of carnage rise.
>
> At last, yet shrouded in the castle's shade,
> Cautious she cross'd its spacious esplanade ;
> Mark'd each strong wall, with towers begirt around,
> The massy keep what lofty turrets crown'd ;
> The boy who never dreamt of war might know
> Those awful ramparts would but mock the foe ;

30   u*

While not one light the abode of man confest,
Or gave the weary pilgrim hope of rest.
Those grated loopholes o'er the gate — ah, there
Perchance her Richard wastes with secret care !
Whose gifts were kingdoms, now by famine dies —
His only prospect those relentless skies,
His only visitant the bats, that prowl
Round the grim tower, or nightly-hooting owl !

Mournful she stood ; but soon the breeze that sighs
Through her lone harp, bids other thoughts arise.
" Yet, yet," she said, " some dear familiar strain
May reach his cell, and bolts and bars be vain ;
While should some jealous warder mark the lay,
'T is but a minstrel sings to cheer his way.
Ah, me ! that air to early love so dear,
Even in the tomb might rouse my Richard's ear ;
Oh ! could I pour his deep clear tones along,
And steal his accents as I steal his song !

' Frown, frown, Clorinda — I would prize
    Thy smile o'er all that arms might gain ;
O'er wealth and fame : yet mock my sighs,
My faded cheek, my tears despise,
    Nor I my fate arraign ;
While every rival's grief I see,
And know that all are scorn'd like me.' "

She ceas'd, — for from on high a fuller tone
Though faint in distance, blended with her own ;
That voice, those words, could come from one alone.

" O smile not, if thou e'er bestow
    On others, grace I think sincere ;
Such smiles are like the beams that glow
On the dark torrent's bridge of snow,
    And wreck the wretch they cheer.
Thine icy heart I well can bear,
But not the love that others share."

Bright hour of rapture! who may dare to tell
In her fond breast what blended feelings swell!
With parted lips, clos'd eyes, and hands comprest,
To still the' impetuous beatings of her breast,
Listening she stood : while conscious memory strays
To that blest hour when first she heard the lays.
Ecstatic dream — at length her faltering tongue
Its grief express'd in emblematic song : —

> " The widow'd dove can never rest,
> The felon kite has robb'd her nest;
> With wing untir'd she seeks her mate,
> To share or change his dreadful fate."

Again she paus'd, and listening, from on high
Caught from the friendly gale the faint reply.

> " But kites a higher power obey ;
> Th' Imperial Eagle claims the prey —
> Hence! to his spacious eyrie go,
> The Eagle is a nobler foe."

She strikes the harp — " Farewell! farewell!"
Her thrilling notes of transport swell : —

> " The monarch bird may build his nest
> On oak, or tower, or mountain crest,
> But love can match his daring flight,
> Can fell the tree, or scale the height."

" Ho! who art thou — " a sturdy warder calls,
" That dar'st to sing beneath Trivallis' walls ?" —
" A wandering bard, good friend, who fain would win
" These awful gates to let the weary in." —
" Nay, hence! nor dare to touch thy harp again,
"And thank thy saints 't was I that heard the strain :
" Tir'd as thou art, fly swiftly o'er the heath,
" And shun these walls. as thou wouldst shun thy death."

But was that pilgrim weary?   Oh! less fleet
The mountain chamois plies its fearless feet:
" Farewell! my ears are blest though not my eyes,
Thy chains shall fall," she warbles as she flies :
" Thou gentle guardian of my steps, my will,
Take my soul's blessing, and direct me still.
At Haguenau soon the empire's magnates meet,
Oh! touch the Eagle's heart—oh! guide my wandering feet."

SUSANNA BLAMIRE,

1747—1794,

WHOSE poetry was so highly esteemed in her own day that she was styled " the Muse of Cumberland," was the daughter of William Blamire, Esq., a gentleman of station and repute in the county named; where she was born in 1747. Losing her mother when she was only seven years of age, she was early thrown upon her own mental resources: and she for some years gave herself completely up to her studies. That her application was effectual, we find from the fact that at the age of nineteen, and even before, she wrote some very excellent poems. She died at Carlisle in 1794 : her writings, however, were not published in a collected form for some years.

The characteristics of Miss Blamire's poetry are considerable tenderness of feeling, very gracefully expressed, and a refined delicacy of imagination, which, whilst it never thrills, always pleases. Her poem called " The Nabob," which describes the return of an Indian adventurer to the home of his youth, is a very affecting and delightful production. Her songs, though not without marks of elaboration, display great simplicity and force of feeling. I select two specimens :

SONG.

What ails this heart o' mine ?
    What ails thy watery ee ?
What gars me a' turn cauld as death
    When I take leave o' thee ?
When thou art far awa'
    Thou 'lt dearer grow to me ;
But change o' place and change o' folk,
    May gar thy fancy jee !

When I gae out at e'en,
   Or walk at morning air,
Ilk rustling bush will seem to say,
   I us'd to meet thee there.
Then I 'll sit down an' cry,
   And live aneath the tree ;
And when a leaf fa's in my lap,
   I 'll ca 't a word frae thee.

I 'll hie me to the bower
   That thou wi' roses tied,
And where wi' many a blushing bud
   I strove myself to hide.
I 'll doat on ilka spot
   Where I ha'e been with thee ;
And ca' to mind some kindly word
   By ilka burn and tree !

Wi' sic thoughts in my mind,
   Time through the world may gae,
And find my heart in twenty years
   The same as 't is to-day.
'T is thoughts that bind the soul,
   And keep friends i' the ee,
And gin I think I see thee aye,
   What can part thee and me !

The authorship of the following well known and justly-admired song was long unknown, but there is now no doubt that it is the production of Miss Blamire.

THE SILLER CROWN.

And ye shall walk in silk attire,
   And siller hae to spare,
Gin ye 'll consent to be his bride,
   Nor think o' Donald mair.

O wha would buy a silken gown
　　Wi' a poor broken heart !
O what 's to me a siller crown
　　Gin frae my love I part !

The mind wha's every wish is pure
　　Far dearer is to me ;
And ere I 'm forced to break my faith,
　　I 'll lay me down and dee !
For I have pledg'd my virgin troth
　　Brave Donald's fate to share ;
And he has gi'en to me his heart
　　Wi' a' its virtues rare !

His gentle manners won my heart,
　　He gratefu' took the gift ;
Could I but think to see it back,
　　It wad be waur than theft !
For longest life can ne'er repay
　　The love he bears to me ;
And ere I'm forc'd to break my troth,
　　I 'll lay me down and dee !

MRS. MARY BRUNTON.

1778—1818.

THIS lady, justly celebrated for her excellent novels of *Self-Control*, *Discipline*, and *Emmeline*, was born in 1778 in the Island of Orkney. Her father, Colonel Balfour, caused her to be more than ordinarily well educated : yet not to the exclusion of household cares and duties. In her thirtieth year she became the wife of the Rev. Alexander Brunton, a clergyman of the Scotch church, late professor of Hebrew in the University of Edinburgh, with whom she lived for many years most happily, and whom she left a sorrowing widower in 1818. Of her novels it is not necessary here to speak ; the more especially as their great merit has been universally acknowledged. Her poetical compositions are extremely few : but they all exhibit the characteristics of her pen — great force of thought and gracefulness of composition. I extract only one of her productions ; which she calls

STANZAS FOR MUSIC.

When thou at eventide art roaming
Along the elm-o'ershaded walk,
Where, past, the eddying stream is foaming
Beneath its tiny cataract,
Where I with thee was wont to talk, —
Think then upon the days gone by,
And heave a sigh!

When sails the moon above the mountains,
And cloudless skies are purely blue,

And sparkle in the light the fountains,
And darker frowns the lonely yew, —
Then be thou melancholy too,
When musing on the hours I prov'd
With thee, belov'd !

When wakes the dawn upon thy dwelling,
And lingering shadows disappear,
And soft the woodland songs are swelling
A choral anthem on thine ear, —
Think — for that hour to thought is dear !
And then her flight remembrance wings
To by-past things.

To me, through every season, dearest,
In every scene — by day, by night,
Thou present to my mind appearest
A quenchless star — for ever bright !
My solitary, sole delight !
Alone — in grove — by shore — at sea,
I think of thee !

31   w

ANNA LÆTITIA BARBAULD,

1743—1825,

Was the daughter of the Reverend John Aiken, D. D., of Kibworth Harcourt, in Leicestershire, where she was born in 1743. She very early evinced a remarkable aptitude for study ; even in infancy she was described by her mother, as " a little girl who was as eager to learn as her instructors could be to teach her ; and who, at two years old, could read sentences and little stories in her *wise book,* roundly, without spelling, and, in half a year more, could read as well as most women."

Her father appears to have feared that she would become too fond of letters ; for, until she was fifteen years of age, he resolutely refused her his permission to study the learned languages. We find, notwithstanding, that she acquired considerable knowledge of both Latin and Greek.

Her first volume of poems was published in 1773, she being then thirty years of age. The success of the work was remarkably great: it passed through four editions within the first year.

In 1774 she became the wife of the Reverend Rochemont Barbauld, a dissenting minister. For a considerable number of years, Mrs. Barbauld was engaged with her husband in the laborious work of tuition : and many individuals now alive can testify to the singular talent she displayed in her arduous vocation. Lord Denman, William Taylor, Esquire, of Norwich, and other eminent persons, whose names escape me, were amongst Mr. Barbauld's pupils.

After a continental tour in 1785, Mr. and Mrs. Barbauld settled at Hampstead, where they remained until 1802 ; in which year they removed to Stoke Newington, where Mrs. Barbauld continued her literary pursuits with great ardour. The death of her husband in 1808, however, interrupted her labours ; and, though she resumed them in 1810, they were not destined to be of long continuance : for some unjust and unkind criticisms upon a poem published in 1812, led her to resolve upon retiring from the literary world. She lived for many years in undisturbed peace, and died in 1825, in the eighty-second year of her age, deeply and deservedly lamented.

Mrs. Barbauld's poetry exhibits, in a high degree, the characteristic qualities of female genius. The quick intuitive perception, the chaste tenderness, the delicate, *musical* flow of thought, that distinguish the female mind, are very forcibly and fully developed by Mrs. Barbauld. In these respects she is second only to Mrs. Hemans ; whilst in many other points of view she is decidedly a greater and more instructive writer.

The following Sonnet is a fair sample of our author's gracefulness of thought and style. She inscribes it —

TO A LADY WITH SOME FLOWERS.

Flowers to the Fair ! to you these flowers I bring,
And strive to greet you with an earlier spring.
Flowers sweet and gay, and delicate like you,
Emblems of innocence and beauty, too.
With flowers the Graces bind their yellow hair,
And flowery wreaths consenting lovers wear.
Flowers, the sole luxury which nature knew,
In Eden's pure and guiltless garden grew.
To loftier forms and rougher tasks assign'd,
The sheltering oak resists the stormy wind, —
The tougher yew repels invading foes,
And the tall pine for future navies grows ;
But this soft family, to cares unknown,
Were born for pleasures and delight alone.
Gay without toil, and lovely without art,
They spring to cheer the sense and glad the heart.
Nor blush, my fair, to own you copy these ;
Your best, your sweetest empire is — to please.

One of Mrs. Barbauld's most admired productions is her " Ode
to Spring : " and I think that the praise commonly bestowed upon
this poem is amply deserved. It is full of beautiful thoughts,
and contains some imagery of the most chaste and elegant
description. It is, moreover, a most happy imitation of the style
of Collins : a very difficult model to copy.

ODE TO SPRING.

Sweet daughter of a rough and stormy sire,
Hoar Winter's blooming child, delightful Spring !
    Whose unshorn locks with leaves
    And swelling buds are crown'd ;

From the green islands of eternal youth,
(Crown'd with fresh blooms, and ever-springing shade)
    Turn, hither turn thy step,
    O thou, whose powerful voice,

More sweet than softest touch of Doric reed,
Or Lydian flute, can soothe the madding winds,
    And through the stormy deep
    Breathe thy own tender calm.

Thee, best belov'd ! the virgin train await,
With songs and festal rites, and joy to rove
    Thy blooming wilds among,
    And vales and dewy lawns,

With untir'd feet ; and cull thy earliest sweets
To weave fresh garlands for the glowing brow
    Of him, the favour'd youth,
    That prompts their whisper'd sigh.

Unlock thy copious stores ; those tender showers
That drop their sweetness on the infant buds,
    And silent dews that swell
    The milky ear's green stem,

And feed the flowering osier's early shoots ;
And calls those winds which through the whispering boughs
    With warm and pleasant breath
    Salute the blowing flowers.

Now let me sit beneath the whitening thorn,
And mark thy spreading tints steal o'er the dale ;
    And watch with patient eye
    Thy fair unfolding charms.

O nymph ! approach, while yet the temperate sun
With bashful forehead, through the cool moist air
    Throws his young maiden beams,
    And with chaste kisses woos

The earth's fair bosom ; while the streaming veil
Of lucid clouds with kind and frequent shade,
    Protects thy modest blooms
    From his severer blaze.

Sweet is thy reign, but short ; the red dog-star
Shall scorch thy tresses, and the mower's scythe
    Thy greens, thy flow'rets all,
    Remorseless shall destroy.

Reluctant shall I bid thee, then, farewell ;
For oh ! not all that Autumn's lap contains,
    Nor summer's ruddiest fruits,
    Can aught for thee atone,

Fair Spring ! whose simplest promise more delights
Than all their largest wealth, and through the heart
    Each joy and new-born hope
    With softest influence breathes.

One of the chief literary faults of the era immediately preceding
our own was a certain *abstractedness* of thought, which I cannot
better describe than by calling it a too strong tendency towards
w*

the Ideal. Our writers shrank from Reality ; shrank, I think, too far from it. They spiritualised all that they attempted to describe ; lifted their subjects into the clouds ; and too often, alas ! left them there. And the result of this error was that they distanced the sympathies, and frequently failed to interest the reader.

The Female poets of the time fell the most readily into the mistake, and well nigh deluged the poetic world with their cloudy abstractions and etherealised personifications. Sentiments, feelings, and passions were all refined into deities, and addressed as if they were superintendents of human fate and conduct. Nothing is more common, in the works of the period referred to, than to meet with poems *To Sensibility* — *To Hope* — *To Wisdom* — *To Indolence* — *To Fear* — *To Health* — *To Simplicity*, and so forth : and nothing can well be more drowsy than the effect of such productions.

Mrs. Barbauld fell partially into this fault. Her poems contain many of these abstractions : and any neglect that her works may have experienced, must, I am inclined to believe, be attributed chiefly to this cause. The following poem is, I think, one of the best samples I can select of the faulty style to which I refer.

HYMN TO CONTENT.

O thou ! the nymph with placid eye !
O seldom found, yet ever nigh !
    Receive my temperate vow :
Not all the storms that shake the pole
Can e'er disturb thy halcyon soul,
    And smooth unalter'd brow.

O come, in simple vest array'd,
With all thy sober cheer display'd,
    To bless my longing sight ;
Thy mien composed, thy even pace,
Thy meek regard, thy matron grace,
    And chaste subdued delight.

No more by varying passions beat,
O gently guide my pilgrim feet
　　To find thy hermit cell ;
Where in some pure and equal sky
Beneath thy soft indulgent eye
　　The modest virtues dwell.

Simplicity in Attic vest,
And Innocence with candid breast,
　　And clear undaunted eye ;
And Hope, who points to distant years,
Fair opening through the vale of tears
　　A vista to the sky.

There Health, through whose calm bosom glide
The temperate joys in even tide,
　　That rarely ebb or flow ;
And Patience there, thy sister meek,
Presents her mild unvarying cheek
　　To meet the offered blow.

Her influence taught the Phrygian sage
A tyrant master's wanton rage
　　With settled smiles to meet ;
Inured to toil and bitter bread,
He bowed his meek submitted head,
　　And kissed thy sainted feet.

But thou, oh nymph, retired and coy,
In what brown hamlet dost thou joy
　　To tell thy tender tale ?
The lowliest children of the ground,
Moss-rose and violet, blossom round,
　　And lily of the vale.

O say, what soft propitious hour,
I best may choose to hail thy power,
　　And court thy gentle sway ?

When Autumn, friendly to the Muse,
Shall thy own modest tints diffuse,
    And shed thy milder day.

When Eve, her dewy star beneath,
Thy balmy spirit loves to breathe,
    And every storm is laid ;
If such an hour was e'er thy choice,
Oft let me hear thy soothing voice
    Low whispering in the shade.

Mrs. Barbauld's muse is highly devotional. Her religious
poems are very purely beautiful in sentiment; and her sense of
reliance on the Deity is very strong and admirable. The following lines will prove it.

ON THE DEITY.

I read God's awful name emblazon'd high
With golden letters on th' illumin'd sky ;
Nor less the mystic characters I see
Wrought in each flower, inscribed on every tree ;
In every leaf that trembles to the breeze
I hear the voice of God among the trees.
With Thee in shady solitudes I walk,
With Thee in busy crowded cities talk ;
In every creature own Thy forming power,
In each event Thy providence adore.

Thy hopes shall animate my drooping soul,
Thy precepts guide me and Thy fear control :
Thus shall I rest, unmov'd by all alarms,
Secure within the temple of Thine arms ;
From anxious cares, from gloomy terrors free,
And feel myself omnipotent in Thee.

Then when the last, the closing hour draws nigh,
And earth recedes before my swimming eye, —

When trembling on the doubtful edge of fate
I stand, and stretch my view to either state : —
Teach me to quit this transitory scene
With decent triumph and a look serene ;
Teach me to fix my ardent hopes on high,
And having lived to Thee, in Thee to die !

It is, indeed, in devotional subjects that Mrs. Barbauld shows
her greatest eloquence and strength. Whilst writing on religion
her faculties seem thoroughly to clear and concentrate themselves :
and then it is that her spirit pours forth its treasures most abun-
dantly and purely. There is something very stirring and thrilling
in this

HYMN.

Jehovah reigns : let every nation hear,
And at his footstool bow with holy fear ;
Let Heaven's high arches echo with His name,
And the wide peopled earth His praise proclaim ;
Then send it down to hell's deep glooms resounding,
Through all her caves in dreadful murmurs sounding.

He rules with wide and absolute command
O'er the broad ocean and the steadfast land :
Jehovah reigns, unbounded and alone,
And all creation hangs beneath His throne.
He reigns alone : let no inferior nature
Usurp or share the throne of the Creator.

He saw the struggling beams of infant light
Shoot through the massy gloom of ancient night ;
His spirit hush'd the elemental strife,
And brooded o'er the kindling seeds of life :
Seasons and months begin the long procession,
And measured o'er the year in bright succession.
    32

The joyful sun sprung up th' ethereal way,
Strong as a giant, as a bridegroom gay ;
And the pale moon diffused her shadowy light,
Superior o'er the dusky brow of night :
Ten thousand glittering lamps the skies adorning,
Numerous as dew-drops from the womb of morning.

Earth's blooming face with rising flowers He dress'd
And spread a verdant mantle o'er her breast ;
Then from the hollow of His hand He pours
The circling waters round her winding shores ;
The new-born world in their cool arms embracing,
And with soft murmurs still her banks caressing.

At length she rose complete in finish'd pride,
All fair and spotless, like a virgin bride ;
Fresh with untarnish'd lustre as she stood,
Her Maker bless'd His work and called it good :
The morning stars with joyful acclamation,
Exulting sung, and hail'd the new creation.

Yet this fair world, the creature of a day,
Though built by God's right hand, must pass away ;
And long oblivion creep o'er mortal things,
The fate of Empires, and the pride of Kings ;
Eternal night shall veil their proudest story,
And drop the curtain o'er all human glory.

The sun himself, with weary clouds opprest,
Shall in his silent dark pavilion rest ;
His golden urn shall broke and useless lie,
Amidst the common ruins of the sky !
The stars rush headlong in the wild commotion,
And bathe their glittering foreheads in the ocean.

But fix'd, O God ! for ever stands Thy throne ;
Jehovah reigns, a universe alone :

Th' eternal fire that feeds each vital flame,
Collected or diffused is still the same.
He dwells within his own unfathom'd essence,
And fills all space with His unbounded presence.

But oh ! our highest notes the theme debase,
And silence is our least injurious praise:
Cease, cease your songs, the daring flight control,
Revere Him in the stillness of the soul.
With silent duty meekly bend before Him,
And deep within your inmost hearts adore Him.

LADY ANNE BARNARD.

1750—1825.

THIS lady was a daughter of James Lindsay, fifth earl of Balcarras, and was born in 1750. She became the wife of Sir Andrew Barnard, librarian to George the Third, in the year 1771. In that year, or in the following, she wrote the touching ballad of *Auld Robin Gray;* the authorship of which she kept a secret until the year 1823, when she divulged it to Sir Walter Scott. Lady Barnard wrote two Continuations to the ballad, which, however, are generally considered to be inferior to the original poem.

AULD ROBIN GRAY.

When the sheep are in the fauld, when the cows come hame,
When a' the weary world to quiet rest are gane,
The woes of my heart fa' in showers frae my ee,
Unkenn'd by my gudeman, who soundly sleeps by me.

Young Jamie loo'd me well, and sought me for his bride,
But saving ae crown-piece, he 'd naething else beside.
To make the crown a pound, my Jamie gaed to sea;
And the crown and the pound, O they were baith for me!

Before he had been gane a twelvemonth and a day,
My father brak his arm, our cow was stown away:
My mother she fell sick — my Jamie was at sea —
And auld Robin Gray —oh! he came a-courting me.

My father cou'dna work — my mother cou'dna spin;
I toil'd day and night, but their bread I cou'dna win;
Auld Rob maintain'd them baith, and, wi tears in his ee,
Said " Jenny, oh, for their sakes, will you marry me?"

My heart it said na, and I look'd for Jamie back ;
But hard blew the winds, and his ship was a wrack :
His ship it was a wrack ! Why didna Jamie dee ?
Or wherefore am I spared to cry out, Woe is me !

My father argued sair — my mother didna speak,
But she look'd in my face till my heart was like to break ;
They gied him my hand, but my heart was in the sea ;
And so auld Robin Gray, he was gudeman to me.

I hadna been his wife, a week but only four,
When mournfu' as I sat on the stane at my door,
I saw my Jamie's ghaist — I cou'dna think it he,
Till he said, " I 'm come hame, my love, to marry thee !"

O sair, sair did we greet, and mickle say of a',
Ae kiss we took, na mair — I bad him gang awa'.
I wish that I were dead, but I 'm no like to dee ;
For O, I 'm but young to cry out, Woe is me !

I gang like a ghaist, and I carena much to spin ;
I darena think of Jamie, for that wad be a sin.
But I will do my best a gude wife aye to be,
For auld Robin Gray, oh ! he is sae kind to me.

x

MRS. ANNE GRANT,

1755—1838,

A CELEBRATED Scotch poetess, was the daughter of an officer in the British army named Macvicar, and was born at Glasgow in the year 1755. Her father's profession leading him into America, he took his family with him, and there Miss Macvicar spent seven of her youthful years. Mr. Macvicar and his family returned to Scotland in 1768; and, in 1779, his daughter married the Reverend James Grant, who subsequently became minister of Laggon, in Inverness-shire. The death of her husband in 1801, left Mrs. Grant and her eight children quite unprovided for: and under these distressing circumstances it was that literature (which had previously been her chief amusement) was now resorted to as a means of subsistence. An education of rough experience, combined with a naturally shrewd, powerful, and sensitive mind, made Mrs. Grant a highly effective and successful writer; and the fame of her literary abilities (even before she published any fruits of them) was so great, that three thousand persons gave her their names as subscribers to her poem of the *Highlanders*. The success of this fine poem relieved her temporarily from her embarrassments, but she still had many privations to bear. In a few years she removed finally to Edinburgh, where she was called upon to endure worse afflictions, in the death of her children, one after another, until only her youngest son was left to her. In 1825, George the Fourth, at the instance of Sir Walter Scott and other friends, granted our authoress a pension of 100*l.* per annum. which she lived to enjoy until 1838, when she died in the eighty-fourth year of her age.

EXTRACT FROM "THE HIGHLANDERS."

No hamlet without some Widow, who is in a great measure supported, and saved from the disgrace of a mendicant life, by the little society.

Where yonder ridgy mountains bound the scene,
The narrow opening glens that intervene
Still shelter, in some lowly nook obscure,
One poorer than the rest, — where all are poor ;
Some *widow'd Matron*, hopeless of relief,
Who to her secret breast confines her grief ;
Dejected sighs the wintry night away,
And lonely muses all the summer day :
Her gallant sons, who, smit with honour's charms,
Pursued the phantom Fame through war's alarms,
Return no more : stretch'd on Hindostan's plain,
Or sunk beneath the' unfathomable main ;
In vain her eyes the watery waste explore,
For heroes — fated to return no more !
Let others bless the morning's reddening beam—
Foe to her peace, it breaks the' illusive dream
That, in their pride of manly bloom confest,
Restor'd the long-lost warriors to her breast ;
And as they strove, with smiles of filial love,
Their widow'd parent's anguish to remove,
Through her small casement broke the' intrusive day,
And chas'd the pleasing images away !
No time can e'er her banish'd joys restore,
For, ah ! a heart once broken heals no more.
The dewy beams that gleam from pity's eye,
The " still small voice" of sacred sympathy,
In vain the mourner's sorrows would beguile,
Or steal from weary woe one languid smile ;
Yet what they can they do, — the scanty store,
So often open'd for the wandering poor,
To her each cottager complacent deals,
While the kind glance the melting heart reveals ;

And still, when evening streaks the west with gold,
The milky tribute from the glowing fold
With cheerful haste officious children bring,
And every smiling flower that decks the Spring :
Ah ! little know the fond attentive train,
That Spring and flowrets smile for her in vain :
Yet hence they learn to reverence modest woe,
And of their little all a part bestow.
Let those to wealth and proud distinction born,
With the cold glance of insolence and scorn
Regard the suppliant wretch, and harshly grieve
The bleeding heart their bounty would relieve, —
Far different these ; — while from a bounteous heart
With the poor sufferer they divide a part ;
Humbly they own that all they have is given
A boon precarious from indulgent Heaven :
And the next blighted crop, or frosty spring,
Themselves to equal indigence may bring.

It is not difficult to distinguish in this passage a touch of simple pathos, such as might have been given by the hand of Goldsmith. Warm, unaffected and homely, Mrs. Grant's strains
might often be mistaken for productions of that fine poet's pen.

Mrs. Grant appears to have been one of the first among modern
writers who drew attention to the striking and romantic features
of Highland life and scenery : and in this respect she may justly
be considered the precursor of Scott and those other writers who
have since attached so much interest to that subject. Her *Letters from the Mountains*, and *Her Essays on the Superstitions
of the Highlanders*, convey much information, and exhibit great
ability.

MRS. ANNE HUNTER,

1742—1821,

WIFE of the celebrated John Hunter, and sister of Sir Everard Home, was born in 1742, and died in 1821. She is the author of several very beautiful poems, of which the following are specimens :

TO-MORROW.

How heavy falls the foot of Time !
How slow the lingering quarters chime,
    Through anxious hours of long delay !
In vain we watch the silent glass,
More slow the sands appear to pass,
    While disappointment marks their way.

To-morrow — still the phantom flies,
Flitting away before our eyes,
    Eludes our grasp, is pass'd and gone ;
Daughter of hope, Night o'er thee flings
The shadow of her raven wings,
    And in the morning thou art flown !

Delusive sprite ! from day to day,
We still pursue thy pathless way :
    Thy promise broken o'er and o'er,
Man still believes, and is thy slave ;
Nor ends the chase but in the grave,
    For there *to-morrow* is no more.

33   x*

The fancy contained in the three last lines of the second stanza of this poem has always appeared to me particularly happy. Such fancies are very frequent in Mrs. Hunter's works.

There is much sweetness, too, in the following

SIMILE.

I saw the wild rose on its parent thorn,
    Half-clos'd, soft blushing, thro' the glittering dew,
Wave on the breeze and scent the breath of morn;
    Lelia, the lovely flower resembled you.

Scarce had it spread to meet the orb of day,
    Its fragrant beauties opening to the view,
When ruffian blasts have torn the rose away: —
    Lelia, — alas! it still resembles you!

So torn by wild and lawless passion's force
    From every social tie thy lot must be;
At last oblivion shades thy future course,
    And still the hapless flower resembles thee!

The beauty of the succeeding extracts will be apparent without comment.

THE LOT OF THOUSANDS.

When hope lies dead within the heart,
    By secret sorrow long conceal'd,
We shrink lest looks or words impart
    What may not be reveal'd.

'T is hard to smile when one would weep,
    To speak when one would silent be;
To wake when one would wish to sleep,
    And wake to agony.

THE NEWS BOY.

Yet such the lot for thousands cast,
Who wander in this world of care,
And bend beneath the bitter blast,
To save them from despair.

Yet Nature waits her guests to greet,
Where disappointment cannot come ;
And Time leads with unerring feet
The weary wanderer home.

THE OCEAN GRAVE.

Friends ! when I die prepare my welcome grave,
Where the eternal Ocean rolls his wave ;
Rough through the blast, still let his free-born breeze,
Which freshness wafts to earth from endless seas,
Sigh o'er my sleep, and let his glancing spray
Weep tear-drops sparkling with a heavenly ray ;
A constant mourner then shall watch my tomb,
And nature deepen while it soothes the gloom.

O let that element whose voice had power
To cheer my darkest, soothe my loneliest hour ;
Which through my life my spirit lov'd so well,
Still o'er my grave its tale of glory tell.
The generous Ocean whose proud waters bear
The spoil and produce they disdain to wear,
Whose wave claims kindred with the azure sky,
From whom reflected stars beam gloriously ;
Emblem of God ! unchanging, infinite,
Awful alike in loveliness and might ;
Rolls still untiring like the tide of Time,
Binds man to man and mingles clime with clime ;
And as the sun, which from each lake and stream,
Through all the world, where'er their waters gleam,
Collects the crowd his heavenly ray conceals,
And slakes the thirst which all creation feels,

So Ocean gathers tribute from each shore,
To bid each climate know its want no more.
Exil'd on earth, a fetter'd prisoner here,
Barr'd from all treasures which my soul holds dear,
The kindred soul, the fame my youth desir'd,
Whilst hope hath fled which once my bosom fir'd ;
Dead to all joy, still to my fancy glow
Dreams of delight which heavenward thoughts bestow,
Not then in death shall I unconscious be
Of that whose whispers are Eternity.

SONG.

Far, far from me my love is fled,
    In a light skiff he tempts the sea,
The young Desires his sails have spread,
    And Hope his pilot deigns to be.

The promis'd land of varied joys,
    Which so delights his fickle mind,
In waking dreams his days employs,
    While I, poor I, sing to the wind.

But young Desires grow old and die,
    And Hope no more the Helm may steer;
Beneath a dark and stormy sky
    Shall fall the late repentant tear.

While I, within my peaceful grot,
    May hear the distant tempest roar,
Contented with my humble lot,
    In safety on the friendly shore.

SONG.

O tuneful voice ! I still deplore
Those accents which, though heard no more,

Still vibrate on my heart;
In echo's cave I long to dwell,
And still would hear the sad farewell
When we were doom'd to part.

Bright eyes! O that the task were mine
To guard the liquid fires that shine,
    And round your orbits play;
To watch them with a Vestal's care,
And feed with smiles a light so fair,
    That it may ne'er decay.

TO MY DAUGHTER,

On being separated from her on her marriage.

Dear to my heart as life's warm stream,
    Which animates this mortal clay,
For thee I court the waking dream,
    And deck with smiles the future day;
And thus beguile the present pain
With hopes that we shall meet again.

Yet will it be, as when the past
    Twin'd every joy and care and thought,
And o'er our minds one mantle cast
    Of kind affections finely wrought?
Ah, no! the groundless hope were vain,
For so we ne'er can meet again!

May he who claims thy tender heart
    Deserve its love, as I have done!
For, kind and gentle as thou art,
    If so belov'd, thou 'rt fairly won.
Bright may the sacred torch remain,
And cheer thee till we meet again!

HESTER LYNCH PIOZZI,

1739—1821,

THE well-known friend of Dr. Johnson, was the daughter of Mr. John Salusbury, of Caernarvonshire. She was born in 1739, and married, first Mr. Thrale, the brewer, who was so warmly attached to Johnson, and subsequently Signor Piozzi, a music-master.

As an authoress, she is chiefly known by her tale called

THE THREE WARNINGS.

The tree of deepest root is found
Least willing still to quit the ground ;
'T was therefore said by ancient sages,
    That love of life increas'd with years
So much, that in our latter stages,
When pain grows sharp, and sickness rages,
    The greatest love of life appears :
This great affection to believe,
Which all confess, but few perceive,
If old assertions can't prevail,
Be pleas'd to hear a modern tale.

When sports went round, and all were gay
On neighbour Dobson's wedding-day,
Death called aside the jocund groom
With him into another room ;
And looking grave, " You must," says he,
" Quit your sweet bride, and come with me."
" With you ! and quit my Susan's side !

" With you !" the hapless husband cried ;
" Young as I am — 't is monstrous hard ;
Besides, in truth I 'm not prepar'd ;
My thoughts on other matters go,
This is my wedding-day, you know."

What more he urg'd I have not heard,
His reasons could not well be stronger ;
So Death the poor delinquent spar'd,
And left to live a little longer.
Yet, calling up a serious look,
His hour-glass trembled while he spoke,
" Neighbour," he said, "farewell ! no more
Shall Death disturb your mirthful hour :
And farther, to avoid all blame
Of cruelty upon my name,
To give you time for preparation,
And fit you for your future station,
Three several warnings you shall have,
Before you 're summoned to the grave :
Willing for once I 'll quit my prey,
    And grant a kind reprieve ;
In hopes you 'll have no more to say,
But when I call again this way,
    Well pleas'd the world will leave."
To these conditions both consented,
And parted, perfectly contented.

What next the hero of our tale befell,
How long he liv'd, how wise, how well,
How roundly he pursued his course,
And smok'd his pipe, and strok'd his horse,
    The willing Muse shall tell :
He chaffer'd then, he bought, he sold,
Nor once perceiv'd his growing old,
    Nor thought of Death as near :
His friends not false, his wife no shrew,
Many his gains, his children few,

He passed his hours in peace :
But while he view'd his wealth increase,
While thus along Life's dusty road
The beaten track content he trod,
Old Time, whose haste no mortal spares,
Uncall'd, unheeded, unawares,
　　Brought on his eightieth year.

And now, one night, in musing mood,
　　As all alone he sat,
The unwelcome messenger of fate
Once more before him stood.

Half kill'd with anger and surprise,
" So soon return'd !" old Dobson cries ;
" So soon d' ye call it ?" Death replies ;
" Surely, my friend, you 're but in jest !
　　Since I was here before,
'T is six and thirty years at least,
　　And you are now fourscore."
" So much the worse," the clown rejoin'd,
" To spare the aged would be kind ;
However, see your search be legal ;
And your authority — is 't regal ?
Else you are come on a fool's errand,
With but a secretary's warrant ;
Besides, you promis'd me Three Warnings,
Which I have look'd for nights and mornings !
But for that loss of time and ease,
I can recover damages."

" I know," cries Death, " that at the best,
I seldom am a welcome guest ;
But don't be captious, friend, at least :
I little thought you 'd still be able
To stump about your farm and stable ;
Your years have run to a great length,
I wish you joy, though, of your strength !"

"Hold" — says the farmer, " not so fast!
I have been lame these four years past."
" And no great wonder," Death replies,
" However, you still keep your eyes :
And sure to see one's loves and friends,
For legs and arms would make amends !"
" Perhaps," says Dobson, " so it might,
But latterly I 've lost my sight."
" This is a shocking story, 'faith,
But there 's some comfort still," says Death ;
" Each strive your sadness to amuse,
I warrant you hear all the news !"
" There 's none," cries he, " and if there were,
I 'm grown so deaf, I could not hear."
" Nay then," the spectre stern rejoin'd,
" These are unjustifiable yearnings ;
If you are lame, and deaf, and blind,
You 've had your Three sufficient Warnings ,
So, come along! no more we 'll part !"
He said, and touch'd him with his dart ;
And now old Dobson, turning pale,
Yields to his fate — so ends my tale.

34   Y

ANN RADCLIFFE,

1764—1823,

WHOSE fame rests, as needs hardly to be said, upon her splendid but terrible novels of *The Italian* and *The Mysteries of Udolpho*, was a poetess of no mean pretensions. The pieces of verse interspersed in her various romances display the same peculiar powers which characterise her prose compositions; they are marked by great energy of imagination, and rich eloquence of style.

Mrs. Radcliffe was born in London, in 1764, of a respectable family named Ward. She married Mr. Radcliffe, a law-student, in 1787 : and died in 1823.

TO THE WINDS.

Viewless, through Heaven's vast vault your course ye steer,
Unknown from whence ye come, or whither go !
Mysterious powers ! I hear you murmur low,
Till swells your loud gust on my startled ear,
And, awful, seems to say — some God is near !
I love to list your midnight voices float
In the dread storm that o'er the ocean rolls,
And, while their charm the angry wave controls,
Mix with its sullen roar, and sink remote.
Then, rising in the pause, a sweeter note,
The dirge of spirits, who your deeds bewail,
A sweeter note oft swells while sleeps the gale !
But soon, ye sightless powers ! your rest is o'er,
Solemn and slow, ye rise upon the air,

Speak in the shrouds, and bid the sea-boy fear,
And the faint-warbled dirge — is heard no more!

Oh! then I deprecate your awful reign!
The loud lament yet bear not on your breath!
Bear not the crash of bark far on the main,
Bear not the cry of men, who cry in vain,
The crew's dread chorus sinking into death!
Oh! give not these, ye powers! I ask alone,
As rapt I climb these dark romantic steeps,
The elemental war, the billow's moan;
I ask the still, sweet tear, that listening Fancy weeps.

THE GLOW-WORM.

How pleasant is the green-wood's deep-matted shade
  On a midsummer's eve when the fresh rain is o'er;
When the yellow beams slope, and sparkle through the glade,
  And swiftly in the thin air the ligh swallows soar!

But sweeter, sweeter still, when the sun sinks to rest,
  And twilight comes on, with the fairies so gay
Tripping through the forest-walk, where flowers unprest
  Bow not their tall heads beneath their frolic play.

To music's softest sounds they dance away the hour,
  Till moonlight steals down among the trembling leaves,
And checkers all the ground, and guides them to the bower,
  The long-haunted bower, where the nightingale grieves.

Then no more they dance, till her sad song is done,
  But, silent as the night, to her mourning attend;
And often as her dying notes their pity have won,
  They vow all her sacred haunts from mortals to defend.

When, down among the mountains, sinks the evening star,
  And the changing moon forsakes this shadowy sphere,
How cheerless would they be, though they fairies are,
  If I, with my pale light, came not near!

Yet cheerless though they'd be, they 're ungrateful to my love!
  For, often when the traveller's benighted on his way,
And I glimmer in his path, and would guide him through the grove,
  They bind me in their magic spells to lead him far astray;

And in the mire to leave him, till the stars are all burnt out,
  While in strange-looking shapes, they frisk about the ground,
And afar in the woods they raise a dismal shout,
  Till I shrink into my cell again, for terror of the sound!

But, see where all the tiny elves come dancing in a ring,
  With the merry, merry pipe, and the tabour, and the horn,
And the timbrel so clear, and the lute with dulcet string,
  Then round about the oak they go till peeping of the morn.

Down yonder glade two lovers steal, to shun the fairy queen,
  Who frowns upon their plighted vows, and jealous is of me,
That yester eve I lighted them, along the dewy green,
  To seek the purple flower whose juice from all her spells can free.

And now to punish me, she keeps afar her jocund band,
  With the merry, merry pipe, and the tabour, and the lute;
If I creep near yonder oak she will wave her fairy wand,
  And to me the dance will cease, and the music all be mute.

Oh! had I but that purple flower whose leaves her charms can foil,
  And knew like fays to draw the juice, and throw it on the wind,
I 'd be her slave no longer, nor the traveller beguile,
  And help all faithful lovers, nor fear the fairy kind!

But soon the vapour of the woods will wander afar,
  And the fickle moon will fade, and the stars disappear,
Then, cheerless will they be, though they fairies are,
  If I with my pale light come not near!

SONG OF A SPIRIT.

In the sightless air I dwell,
On the sloping sunbeams play;
Delve the cavern's inmost cell,
Where never yet did daylight stray.

I dive beneath the green sea-waves,
And gambol in the briny deeps;
Skim every shore that Neptune laves,
From Lapland's plains to India's steeps.

Oft I mount with rapid force,
Above the wide earth's shadowy zone;
Follow the day-star's flaming course,
Through realms of space to thought unknown;

And listen to celestial sounds
That swell in air, unheard of men,
As I watch my nightly rounds
O'er woody steep and silent glen.

Under the shade of waving trees,
On the green bank of fountain clear,
At pensive eve I sit at ease,
While dying music murmurs near.

And oft, on point of airy clift
That hangs upon the western main,
I watch the gay tints passing swift,
And twilight veil the liquid plain.

Then, when the breeze has sunk away,
And Ocean scarce is heard to lave,
For me the sea-nymphs softly play
Their dulcet shells beneath the wave.

Y*

Their dulcet shells ! — I hear them now ;
  Slow swells the strain upon mine ear ;
Now faintly falls — now warbles low,
  Till rapture melts into a tear.

The ray that silvers o'er the dew,
  And trembles through the leafy shade,
And tints the scene with softer hue,
  Calls me to rove the lonely glade ;

Or hie me to some ruin'd tower,
  Faintly shown by moonlight gleam,
When the lone wanderer owns my power,
  In shadows dire that substance seem ;

In thrilling sounds that murmur woe,
  And pausing silence make more dread ;
In music breathing from below
  Sad, solemn strains, that wake the dead.

Unseen I move — unknown am fear'd ;
  Fancy's wildest dreams I weave ;
And oft by bards my voice is heard
  To die along the gales of eve.

MRS. HENRY ROLLS.

I AM not able to give any account at all of this lady. The following productions have been extracted from common-place books: the poetry, however, is any thing but common-place.

SIGHS.

There is a sigh — that half supprest,
    Seems scarce to heave the bosom fair;
It rises from the spotless breast,
    The first fair dawn of tender care.

There is a sigh —so soft, so sweet,
    It breathes not from the lip of woe;
'T is heard where conscious lovers meet.
    Whilst yet untold young passions glow.

There is a sigh — short, deep and strong,
    That on the lip of rapture dies;
It floats mild evening's shade along,
    When meet the fond consenting eyes.

There is a sigh — that speaks regret,
    Yet seems scarce conscious of its pain;
It tells of bliss remember'd yet,
    Of bliss that ne'er must wake again.

There is a sigh — that, deeply breathed,
    Bespeaks the bosom's secret woe;
It says the flowers which Love had wreathed,
    Are wither'd, ne'er again to blow.

There is a sigh — that slowly swells,
   Then deeply breathes its load of care ;
It speaks that in that bosom dwells
   That last, worst pang, fond love's despair.

SMILES.

What is that smile that o'er the cheek
   Of artless blooming childhood strays ;
That revels in the dimple sleek —
   That charms the mother's tender gaze ?

'T is the bright sun of April's morn,
   That rises with unsullied ray ;
Nor marks the clouds, that swift are borne,
   To wrap in shades the future day !

What is that soft, that languid smile,
   That mingles with a tender sigh ;
Light spreads the timid blush the while,
   And sweetly sinks the melting eye ?

'T is the bright dew-drop on the rose,
   Sweet remnant of the early shower,
That will its ripen'd leaves unclose,
   And to full fragrance spread the flower !

What is that smile, whose rapturous glow
   Passion's impetuous breast inspires,
Whilst Pleasure's gaudy blossoms blow,
   And the eye beams with guilty fires ?

'T is the volcano's baleful blaze
   That pours around a fatal light ;
Whose victim dies that stops to gaze ;
   Whence safety is but found in flight !

Whence is that sad, that transient smile
  That dawns upon the lip of woe;
That checks the deep-drawn sigh awhile,
  And stays the tear that starts to flow ?

'T is but a veil cast o'er the heart,
  When youth's gay dreams have pass'd away
When joy's faint lingering rays depart,
  And the last gleams of hope decay !

What is that bright, that fearful smile,
  Quick flashing o'er the brow of care ;
When fades each fruit of mental toil,
  And nought remains to check despair ?

'T is the wild lurid lightning's gleam,
  Swift bursting from a stormy cloud ;
That spreads a bright destructive beam,
  Then sinks into its sable shroud !

What is that smile, calm, fix'd at last,
  On the hoar brow of reverend age,
When the world's changing scenes are past,
  And nearly clos'd life's varied page ?

'T is the rich glowing western beam,
  Bright spreading o'er the dark'ning skies ;
That shows, by its mild parting gleam,
  A cloudless heavenly morn shall rise !

THE WARRIORS' SONG.

Fill high the bowl ! 't is perhaps the last
  The kindred warriors e'er may drain !
Oh, when to-morrow's fight is past,
  How few to pledge it may remain !
35

Fill high the bowl ! 't is perhaps the last
  That Beauty's hand may yield to thine!
Oh, when it o'er her lip has pass'd,
  It gives a joy more sweet than wine.

Fill high the bowl! 't is perhaps the last
  That will beneath this roof be crown'd;
Soon the wild breeze that murmurs past
  May sweep its ruin'd wall around.

Fill high the bowl! 't is perhaps the last
  In which we hail our fathers' fame ;
Oh, when 't is by our children pass'd,
  May added glories gild their name !

Fill high the bowl ! 't is perhaps the last —
  In it come pledge the hero's grave !
For him Death's pang, ere felt, is past,
  It lingers only to the slave.

LADY BURRELL

Wrote two volumes of poems, in 1793. They display considerable liveliness of fancy, but are occasionally coarse and vulgar. The two poems which the reader finds below are about the best in the collection.

CHLOE AND MYRA.

Chloe is elegant and pretty,
  But silly and affected;
Myra is sensible and witty,
  And by the wise respected.

When pretty Chloe I behold,
  I think myself her lover;
But ere I have my passion told,
  Her failings I discover.

When Myra talks, I'm pleased to hear,
  And venerate her mind:
But in her face no charms appear,
  My wavering heart to bind.

Blindfold I should to Myra run,
  And swear to love her ever;
Yet when the bandage was undone,
  Should only think her clever.

With the full usage of my eyes,
  I Chloe should decide for;
But when she talks, I *her* despise,
  Whom, dumb, I could have died for!

My ear or eye must tortur'd be
If I make choice of either ;
'T is therefore best I should agree —
Ladies ! —to marry neither !

TO EMMA.

Why, pretty rogue ! do you protest
The trick of stealing you detest?
'T is what you are doing every day,
Either in earnest or in play.
Cupid and you, 't is said, are cousins,
(*Au fait* in stealing hearts by dozens,)
Who make no more of shooting sparks,
Than schoolboys do of wounding larks ;
Nay, what is worse, 't is my belief,
Though known to be an arrant thief,
Such powers of witchcraft are your own,
That Justice slumbers on her throne ;
And should you be arraign'd in court
For practising this cruel sport,
In spite of all the plaintiff's fury
Your smile would bribe both judge and jury.

LUCY AIKIN,

THE daughter of Dr. John Aikin, and niece of Mrs. Barbauld, seems to have inherited no small share of the genius of her family. Miss Aikin has been engaged in various literary undertakings, in none of which perhaps has she been more successful than in her Poetry for Children, which is, probably, the most difficult style of verse that can be attempted. Miss Aikin very ably avoids a too great simplicity on the one hand, and a too refined diction on the other: and thus grasps the youthful mind with a sure hold.

THE BEGGAR MAN.

Around the fire, one winter night,
  The farmer's rosy children sat;
The faggot lent its blazing light,
  And jokes went round, and careless chat.

When, hark! a gentle hand they hear
  Low tapping at the bolted door;
And thus to gain their willing ear,
  A feeble voice was heard t' implore: —

" Cold blows the blast across the moor:
  The sleet drives hissing in the wind:
Yon toilsome mountain lies before;
  A dreary treeless waste behind.

" My eyes are weak and dim with age;
  No road, no path, can I descry;
And these poor rags ill stand the rage
  Of such a keen inclement sky.

z

" So faint I am — these tottering feet
    No more my feeble frame can bear ;
My sinking heart forgets to beat,
    And drifting snows my tomb prepare.

" Open your hospitable door :
    And shield me from the biting blast ;
Cold, cold it blows across the moor
    The weary moor that I have pass'd ! "

With hasty step the farmer ran,
    And close beside the fire they place
The poor half-frozen beggar-man,
    With shaking limbs and pallid face.

The little children flocking came,
    And warm'd his stiffening hands in theirs ;
And busily the good old dame
    A comfortable mess prepares.

Their kindness cheer'd his drooping soul ;
    And slowly down his wrinkled cheek
The big round tears were seen to roll,
    And told the thanks he could not speak.

The children, too, began to sigh,
    And all their merry chat was o'er ;
And yet they felt, they knew not why,
    More glad than they had done before.

This last verse has quite the manner and spirit of Wordsworth : indeed, the whole composition is full of the finest and
most tender feeling.

As a sample of the clever manner in which Miss Aikin combines information with amusement, I select her little poem called

ARABIA.

O'er Arabia's desert sands
  The patient camel walks ;
Mid lonely caves and rocky lands
  The fell hyæna stalks.
On the cool and shady hills
  Coffee shrubs and tamarinds grow,
Headlong fall the welcome rills
  Down the fruitful dells below.

The fragrant myrrh and healing balm
  Perfume the passing gale ;
Thick hung with dates, the spreading palm
  Tow'rs o'er the peopled vale.
Locusts oft, a living cloud,
  Hover in the darken'd air ;
Like a torrent dashing loud,
  Bringing famine and despair.

And often o'er the level waste
  The stifling hot winds fly ;
Down falls the swain with trembling haste,
  The gasping cattle die.
Shepherd people on the plain
  Pitch their tents and wander free ;
Wealthy cities they disdain,
  Poor, — yet blest with liberty.

MRS. AMELIA OPIE.

THIS estimable lady, who is a member of the Society of
Friends, is chiefly known for her admirable prose stories, in
which is contained a pure, simple, and sweet morality, not surpassed by any writer in our literature.   She, however, published,
in 1802, a volume of miscellaneous Poems, and, in 1834, a work
entitled " *Lays for the Dead*," both of which are characterised
by great tenderness and grace of feeling.   Her song of *The Orphan Boy* is one of the most touching productions contained in
our language.

THE ORPHAN BOY'S TALE.

Stay, Lady, stay for mercy's sake,
    And hear a helpless orphan's tale ;
Ah ! sure my looks must pity wake,
    'T is want that makes my cheek so pale.
Yet I was once a mother's pride,
    And my brave father's hope and joy ;
But in the Nile's proud fight he died,
    And I am now an orphan boy.

Poor foolish child ! how pleas'd was I,
    When news of Nelson's victory came,
Along the crowded streets to fly,
    And see the lighted windows flame !
To force me home my mother sought,
    She could not bear to see my joy ;
For with my father's life 't was bought,
    And made me a poor orphan boy.

The people's shouts were long and loud,
　My mother shuddering closed her ears ;
" Rejoice, rejoice," still cried the crowd,
　My mother answer'd with her tears.
" Why are you crying thus," said I,
　" While others laugh and shout with joy ?"
She kiss'd me — and with such a sigh !
　She call'd me her poor orphan boy.

" What is an orphan boy ?" I cried,
　As in her face I look'd and smil'd ;
My mother through her tears replied,
　" You 'll know too soon, ill fated child !"
And now they 've toll'd my mother's knell,
　And I 'm no more a parent's joy,
O Lady ! I have learnt too well
　What 't is to be an orphan boy.

O were I by your bounty fed !
　— Nay, gentle Lady, do not chide, —
Trust me, I mean to earn my bread ;
　The sailor's orphan boy has pride.
Lady, you weep ! — ha ! — this to me ?
　You 'll give me clothing, food, employ ?
Look down, dear parents ! look and see
　Your happy, happy orphan boy.

It is a fault of the Female Poets of the last century that they expended their strength rather on sentiment than on feeling. This makes most of the verse which they produced, appear tame and unimpassioned ; and it is a reason, perhaps the chief reason, why so many of their names have nearly passed into oblivion : for sentiment is, in its very nature, evanescent : and, even when painted in its brightest colours, lasts but a little while. It is a phosphorescent flame, flashing for a moment through the mental atmosphere, but giving neither warmth nor light : whilst true passion is a ray shot from the everlasting sun of the spiritual

36　　　　　　　z*

firmament, shedding a glow and a brightness upon all time. Of
this true sterling sort is the pathos of Mrs. Opie.

SONG.

Go, youth belov'd, in distant glades
New friends, new hopes, new joys to find!
Yet sometimes deign, 'midst fairer maids,
To think on her thou leav'st behind.
Thy love, thy fate, dear youth, to share
Must never be my happy lot;
But thou mayst grant this humble prayer,
Forget me not, forget me not.

Yet, should the thought of my distress
Too painful to thy feelings be,
Heed not the wish I now express,
Nor ever deign to think on me :
But, oh! if grief thy steps attend,
If want, if sickness be thy lot,
And thou require a soothing friend,
Forget me not, forget me not!

From Mrs. Opie's numerous devotional poems I extract the
subjoined

HYMN.

There's not a leaf within the bower ;
There's not a bird upon the tree ;
There's not a dewdrop on the flower,
But bears the impress, Lord! of Thee.

Thy hand the varied leaf design'd,
And gave the bird its thrilling tone :
Thy power the dewdrop's tints combined,
Till like a diamond's blaze they shone.

Yes: dewdrops, leaves, and birds, and all,
    The smallest like the greatest things;
The sea's vast space, the earth's wide ball,
    Alike proclaim Thee King of Kings.

But man alone to bounteous Heaven
    Thanksgiving's conscious strains can raise;
To favour'd man alone 't is given
    To join the angelic choir in praise.

Mrs. Opie's poems bear fresh evidence to the truth of an
assertion more than once made in this work, that woman's moral
sentiments are generally in advance of man's. Those who doubt
the fact will do well to remember how continually man's verse
celebrates the infernal glories of war, the cruel excitements of the
chase, or the selfish pleasures of bacchanalian enjoyment; and,
on the other hand, how unceasingly woman's verse exposes the
wickedness and folly of such pursuits. Very rarely do we find
in the writings of the male sex, passages like the following, though
we continually see similar sentiments in the works of our female
writers : —

Alas! to think one Christian soul
    At War's red shrine can worship still,
Nor heed, though seas of carnage roll,
    Those awful words — " THOU SHALT NOT KILL ! "

O Lord of all, and Prince of Peace,
    Speed, speed the long-predicted day,
When War throughout the world shall cease,
    And Love shall hold eternal sway !

Mrs. Opie's *Lays for the Dead* is a book of truest beauty : and,
although the perusal of it resembles (from the mournfulness of its
subjects) a visit to a churchyard, the effect it produces upon us is
of a most pleasing character. It hushes all unquiet emotion ;
bids the cares of earth far into the distance ; and awakens a calm
sweet pensiveness of feeling, which nothing could make us wish

to change. We seem to converse with the Past and the Departed, and to stand on the very shore of the great ocean of Eternity.

It is very difficult to select fair samples of this book; for it is *as a whole* that its exquisite beauty is apparent: but I nevertheless subjoin two extracts, to show the pure tone which marks the volume.

REMEMBRANCE.

Where'er I stray, thou dear departed one,
I see thy form, thy voice I seem to hear!
And though thou art to brighter regions gone,
Thy smile still charms my eye, thy tones my ear!

Whene'er adown thy favourite walk I go,
Still, still I feel the pressure of thy arm;
And oh! so strong the sweet illusions grow,
I shun, I loathe whatever breaks the charm.

In vain I 'm urged to join the social scene;
This silent shade alone has charms for me:
I love to be where I with thee have been;
And home, though desolate, is full of thee!

It is not difficult to perceive that the foregoing, as well as the following, lines refer to her excellent husband, the late John Opie, of the Royal Academy. It is impossible for sentiment to be more exquisitely feminine than this:

A LAMENT.

There was an eye, whose partial glance
Could ne'er my numerous failings see;
There was an ear that heard untired
When others spoke in praise of me.

There was a heart time only taught
With warmer love for me to burn;

A heart whene'er from home I roved
Which fondly pined for my return.

There was a lip which always breathed,
E'en short farewells in tones of sadness ;
There was a voice whose eager sound
My welcome spoke with heartfelt gladness.

There was a mind whose vigorous power
On mine its own effulgence threw,
And called my humble talents forth,
While thence its dearest joys it drew.

There was a love, which for my weal
With anxious fears would overflow ;
Which wept, which pray'd, for me, and sought
From future ills to guard — But now ! —

That eye is closed, and deaf that ear,
That lip and voice are mute for ever;
And cold that heart of anxious love,
Which death alone from mine could sever :

And lost to me that ardent mind,
Which loved my various tasks to see ;
And oh ! of all the praise I gain'd,
His was the dearest far to me !

Now I unloved, uncheer'd, *alone*,
Life's dreary wilderness must tread,
Till He who heals the broken heart
In mercy bids me join the dead.

O Thou ! who from thy throne on high,
Can'st heed the mourner's deep distress ;
O Thou, who hear'st the widow's cry,
Thou ! Father of the fatherless !

Though now I am a faded leaf,
That 's sever'd from its parent tree,
And thrown upon a stormy tide,
Life's awful tide that leads to Thee ! —

Still, gracious Lord ! the voice of praise
Shall spring spontaneous from my breast ;
Since, though I tread a weary way,
I trust that he I mourn is blest.

JOANNA BAILLIE.

THIS distinguished lady, in many respects the most remarkable of our Female Poets, has attempted almost every kind of verse, and has succeeded in all she has tried. Lyrical, social, devotional, heroic, and domestic poems have alike proceeded from her pen, and in strains of equal beauty : while her muse has undeniably accomplished

> " Things unattempted yet in prose or rhyme "

by any other writer of her sex. Her *Plays on the Passions* would have been marvellous productions, even had they been the work of a *Man*, of long and varied experience : but they become infinitely more so when we reflect that they were composed by a young *Female* writer, whose sex and station must have kept her comparatively secluded from the world of active life and emotion. Sir Walter Scott had, therefore, good reasons for saying —

> " That Avon's swans, while rang the grove
> With Monfort's hate and Basil's love, —
> Awakening at the inspired strain,
> Deem'd their own Shakspere lived again."

I think that Mrs. Baillie may be said to be the most purely and serenely intellectual of all our Female Poets. There is a clearness, a plainness, a massiveness in her genius, which reminds one of the simple but severe perfection of a Doric column. Strength rather than elegance, chasteness rather than beauty, and proportion rather than grace, distinguish her productions. I do not mean to say that they want warmth ; no verse can be more *living* and *thrilling* than hers is : but I mean that they have none of that glare which is often mistaken for true poetic fire, but is in fact

only the unreal brilliancy of an *ignis fatuus*.   There is nothing
phosphorescent or stage-firelike in Mrs. Baillie's poetry : it is the
calm, soft, refreshing, wholesome sunshine of a clear spring
morning.   Sir Walter Scott has likened Mrs. Baillie's muse to
Shakspere's ; I venture to think that it is more like Chaucer's.

The great characteristics of Mrs. Baillie's general style are
vigour, clearness, and simplicity.   Nothing can exceed the force
and transparency of her compositions.   I do not think that a
strained, turgid, or unintelligible expression is to be found in her
writings : every thought is plain, every image distinct, every
conclusion unmistakeable.   Much as Mrs. Baillie has published,
I cannot call to mind a single hurried idea or undigested sentiment.
We never meet with noise or bustle in her works : she is not at
all of the steam-engine class of poets : everything is calm,
unconscious, and serene.   Deep as may be the emotions which
she describes, she exhibits no symptoms of self disturbance.   She
is *above* her subject, just as a Shakspere or a Goethe is.   There
is none of the strained sentimentalism, none of the spasmodic
effort, that we find in the productions of second-rate minds ;
but with a firm strong hand she grasps the very heart of passion,
and lays its inmost secrets bare.

Before I speak of Mrs. Baillie's chief poetical efforts, her
Tragedies, I would direct the reader's attention briefly to her
miscellaneous poems.

A good idea of her simple style and natural sentiments will be
gathered from the following lines

TO A CHILD.

Whose imp art thou, with dimpled cheek,
    And curly pate and merry eye,
And arm and shoulder round and sleek,
    And soft and fair ? — thou urchin sly !

What boots it who, with sweet caresses,
    First called thee his, — or squire or hind ?
Since thou in every wight that passes,
    Dost now a friendly playmate find.

Thy downcast glances, grave but cunning,
  As fringed eyelids rise and fall ;
Thy shyness swiftly from me running,
  Is infantine coquetry all.

But far afield thou hast not flown ,
  With mocks and threats, half lisped, half spoken,
I feel thee pulling at my gown,
  Of right good will thy simple token.

And thou must laugh and wrestle, too,
  A mimic warfare with me waging ;
To make, as wily lovers do,
  Thy after-kindness more engaging.

The wilding rose, sweet as thyself,
  And new-cropt daisies are thy treasure ;
I 'd gladly part with worldly pelf
  To taste again thy youthful pleasure.

But yet for all thy merry look,
  Thy frisks and wiles, the time is coming
When thou shalt sit in cheerless nook
  Thy weary spell or horn-book thumbing.

Well, let it be ! — through weal and woe,
  Thou know'st not now thy future range ;
Life is a motley shifting show,
  And thou a thing of hope and change.

As a further specimen of Mrs. Baillie's womanly tenderness of feeling, and also of her terse and concentrative style, I may quote her poem entitled —

A MOTHER TO HER WAKING INFANT.

Now in thy dazzled, half-oped eye,
Thy curled nose and lip awry,

37   AA

Uphoisted arms and noddling head,
And little chin with crystal spread,
Poor helpless thing! what do I see
That I should sing of thee?

From thy poor tongue no accents come,
Which can but rub thy toothless gum:
Small understanding boasts thy face;
Thy shapeless limbs nor step nor grace:
A few short words thy feats may tell;
And yet I love thee well.

When wakes the sudden bitter shriek,
And redder swells thy little cheek;
When rattled keys thy woes beguile,
And through thy eyelids gleams the smile;
Still for thy weakly self is spent
Thy little silly plaint.

But when thy friends are in distress,
Thou 'lt laugh and chuckle ne'ertheless;
Nor with kind sympathy be smitten
Though all are sad but thee and kitten;
Yet, puny varlet that thou art,
Thou twitchest at the heart.

Thy smooth round cheek so soft and warm;
Thy pinky hand and dimpled arm;
Thy silken locks that scantly peep,
With gold-tipp'd ends, where circles deep,
Around thy neck in harmless grace
So soft and sleekly hold their place,
Might harder hearts with kindness fill,
And gain our right good will.

Each passing clown bestows his blessing,
Thy mouth is worn with old wives' kissing:
E'en lighter looks the gloomy eye

Of surly sense when thou art by ;
And yet, I think, whoe'er they be,
They love thee not like me.

Perhaps when time shall add a few
Short months to thee, thou 'lt love me too ;
And after that, through life's long way
Become my sure and cheering stay ;
Wilt care for me and be my hold,
When I am weak and old.

Thou 'lt listen to my lengthen'd tale,
And pity me when I am frail * —
— But see ! the sweepy swimming fly,
Upon the window takes thine eye.
Go to thy little senseless play ;
Thou dost not heed my lay.

Mrs. Baillie takes high rank as a *Lyric* poet. Her Songs and Hymns have singular merit. For conciseness and vigour of expression they stand almost alone amongst the lyrical productions of the period. There is a Scott-like spirit in the following song, from *The Beacon :* —

Up ! quit thy bower, late wears the hour ;
Long have the rooks caw'd round thy tower ;
On flower and tree, loud hums the bee ;
The wilding kid sports merrily :
A day so bright, so fresh, so clear,
Shineth when good fortune 's near.

Up ! lady fair, and braid thy hair,
And rouse thee in the breezy air ;
The lulling stream, that soothed thy dream,
Is dancing in the sunny beam ;
And hours so sweet, so bright, so gay,
Will waft good fortune on its way.

* *Feeble.*

Up ! time will tell ; the friar's bell
Its service sound hath chiméd well ;
The aged crone keeps house alone,
And reapers to the field are gone ;
The active day so boon and bright,
May bring good fortune ere the night.

As a *sentimental* song-writer Mrs. Baillie is perhaps not so successful. Her style is too intense and terse for this species of composition : and she is apparently deficient in that mere prettiness of fancy which seems essential to a poet of this class. She can, however, at times be very sweetly plaintive, as we may see by the following

SONG.

What voice is this, thou evening gale !
That mingles with thy rising wail ;
And as it passes sadly seems
The faint return of youthful dreams ?

Though now its strain is wild and drear,
Blythe was it once, as skylark's cheer —
Sweet as the night-bird's sweetest song —
Dear as the lisp of infant's tongue.

It was the voice at whose sweet flow
The heart did beat and cheek did glow,
And lip did smile, and eye did weep,
And motion'd love the measure keep.

Oft be thy sound, soft gale of even,
Thus to my wistful fancy given ;
And as I list the swelling strain,
The dead shall seem to live again.

Mrs. Baillie's genius is seen to great advantage in her devotional Poems. Her peculiar compression of thought and strength of style are very effective in this kind of composition. The sens

of religion, too, is in her very serene and lofty. The two following hymns seem to me among the best of such productions : —

I.

O God ! who mad'st earth, sea, and air,
And living creatures, free and fair,
Thy hallow'd praise is everywhere,
  Halleluja !

All blended in the swelling song
Are wise and simple, weak and strong,
Sweet woman's voice and infant's tongue,
  Halleluja !

Yea, woods and winds and waves convey
To the rapt ear a hymn, and say
" He who hath made us we obey,
  Halleluja !"

II.

Up ! sluggard soul ! awake and raise
To thy blest Lord a song of praise,
Who lifts thee from the gloomy grave
 When low on earth thou liest, —
To Him who lived and died to save,
 Hosanna in the highest !

To Him, thy friend of friends, whose love
Invites thee to a home above,
When thou, the world's poor outcast slave,
 In grief and anguish criest, —
To Him who lived and died to save,
 Hosanna in the highest !

His love a living stream hath found
For pilgrims faint on barren ground,
Their parched and languid souls to lave,
 When earthly streams are driest, —
To Him who lived and died to save,
 Hosanna in the highest !

AA*

In the *Metrical Legends* Mrs. Baillie strongly reminds the
reader of Scott. There is, it is true, more reflection and more
seriousness in them than in Scott's poems; but still the likeness
is great. Her *Christopher Columbus* is a very spirited, and,
withal, very affecting poem; the following passage seems to me
exceedingly fine : —

THE GRAVE OF COLUMBUS.

Silence, solemn, awful, deep,
Doth in that hall of death her empire keep;
Save when at times the hollow pavement, smote
    By solitary wanderer's foot, amain
From lofty dome and arch and aisle remote,
    A circling loud response receives again.
The stranger starts to hear the growing sound,
    And sees the blazon'd trophies waving near;
" Ha ! tread my feet so near that sacred ground !"
He stops and bows his head : —" Columbus resteth here !"

Some ardent youth, perhaps, ere from his home
He launch his vent'rous bark, will hither come;
Read fondly o'er and o'er his graven name,
With feelings keenly touch'd,—with heart of flame,
Till wrapp'd in fancy's wild delusive dream,
Times past, and long forgotten, present seem;
To his charm'd ear the east-wind rising shrill,
Seems through the Hero's shroud to whistle still.
The clock's deep pendulum swinging, through the blast
Sounds like the rocking of the lofty mast;
While fitful gusts rave like his clam'rous band
Mix'd with the accents of his high command.
Slowly the stripling quits the pensive scene,
And burns, and sighs, and weeps to be what he has been.

Oh! who shall lightly say that fame
Is nothing but an empty name !
Whilst in that sound there is a charm

The nerves to brace, the heart to warm ;
As thinking of the mighty dead,
    The young from slothful couch will start,
And vow, with lifted hands outspread,
    Like them to act a noble part.

Oh ! who shall lightly say that fame
Is nothing but an empty name !
When but for those our mighty dead,
    All ages past a blank would be,
Sunk in oblivion's murky bed,
    A desert bare, a shipless sea !
They are the distant objects seen,—
The lofty marks of what hath been.

Oh ! who shall lightly say that fame
Is nothing but an empty name !
When memory of the mighty dead
    To earth-worn pilgrims' wistful eye
The brightest rays of cheering shed
    That point to immortality ?

A twinkling speck, but fix'd and bright,
To guide us through the dreary night,
    Each hero shines, and lures the soul
    To gain the distant happy goal.
For is there one who musing o'er the grave
Where lies interr'd the good, the wise, the brave,
Can poorly think beneath the mouldering heap,
That noble being shall for ever sleep ?
" No !" saith the generous heart, and proudly swells,—
" Though his cered corpse lies here, with GOD his spirit
    dwells !"

But it is of course by her Plays that Mrs. Baillie will hereafter
be chiefly known. To these productions, therefore, we must turn
for our best view of her genius.

I quite agree with the opinion expressed by an eminent critic that " no female has ever struck at once into so high a vein of poetry, or obtained so much success, in the noblest and most consummate branch of poetic composition as Mrs. Baillie has done in her Tragic Dramas." The aim, the tone, the style and the moral are alike lofty, fresh, and pure. Intensely natural, the emotions she depicts are yet always free from that familiar *nearness* which makes passion coarse and vulgar. Though casting aside poetical *decorations*, she ever writes in the *spirit* of poetry. She disdains the use of the conventionalisms which weak writers have employed to depict impassioned feeling, and, with the true originality of genius, chooses rather to trace the passions to their sources for herself, and describe them as she finds them.

To acquire a just idea of Mrs. Baillie's merit, we must recollect what was the aspect of dramatic literature when she produced her first volume of plays. The German school was then in full vogue. Kotzebue and his vicious style were on the very pinnacle of public favour. Rant, fustian, violence, noise and heroics were the chief ingredients of dramatic composition, and passion had become lost in contortion. Great, then, must have been the genius that first saw the deep mistake of this departure from nature : and resolute the spirit that could at once and alone set itself to oppose so strong a tide of error. I see in Mrs. Baillie, therefore, not merely a powerful and successful dramatist, but a great literary reformer : if not the *very* first, at least *amongst* the first, of those who once again placed our poetry under the dominion of nature. She preceded and heralded the school of Wordsworth ; and may be safely said to have done more for the restoration of our national drama than any living writer.

It is not necessary to speak much of Mrs. Baillie's Plays as connected with their fitness for theatrical representation. The success which has attended the performance of *The Separation* and *Henriquez* clearly shows that with performers sedulously bent on carrying out the author's design, and willing to sacrifice momentary applause for ultimate appreciation, Mrs. Baillie's Plays would be as forcible in action as they are striking on perusal. But our Stage is too melodramatic for this at present : and possibly the taste of the public too melodramatic also. There is too great a love for blue-fire, and tin-foil, and broadsword-combats as yet: when once this taste for mere show is rendered subservient to the higher effects of moral beauty and fitness, the Plays on the Passions cannot fail to become popular upon the Stage.

It may be as well to say, however, that all Joanna Baillie's poetical gifts are seen to the greatest advantage in her Plays. Her clear style, energetic diction, and keen direct vision are there quite in place, and contribute very materially to the success which she undoubtedly achieves. It is impossible to dispute the power and dramatic skill of the following scene from *De Monfort*.

[DE MONFORT is revealing to his sister JANE his hatred of REZENVELT, which at last hurries him into the crime of murder.]

DE MONFORT.

No more, my sister, urge me not again ;
My secret troubles cannot be revealed.
From all participation of its thoughts
My heart recoils : I pray thee be contented.

JANE.

What, must I, like a distant humble friend,
Observe thy restless eye, and gait disturbed,
In timid silence, whilst with yearning heart
I turn aside to weep ? O no ! De Monfort !
A nobler task thy noble mind will give ;
Thy true intrusted friend I still shall be.

DE MONFORT.

Ah, Jane, forbear ! I cannot e'en to thee.

JANE.

Then fie upon it ! fie upon it, Monfort !
There was a time when e'en with murder stain'd,
Had it been possible that such dire deed
Could e'er have been the crime of one so piteous,
Thou wouldst have told it me.

38

DE MONFORT.

So would I now — but ask of this no more.
All other trouble but the one I feel
I had disclosed to thee.   I pray thee spare me.
It is the secret weakness of my nature.

JANE.

Then secret let it be : I urge no farther.
The eldest of our valiant father's hopes,
So sadly orphan'd, side by side we stood,
Like two young trees, whose boughs, in early strength,
Screen the weak saplings of the rising grove,
And brave the storm together —
I have so long, as if by nature's right,
Thy bosom's inmate and adviser been,
I thought through life I should have so remain'd,
Nor ever known a change.   Forgive me, Monfort,
A humbler station will I take by thee :
The close attendant of thy wandering steps ;
The cheerer of this home, by strangers sought :
The soother of those griefs I must not know,
This is mine office now : I ask no more.

DE MONFORT.

Oh Jane ! thou dost constrain me with thy love !
Would I could tell it thee !

JANE.

Thou shalt not tell me.   Nay, I'll stop mine ears,
Nor from the yearnings of affection wring
What shrinks from utterance.   Let it pass, my brother.
I'll stay by thee : I'll cheer thee, comfort thee :
Pursue with thee the study of some art,
Or nobler science, that compels the mind
To steady thought progressive, driving forth
All floating, wild, unhappy fantasies :
Till thou, with brow unclouded, smil'st again,
Like one who from dark visions of the night,

When th' active soul within its lifeless cell
Holds its own world, with dreadful fancy press'd
Of some dire, terrible, or murd'rous deed,
Wakes to the dawning morn, and blesses heaven.

DE MONFORT.

It will not pass away : 't will haunt me still.

JANE.

Ah ! say not so, for I will haunt thee too ;
And be to it so close an adversary,
That though I wrestle darkling with the fiend,
I shall o'ercome it.

DE MONFORT.

Thou most generous woman!
Why do I treat thee thus ? It should not be —
And yet I cannot — O that cursed villain !
He will not let me be the man I would.

JANE.

What say'st thou, Monfort ?   Oh ! what words are these ?
They have awaked my soul to dreadful thoughts.
I do beseech thee speak !
    [*He shakes his head, and turns from her : she following him.*]
By the affection thou didst ever bear me,
By the dear memory of our infant days ;
By kindred living ties, ay, and by those
Who sleep i' the tomb, and cannot call to thee,
I do conjure thee speak.
                    [*He waves her off with his hand.*]
                Ha ! wilt thou not ?
Then, if affection, most unwearied love,
Tried early, long, and never wanting found,
O'er generous man hath more authority,
More rightful power than crown and sceptre give,
I do command thee.
                [*He sinks into a chair, greatly agitated.*]

De Monfort, do not thus resist my love.
Here I entreat thee on my bended knees.

                                        [*Kneeling.*]
Alas ! my brother !
 [DE MONFORT *starts up, raises her, and kneels at her feet.*]

DE MONFORT.

Thus let him kneel who should the abased be,
And at thine honoured feet confession make.
I 'll tell thee all — but oh ! thou wilt despise me.
For in my breast a raging passion burns,
To which thy soul no sympathy will own.
A passion which hath made my nightly couch
A place of torment ; and the light of day,
With the gay intercourse of social man,
Feel like th' oppressive airless pestilence.
O Jane ! thou wilt despise me.

JANE.

      Say not so :
I never can despise thee, gentle brother.
A lover's jealousy and hopeless pangs
No kindly heart contemns.

DE MONFORT.

     A lover, say'st thou ?
No, it is hate ! black, lasting, deadly hate ;
Which thus hath driven me forth from kindred peace,
From social pleasure, from my native home,
To be a sullen wanderer on the earth,
Avoiding all men, cursing and accurs'd.

JANE.

De Monfort, this is fiendlike, frightful, terrible !
What being, by the Almighty Father formed,
Of flesh and blood, created even as thou,
Could in thy breast such horrid tempest wake,
Who art thyself his fellow ?

Unknit thy brows, and spread those wrath-clench'd hands :
Some sprite accurs'd within thy bosom mates
To work thy ruin.   Strive with it, my brother !
Strive bravely with it : drive it from thy breast :
'T is the degrader of a noble heart ;
Curse it, and bid it part.

DE MONFORT.

It will not part.   I 've lodged it here too long ;
With my first cares I felt its rankling touch,
I loath'd him when a boy.

JANE.

Who didst thou say ?

DE MONFORT.

Oh ! that detested Rezenvelt ?
E'en in our early sports, like two young whelps
Of hostile breed, instinctively averse,
Each 'gainst the other pitch'd his ready pledge,
And frown'd defiance.   As we onward pass'd
From youth to man's estate, his narrow art,
And envious gibing malice, poorly veil'd
In the affected carelessness of mirth,
Still more detestable and odious grew.
There is no living being on this earth
Who can conceive the malice of his soul,
With all his gay and damned merriment,
To those, by fortune or by merit plac'd
Above his paltry self.   When, low in fortune,
He look'd upon the state of prosperous men,
As nightly birds, rous'd from their murky holes,
Do scowl and chatter at the light of day,
I could endure it ; even as we bear
The' impotent bite of some half-trodden worm,
I could endure it.   But when honours came,
And wealth and new-got titles fed his pride ;
Whilst flattering knaves did trumpet forth his praise,

BB

And grov'ling idiots grinn'd applauses on him;
Oh! then I could no longer suffer it!
It drove me frantic. — What! what would I give!
What would I give to crush the bloated toad,
So rankly do I loathe him!

JANE.

And would thy hatred crush the very man
Who gave to thee that life he might have ta'en?
That life which thou so rashly didst expose
To aim at his! oh! this is horrible!

DE MONFORT.

Ha! thou hast heard it, then? From all the world,
But most of all from thee, I thought it hid.

JANE.

I heard a secret whisper, and resolv'd
Upon the instant to return to thee.
Didst thou receive my letter?

DE MONFORT.

I did! I did! 'twas that which drove me hither.
I could not bear to meet thine eye again.

JANE.

Alas! that, tempted by a sister's tears,
I ever left thy house! These few past months,
These absent months, have brought us all this woe.
Had I remain'd with thee it had not been.
And yet, methinks, it should not move you thus.
You dar'd him to the field; both bravely fought;
He, more adroit, disarm'd you; courteously
Return'd the forfeit sword, which, so return'd,
You did refuse to use against him more;
And then, as says report, you parted friends.

DE MONFORT.

When he disarm'd this curs'd, this worthless hand,
Of its most worthless weapon, he but spar'd
From devilish pride, which now derives a bliss
In seeing me thus fetter'd, sham'd, subjected
With the vile favour of his poor forbearance;
Whilst he securely sits with gibing brow,
And basely baits me, like a muzzled cur
Who cannot turn again.—
Until that day, till that accursed day,
I knew not half the torment of this hell
Which burns within my breast.
Heaven's lightnings blast him !

JANE.

O this is horrible ! Forbear, forbear !
Lest Heaven's vengeance light upon thy head,
For this most impious wish.

DE MONFORT.

Then let it light.
Torments more fell than I have felt already
It cannot send. To be annihilated —
What all men shrink from — to be dust, be nothing,
Were bliss to me, compared to what I am.

There is consummate strength and skill, too, in the following passage from the magnificent play of *Henriquez*.

Henriquez, a favourite general of King Alonzo, moved by strong, but, as it turns out, groundless jealousy, kills his friend, Don Juan. A youth named Antonio is seized on suspicion of having committed the murder, and thrown into prison. Henriquez, stung by overpowering remorse, resolves to explain the true facts of the case. The King has at a former time promised to grant him any favour he may ask from him on the production of a certain ring. At the period fixed for the examination of the supposed culprit, Henriquez suddenly appears in the presence-chamber. The scene is wrought with surpassing power.

[Enter Henriquez, *followed by* Carlos *and* Antonio, *the prisoner, fettered and manacled.]*

KING.

Thou, too, my valiant friend, a suitor here?

HENRIQUEZ.

A humble supplicant.

KING.

Who needs not sue.
Say freely what thou would'st, and it is granted.

HENRIQUEZ.

But what I beg, an earnest boon, must be
Confirmed to me with all solemnity
Before I utter it.

KING.

A strange request!
But that thy services have been to me
Beyond all recompense, and that I know
Thy country's welfare and thy sovereign's honour
Are dear to thee, as thou full well hast prov'd,
I should with some precaution give my word;
But be it so: I say thy suit is granted.

HENRIQUEZ.

Nay, swear it on this sword.

KING.

Where doth this tend? Doubt'st thou my royal word?

HENRIQUEZ.

When honoured lately by your princely presence,
You gave to me this ring with words of favour;
And said if I should e'er, by fortune press'd,
Return the same to you, whatever grace
I then might ask should be conceded to me.

[Giving the ring.]

Receive your royal token: my request
Is that you swear upon my sword to grant
This boon which I shall beg.
    [*Holds sword to the* KING, *who lays his hand upon it.*]

KING.

This sword, this honour'd blade, I know it well;
Which thou in battle from the princely Moor
So valiantly did win: why should I shrink
From any oath that should be sworn on this?
I swear by the fair honour of a soldier,
To grant thy boon, whatever it may be.
Declare it then, Henriquez.
                          [*A pause.*]
              Thou art pale,
And silent, too. I wait upon thy words.

HENRIQUEZ.

My breath forsook me. 'T is a passing weakness:
I have power now. — There is a criminal,
Whose guilt before your Highness in due form
Shall shortly be attested: and my boon
Is, that your Highness will not pardon him,
However strongly you may be inclined
To royal clemency, — however strongly
Entreated so to do.

KING.

This much amazes me. Ever till now
Thou 'st been inclined to mercy, not to blood.

HENRIQUEZ.

Yea, but this criminal, with selfish cruelty,
With black ingratitude, with base disloyalty
To all that sacred is in virtuous ties,
Knitting man's heart to man — What shall I say?
I have no room to breathe
          [*Tearing open his doublet with violence*]
39   BB*

He had a friend,
Ingenuous, faithful, generous and noble :
Even but to look on him had been full warrant
Against the accusing tongue of man or angel,
To all the world beside, — and yet he slew him.
A friend whose fostering love had been the stay,
The guide, the solace of his wayward youth, —
Love steady, tried, unwearied, — yet he slew him.
A friend, who in his best devoted thoughts,
His happiness on earth, his bliss in heaven,
Intwin'd his image, and could nought devise
Of separate good, — and yet he basely slew him ;
Rush'd on him like a ruffian in the dark,
And thrust him forth from life, from light, from nature,
Unwitting, unprepared for the awful change
Death brings to all.   This act, so foul, so damned,
This he hath done : therefore upon his head
Let fall the law's unmitigated justice !

KING.

And wherefore doubt'st thou that from such a man
I will withhold all grace ?   Were he my brother
I would not pardon him.   Produce your criminal.
                    [*Attendants lead forward* ANTONIO.]

HENRIQUEZ.
              [*Motioning with his hand to forbid them.*]
Undo his shackles,
He is innocent !

KING.

What meaneth this ?   Produce your criminal.

HENRIQUEZ.
                              [*Kneeling.*]
My Royal Master, — he is at your feet !

The King endeavours to save Henriquez, but in vain.   He
persists in dying on the scaffold.

MRS. MARGARET HODSON.

(Formerly Miss Holford.)

THIS lady is the author of *Wallace, or the Fight of Falkirk ; Margaret of Anjou ;* and some Miscellaneous Verses, which, I believe, have not yet appeared in a collected form. Her poetical writings display a strong, romantic, vigorous genius, lofty and daring in its flight, and essentially firm and healthy in its constitution. She presents a fine contrast to those gossamer Poetesses who have since appeared among us so frequently. Like Mrs. Baillie, she finds that simplicity is the truest strength : and she never exhibits the slightest leaning towards the rhapsodical, the sentimental, or the spasmodic. Clear in thought and intelligible in style, she is one of the most agreeable Poets we possess. Her narratives flow on as gracefully and smoothly as Scott's : she closely resembles that great writer, indeed, in many respects, although as regards dramatic skill she is certainly superior. Her stories are very skilfully conducted, and a strong chain of interest runs through them from the first page to the last. In her spirited descriptions of " broil and battle," few writers in our language surpass her : and one cannot but feel surprised that a lady of our peaceful age should be so thoroughly imbued with the martial spirit of our warlike ancestors. The fact proves not merely the strength of the human imagination, but also that the imagination is not sexual.

The reader will find ample specimens of Mrs. Hodson's poetical powers in the subjoined extracts.

THE DREAM OF GRÆME.

(From " Wallace.")

Wallace in sober mood revolves
High-soaring hopes and deep resolves :

Sees victory gain'd, the day his own,
A native monarch on the throne, —
And hears his much-loved country shed
A thousand blessings on his head !

'T was a gay dream, — the voice of Græme
    Dispers'd it, and it fled away,
As fly from morning's ruddy beam
    The mists of early day :

As its accents came to Wallace' ear,
They sounded with half their wonted cheer ;
And when he rais'd his speaking eye,
It sparkled with half the usual joy ;
For who so blithe as the gallant Græme,
When he stood on the edge of the hour of fame !
But now a strange unwelcome guest
O'erclouds his brow, and chills his breast ;
His generous heart disdain'd to bear
The ponderous weight of untold care ;
Though half asham'd, his lips confess
His fancy's dreary dreams, his bosom's heaviness.

" Wallace, in many a busy hour
We have look'd on death together :
We have seen the fiercest war-clouds lower,
Stood calm 'mid many an iron-shower,
    And mock'd the pelting weather ;
    And smil'd to see our burnish'd mail
    Turn the thick storm of arrowy hail ;
    For still, wherever Wallace trod,
    My foot as firmly press'd the sod ;
    My heart's first boast, my dearest pride,
    To stand or fall by Wallace' side !
    How wilt thou marvel then to hear,
    That gossip tales and baby fear,
    Sleep's flimsy shades — night's mockeries,
    With magic film delude my eyes,

Till to my heart the future seems
Crowded with sanguine forms, a scene of ghastly dreams.

" Nay, Wallace, smile not on thy friend ;
    'T is pressing on a thorn :
Chide, and thy voice shall not offend ;
    But Græme endures not scorn !

" Of late in great Kincardine's tower,
Subdued by slumber's welcome power,
    In willing thrall I lay ;
When to my eyes a phantom rose,
Which scar'd the angel of repose,
    And fill'd me with dismay :
All shivering, wan, and smear'd with blood,
Close to my couch Sir Patrick stood ;
His pale, pale cheek and clotted hair,
His hollow eyes' unearthly glare,
Appall'd my senses, from my brow
The beads of fear began to flow ;
The phantom shook its gory head —
' Art thou a Græme ? ' it sternly said ;
' Art thou a Græme ? and does thine eye
Shrink to behold war's livery ?
The Fates, enamour'd of our name,
Loudly demand another Græme ;
Thy death-word is pronounc'd on high
The last of all thy fields is nigh !
Farewell, thy task shall soon be o'er ;
We meet ere long, to part no more ! '

" I sprang from my couch as the dawn arose,
    And thought in my restless mind,
That the grizzly forms of vex'd repose
    Would flee from the morning wind ;
And I climb'd to the brow of the upland heath,
To taste of the gale the freshest breath ;
A cloud was on Craig Rossie's brow,

Dark gloom'd Kincardine's towers below ;
And the winding Ruthven's rippling swell
Murmur'd low on mine ear, ' Farewell, farewell!'
Then I thought on thee, and thy loyal tryste,
    And I sprang on my berry-brown steed ;
That it might not be said that Græme was miss'd
    In the hour of Scotland's need ;
But still as I rode, I turn'd me round,
To list to the Ruthven's mournful sound,
And thou canst not think how its voice was dear,
When its last faint murmur met mine ear !
For prophetic was my answering sigh
To the stream which I lov'd in infancy !"

ON MEMORY.

Written at Aix-la-Chapelle.

No ! this is not the land of Memory,
    It is not the home where she dwells;
Though her wandering, wayward votary
    Is ever the thrall of her spells.
Far off were the fetters woven which bind
Still closer and closer the Exile's mind.

Yet this land was the boast of minstrelsy,
    And the song of the Troubadour ;
Where Charlemagne led his chivalry
    To the fields which were fought of yore ;
Still the eye of Fancy may see them glance,
Gilded banner and quivering lance !

But Memory from Fancy turns away,
    She hath wealth of her own to guard ;
And whisperings come to her ear which say
    Sweeter things than the song of the bard.

They are solemn and low, and none can hear
The whispers which come to Memory's ear!

They tell of the dews that brightened the way
    By our earliest footsteps prest;
They tell of the visions hopeful and gay,
    Which were born, and which died, in the breast;
They recall the accents which sweetly spake
To the soul, when the soul was first awake.

In Memory's land springs never a flower,
    Nor the lowliest daisy blooms ;
Ne'er a robin chirps from its russet bower,
    But to call from their silent tombs
The thoughts and the things which Time's pitiless sway
Has long since swept from the world away !

In Memory's land waves never a leaf,
    There never a summer-breeze blows,
But some long-smother'd thought of joy or grief
    Starts up from its long repose :
And forms are living and visible there,
Which vanish'd long since from our earthly sphere !

I would not escape from Memory's land
    For all that the eye can view ;
For there 's dearer dust in Memory's land
    Than the ore of rich Peru.
I clasp the fetters by Memory twin'd,
The wanderer's heart and soul to bind !

Mrs. Hodson's chief work is doubtless the fine poem entitled
Margaret of Anjou. The fate of this royal lady seems to have
called forth the warm sympathy of her sex ; for her career has
met with many female historians. None, however, have traced
her story so eloquently and graphically as Mrs. Hodson. Her
portrait is masterly :

Now who is she, whose awful mien,
Whose dauntless step's firm dignity,
Whose high arch'd brow, sedate, serene,
Whose eye, unbending, strong and keen,
The solemn presence hint of conscious majesty ?

*   *   *   *

But she is calm : — a peace profound
On the unruffled surface rests ;
Yet is that breast in iron bound,
And fill'd with rude and sullen guests ;
No female weakness harbour'd there,
Relentings soft, nor shrinking fear,
Within its centre deep abide :
The stern resolve, the purpose dire,
And grim revenge's quenchless fire,
The intrepid thought, cold, thawless pride,
And fortitude in torture tried, —
These are its gentlest inmates now,
Tho' lawless love, they say, once heard its secret vow.

Very exquisitely does our fair author from time to time cause
the beautiful ray of maternal love to light up this dark and gloomy
heart. We will take here a brief specimen. When the Queen's
son, Prince Edward, after the unsuccessful battle of Hexham,
falls fainting at her feet, overcome with exertion and dispirited by
defeat, —

In Margaret's fierce and stormy breast
A thousand warring passions strove ;
Yet now, unbid, a stranger-guest
Dispers'd and silenc'd all the rest —
Thy voice, Maternal Love !
Ambition, Hatred, Vengeance wild,
Hot Ire, and frozen Pride were flown,
While gazing on her lifeless child,
On heaven she cried, in frenzied tone,
" Oh, save my gallant boy ! oh, Edward ! oh, my son !"

The description of the preservation of the fainting Prince by the robbers is given with remarkable spirit.

There is great force in the picture which the poetess gives us of the awe which the queenly Margaret wields over the fierce robber Rudolph.

> The bloodhound darting on his prey
> Checks when his master bids him stay,
> Crouches and cowers at his command,
> And licks with gory tongue his hand :
> Rudolph, the forest's ruffian child,
> As shaggy bloodhound fierce and wild,
> Of lion heart and iron frame,
> Beneath Queen Margaret's eye was tame,
> And by mysterious impulse sway'd,
> In unseen fetters held, he listen'd and obey'd !

In the fourth canto of this poem there is a striking episode descriptive of the unwitting slaughter by a knight of his unrecognised brother. The whole passage is too long for quotation, but I extract a portion of it.

The three children of Lord Edric part on that nobleman's death. Two of them, Sir Gerald and Geraldine, are placed under the charge of a lawless baron, while Edwin, the other son, departs to Spain to offer a relique upon the shrine of St. Jago, pursuant to his deceased mother's injunctions. Gerald and his sister, sorely oppressed by their wicked guardian, fled from their home,

> . . . . and gave
> Their fortunes to the bounding wave.

A storm overtakes them, their vessel founders, and all are lost but Sir Gerald, who is rescued from the waves by a hardy crew of sailors. He is carried to a neighbouring castle, where he is trained to knightly deeds. At length he seeks the field of fame, and fights under the banner of the Red Rose. After describing a disastrous conflict in which he had been engaged, he continues,—

40   cc

Stoutly we strove, till hope declined
In every brave Lancastrian's mind,
No more to conquer then we fought,
That thought, that cheering thought was chill'd,
And now the prize for which we sought
Was death upon the hostile field!
Yet ill to strife like this inur'd,
My manly strength but half-matur'd,
And stung with sorrow and disdain
To find we had but striven in vain,
I paus'd a little while to breathe,
And cast a hopeless look around that dismal heath.

While thus I stood, for long before
My steed had dropp'd to rise no more,
A brook's refreshing murmurs stole
Like music o'er my harass'd soul;
I turn'd to seek the cooling tide,
Resolv'd to taste it ere I died;
Alas! commissioned from on high!
That brook entic'd my steps, its voice was destiny!

Just as I gain'd the sparkling flood,
A martial form beside it stood,
Whose towering mien and bearing bold,
A noble soldier's presence told;
"That rill," he said, "to toil and pain
Lends grateful solace! Bright success
May only for a while sustain
Man's feeble spirit! — Weariness
E'en Fortune's minions must confess!
Our task is over!" — I perceiv'd
My badgeless coat his eye deceiv'd;
While, all unwittingly, his tongue
Thus with a victor's boast, a foe's proud bosom stung!

"Thou dost mistake! — One struggle more
Awaits us ere our task is o'er!

Oh ! ere yon glorious orb shall set,
One struggle for the Red Rose yet!"

" Alas ! young knight," he cried, " methinks
Too much of precious British blood
The mother soil already drinks !
If but hope's shadow linger'd yet
To nerve thine arm and edge thy sword,
I am no recreant, and my word
Should ne'er oppose thy gallant will !"

" What ! thinkest thou to see me led
Thy rebel party's scorn and mock,
Meekly to lay my captive head
An offering on your tyrant's block !
Oh no ! that felon lot to shun,
I 'll perish with my armour on !"

" Brave youth ! be rul'd ! Seem but to yield,
Quit thou this blood-stain'd heath with me,
This night my voice shall be thy shield,
To-morrow thou shalt wander free !"

A fatal fire was in my heart,
Lit by the Furies ; " From my grasp,"
I cried, " this sword shall ne'er depart
Till I have breath'd life's latest gasp !
And yet, methinks, I too would fain
From slaughter and from toil refrain ;
And since to thee it seems not vile
To yield up liberty awhile,
Give me *thy* sword and purchase peace,
And do thou follow me, and let our parley cease !"

His soul was rous'd : " Insulting boy !
I would have spar'd thee ! — Heav'n record
How all unwilling to destroy,
Provok'd, I lift the sated sword,

Which to the hilt in slaughter dyed,
Appeas'd, would fain have turn'd aside
And shunn'd the useless homicide !"

We fought : — and tho' the stranger's brand
Seem'd wielded with a veteran's hand,
Tho' all my strokes were spent in air,
Incens'd I saw his skilful care
Was bent his foeman's life to spare :
I paus'd : — " Come on, Sir Knight," I cried,
" By heaven ! thou holdest me at bay !
I cannot brook thy scornful pride,
Mock not a man with childish play ! "
Again we strove, — a mortal stroke
The stranger's brittle cuirass broke !
Backward he reel'd, and from his side
Impetuous rush'd the boiling tide ;
Oh ! why do I survive to tell,
The stroke was death ! — The stranger fell !

Then, all too late, wrath's wasteful flame
Expir'd extinguish'd and supprest,
And a still voice within my breast
Did greet me with the murderer's name !
The Fury which had urged me on,
Forsook me when her work was done.
Now by the fallen warrior's side
I knelt, and gently rais'd his head
From off its cold and bloody bed,
And many a fruitless aid supplied :
And, eager in the futile task,
I flung aside the heavy casque,
And vainly hop'd the evening breath
Would chase away the damps of death !
I met the stranger's lifted eye,
It beamed forgiveness ; yet, methought,
With heaven's blue bolt that glance was fraught !
I turn'd me shuddering from his look,

The solid earth beneath me shook,
I shriek'd "My brother!" — Oh! my hand
Was with a brother's life-blood stain'd,
And my accursed sword its noble source had drain'd!

Oh! when my dying brother found
What hand had dealt the fatal wound,
And when he saw the frantic woe
Which tortur'd his unnatural foe,
The hero melting into man
Swift down his cheeks the big drop ran;
"Oh, Gerald! while mine eyes can see,
Oh, quick that envious helm embrace!
Alas! I yearn to look on thee,
And gaze once more upon thy face!
Where is our sister?"—"Drown'd," I cried,
"And would to God my bones lay bleaching by her side!"

There is a passage of extraordinary power in the seventh canto
of this Poem. It describes the visit of Margaret and a band of
followers to the cave of a sorceress — "The haggard Woman of
the Wold." The mind is excellently prepared for the interview
by the description of the scenery: —

All nature sleeping seem'd, or dead;
The air was motionless — unheard
Or insects' hum, or song of bird, —
And underneath or overhead
No living thing around them stirr'd!
E'en the strange bird, whose circling flight
Still heralds in approaching night,
His task forewent, — nor heavily
The drowsy dorr fled buzzing by:
Still on they trod, — the ghastly light,
Which hither led them, past away, —
Thick rolling clouds obscured the night,
And to assist their baffled sight
Not one small star shone forth its ray.

cc*

At once upon the darkness burst
A blaze so dazzling that each eye,
Abash'd and baffled, clos'd at first,
Abiding not its brilliancy !
Their senses reel'd, — for every sound
Which the ear loves not, fill'd the air;
Each din that reason might confound
Echoed in ceaseless tumult there !
Swift whirling wheels, — the shriek intense
Of one who dies by violence ;
Yells, hoarse and deep, from bloodhound's throat;
The night-crow's evil boding note ;
Such wild and chattering sounds as throng
Upon the moon-struck idiot's tongue;
The roar of bursting flames, the dash
Of waters wildly swelling round,
Which, unrestrained by dyke or mound,
Leap down at once with hideous crash, —
And sounds without a name, — so drear,
So full of wonder and of fear,
As seldom come to those who walk this middle sphere !

This din unearthly so prevail'd
That e'en the Queen's high spirit fail'd ;
With fainting heart, and freezing blood,
And trembling limbs, the Lady stood !
As yet nor she nor Rudolph rais'd
Their eyelids, lest some hideous sight
Might quell their tottering senses quite,
By that dire chorus sore amaz'd :
At once it ceased ; for over all
They heard a voice in thunder call
" Silence ! "   Once, twice, and thrice it cried,
Then all those deafening sounds sank on the ear and died !
        *   *   *   *
" If my word has force to bind
The riders of the midnight wind,
If from ocean's weltering wave,

If from the firm earth's midmost cave,
If from that region, cold and dim,
The wintry land of Fiacim,
Where all is still, and frozen sleep
Chains e'en the billows of the deep;
Whether amid the halo pale
Around the wat'ry moon ye sail,
Or ye be they who love to dwell
In some dank cemetery's cell,
And drink the yellow dews that fall
In slow drops from the stained wall,—
If each has felt that word of might
Which quells the disobedient sprite,
And grasps him in his swiftest flight;
If Balkin, and if Luridane,
Strong spirits, tremble in my chain,
And tread my circle,— now let all,
Mute and unseen, attend my call,
And all within, around, and over
The magic ringlet, closely hover! —
Lady, now unclose thine eyes!
Behold! behold our mysteries!"

*   *   *   *

Now bright, and brighter still, I ween,
The magic tapers blaze!
And with wond'ring heart the dauntless Queen
Beholds how quickly shifts the scene,
Beneath her deep fix'd gaze!

On either side, in double row,
Do massy pillars rise!
Majestic o'er the Lady's brow
The high roof arches! and below
A chequer'd pavement lies!

And hark! for the trumpet brays without,
And the organ peals within!
And louder yet from a festive rout

Echoes the wild triumphant shout,
A joy-proclaiming din !

Now open spreads the ponderous door,
And lo ! a princely band,
With golden censers toss'd before,
Come sweeping o'er the chequer'd floor,
Link'd kindly hand in hand !

Now Margaret well her sight may strain,
And doubt if sooth it be,
Or some strange error of the brain
That first amid that pompous train,
Her haughty self she see !

Oh ! scarce might the indignant tide
Within her breast be stay'd,
When by that shadowy Lady's side,
Like gallant bridegroom leading bride,
Earl Warwick she survey'd !

Next Edward comes, of Lancaster
The only hope and pride ;
But his cheek was wan and his look was drear,
And a tear-drop dimm'd his eye so clear,
And heavily he sigh'd !

Now wherefore, wherefore sigheth he ?
Why wet with tears the hour ?
Since smiling by his side, ye see
Of all that noble company
The bright and peerless flow'r !

For by the lily hand he held
Proud Warwick's beauteous heir !
While joy, by fair decorum quell'd,
Within the Lady's bosom swell'd,
His foster'd black despair !

Anon that fair and princely pair
Were link'd in golden chain ! —
Then — all the pageant shrank in air,
Nor aught of all that glitter'd there
E'en now, doth now remain !

This does not satisfy the impatient Queen.

She cries, " Oh wondrous woman, more !
Let me Fate's awful page explore !
Leaf after leaf would I unfold,
E'en to the final word ! — till *all* the tale be told !"
Scarce had she spoken, when behold
The gloomy night seem'd fled away !
Two mighty armies, fierce and bold,
Await the sign in firm array,
And armour glanc'd, and courser neigh'd ;
And the sun on many a bickering blade
And many a gaudy banner play'd !
On this side rear'd Lancastria's flow'r
Its bright and blushing head ;
And high above th' opposing pow'r
Her paler leaf the rival spread !
And, hark ! the signal ! — Now begin,
Of those who lose and those who win,
The strife, the shout, the mortal din !
Behold ! — they meet ! — they clash ! — they close ! —
They mix ! — Sworn friends and deadly foes,
In one dire mass, one struggling host,
All order and distinction lost,
Roll headlong, guideless, blind, like waves together toss'd !

But mark the Queen ! — the hue of death
Blanches her cheek ! — her lab'ring breath,
Her hard-clasp'd hands, her blood-shot eye,
Speak nature's utmost agony !
The cold drops on her writhed brow
Her heart's convulsive struggles show,

41

And — hark ! that scream ! — scarce can the ear
Its shrill and piercing echo bear !
" Hold ! monsters ! fiends in human mould !
Oh ! stay your bloody hands ! remorseless monsters, hold !"

" Come, cheer thee ! cheer thee, mighty Dame !
These are but toys of airy frame ;
Faint shadowings forth of things to be ;
Mere mockings of futurity !
But see ! — like morning mists they fly, —
See how they melt in vacancy !
Oh, bid them quit thy mind as they elude thine eye !

" Now, ere our royal guests go hence,
One pageant more our art must show,—
Come, let us stir each mortal sense
Till rage or transport, joy or woe,
In either bosom overflow !
Night wanes apace ! — prepare, prepare !
'T is time, — 't is time our task were done !
My sprites and I must journey far
Ere the grey dawning shall declare
The coming of the sun !
Prepare !"

With crowned head and ermin'd robe
Grasping the sceptre and the globe,
While a vile rabble's uncheck'd tide
Roll'd after swells his regal pride,
Stalks slowly round the charmed ring,
What seems in act and state a king !
Amid the gems which deck his brow
Triumphant nods the Rose of Snow,
While, crush'd beneath the despot's tread,
The Red Rose droops her blushing head !
What lightnings flash from Margaret's eyes
While " Long live Richard !" rends the skies !
For he it is, in shapeless frame,

Dark scowl, and halting step, the same
Before him waves his well-known crest,
That symbol of his soul, the grizzly arctic beast!

In the tenth and last canto, the poet gives a vivid description of the battle of Tewksbury, into the spirit of which she enters with all the vivacity and energy of a "warrior tried." Margaret's bravery and conduct on the fatal field are most characteristic, and are powerfully drawn. Before the conflict, a priest appeals to the Queen, and prays her to stay the shedding of more English blood, adjuring her by the mandates of religion. Very fine is her reply : —

Oh, holy father! if indeed
To mutter'd prayer, or counted bead,
The distant powers of heaven give heed,
I know not : — But 't is now too late
By humbleness to conquer fate!
Long since these eyes have done with tears!
Harden'd by many wintry years,
My heart its wrongs unshrinking bears!
My lips have ceased to supplicate,
My knees to bend, and I do wait
With resolute and settled soul
Till I have seen, and prov'd the whole!

The battle-scene is too long to be transcribed, and too complete a picture to admit of an extract. I give, therefore, the conclusion of the poem only ; descriptive of the death of the two royal prisoners, the Queen and Prince Edward.

In Tewksbury's walls triumphant York
Refresh'd him from his bloody work,
While Gloster, Clarence, Hastings, Grey,
Blythe sharers in th' eventful fray,
Boast o'er the perils of the day ;
And they have wash'd their crimson hands,
And sheath'd their weary swords, when lo !

In helpless plight before them stands
The battle's crown,— their royal foe !

    *   *   *   *

Alone, defenceless, Edward stood
Encompass'd by these men of blood !
E'en yet a spark of royal pride
Flash'd from his eye, the hectic bloom
Rush'd o'er his features, and defied,
With gallant show, th' impending doom ;
Such mournful, stern, majestic grace
Dwells on the ruin'd Prince's face,
That they who hate him, half respect
The virtue by their fury wreck'd !
E'en York deliberates, and surveys
His victim's form with troubled gaze,—
Did he relent ? No ! — From his breast
He drove in scorn th' intrusive guest,
And then, in thund'ring voice, his captive foe address'd :

" Who art thou, stripling ? what impell'd
Thy puny pride to wake the ire
Which has consum'd thee in its fire ?
Who taught thy boyish arm to wield
Rebellion's blade ?   What frantic rage,
What demon was 't, who bade thee dare
With fate the desperate fight to wage,
And brave thy sov'reign to the war ?
Kneel, stubborn traitor ! and confess
What message from below provok'd thee to transgress ?"

" Dost thou not know me, York ? 'T is strange
How memory fails with fortune's change !
But I will tell thee,—I am one
To whom thy knee, unbid, should bend ;
I came to claim my father's throne,
And my fair birthright to defend,
And with God's favour, to chastise
Mine own and England's enemies !

Now thou art answer'd ! — and my tongue
Would do its royal office wrong
To parley with thee more ! Thou knowest
Full well, usurping York, to whom that place thou owest !"

Nor needed farther to provoke
Of fell revenge the savage stroke ;
York rush'd upon the unarm'd youth
And smote him rudely on the mouth
With mailed hand ; — that outrage borne
The rest was easy ! Edward's soul,
Rejoicing, from its spoils forlorn,
Escapes to its eternal goal
And closes with a thankful sigh,
Life's long and lingering tragedy !

    *   *   *   *

Now from without, a parley rude
Does on their wondering ears intrude :
York shudder'd,— e'en his callous breast
Trembled to meet th' unwelcome guest
Whose voice claim'd entrance ! It was she,
She who *was* Queen of England ! — late
The people's gaze, the voice of fate,
To whom the loftiest bent his knee !
A fond fallacious hope had led
The mother's frantic footsteps thither,—
She look'd upon the weapons red,
She guess'd what blood their points had shed,
And felt that fond hope wither !
" Then ye have done the deed ! " she said :
" I come too late ! — Ye might have staid
One moment longer ! I would fain
Have kiss'd my living son again,
And whisper'd somewhat in his ear
Ere he began th' unknown career
On which ye sent him ! — Hark ye, Lords !
I long to feel those reeking swords !
In mercy kill me ! Will ye not ?

DD

Ye sons of York, have ye forgot
How many a deep and bitter debt
Ye owe the hated Margaret?
Where is my child? Mine only one!
Oh, God! Oh, God! Is this my son?

" Cold, cold and pale! — Some flatterers said
That heav'n still guards the holy head!
Why this grim heap did late contain
A soul which never crime did stain,
Pure, gentle, innocent! — And yet
Your swords are with his life-blood wet,
And heav'n the while look'd smiling on
Nor aim'd its thunderbolts, when the black deed was done!

"Monsters! A mother's curse lie strong
And heavy on you! May the tongue,
The ceaseless tongue which well I ween
Lives in the murderer's murky breast,
With goading whispers, fell and keen,
Make havoc of your rest!
For ever in your midnight dream
May the wan, wintry smile, which stays
On yon cold lips, appal your gaze,
And many a madden'd mother's scream
Ring in your ears, till ye awake
And every unstrung limb with horror's palsy shake!"

An impulse like the grasp of death
Now hardly held her gasping breath!
Dire was the conflict! Mute she stood,
Striving and fain to utter more,
Her writhing features struggled sore
With black convulsion; till the blood
Burst from her lips, a ghastly flood,
Then Nature gave the combat o'er,
And the heart-stricken Queen fell senseless on the floor!

MARY RUSSELL MITFORD.

MISS MITFORD is, I think, the most thoroughly English of all our Female Poets, — I mean *Saxon*-English. Her verse, like her prose, has the strong, sanguine, cheerful robustness which seems characteristic of the Anglo-Saxon constitution. Miss Mitford's writings always suggest to me golden hair, blue eyes, ruddy cheeks and vigorous limbs : — and her thoughts have a large, full, dimpled, rounded expression which is very healthful and cheerful to look upon. I never read Miss Mitford's Poems without feeling that I have before me a sound, comprehensive, true-seeing, and widely sympathising mind, very just in its views, utterly unaffected in its sentiments, and unwaveringly true in its philosophy : — whilst her mode of expression is marked by a graceful and refreshing simplicity which is very rare in minds so fully stored.

Miss Mitford's poetical works comprise almost every variety of verse, from the simplest to the loftiest; and she displays the same power and excellence in all. There is less inequality in Miss Mitford's writings, wide as is their grasp, than in the productions of almost any other author in the language. You see her whole mind in all she does ; and a beautiful, loveable mind it is. Whether the work be Sonnet or Tragedy, Song or Descriptive Poem ; whether the subject be homely or heavenly, rustic or classical ; the same strong, unaffected, sympathetic spirit is similarly manifest : and, let her write what she will, she is always in earnest. A Daisy in her garden is the source of as true an emotion as the picture of Jerusalem during the Crucifixion; and her sympathy is as powerfully excited towards the little Forget-me-not " that loves on shadowy banks to lie," as towards the noble Rienzi, or the martyred Charles Stuart.

I subjoin without comment some varied extracts, in order that Miss Mitford's wide range of sympathy may be fairly seen.

I. INFANT LOVE.

(*From Blanch, a Poem.*)

If in this world of breathing harm,
There lurk one universal charm,
One power, which, to no clime confin'd,
Sways either sex and every mind ;
Which cheers the monarch on his throne ;
The slave beneath the torrid zone ;
The soldier rough, the letter'd sage,
And careless youth, and helpless age ;
And all that live, and breathe, and move, —
'T is the pure kiss of infant love !

II. THE MARCH OF MIND.

Fair Nature smiled in all her bowers,
    But man, the master-work of God,
Unconscious of his latent powers,
    The tangled forest trod.
Without a hope, without an aim
    Beyond the sloth's, the tiger's life,
    His only pleasure sleep or strife,
And war his only fame.

Furious alike and causeless beam'd
    His lasting hate, his transient love :
And e'en the mother's fondness seem'd
    The instinct of the dove.
The mental world was wrapp'd in night
    Though some, the diamonds of the mine,
    Burst through the shrouding gloom to shine
With self-emitted light.

But see the glorious dawn unfold
  The brightest day that lurks behind !
The march of armies may be told,
  But not the *march of mind.*
Instruction ! child of Heaven and earth!
  As heat expands the vernal flower,
  So wisdom, goodness, freedom, power,
From thee derive their birth.

From thee, all mortal bliss we draw ;
  From thee, Religion's blessed fruit ;
From thee, the good of social law,
  And man redeem'd from brute.
From thee, all ties to virtue dear,
  The father's, brother's, husband's name :
  From thee the sweet and holy fame
That never cost a tear.

Oh ! breathe thy soul along the gale,
  That Britons still, in generous strife,
Knowledge and freedom may inhale,—
  The mingled breath of life !
So shall they share what they possess,
  And show to distant worlds thy charms :
  Wisdom and peace their only arms,
Their only aim to bless.

III. THE VOICE OF PRAISE.

There is a voice of magic power
  To charm the old, delight the young —
In lordly hall, in rustic bower,
  In every clime, in every tongue ;
  Howe'er its sweet vibration rung,
In whispers low, in poet's lays,
  There lives not one who has not hung
Enraptur'd on the voice of praise.

42   DD*

The timid child, at that soft voice
   Lifts for a moment's space the eye ;
It bids the fluttering heart rejoice,
   And stays the step prepar'd to fly :
   'T is pleasure breathes that short quick sigh,
And flushes o'er that rosy face ;
   Whilst shame and infant modesty
Shrink back with hesitating grace.

The lovely maiden's dimpled cheek
   At that sweet voice still deeper glows ;
Her quivering lips in vain would seek,
   To hide the bliss her eyes disclose ;
   The charm her sweet confusion shows
Oft springs from some low broken word :
   O Praise ! to her how sweetly flows
Thine accent from the lov'd one heard !

The hero, when a people's voice
   Proclaims their darling victor near,
Feels he not then his soul rejoice,
   The shouts of love, of praise, to hear ?
   Yes ! fame to generous minds is dear —
It pierces to their inmost core :
   He weeps, who never shed a tear ;
He trembles, who ne'er shook before.

The poet, too ; — ah ! well I deem
   Small is the need the tale to tell ;
Who knows not that his thought, his dream,
   On thee at noon, at midnight, dwell ?
   Who knows not that thy magic spell
Can charm his every care away ?
   In memory, cheer his gloomy cell ;
In hope, can lend a deathless day ?

'T is sweet to watch Affection's eye :
   To mark the tear with love replete ;

To feel the softly-breathing sigh,
    When Friendship's lips the tones repeat;
But oh ! a thousand times more sweet
The praise of those we love to hear !
    Like balmy showers in summer heat,
It falls upon the greedy ear.

The lover lulls his rankling wound,
    By dwelling on his fair one's name ;
The mother listens for the sound
    Of her young warrior's growing fame.
    Thy voice can soothe the mourning dame
Of her soul's wedded partner riven,
    Who cherishes the hallow'd flame,
Parted on earth, to meet in heaven ! —

That voice can quiet passion's mood,
    Can humble merit raise on high ;
And from the wise, and from the good,
    It breathes of immortality !
    There is a lip, there is an eye
Where most I love to see it shine,
    To hear it speak, to feel it sigh, —
My mother ! need I say 't is thine !

IV. ON A PICTURE OF JERUSALEM AT THE TIME OF THE
CRUCIFIXION.

Jerusalem ! and at the fatal hour !
    No need of dull and frivolous question here !
    No need of human agents to make clear
The most tremendous act of human power !
The distant cross ; the rent and fallen tower ;
    The opening graves, from which the dead uprear

Their buried forms ; the elemental fear,
When horrid light and horrid darkness lower ;
All tell the holy tale : the mystery
And solace of our souls.   Awe-struck we gaze
  Oh this so mute yet eloquent history !
Awe-struck and sad, at length our eyes we raise
  To go : — yet oft return that scene to see,
Too full of the great theme to think of praise.

How varied is the style of these four Poems ! We have, first,
the simplicity of a child ; next a pure and noble intellectuality :
then a frank and picturesque burst of moral eloquence ; and,
lastly, a fine religious bending of the spirit until it seems to
become almost speechless with the awe it feels.   But for a full
view of our fair Poet's powers we must go farther still.   I especially refer the reader to the following Poem of

ANTIGONE.

'T was noon ; beneath the ardent ray
Proud Thebes in all her glory lay ;
On pillar'd porch, on marble wall,
On temple, portico and hall,
The summer sunbeams gaily fall ;
Bathing, as in a flood of light,
Each sculptur'd frieze and column bright.
Dirce's pure stream meanders there,
A silver mirror clear and fair ;
Now giving back the deep-blue sky,
And now the city proud and high,
  And now the sacred grove ;
And sometimes on its wave a shade,
Making the light more lovely, play'd,
  When some close-brooding dove
Flew from her nest, on rapid wing,
For needful food across the spring,
  Or sought her home of love.
The very air in that calm hour,

Seem'd trembling with the conscious power
Of its own balminess ;
The herbage, if by light foot press'd,
Sent up sweet odours from its breast ; —
Sure, if coy happiness
E'er dwelt on earth, 't was in that clime
Of beauty, in that noon-day prime
Of thrilling pleasantness !

But who are they before the gate
Of Thebes conven'd in silent state ?
Sad, grey-hair'd men, with looks bow'd down,
Slaves to a tyrant's haughty frown ;
And he the wicked king, and she
The royal maid Antigone,
Passing to death. Awhile she laid
Her clasp'd hands on her heart, and stay'd
Her firmer step, as if to look
On the fair world which she forsook ;
And then the sunbeams on her face
Fell, as on sculptur'd Nymph or Grace,
Lighting her features with a glow
That seemed to mock their patient woe.

She stay'd her onward step, and stood
A moment's space ; — oh, what a flood
Of recollected anguish stole
In that brief moment o'er her soul !
The concentrated grief of years,
The mystery, horror, guilt and tears,
The story of her life past by,
E'en in the heaving of a sigh !

She thought upon the blissful hour
Of infancy, when, as a flower
Set in the sun, she grew,
Without a fear, without a care,
Enjoying, innocent and fair,

As buoyant as the mountain air,
  As pure as morning dew ;
'Till burst at once like lightning's flame,
The tale we tremble but to name,
Of them from whom her being came,
  Poor Œdipus, and one,
The wretched yet unconscious dame,
  Who wedded with her son !

Then horror fast on horror rose :
She maddening died beneath her woes,
Whilst crownless, sightless, hopeless, *he*
Dared to outlive that agony.
Through many a trackless path and wild
The blind man and his duteous child
Wandered, 'till pitying Theseus gave
The shelter brief, the mystic grave.
One weary heart finds rest at last :
But, when to Thebes the maiden pass'd,
  The god's stern wrath was there : —
Her brothers each by other slain,
And one upon the bloody plain
Left festering in the sun and rain,
  Tainting the very air ;
For none, the haughty Creon said,
On pain of death should yield the dead
  Burial, or tear, or sigh ;
And, for alone she feebly strove
To pay the decent rites of love,
  The pious maid must die.

She paus'd — and in that moment rose
As in a mirror all her woes ;
She spake — the flush across her cheek
Told of the woe she would not speak,
As a brief thought of Hæmon stole
With bitter love across her soul.
" I die,— and what is death to me

But freedom from long misery ?
Joyful to fall before my time,
I die ; and, tyrant, hear my crime :
I did but strive his limbs to shield
From the gaunt prowlers of the field ;
I did but weave, as nature weaves,
A shroud of grass and moss and leaves ;
I did but scatter dust to dust,
As the desert wind on marble bust ;
I did but as the patient wren
And the kind redbreast do for men.
I die — and what is death to me ?
But tremble in thy tyranny,
Tyrant ! and ye, base slaves of power,
Tremble at freedom's coming hour !
I die — and death is bliss to me !"
Then, with a step erect and free,
With brow upraised and even breath,
The royal virgin passed to death.

Nothing, I think, can exceed the pure taste which characterises this exquisite poem. Nowhere is a classical story more classically treated. The spirit of the poem is wholly Greek. Yet it has a charm which is more than classical. There is a *life* in it which we rarely find in the classical models. To the statuesque Miss Mitford adds the picturesque ; to correctness of form she adds beauty of colour ; to chasteness of design she adds beauty of expression. The foregoing poem amply illustrates these assertions. How beautifully Thebes is pictured to form the background of the scene ! And how the whole description is made instinct with moving life, as the

——— " close brooding dove,
Flies from her nest, on rapid wing,
For needful food across the spring."

It is in passages like this that Miss Mitford's strength is best seen : and they abound in every page of her poetry.

It has been said that purity of sentiment will always produce purity of style. Miss Mitford's compositions certainly bear out the assertion. I offer the following sweetly-expressed Sonnet in proof: I might select any our poetess has written, for the same purpose.

TO MY MOTHER SLEEPING.

Sleep on, my mother! sweet and innocent dreams
    Attend thee, best and dearest! Dreams that gild
    Life's clouds like setting suns, with pleasure filled,
And saintly joy, such as thy mind beseems,—
Thy mind where never stormy passion gleams,
    Where their soft nest the dovelike virtues build,
And calmest thoughts, like violets distill'd,
Their fragrance mingle with bright wisdom's beams.
    Sleep on, my mother! not the lily's bell
So sweet; not the enamour'd west-wind's sighs
    That shake the dew-drop from her snowy cell
So gentle; not that dew-drop ere it flies
So pure. E'en slumber loves with thee to dwell,
Oh, model most beloved of good and wise.

No reader of "Our Village" can have failed to notice the countless dramatic touches which those delightful prose sketches exhibit: no reader will therefore quarrel with me for saying that Miss Mitford's genius is essentially of a dramatic kind. The picturesqueness of her style, the universality of her sympathies, and the perspicacity of her mental vision, all tend to make her a dramatist. And a very powerful dramatist she proves herself. No one who reads her volume of *Dramatic Scenes* can doubt my assertion. These scenes display not merely a large measure of the creative faculty which results in the invention of striking incidents and effective situations, but the existence in a high degree of that *individualising* faculty which selects, animates, and sustains human character, which surrounds the fictitious creation of the stage with real human interest, and which makes each person on the scene a separate, complete, and consistent being. Besides this, Miss Mitford exhibits that spiritualising faculty which alone elevates Drama into Poetry. She always avoids harsh outline and too-literal fact, and she gives her creations an air of remoteness which effectually preserves them from ever degenerating into common-place. She embellishes her scenes, too, with such sweet flowers of fancy, that our very taste is moralised by her, and our conception detached from all that is gross, vulgar, and sensual.

So many fine passages in illustration of these remarks crowd upon my memory that I find the greatest difficulty in selecting a specimen. *Cunigunda's Vow*, in which a proud heart is proudly punished, *The Painter's Daughter*, the death of *Fair Rosamond*, *The Bridal Eve*, *The Captive*, all claim a place, whilst I have scarcely space for one of them. But as I am obliged to resolve, I choose

THE MASQUE OF THE SEASONS.

GIACOMO.

Where is Fiesco now?

ISABELLA.

Oh, you should see him!
Celia is showing him her gay saloon
Sparkling with lamps and flowers, and her quaint masque
Of country lasses, cunningly prankt out
With rustic fancy. The little thief
Hath stolen all my roses — all save this —
To deck the pretty damsel she calls Spring,
And there is she turning them round and round
To be admired; and there are they, all blushes,
Curtsying with coy and shame-faced bashfulness,
Yet full of a strange joy; and there is he,
Dropping kind words and kinder smiles about,
Delighting and delighted. We must join them.

43   EE

THE MASQUE.

Enter Spring.

SPRING.

Room for the jocund queen of new-born flowers!
Bathed in light fragrant airs and sunny showers
I come. Beneath my steps the grass is set
With violets, cowslips, daffodils, all wet
With freshest dew as any crystal clear.
The youth, the smile, the music of the year
Am I. Who loves not Spring? Gay songs of birds
Tell my delights, and rough uncouthest words
Of shepherds. Fairest ladies, here are posies
Of crisp curled hyacinths, pale maiden roses,
And bright anemonies of richer dyes
Than rubies, amethysts, or azure eyes
Of sapphires. Summer! hasten, leafy queen!
And Autumn help to bind my garlands sheen!

Enter Summer.

SUMMER.

In a green nook, whose mossy bed receives
Shade from my own unnumbered world of leaves,
I heard a voice called Summer.

SPRING.

Hast thou not
Brought flowery tribute? To thy favourite grot
I sent my deftist, trustiest messenger,
A dappled butterfly, whose pinions whir
Like thy mailed beetle's. He was charg'd to say
That great Doria would be here to-day —
Did not that rouse thee?

SUMMER.

                                    Yes ! his name hath won
To my deep solitudes, where scarce the sun
Can pierce the heavy umbrage.   The cool places
To which the sweltering noon the wild deer chases ;
The shelter'd pools, which oft the swallow's winglet
Skims, or where lazily her darker ringlet
Some Naiad floating in her beauty laves ;
The little bubbling springs, whose tiny waves
Do murmur gently round old pollard trees,
Mingling their music with the stir of bees ;
All these are mine : mine the wild forest glade
Where the bright sun comes flickering through the shade,
Gilding the turfy wood-walks ; and his name
Is wafted through them with an odorous fame,
Balm breathing.   Take my tribute.   Strawberries bred
In shrubby dingles : cherries round and red,
And flowers that love the sun.

SPRING.

                                Sweet flowers are thine,
Carnation, pink, acacia, jessamine,
With coral-budded myrtle, which discloses
White pearly blossoms, and perfumed musk roses.

Enter AUTUMN.

AUTUMN.

Fair queen of leaves and flowers, give way to me,
To Autumn and his fruits.   Do you not see
How I am laden ?   Corn and grapes are here
And olives.   Of the riches of the year
I am the joyful gatherer.   Merry nights
Have I at harvest-time, and rare delights
When the brown vintagers beneath the trees
Dance and drink in the sunset and the breeze.
And I have brought young tendrils of the vine
Amidst your gayer garlands to entwine
For great Doria.

Enter WINTER.

SPRING.

Ah ! what form is this ?
Stern Winter, hence ! Come not to mar our bliss
With frosts and tempests. Icy season, hence !
See, Summer sickens at thy influence,
And I can feel my coronet withering.

WINTER.

Hence then, thyself, fair, dainty, delicate thing !
Light fluttering playmate of the infant loves,
Mistress of butterflies and turtle-doves,
Hence ! and bear with thee that gay blooming toy,
To a fair girl from an enamoured boy
Fit homage, not for heroes. In this form
Thou hail'st a friend, Doria ! The wild storm,
The raging of the elements, the wave
That Winter flings aloft, are to the brave
A victory and a glory. Thou hast breasted
My billows, mountain-high and foamy-crested,
And vanquished them. And I can guerdon thee,
I, barren Winter, from the unfading tree
To valour consecrate. This laurel crown
Wear ! as it clips thy temples, thy renown
Will cast upon its shining leaves a light
Ineffable. Approach, ye Seasons bright,
With gifts and garlands ; let us offer here
The blended homage of the circling year.

Some exquisite snatches of song, sometimes of Shaksperean
character, occur occasionally in the Dramatic Scenes. One of
them I transcribe.

BRIDAL SONG.

Forth the lovely bride ye bring ;
Gayest flowers before her fling,

From your high-piled baskets spread,
Maidens of the fairy tread !
Strew them far, and wide, and high,
A rosy shower 'twixt earth and sky !
 Strew about ! Strew about !
Bright jonquil, in golden pride,
Fair carnation, freak'd and dyed,
 Strew about ! Strew about !
Dark-eyed pinks, with fringes light,
Rich geraniums, clustering bright,
 Strew about ! Strew about !
Flaunting pea, and harebell blue,
And damask-rose of deepest hue,
And purest lilies, maidens, strew !
 Strew about ! Strew about !
Home the lovely bride ye bring :
Choicest flowers before her fling,
Till dizzying streams of rich perfume
Fill the lofty banquet-room !
Strew the tender citron there,
The crushed magnolia proud and rare,
 Strew about ! Strew about !
Orange blossoms, newly dropp'd,
Chains from high acacia cropp'd,
 Strew about ! Strew about !
Pale musk-rose, so light and fine,
Cloves, and stars of jessamine,
 Strew about ! Strew about !
Tops of myrtle, wet with dew,
Nipp'd where the leaflets sprout anew,
Fragrant bay-leaves, maidens, strew !
 Strew about ! Strew about !

But to gain a just appreciation of Miss Mitford's dramatic genius, we must go to her Plays. It is in them that she puts forth all her strength, and it will doubtless be by them that posterity will mainly judge her. *Julian, Rienzi, Charles the First,* and
EE*

The Vespers of Palermo, are the names of her Plays: and all of them display more or less the dramatic qualities which I have heretofore attributed to her. *Charles the First* and *Rienzi* are the two which have taken the strongest hold of the public mind ; and I see no reason to dispute the verdict. Both are noble plays — full of poetry and characterisation. I take, however, one of them only for my illustrations. It shall be *Rienzi*.

There could not well be a more dramatic story than that of Rienzi. The dazzling and strange career of " The Last of the Tribunes" presents more than most histories those strong and startling points of interest which contribute so materially to dramatic success. The time, the place, the men, the events, all attract and fasten the attention. The scene is Rome : the subject Liberty : the passions addressed are amongst the intensest that belong to human nature. All these concurrent circumstances no doubt contributed materially to Miss Mitford's success : but still there seems to me no question that the story owes more to her than she to the story. Some of the chief dramatic faculties are displayed by the fair author of this work in a remarkable degree. There is great constructiveness in it: the piece is extremely well put together: the occurrences happen naturally and truthfully. The main points are most judiciously kept in view throughout, and the minor ones duly subordinated. There is a consistency, too, a coherency in the Play, which is essentially dramatic. There is no flying off at a tangent ; no forgetting the great object in view, even for a moment. The characters are brought upon the scene easily and naturally : and they speak not at all like automata, but like men and women of actual flesh and blood. The passions displayed in the Tragedy are, moreover, most correctly and affectingly delineated : there is not a syllable of false feeling or unreal sentiment in the whole composition. Besides this, there is an amazing range of sympathy shown by the writer. The proud, ambitious, fiery Rienzi, the gentle and innocent Claudia, the brave but indecisive and haughty Angelo, the revengeful Lady Colonna, and the fierce Ursini, are all so powerfully and sympathetically portrayed, that the mind of the author must have inhabited for a time the soul of each, and must have really felt as they are made to feel. The mere composition, too, is eminently dramatic in its character. It is terse, vigorous, and suggestive. The writer never forgets that she is *depicting*, not *describing*.

Here is the portrait of Rienzi: there is absolute, moving, speaking *life* in it. Lady Colonna calls him

> A sad, wise man, of daring eye and free
> Yet mystic speech. While others laugh'd, I still
> Have shudder'd, for his darkling words oft fell
> Like oracles, answering with dim response
> To my unspoken thoughts, so that my spirit,
> Albeit unus'd to womanish fear, hath quail'd
> To hear his voice's deep vibration. Watch him!
> Be sure he is ambitious. Watch him, lords!

To complete the picture, here are touches by his daughter, Claudia.

> Alas! I've learned to fear him : — he is chang'd,
> Grievously chang'd : still good and kind, but full
> Of fond relentings — cross'd by sudden gusts
> Of wild and stormy passion. Then he 's so silent : —
> He once was eloquent. Now he sits mute,
> His serious eyes bent on the ground : — each sense
> Turn'd inward.

A dangerous man, this, one would say, in a wicked state! — especially when he begins to talk about

> —— " the will of man, the hallow'd names
> Of Freedom and of Country."

But let us listen to him. He is speaking to the Romans of their wrongs : — incited by wrongs of his own.

> Friends,
> I come not here to talk. Ye know too well
> The story of our thraldom. We are slaves!

The bright sun rises to his course, and lights
A race of slaves ! — He sets, and his last beam
Falls on a slave.   Not such as swept along
By the full tide of power the conqueror leads
To crimson glory and undying fame —
But base ignoble slaves, slaves to a horde
Of petty despots, feudal tyrants : — lords
Rich in some dozen paltry villages,
Strong in some hundred spearmen, only great
In that strange spell, a name.   Each hour dark fraud
Or open rapine, or protected murder,
Cry out against them.   But this very day
An honest man, my neighbour — there he stands —
Was struck — struck like a dog, by one who wore
The badge of Ursini, because forsooth,
He toss'd not high his ready cap in air,
Nor lifted up his voice in servile shouts
At sight of that great ruffian.   Be we men,
And suffer such dishonour ?   Men, and wash not
The stain away in blood ?   Such shames are common :
I have known deeper wrongs.   I that speak to ye.
I had a brother once, a gracious boy,
Full of all gentleness, of calmest hope,
Of sweet and quiet joy.   Oh how I lov'd
That gracious boy !   Younger by fifteen years,
Brother at once and son !   He left my side ;
A summer-bloom on his fair cheeks, a smile
Parting his innocent lips.   In one short hour
The pretty harmless boy was slain !   I saw
His corse, his mangled corse ; and when I cried
For vengeance — Rouse ye, Romans ! rouse ye, slaves !
Have ye brave sons ?   Look in the next fierce brawl
To see them die.   Have ye fair daughters ?   Look
Ye to see them live, torn from your arms ; distained,
Dishonor'd ; and if ye dare to call for justice,
Be answer'd with — the lash !   Yet this is Rome,
That sat on her seven hills, and from her throne
Of beauty rul'd the world !   And we are Romans !

Why in that elder day to be a Roman
Was greater than a king! And once again —
Hear me, ye walls that echoed to the tread
Of either Brutus! Once again, I swear,
The eternal city shall be free! Her sons
Shall walk with princes!

Very consistent is the bearing of Rienzi when lifted to the
height of power. True to his nature, his ambition has *grown* in
him, and is become selfish and infatuating. Still his great spirit
remains true and noble. His sway must be just, however despotic. Lordly fraud swings on the same gibbet with plebeian
theft: there is no partial hand interposed for either. Though
the head of the Ursini is the offender, he must hang with the rest
of the criminals. The scene wherein Rienzi refuses mercy to
the patrician culprit is a very fine and characteristic one.

[The Nobles are come to intercede with *Rienzi* for *Ursini*. *Colonna* begins.]

COLONNA.

Sir, I come
A suitor to thee. Martin Ursini —

RIENZI.

When last his name was on thy lips — Well, Sir,
Thy suit, thy suit? If *pardon*, take at once
My answer.— No!

ANGELO.

Yet, mercy —

RIENZI.

Angelo,
Waste not thy pleadings on a desperate cause,
And a resolvëd spirit. My Lord Colonna,
This is a needful justice.
    44

COLONNA.

Noble Tribune,
It is a crime which custom —

RIENZI.

Aye, the law
Of the strong against the weak,— *your* law, the law
Of the sword and spear.   But, gentles, now ye live
Under the good estate.

SAVELLI.

He is noble !

RIENZI.

Therefore
A thousand times, he dies.   Ye are noble, Sirs,
And need a warning.

COLONNA.

Sick, almost to death.

RIENZI.

Ye have less cause to grieve.

FRANGIPANI.

New wedded.

RIENZI.

Aye,
Madonna Laura is a blooming dame,
And will become her weeds.

CAFARELLO.

Remember, Tribune,
He hath two uncles, cardinals.   Would'st outrage
The sacred College ?

RIENZI.

The Lord Cardinals,
Meek, pious, lowly men, and loving virtue,
Will render thanks to him who wipes a blot
So flagrant from their name !

COLONNA.

An Ursini,
Head of the Ursini !

JOHN OF URSINI.

My brother !

RIENZI.

And dar'st *thou* talk to me of *brothers ?* Thou,
Whose groom — Would'st have me break my own just laws
To save thy brother ? *Thine!* Hast thou forgotten
When that most beautiful and blameless boy,
The prettiest piece of innocence that ever
Breath'd in this sinful world, lay at thy feet,
Slain by thy pamper'd minion, and I knelt
Before thee for redress,— whilst thou — Didst never
Hear talk of *retribution ?* This is justice —
Pure justice, not revenge ! mark well, my Lords,
Pure equal justice. Martin Ursini
Had open trial, is guilty, is condemn'd,
And he shall die !

COLONNA.

Yet listen to us —

RIENZI.

Lords,
If ye could range before me all the peers,
Prelates, and potentates of Christendom,
The holy Pontiff kneeling at my knee,
And emperors crouching at my feet, to sue
For this great robber, still I should be blind

As Justice.   But this very day a wife,
One infant hanging at her breast, and two,
Scarce bigger, first-born twins of misery,
Clinging to the poor rags that scarcely hid
Her squalid form, grasped at my bridle-rein
To beg her husband's life, condemned to die
For some vile petty theft, some paltry scudi :
And whilst the fiery war-horse chaf'd and rear'd,
Shaking his crest and plunging to get free,
There 'midst the dangerous coil unmov'd she stood,
Pleading in broken words, and piercing shrieks,
And hoarse low shivering sobs, the very cry
Of Nature.   And when I at last said No,—
For I said No to her — she flung herself
And those poor innocent babes between the stones
And my hot Arab's hoofs.   We sav'd them all,
Thank Heaven we sav'd them all !   But I said No
To that sad woman midst her shrieks.   Ye dare not
Ask me for mercy now !

All this is in the highest degree dramatic, and most truly fitted
to the character of the man who utters it.

In his zenith of triumph, Rienzi is Reinzi still.   The ambitious,
unquiet spirit can find no rest, even when most successful.   We
see that now

He bears him like a prince, save that he lacks
The port serene of majesty.   His mood
Is fitful : stately now, and sad ; anon,
Full of a hurried mirth ; courteous awhile,
And mild : — then bursting, on a sudden, forth
Into sharp biting taunts.

But the intoxication of ambition increases in him ;

———— " his new power
Mounts to his brain like wine : —"

He becomes reckless, hated, despised, deserted by' those who
raised him to his giddying elevation.   Rebellion, turmoil, riot,
meet him at every turn ; until at last his awakened spirit sees the
vanity of the dream in which he has indulged.

> " For this," (he cries) I left
> The assur'd condition of my lowliness,—
> The laughing days, the peaceful nights, the joys,
> Of my small quiet home ; for such I risk'd
> Thy peace, my daughter!   O had I laid
> All earthly passion, pride, and pomp, and power,
> And high ambition and hot lust of rule,
> Like sacrificial fruits upon the altar
> Of Liberty, divinest Liberty ! —
> Then — but the dream that fill'd my soul was vast
> As his whose mad ambition thinn'd the ranks
> Of the seraphim, and peopled hell !

And so he falls — like a star from the sky — into the black-
ness of darkness.   Oh, ambition !

> By that sin fell the angels — how shall man, then,
> The image of his Maker, hope to profit by 't ?

Thy dream is a sick and a vain one, and thy waking is to misery and the tomb.   " Madness is in thee, and Death — thy end
is Bedlam and the Grave."

FF

MARY HOWITT,

The poetess alike of the Fireside and of the Field, and perhaps the most popular of all our female writers, takes a rank second to none among the fair poets of our country. Not less harmonious and graceful than Mrs. Hemans, she is infinitely more spirited, natural, and powerful ; and whilst her sympathies are possibly less subtle and sentimental than those of the lady referred to, they are much more strong, more extended, and more human. She feels equally for creation, but more for humanity. She writes with a more direct and earnest purpose, too, than Mrs. Hemans does : Mrs. Hemans delights, Mrs. Howitt instructs us. In a word, I find in Mrs. Hemans *music ;* in Mrs. Howitt musical *speech.*

In force and character of style, and in bold nervousness of thought, Mrs. Howitt may challenge comparison with most writers in our literature. There is a strength approaching to massiveness in the following noble Sonnets on

TYRE.

I.

In thought I saw the palace domes of Tyre :
   The gorgeous treasures of her merchandize ;
All her proud people in their brave attire,
   Thronging her streets for sport or sacrifice.
I saw her precious stones and spiceries ;
   The singing-girl, with flower-wreathed instrument ;
   And slaves whose beauty ask'd a monarch's price :
Forth from all lands all nations to her went,
And kings to her on embassy were sent.
   I saw with gilded prow and silken sail,

Her ships that of the sea had government.
O gallant ships, 'gainst you what might prevail!
She stood upon her rock, and in her pride
Of strength and beauty, waste and woe defied.

II.

I looked again — I saw a lonely shore;
    A rock amid the waters, and a waste
Of trackless sand : I heard the bleak sea's roar,
    And winds that rose and fell with gusty haste.
There was one scathëd tree, by storm defaced,
Round which the sea-birds wheeled with screaming cry.
    Ere long came on a traveller, slowly paced :
Now east, then west, he turn'd with curious eye,
Like one perplexed with an uncertainty.
    Awhile he looked upon the sea, — and then
Upon a book as if it might supply
    The thing he lack'd : — he read and gazed again —
Yet as if unbelief so on him wrought,
He might not deem this shore the shore he sought.

III.

Again I saw him come : — 't was eventide;
    The sun shone on the rock amid the sea;
The winds were hush'd : — the quiet billows sighed
    With a low swell : — the birds winged silently
    Their evening flight around the scathëd tree;
The fisher safely put into the bay
    And push'd his boat ashore; then gathered he
His nets, and hastening up the rocky way,
Spread them to catch the sun's warm evening ray.
    I saw that stranger's eye gaze on the scene :
And this was Tyre," — said he : how has decay
    Within her palaces a despot been.
Ruin and silence in her courts have met,
And on the city rock the fisher spreads his net.

Not content with showing that she possesses noble powers,
Mrs. Howitt exhibits the rare ambition of using her gifts nobly :
and, with an earnest eloquence, which often reaches sublimity,
she proclaims herself the poet of the Young and the Humble and
the Poor.   Her sympathies with all classes are strong,

> —— " all tears
> Which human sorrow sheds are dear to her;"

but with these classes they are overpowering.   Childhood has
for her an inexpressible charm : a reminiscence of childhood
takes precedence of everything besides.   We see this in her
lines respecting Smyrna.

> "Of Smyrna nought I know,
> Except that Homer was *a child*
> In Smyrna long ago :"

indeed the sentiment is ever uppermost in her poetry : and never
is it more graceful and beautiful than when allied to her delicate
womanly sympathy for the poor.   Take the following, for instance : —

> My heart o'erfloweth to mine eyes,
> And a prayer is on my tongue,
> When I see the poor man's children,
> The toiling, though the young,
> Gathering with sunburnt hands
> The dusty wayside flowers !
> Alas ! that pastime symbolleth
> Life's after, darker, hours !

And how eloquently and touchingly she pleads for the children
of the poor.   I find the finest possible oratory in the subjoined
beautiful extract from her *Lyrics of Life :*—

THE CHILDREN.

Beautiful the children's faces !
   Spite of all that mars and sears:
To my inmost heart appealing ;
Calling forth love's tenderest feeling ;
   Steeping all my soul with tears.

Eloquent the children's faces —
   Poverty's lean look, which saith,
Save us ! save us ! woe surrounds us ;
Little knowledge sore confounds us :
   Life is but a lingering death !

Give us light amid our darkness ;
   Let us know the good from ill ;
Hate us not for all our blindness ;
Love us, lead us, show us kindness —
   You can make us what you will.

We are willing ; we are ready ;
   We would learn, if you would teach ;
We have hearts that yearn towards duty ;
We have minds alive to beauty ;
   Souls that any heights can reach !

Raise us by your Christian knowledge :
   Consecrate to man our powers ;
Let us take our proper station ;
We, the rising generation,
   Let us stamp the age as ours !

We shall be what you will make us : —
   Make us wise, and make us good !
Make us strong for time of trial ;
Teach us temperance, self-denial,
   Patience, kindness, fortitude !

45   FF *

Look into our childish faces ;
    See ye not our willing hearts ?
Only love us, only lead us ;
Only let us know you need us,
    And we all will do our parts.

We are thousands, many thousands !
    Every day our ranks increase ;
Let us march beneath your banner,
We, the legion of true honour,
    Combating for love and peace !

Train us ! try us ! days slide onward,
    They can ne'er be ours again :
Save us, save ! from our undoing !
Save from ignorance and ruin ;
    Make us worthy to be MEN !

Send us to our weeping mothers,
    Angel-stamped in heart and brow !
We may be our father's teachers :
We may be the mightiest preachers,
    In the day that dawneth now !

Such the children's mute appealing,
    All my inmost soul was stirred ;
And my heart was bowed with sadness,
When a cry, like summer's gladness,
    Said, " The children's prayer is heard !"

There is a line in the preface to Mrs. Howitt's Ballads, which
very happily describes her: the line that speaks of " love for
flowers, and *Christ*, and *little children ;*" Beauty, Humility, and
Dependence. Her sense of beauty is truly exquisite. It is not
the soft semi-voluptuous, undefined sentiment of Mrs. Hemans,
nor the rich, showy, brilliant conception of Miss Landon : but a
clear, honest, happy, grateful appreciation of what is harmonious
and loveable and elevating. There is nothing dreamy in her idea

of beauty. It is a real existence : something that may be clasped to the heart, and felt, and transmitted. She says —

> Make beauty a familiar guest,
> So shalt thou elevate thy mind !
> And let their glorious names be bless'd,
> Who leave one thought of grace behind,
> Be it in form or word express'd,
> For such are benefactors of mankind !

Equally fine is her sympathy with lowliness. Anything that is humble, or dependent, or patient, or uncomplaining, or enduring, has a charm which attracts the whole intellect and heart of Mrs. Howitt at once. And such sympathies proclaim her to be the possessor of one of those true, earnest, loving souls which alone (humanly speaking) can save us from sinking into that yawning gulf of pride and selfishness which now threatens to devour and close over all that is noble and self-denying in the heart of man. We need to be more *child*like : and to be this we want writers who see with the true eyes, and speak with the fearless souls of children. This our author does. With one single exception (Jane Taylor) Mary Howitt has written more charmingly *for* children and *of* children, than any writer of poetry in our language. And whilst in all respects she is equal, in one respect she is far superior to the exception named : the information she conveys is of a higher and more solid order. In her volume entitled *Birds and Flowers*, there is a large amount of positive instruction : and most delightfully it is conveyed to the mind of the youthful reader ; not merely inculcating facts, but inducting sympathies : not merely fastening the young mind on intellectual Knowledge, but fixing it deeply in the rock of moral Truth. Her style contains everything that can attract the young imagination ; fervour, simplicity, harmony, affectionateness, and pictorial power. Take the following lines : —

BIRDS IN SUMMER.

> How pleasant the life of a bird must be,
> Flitting about in each leafy tree ;

In the leafy trees, so broad and tall,
Like a green and beautiful palace hall;
With its airy chambers, light and boon,
That open to sun and stars and moon,
That open unto the bright blue sky,
And the frolicsome winds as they wander by.

They have left their nests in the forest bough,
Those homes of delight they need not now;
And the young and the old they wander out,
And traverse their green world round about:
And hark! at the top of this leafy hall,
How one to the other they lovingly call;
" Come up, come up!" they seem to say,
" Where the topmost twigs in the breezes sway!"

" Come up, come up, for the world is fair,
Where the merry leaves dance in the summer air!"
And the birds below give back the cry,
" We come, we come, to the branches high!"
How pleasant the life of a bird must be,
Flitting about in a leafy tree;
And away through the air what joy to go,
And to look on the green bright earth below.

How pleasant the life of a bird must be,
Skimming about on the breezy sea;
Cresting the billows like silvery foam,
And then wheeling away to its cliff-built home!.
What joy it must be, to sail, upborne
By a strong free wing, through the rosy morn,
To meet the young sun face to face,
And pierce like a shaft the boundless space!

How pleasant the life of a bird must be,
Wherever it listeth, there to flee;
To go when a joyful fancy calls
Dashing adown 'mong the waterfalls;

Then wheeling about with its mates at play,
Above and below, and among the spray,
Hither and hither, with screams as wild
As the laughing mirth of a rosy child!

What joy it must be, like a living breeze,
To flutter about 'mong the flowering trees;
Lightly to soar, and to see beneath
The wastes of the blossoming purple heath,
And the yellow furze, like fields of gold,
That gladden some fairy region old!
On mountain tops, on the billowy sea,
On the leafy stems of the forest tree,
How pleasant the life of a bird must be!

I quote next a little Poem full of sweet, simple tenderness,
quite characteristic of Mrs. Howitt, and entitled

MOUNTAIN CHILDREN.

Dwellers by lake and hill!
Merry companions of the bird and bee!
Go, gladly forth, and drink of joy your fill,
With unconstrainéd step, and spirits free!

No crowd impedes your way,
No city wall impedes your further bounds:
Where the wild flock can wander, ye may stray
The long day through, 'mid summer sights and sounds.

The sunshine and the flowers,
And the old trees that cast a solemn shade;
The pleasant evening, the fresh dewy hours,
And the green hills whereon your fathers played; —

The grey and ancient peaks
Round which the silent clouds hang day and night;
And the low voice of water as it makes,
Like a glad creature, murmurings of delight; —

These are your joys ! Go forth —
Give your hearts up unto their mighty power ;
  For in his spirit God has clothed the earth,
And speaketh solemnly from tree and flower.

The voice of hidden rills
Its quiet way into your spirit finds ;
  And awfully the everlasting hills
Address you in their many tonëd winds.

Ye sit upon the earth
Twining its flowers, and shouting full of glee ;
  And a pure mighty influence, 'mid your mirth,
Moulds your unconscious spirits silently.

Hence is it that the lands
Of storm and mountain have the noblest sons ;
  Whom the world reverences.   The patriot bands
Were of the hills like you, ye little ones !

Children of pleasant song
Are taught within the mountain solitudes ;
  For hoary legends to your wilds belong,
And yours are haunts where inspiration broods.

Then go forth — earth and sky
To you are tributary ; joys are spread,
  Profusely, like the summer flowers that lie
In the green path, beneath your gamesome tread !

Beautifully in the foregoing verses does the poet sympathize
with Freedom and its joys :— but she has a heart that feels for
the Captive, too.   " Look on *that* picture, and on *this !* "

PAUPER ORPHANS.

They never knew what 't was to play,
Without control, the long long day,

W. Page, pinxt   J.J. Pease, sculp.

THE STRAWBERRY GIRL.

In wood and field at will;
They knew no tree, no bird, no bud,
They got no strawberries from the wood,
No wild thyme from the hill.

They play'd not on a mother's floor;
They toil'd amidst the hum and roar
Of bobbins and of wheels; —
The air they drew was not the mild
Bounty of Nature, but defiled,—
And scanty were their meals.

Their lives can know no passing joy,
Dwindled and dwarfed are girl and boy,
And even in childhood old;
With hollow eye and anxious air,
As if a heavy grasping care
Their spirits did infold.

Their limbs are swollen, their bodies bent,
And worse, no noble sentiment
Their darken'd minds pervade;
Feeble and blemish'd by disease,
Nothing their marble hearts can please,
But doings that degrade.

Oh, hapless heirs of want and woe!
What hope of comfort can they know?
Them man and law condemn;
They have no guide to lead them right,
Darkness they have not known from light,—
HEAVEN be a friend to them!

This seems to me a noble instance of the strength of Mrs.
Howitt's moral sympathies. Very few writers equal this "finely
touched" spirit. As a further illustration I quote her poem of

A CITY STREET.

I love the fields, the woods, the streams,
   The wild flowers fresh and sweet,
And yet I love, no less than these,
   The crowded city street:
For haunts of men, where'er they be,
Awake my deepest sympathy.

I see within the city street
   Life's most extreme estates,
The gorgeous domes of palaces ;
   The prison's doleful gates ;
The hearths by household virtues blest,
The dens that are the serpent's nest.

I see the rich man, proudly fed,
   And richly clothed, pass by ;
I see the shivering homeless wretch,
   With hunger in his eye :
For life's severest contrasts meet
   For ever in the city street.

Infinitely varied as are the styles in which Mrs. Howitt has written, it is not saying too much to affirm that she is successful in all. Perhaps, however, her "BALLADS" are her master-pieces. Nothing can exceed the simple, plaintive tenderness, the unaffected, overpowering pathos of these beautiful compositions. Adopting the manner, she has caught the spirit, of our old Balladists : adding, moreover, a refinement of sentiment which few of our ancient writers display. As a very interesting specimen of Mrs. Howitt's Ballad style, I present her poem called

THE SALE OF THE PET LAMB.

Oh ! poverty is a weary thing, 't is full of grief and pain,
It boweth down the heart of man, and dulls his cunning brain :
It maketh even the little child with heavy sighs complain !

The children of the rich man have not their bread to win ;
They hardly know how labour is the penalty of sin ;
Even as the lilies of the field, they neither toil nor spin.

And year by year, as life wears on, no wants have they to bear ;
In all the luxury of the earth they have abundant share :
They walk among life's pleasant ways, where all is rich and fair.

The children of the poor man,— though they be young each one,
Must rise betime each morning, before the rising sun :
And scarcely when the sun is set their daily task is done.

Few things have they to call their own, to fill their hearts with
        pride,
The sunshine and the summer flowers upon the highway side,
And their own free companionship on heathy commons wide.

Hunger, and cold, and weariness, these are a frightful three,
But another curse there is beside, that darkens poverty ;
It may not have one thing *to love*, how small soe'er it be !

A thousand flocks were on the hills, a thousand flocks and more,
Feeding in sunshine pleasantly ; they were the rich man's store :
— There was the while one little lamb beside the cottage door :

A little lamb that rested with the children 'neath the tree,
That ate, meek creature, from their hands, and nestled to their
        knee ;
That had a place within their hearts, as one of the family.

But want, even as an armëd man, came down upon their shed,
The father laboured all day long, that his children might be fed,
And, one by one, their household things were sold to buy them
        bread.

That father, with a downcast eye, upon his threshold stood ;
Gaunt poverty each pleasant thought had in his heart subdued :
" What is the creature's life to us ?" said he — 't will buy us food !

46   GG

" Ay, though the children weep all day, and with down-drooping
    head
Each does his small task mournfully, the hungry must be fed :
And that which has a price to bring must go to buy us bread."

It went.   Oh! parting has a pang the hardest heart to wring:
But the tender soul of a little child with fervent love doth cling,
With love that hath no feignings false, unto each gentle thing!

Therefore most sorrowful it was those children small to see,
Most sorrowful to hear them plead for the lamb so piteously ;
" Oh! mother dear! it loveth us ; and what beside have we?"

" Let's take him off to the broad green hill!" in his impotent
    despair
Said one strong boy : " let's take him off ; — the hills are wide
    and fair,
I know a little hiding place, and we will keep him there!"

Oh vain! they took the little lamb, and straightway tied him
    down,
With a strong cord they tied him fast; and o'er the common
    brown
And o'er the hot and flinty roads, they took him to the town.

The little children through that day and throughout all the mor-
    row,
From everything about the house a mournful thought did borrow ;
The very bread they had to eat was food unto their sorrow.

O poverty is a weary thing, 't is full of grief and pain,
It keepeth down the soul of man as with an iron chain ;
It maketh even the little child with heavy sighs complain.

    Like the great majority of her Sister-Poets, Mrs. Howitt is
truly devotional.   A fine spirit of piety breathes through all her
works.   As a specimen I take her well-known·lines called

THOUGHTS OF HEAVEN.

Thoughts of heaven! they come when low
The summer even breeze doth faintly blow;
When the mighty sea shines clear, unstirr'd
By the wavering tide, or the dipping bird:
They come in the rush of the surging storm,
When the blackening waves rear their giant form, —
When o'er the dark rocks curl the breakers white,
And the terrible lightnings rend the night, —
When the noble ship hath vainly striven
With the tempest's might, come thoughts of heaven.

They come where man doth not intrude,
In the untrack'd forest's solitude;
In the stillness of the gray rock's height,
Where the lonely eagle takes his flight;
On peaks where lie the eternal snows;
In the sunbright isle, 'mid its rich repose.
In the healthy glen, by the dark clear lake,
When the fair swan sails from her silent brake;
When Nature reigns in her deepest rest,
Pure thoughts of heaven come unrepress'd.

They come as we gaze on the midnight sky
When the star-gemm'd vault looks dark and high,
And the soul, on the wings of thought sublime,
Soars from the dim world, and the bounds of time.
Till the mental eye becomes unseal'd,
And the mystery of being in light revealed.
They rise in the Gothic chapel dim,
When slowly comes forth the holy hymn,
And the organ's rich tones swell full and high,
Till the roof peals back the melody.

Thoughts of heaven! from his joy beguiled,
They come to the bright-eyed, sinless child;

To man of age in his dim decay,
Bringing hope that his youth had borne away ;
To the woe-smit soul in its dark distress,
As flowers spring up in the wilderness :
And in silent chambers of the dead,
When the mourner goes with soundless tread ;
For, as the day-beams freely fall,
Pure thoughts of heaven are sent to all.

Highly religious, however, as Mrs. Howitt is, she is not in the slightest degree bigoted.   She can appreciate piety in any of its shapes.

Creeds matter not to her.   She asks no more
Than that the one Great Father, men adore :
For loving Him, with better right we call
On God as Father, who hath loved us all.

Her *Faith* is the earnest trust of a true and childlike soul, unfettered by wordy dogmas : her *Hope* is the cheerful expectation of a spirit confident of a coming immortality, to be shared with people of every clime and kindred and nation and tongue : her *Charity* is of the kind that " envieth not, and thinketh no evil,''
—that can extend the hand of fellowship to all who bear the human form, and find in the poorest of the species a brother and a friend.

In the subjoined lines the spirit of true religion is very sweetly apparent ; and combined with it there is a touch of sound philosophy such as we should do well to take closely to our hearts. The Mammonism of the age is powerfully described ; and the purifying influences of religion become all the more evident from the contrast.   The passage is quite a characteristic one.

ENGLISH CHURCHES.

How beautiful they stand,
Those ancient altars of our native land !
Amid the pasture fields and dark green woods,
Amid the mountain's cloudy solitudes ;

By rivers broad that rush into the sea ;
    By little brooks that with a lapsing sound,
Like playful children, run by copse and lea :
    Each in its little plot of holy ground,
        How beautiful they stand,
Those old grey churches of our native land !

    Our lives are all turmoil ;
Our souls are in a weary strife and toil,
Grasping and straining — tasking nerve and brain,
— Both day and night for gain !
We have grown worldly : have made gold our god :
    Have turned our hearts away from lowly things :
We seek not now the wild flower on the sod ;
    We see not snowy-folded angels' wings
        Amid the summer-skies ;
For visions come not to polluted eyes !

    Yet, blessed quiet fanes !
Still piety, still poetry remains,
And shall remain, whilst ever on the air
One chapel-bell calls high and low to prayer,—
Whilst ever green and sunny churchyards keep
    The dust of one beloved, and tears are shed,
From founts which in the human heart lie deep !
    Something in these aspiring days we need
        To keep our spirits lowly,
To set within our hearts sweet thoughts and holy !

    And 't is for this they stand,
The old grey churches of our native land !
And even in the gold-corrupted mart,
In the great city's heart,
They stand ; and chanting dim and organ sound
    And stated services of prayer and praise,
Like to the righteous ten who were not found
    For the polluted city, shall upraise,
        Meek faith and love sincere,—
Better in time of need than shield and spear !

GG*

Occasionally we find in Mrs. Howitt's writings a more lofty
and ambitious aim than that simple one which generally characterises them : or perhaps I should rather say that she seeks to
effect the same object which she has commonly in view, by loftier means. In her poem called *The Seven Temptations*, one
of the finest works ever pritten by a woman, with touches, now
like Byron's, now like Goethe's, now almost Miltonic, we find
her analysing the nature and tracing the operations of the principle of Evil : and although it is not to be expected that she should
make this awful matter plain, still she often discourses most eloquently and instructively upon it. The following lines are, I
think, very nobly conceived : they mount, indeed, into true sublimity.

Thou, that createdst with a word each star ;
   Who out of nothingness brought systems forth ;
Yet didst exalt beyond creation, far,
   The human soul, immortal at its birth ; —
Thou gavest light and darkness ; life and death;
     Thou gavest good and ill,
     Twin powers, to be
Companions of its mortal devious path ;
     Yet left the human will
     Unlimited and free !
We know how pain and woe,
   Sorrow and sin make up the sum of life!
How good and evil are at ceaseless strife,
And how the soul doth err in choice we know !
Yet not for this droop we, nor are afraid ;
   We know thy goodness, we behold thy might ;
We know thy truth can never be gainsaid,
   And what thou dost is right !
We glorify thy name that thus it is ;
We glorify thy name for more than this !
We know that out of darkness shines thy light;
   That out of evil cometh forth thy good ;
That none shall circumvent the Infinite,
Nor can Omnipotence be e'er subdued !

We know that doubt shall cease, and feeble terror ;
  That thou wilt wipe all tears from every eye ;
  That Thine Almighty Truth shall vanquish Error,
      And Death shall die !
      We know that this shall be,
      Therefore we trust in Thee,
  And pour in balm to human hearts that bleed ;
  And bind the broken and the bruisëd reed ;
      And say, Rejoice, Rejoice !
        For Truth is strong :
        Exalt ye every voice
          In one triumphant song —
  For Truth is God, and He shall make you free !
  Evil is but of Time ; — Good, of Eternity !

To give a just and complete idea of Mrs. Howitt's varied and
voluminous writings requires far more space than the limits of
this work will afford : the reader, therefore, who desires — and
who will not ? — to make a more familiar acquaintance with this
gifted lady's muse, must turn to her works for himself.   He must
go to her book of *Birds and Flowers*, and follow her through
wood and copse, by lake and stream,

> " And think of angels' voices
> When the birds' songs he hears : " —

and he must turn to her volume of *Fireside Verses*, and read of
little Marien —

> " The angel of the poor," —

and of Mabel on Midsummer-day : and of The Boy of the
Southern Isle, in whom he will find a spirit akin to that of
Coleridge's Ancient Mariner.   And above all he must acquaint
himself with her *Book of Ballads ;* mourn with the desolate
Magdalene ; hie with Mary to the top of the Caldon Low ; search
the woods for little Lilien May ; and listen to the angel-words
of The Boy of Heaven.   He will find before long that he is in

company with one of the most richly freighted spirits that ever sailed down the stream of Time.

In summing up my imperfect estimate of Mary Howitt, I would say that no Female Poet in our literature surpasses her, and that but few equal her. As a versifier, as a moralist, and as a philosopher, she may safely challenge comparison with any writer of her own sex, and with most of the writers of the other sex : whilst as regards grace, pathos, womanly sentiment, and Christian sympathy, she has scarcely " a rival near her throne." I believe that her writings have done more to elevate our idea of woman's intellectual character, than all the treatises on that subject in our language : I believe further, that her works tend most powerfully to ameliorate, exalt, and purify the heart of the world ; and I believe, finally, that she is the truest representative we have among our Poets of that fervent, practical, beautiful Christianity which was prophesied in the song of the angels at Bethlehem, — PEACE ON EARTH AND GOOD WILL AMONG MEN. Mrs. Howitt is indeed a writer of whom England may be, and will be eternally proud.

THE LOST ONE.

We meet around the board, thou art not there ;
    Over our household joys hath passed a gloom;
Beside the fire we see thy empty chair,
    And miss thy sweet voice in the silent room.
    What hopeless longings after thee arise !
Even for the touch of thy small hand I pine ;
    And for the sound of thy dear little feet.
        Alas ! tears dim mine eyes,
Meeting in every place some joy of thine,
    Or when fair children pass me in the street.

Beauty was on thy cheek ; and thou didst seem
    A privileged being, chartered from decay ;

And thy free spirit, like a mountain stream
   That hath no ebb, kept on its cheerful way.
      Thy laugh was like the inspiring breath of spring,
That thrills the heart, and cannot be unfelt.
   The sun, the moon, the green leaves and the flowers,
      And every living thing,
Were a strong joy to thee; thy spirit dwelt
   Gladly in life, rejoicing in its powers.

Oh! what had death to do with one like thee,
   Thou young and loving one; whose soul did cling,
Even as the ivy clings unto the tree,
      To those that loved thee? Thou, whose tears would spring
      Dreading a short day's absence, didst thou go
Alone into the future world unseen,
   Solving each awful untried mystery,
      The dread unknown to know;
To be where mortal traveller hath not been,
   Whence welcome tidings cannot come from thee?

My happy boy! and murmur I that death
   Over thy young and buoyant frame had power?
In yon bright land love never perisheth,
   Hope may not mock, nor grief the heart devour.
      The Beautiful are round thee; thou dost keep
Within the Eternal Presence; and no more
   Mayst death, or pain, or separation dread:
      Thy bright eyes cannot weep,
Nor they with whom thou art thy loss deplore;
   For ye are of the living, not the dead.

Thou dweller with the unseen, who hast explored
   The immense unknown; thou to whom death and heaven
Are mysteries no more; whose soul is stored
      With knowledge for which man hath vainly striven;
      Beloved child, oh! when shall I lie down
With thee beneath fair trees that cannot fade?
   When from the immortal rivers quench my thirst?
47

Life's journey speedeth on ;
Yet for a little while we walk in shade ;
Anon, by death the cloud is all dispersed ;
Then o'er the hills of heaven the eternal day doth burst.

TIBBIE INGLIS, OR THE SCHOLAR'S WOOING.

Bonny Tibbie Inglis !
     Through sun and stormy weather,
She kept upon the broomy hills
     Her father's flock together.

Sixteen summers had she seen,
     A rose-bud just unsealing,
Without sorrow, without fear,
     In her mountain shieling.

She was made for happy thoughts,
     For playful wit and laughter,
Singing on the hills alone,
     With echo singing after.

She had hair as deeply black
     As the cloud of thunder ;
She had brows so beautiful,
     And dark eyes flashing under.

Bright and witty shepherd girl !
     Beside a mountain water
I found her, whom a king himself
     Would proudly call his daughter.

She was sitting 'mong the crags,
     Wild and mossed and hoary,
Reading in an ancient book
     Some old martyr story.

Tears were starting to her eyes,
   Solemn thought was o'er her;
When she saw in that lone place
   A stranger stand before her.

Crimson was her sunny cheek,
   And her lips seemed moving
With the beatings of her heart —
   How could I help loving!

On a crag I sat me down,
   Upon the mountain hoary,
And made her read again to me
   That old pathetic story.

Then she sang me mountain songs,
   Till the air was ringing
With her clear and warbling voice
   Like a sky-lark singing.

And when eve came on at length,
   Among the blooming heather,
We herded on the mountain side
   Her father's flock together.

And near unto her father's house,
   I said " Good night" with sorrow,
And inly wished that I might say,
   " We 'll meet again to-morrow!"

I watched her tripping to her home;
   I saw her meet her mother;
" Among a thousand maids," I cried,
   " There is not such another!"

I wandered to my scholar's home,
   It lonesome looked and dreary;
I took my books but could not read,
   Methought that I was weary.

I laid me down upon my bed,
  My heart with'sadness laden ;
I dreamed but of the mountain wild,
  And of the mountain maiden.

I saw her of her ancient book
  The pages turning slowly;
I saw her lovely crimson cheek,
  And dark eye drooping lowly.

The dream was, like the day's delight,
  A life of pain's o'erpayment.
I rose, and with unwonted care
  Put on my sabbath-raiment.

To none I told my secret thoughts,
  Not even to my mother,
Nor to the friend who, from my youth,
  Was dear as is a brother.

I got me to the hills again ;
  The little flock was feeding,
And there young Tibbie Inglis sate,
  But not the old book reading.

She sate, as if absorbing thought
  With heavy spells had bound her,
As silent as the mossy crags
  Upon the mountains round her.

I thought not of my sabbath dress ;
  I thought not of my learning ;
I thought but of the gentle maid,
  Who, I believed, was mourning.

Bonny Tibby Inglis !
  How her beauty brightened,
Looking at me, half-abashed,
  With eyes that flashed and lightened !

There was no sorrow then I saw,
  There was no thought of sadness.
Oh life ! what after-joy hast thou
  Like love's first certain gladness !

I sate me down among the crags,
  Upon the mountain hoary ;
But read not then the ancient book,—
  Love was our pleasant story.

And then she sang me songs again,
  Old songs of love and sorrow,
For our sufficient happiness
  Great charm from woe could borrow.

And many hours we talked in joy,
  Yet too much blessed for laughter :
I was a happy man that day,
  And happy ever after !

                HH

MRS. SOUTHEY,

FORMERLY Miss Caroline Bowles, is the daughter of the late
Reverend William Lisle Bowles, and the widow of the late Robert
Southey, the poet. She has written several poetical works, all
of which have been received with the favour due to the author's
genius.

It would be difficult, I think, to find among our Female Poets
one who in vigour of mind, intensity of feeling, and gracefulness
of expression, excels Mrs. Southey. Her poems have a simplicity, a naturalness, which is as pleasing as it is rare. Her verses
are the very perfection of direct and inartificial thought. In terse
force of style I do not know her superior: whilst at the same
time she has the quickness of vision and the sensitiveness of
sympathy which characterise her sex. It is impossible not to
notice the freeness of the touches which compose the following
fine picture of

THE PAUPER'S DEATHBED.

Tread softly ! — bow the head —
In reverent silence bow ! —
No passing bell doth toll,
Yet an immortal soul
Is passing now.

Stranger ! however great,
With lowly reverence bow :
There's one in that poor shed —
One by that paltry bed,
Greater than thou.

Beneath that beggar's roof,
  Lo ! Death doth keep his state ;
Enter ! — no crowds attend —
Enter ! — no guards defend
  This palace-gate !

That pavement damp and cold,
  No smiling courtiers tread ;
One silent woman stands
Lifting with meagre hands
  A dying head.

No mingling voices sound —
  An infant wail alone;
A sob suppress'd — again
That short deep gasp, and then
  The parting groan.

Oh, change ! oh, wondrous change —
  Burst are the prison bars —
This moment there, so low,
So agonized, and now
  Beyond the stars !

Oh, change — stupendous change !
  There lies the soulless clod :
The sun eternal breaks —
The new immortal wakes —
  Wakes with his God.

For depth and irresistible force of natural pathos I think I may challenge our literature to produce a more perfect specimen than Mrs. Southey's poem called

THE DYING MOTHER TO HER INFANT.

My baby ! my poor little one ! thou 'rt come a winter flower,
A pale and tender blossom, in a cold unkindly hour ;

Thou comest like the snow-drop, and like that pretty thing,
The power that calls my bud to life will shield its blossoming.

The snow-drop hath no guardian leaves, to fold her safe and warm
Yet well she bides the bitter blast, and weathers out the storm ;
I shall not long enfold thee thus — not long, but well I know
The everlasting arms, my Babe ! will never let thee go.

The snow-drop — how it haunts me still ! hangs down her fair
          young head ;
So thine may droop in days to come, when I have long been dead.
And yet the little snow-drop 's safe — from her instruction seek ;
For who would crush the motherless, the lowly, and the meek ?

Yet motherless thou 'lt not be long — not long *in name*, my life !
Thy father soon will bring him home another, fairer, wife :
Be loving, dutiful to her — find favour in her sight —
— But never, O my child, forget thine own poor mother quite.

But who will speak to thee of her ? — The gravestone at her head
Will only tell the name and age and lineage of the dead :
But not a word of all the love — the mighty love for thee
That crowded years into an hour of brief maternity.

They 'll put my picture from its place to fix another's there,
That picture that was thought so like, and then so passing fair !
Some chamber in thy father's house they 'll let thee call thine own ;
Oh ! take it there to look upon, when thou art all alone —

To breathe thine early griefs unto, if such assail my child ;
To turn to from less loving looks, from faces not so mild.
Alas ! unconscious little one, thou 'lt never know that best,
That holiest home of all the earth, a living mother's breast.

I do repent me now too late of each impatient thought,
That would not let me tarry out God's leisure as I ought :
I 've been too hasty, peevish, proud : I long'd to go away ;
And now I 'd fain live on for thee, God will not let me stay.

Oh! when I think of what I was, and what I *might have been*,
A bride last year — and now to die! — and I am scarce nineteen;
And just, just opening in my heart a fount of love so new!
So deep! Could *that* have run to waste? Could that have
    fail'd me, too?

The bliss it would have been to see my daughter at my side!
My prime of life scarce overblown, and hers in all its pride:
To deck her with my finest things, with all I 've rich and rare:
To hear it said, " How beautiful! and good as she is fair!"

And then to place the marriage-wreath upon that bright young
    brow, —
Oh! no — not *that* — 't is full of thorns. — Alas! I 'm wander-
    ing now.
This weak, weak head! this foolish heart! they 'll cheat me to
    the last:
I 've been a dreamer all my life, and now that life is past!

Thou 'lt have thy father's eyes, my child! Oh! once how kind
    they were!
His long black lashes, his own smile, and just such raven hair.
But here 's a mark — Poor innocent! he 'll love thee for 't the
    less —
Like that upon thy mother's cheek, his lips were wont to press.

And yet perhaps I do him wrong: — perhaps, when all 's forgot
But our young loves, in memory's mood he 'll kiss this very
    spot.
Oh! then, my dearest! clasp thine arms about his neck full fast;
And whisper that I bless'd him now, and loved him to the last.

I 've heard that little infants converse by smiles and signs
With the guardian band of angels that round about them shines,
Unseen by grosser senses; belovëd one! dost thou
Smile so upon thy heavenly friends, and commune with them
    now?

48   HH*

And hast thou not one look for me? Those little restless eyes
Are wand'ring, wand'ring everywhere, the while thy mother dies;
And yet, perhaps thou 'rt seeking me, expecting me, mine own!
Come, Death! and make me to my child at least in spirit known.

The beauty of the following, as of the foregoing extracts, will
be manifest without comment: indeed, Mrs. Southey is one of
those particularly natural and lucid writers, whose genius is
apparent without the aid of critic or eulogist.

THE RIVER.

River! river! little river!
  Bright you sparkle on your way;
O'er the yellow pebbles dancing,
Through the flowers and foliage glancing,
  Like a child at play.

River! river! swelling river!
  On you rush o'er rough and smooth;
Louder, faster, brawling, leaping
Over rocks, by rose-banks sweeping,
  Like impetuous youth.

River! river! brimming river!
  Broad, and deep, and *still* as Time;
Seeming *still*, yet still in motion,
Tending onward to the ocean,
  Just like mortal prime.

River! river! rapid river!
  Swifter now you slip away;
Swift and silent as an arrow,
Through a channel dark and narrow,
  Like life's closing day.

River ! river ! headlong river!
  Down you dash into the sea ;
Sea, that line hath never sounded,
Sea, that voyage hath never rounded,
  Like Eternity.

THE DEATH OF THE FLOWERS.

How happily, how happily, the flowers die away !
Oh, could we but return to earth as easily as they !
Just live a life of sunshine, of innocence, and bloom :
Then drop without decrepitude or pain into the tomb.

The gay and glorious creatures ! " They neither toil nor spin,"
Yet lo ! what goodly raiment they are all apparell'd in ;
No tears are on their beauty, but dewy gems more bright
Than ever brow of Eastern queen endiadem'd with light.

The young rejoicing creatures ! their pleasures never pall,
Nor lose in sweet contentment, because so free to all ;
The dew, the shower, the sunshine, the balmy blessed air
Spend nothing of their freshness, though all may freely share.

The happy careless creatures ! of time they take no heed ;
Nor weary of his creeping, nor tremble at his speed ;
Nor sigh with sick impatience, and wish the light away ;
Nor when 't is gone cry dolefully, " Would God that it were day !"

And when their lives are over, they drop away to rest,
Unconscious of the penal doom, on holy Nature's breast.
No pain have they in dying — no shrinking from decay ;
Oh, could we but return to earth as easily as they !

MARINER'S HYMN.

Launch thy bark, mariner!
  Christian, God speed thee!
Let loose the rudder-bands —
  Good angels lead thee!
Set thy sails warily,
  Tempests will come;
Steer thy course steadily;
  Christian, steer home!

Look to the weather-bow,
  Breakers are round thee;
Let fall the plummet now,
  Shallows may ground thee.
Reef in the foresail, there!
  Hold the helm fast!
So — let the vessel wear —
  There swept the blast.

" What of the night, watchman?
  What of the night?"
" Cloudy, all quiet,
  No land yet — all's right."
Be wakeful, be vigilant;
  Danger may be
At an hour when all seemeth
  Securest to thee.

How! gains the leak so fast!
  Clean out the hold;
Hoist up thy merchandise,
  Heave out thy gold;
There — let the ingots go —
  Now the ship rights;
Hurrah! the harbour's near,
  Lo! the red lights!

Slacken not sail yet
At inlet or island;
Straight for the beacon steer,
Straight for the high land;
Crowd all thy canvass on,
Cut through the foam :
Christian! cast anchor now,
Heaven is thy home !

THE LAST JOURNEY.

Michaud, in his description of an Egyptian funeral procession, which he met on its way to the cemetery of Rosetta, says — "The procession we saw pass stopped before certain houses, and sometimes receded a few steps. I was told that the dead stopped thus before the doors of their friends to bid them a last farewell, and before those of their enemies to effect a reconciliation before they parted for ever." — *Correspondance d'Orient, par* MM. MICHAUD *et* POUJOULAT.

Slowly, with measured tread,
Onward, we bear the dead
    To his long home.
Short grows the homeward road,
On with your mortal load.
    O Grave! we come.

Yet, yet — ah! hasten not
Past each familiar spot
    Where he hath been;
Where late he walked in glee,
There from henceforth to be
    Never more seen.

Yet, yet — ah! slowly move —
Bear not the form we love
    Fast from our sight —

Let the air breathe on him,
And the sun leave on him
        Last looks of light.

Rest ye — set down the bier,
One he loved dwelleth here.
        Let the dead lie
A moment that door beside,
Wont to fly open wide
        Ere he came nigh.

Hearken ! — he speaketh yet —
"Oh, friend ! wilt thou forget
        (Friend more than brother !)
How hand in hand we 've gone,
Heart with heart linked in one —
        All to each other ?

" Oh, friend ! I go from thee,
Where the worm feasteth free,
        Darkly to dwell —
Giv'st thou no parting kiss ?
Friend ! is it come to this ?
        Oh, friend, farewell !"

Uplift your load again,
Take up the mourning strain !
        Pour the deep wail !
Lo ! the expected one
To his place passeth on —
        Grave ! bid him hail.

Yet, yet — ah ! —slowly move ;
Bear not the form we love
        Fast from our sight —
Let the air breathe on him,
And the sun leave on him
        Last looks of light.

Here dwells his mortal foe ;
Lay the departed low,
  E'en at his gate. —
Will the dead speak again ?
Uttering proud boasts and vain,
  Last words of hate ?

Lo ! the dead lips unclose —
List ! list ! what sounds are those,
  Plaintive and low ?
" Oh thou, mine enemy !
Come forth and look on me
  Ere hence I go.

" Curse not thy foeman now —
Mark ! on his pallid brow
  Whose seal is set !
Pard'ning I past away —
Thou — wage not war with clay —
  Pardon — forget."

Now his last labour 's done !
Now, now the goal is won !
  Oh, Grave ! we come.
Seal up this precious dust —
Land of the good and just,
  Take the soul home !

I NEVER CAST A FLOWER AWAY.

I never cast a flower away,
 The gift of one who cared for me —
A little flower — a faded flower —
 But it was done reluctantly.

I never looked a last adieu
    To things familiar, but my heart
Shrank with a feeling almost pain,
    Even from their lifelessness to part.

I never spoke the word " Farewell,"
    But with an utterance faint and broken;
An earth-sick longing for the time
    When it shall never more be spoken.

TO DEATH.

Come not in terrors clad, to claim
    An unresisting prey —
Come like an evening shadow, Death !
    So stealthily ! so silently :
And shut mine eyes, and steal my breath —
    Then willingly — oh ! willingly
With thee I 'll go away.

What need to clutch with iron grasp
    What gentlest touch may take ?
What need, with aspect dark, to scare,
    So awfully — so terribly,
The weary soul would hardly care,
    Called quietly, called tenderly,
    From thy dread power to break ?

'T is not as when thou markest out
    The young — the blest — the gay ;
The loved, the loving ; they who dream
    So happily, so hopefully ;
Then harsh thy kindest call may seem,
    And shrinkingly — reluctantly —
The summoned may obey.

But I have drunk enough of life
(The cup assigned to me
Dashed with a little sweet at best,
So scantily — so scantily) —
To know full well that all the rest,
More bitterly — more bitterly
Drugged to the last will be : —

And I may live to pain some heart
That kindly cares for me —
To pain, but not to bless.   O Death !
Come quietly — come lovingly,
And shut mine eyes, and steal my breath :
Then willingly — oh ! willingly
With thee I 'll go away.

49   II

FELICIA HEMANS.

IT would be as much out of good taste as it is unnecessary, to prefix a memoir of Mrs. Hemans to this brief estimate of her writings. The melancholy circumstances connected with her history are too generally known already, and should be screened rather than unveiled.

Suffice it to say, therefore, that Mrs. Hemans was born in 1793, of a highly respectable family ; that she was married early in life to Captain Hemans, from whom she subsequently separated ; and that, after a life of singular purity and goodness, she died in 1835.

I think there can be no doubt that Mrs. Hemans takes decidedly one of the most prominent places among our Female Poets. She seems to me to represent and unite as purely and completely as any other writer in our literature the peculiar and specific qualities of the female mind. Her works are to my mind a perfect embodiment of woman's soul : — I would say that they are *intensely* feminine. The delicacy, the softness, the pureness, the quick observant vision, the ready sensibility, the devotedness, the faith of woman's nature find in Mrs. Hemans their ultra representative. The very diffuseness of her style is feminine, and one would not wish it altered. Diction, manner, sentiment, passion, and belief are in her as delicately *rounded off* as are the bones and muscles of the Medicean Venus. There is not a harsh or angular line in her whole mental contour. I do not know a violent, spasmodic, or contorted idea in all her writings ; but every page is full of grace, harmony, and expressive glowing beauty.

In nothing can one trace her feminine spirit more strikingly than in her domestic *home*-loving ideas. Her first volume, written before she was fifteen, is chiefly about home : it is entitled *The Domestic Affections ;* and is full of calm sweet pictures of most gentle and refining tendency.

I would particularly refer the reader to that exquisite passage in the poem where Domestic Bliss is compared to the Violet, smiling in the vale. The image is very purely conceived, and the spirit and treatment of it are most spiritual and elevating.

No where, indeed, can we find a more pure and refined idea of home than that which pervades Mrs. Hemans's writings on the subject. She reproduces the conception in very many instances, and always with the same chasteness. The beautiful lines entitled *The Homes of England*, in which every class is made to participate in domestic pleasures ; those called *A Domestic Scene*, where the father is represented as reading the evening Psalms in the soft sunset, while on his face shines —

> " A radiance all the spirit's own,
> Caught not from sun or star ;"

and many more passages of similar character, might be cited in illustration.

And not only of the homes of *earth* has Mrs. Hemans a fervent and beautiful conception ; but of a

> . . " home more pure than this,
> Set in the deathless azure of the sky," —

she fails not to speak also. The Temporal home suggests the Spiritual. The Mortal's resting-place on Earth prefigures the *Immortal's* resting-place in Heaven. The idea of heaven as a *home* is beautifully wrought out in her lines called *The Two Homes*, wherein a desolate stranger has a glowing picture of a happy home placed before him, and then is asked to describe his own. How touching is the sadness of the reply ! —

> . . . " In solemn peace 't is lying
> Far o'er the deserts and the tombs away ;
> 'T is where I, too, am loved with love undying,
> And fond hearts wait my step : — But where are they ?

> " Ask where the earth's departed have their dwelling,
>   Ask of the clouds, the stars, the trackless air ;
> I know it not, yet trust the whisper, telling
>   My lonely heart that love unchanged is there."

In another very important respect Mrs. Hemans finely represents the pure sentiment of her sex : I mean in her sensitive, deep, and clinging sense of affection. Her lovingness of feeling is exquisite. To *passion* she is well nigh a stranger; but it may be questioned whether passion ever proceeds from so great or so true a love as that more pervading and more sympathetic feeling which expresses itself less wildly. Passion may be said to be a sort of madness, resulting from an overpowering sense of beauty or desire ; and seems to have in it but little of the true nature of love at all. Real affection is ever mild, ever gracious and benign. It never *raves* till it becomes selfish ; and then it ceases to be love, and grows into a kind of guilt.

Byron is a poet of passion — indeed, of all others *the* poet of passion. Love is with him a selfish and unrestrainable idolatry — wild and mighty, but fickle and forgetful. It is, while it lasts, a tempest, a hurricane, and it scathes where it alights ; but its force is soon spent, and then there is no trace of it, but in the ruin it has wrought.

Far different is Mrs. Hemans. Affection is with her a serene, radiating principle, mild and ethereal in its nature, gentle in its attributes, pervading and lasting in its effects. Her soul is full of sympathies; and the refusal of sympathy seems to her almost the height of crime. This is pathetically shown in her poem entitled *The Burial of the Forest*, founded on the following incident : —

An Indian who had established himself in a township of Maine, feeling indignantly the want of sympathy evinced towards him by the white inhabitants, particularly on the death of his only child, gave up his farm soon afterwards, dug up the body of his child, and carried it with him two hundred miles through the forest, to join his tribe of the Canadian Indians.

Mrs. Hemans's Poem is a truly poetical version of this touching fact. Very nobly speaks the high-souled father as —

" With spirit high and fearless,
As by mighty wings upborne,"—

he pursues his solitary way.

I have rais'd thee from the grave-sod,
By the white man's path defiled ;
On to the ancestral wilderness
I bear thy dust, my child.

I have ask'd the ancient desert
To give my dead a place,
Where the stately footsteps of the free
Alone should leave a trace.

And the tossing pines made answer —
" Go, bring us back thine own ;"
And the streams from all the hunter's hills
Rush'd with an echoing tone.

Thou shalt rest by sounding waters
That yet untamed may roll ;
The voices of that chainless host
With joy shall fill thy soul.

To the forests, to the cedars,
To the warrior and his bow,
Back, back ! — I bore thee laughing thence,
I bear thee slumbering now !

I bear thee unto burial
With the mighty hunters gone ;
I shall hear thee in the forest-breeze,
Thou wilt speak of joy, my son !

In the silence of the midnight
I journey with the dead ;
But my heart is strong, my step is fleet,
My father's path I tread.

Mrs. Hemans has all the harmony of expression, all the subtle
perception and refined love of beauty, which distinguish her sex.
Her verses are at once pictures and music.   What versification
can be more beautiful and harmonious than this, from the *Voice of
Spring?* —-

> I come, I come! ye have call'd me long;
> I come o'er the mountains with light and song!
> Ye may trace my steps o'er the wakening earth,
> By the winds which tell of the violet's birth;
> By the primrose stars in the shadowy grass,
> By the green leaves opening as I pass.

The sensibility of Mrs. Hemans to the influences of beauty is
strikingly seen in her passion for flowers.   Nothing can be more
refined.   Some poets write of flowers in the spirit of botanists.
Not so our author.   Her worship is paid to the *spirit* of beauty
indwelling in them — and no logic can explain her devotion to
her.   She asks in one place —

> .   .   .   By what strange spell
> Is it, that ever when I gaze on flowers
> I dream of *music?*   Something in their hues
> All melting into colour'd harmonies,
> Wafts a swift thought of interwoven chords,
> Of blended singing tones, that swell and die
> In tenderest falls away.

I see in that simple inquiry a plummet sounding the lowest
deep of Truth.   I see in it a recognition of the infinite fact, that,
as the heart of Nature is everywhere beauty, so it is everywhere
music.

But, after all, it is chiefly in the strength of her religious sentiment that Mrs. Hemans most completely typifies and represents
her sex.   It has not now to be proved, I imagine, that in simple
steadfastness of faith, in gentle calmness of hope, and in sweet
enthusiasm of piety, woman far surpasses man.   She has more
awe, more reverence, more reliance, more implicitness, than he:

and hence her greater fervour of religion.   The mild, forgiving, loving doctrines of the Man of Sorrows, too, find a readier home in her heart than in man's: and hence her prominence in all works of charity and goodness.   But for this, man, with his wars, strifes, and passions, would long since have turned this earth into a hell.

Mrs. Hemans, I repeat, embodies woman's religious excellence most completely.   Religion is with her both an intellectual conviction and a moral persuasion.   We may see here how she argues on the subject.

EXTRACT FROM THE SCEPTIC.

But hop'st thou, in thy panoply of pride,
Heaven's messenger, Affliction, to deride?
In thine own strength unaided to defy,
With Stoic smile, the arrows of the sky?
Torn by the Vulture, fettered to the rock,
Still, demigod! the tempest wilt thou mock?
Alas! the tower that crests the mountain's brow
A thousand years may awe the vale below,
Yet not the less be shatter'd on its height,
By one dread moment of the earthquake's might!
A thousand pangs thy bosom may have borne,
In silent fortitude, or haughty scorn,
Till comes the one, the master-anguish, sent
To break the mighty heart that ne'er was bent.

Oh! what is Nature's strength? — the vacant eye,
By mind deserted, hath a dread reply!
The wild delirious laughter of despair,
The mirth of frenzy — seek an answer there!
Turn not away, though Pity's cheek grow pale,
Close not thine ear against their awful tale.
They tell thee, Reason, wandering from the ray
Of faith, the blazing pillar of her way,
In the mid-darkness of the stormy wave,
Forsook the struggling soul she could not save!

Weep not, sad moralist ! o'er desert plains,
Strew'd with the wrecks of grandeur, mouldering fanes,
Arches of triumph, long with weeds o'ergrown,
And regal cities, now the serpent's own :
Earth has more awful ruins — one lost mind,
Whose star is quench'd, hath lessons for mankind
Of deeper import than each prostrate dome,
Mingling its marble with the dust of Rome.

NOTE. — It is a source of deep regret to the Compiler, that he has not been at liberty to extract a single entire poem from the works of Mrs. Hemans. The genius of this gifted lady undoubtedly demands the most ample and copious illustration from any one who pretends to criticise it; and the Author originally selected a sufficient, yet a comparatively small, number of passages to support the title of Mrs. Hemans to the high place which he meant to claim for her amongst our Poetesses.   The Proprietor of the Copy-right, however, declined to permit the republication of even the few selections which were made ; and hence the Compiler has been compelled to offer his opinions, without presenting any illustrations in support of them.   He feels bound to mention this, lest it should be said, as it might very justly, that the writings of Mrs. Hemans have not been considered so fully as they ought to have been.

(The holders of the copy-right of Mrs. Hemans's Works having prevented the editor of this volume from illustrating his criticisms with the liberal extracts he otherwise would have made,
the following poems are added in the present edition.)

THE AMERICAN FOREST GIRL.

A fearful gift upon thy heart is laid,
Woman ! — a power to suffer and to love,
Therefore thou so canst pity.

Wildly and mournfully the Indian drum
On the deep hush of moonlight forests broke ; —
" Sing us a death-song, for thine hour is come," —
So the red warriors to their captive spoke.

Still, and amidst those dusky forms alone,
  A youth, a fair-haired youth of England stood,
Like a king's son ; though from his cheek had flown
  The mantling crimson of the island-blood,
And his pressed lips looked marble. — Fiercely bright,
And high around him, blazed the fires of night,
Rocking beneath the cedars to and fro,
As the wind passed, and with a fitful glow,
Lighting the victim's face : — But who could tell
Of what within his secret heart befel,
Known but to Heaven that hour ? — Perchance a thought
Of his far home then so intensely wrought.
That its full image, pictured to his eye
On the dark ground of mortal agony
Rose clear as day ! —and he might *see* the band
Of his young sisters wandering hand in hand,
Where the laburnum drooped ; or haply binding
The jasmine, up the door's low pillars winding :
Or, as day closed upon their gentle mirth,
Gathering with braided hair, around the hearth
Where sat their mother ; — and that mother's face
Its grave sweet smile yet wearing in the place
Where so it ever smiled ! — Perchance the prayer
Learned at her knee came back on his despair :
The blessing from her voice, the very tone
Of her "*Good-night,*" might breathe from boyhood gone !—
He started and looked up : — thick cypress boughs
    Full of strange sound, waved o'er him, darkly red
In the red stormy firelight ; — savage brows,
    With tall plumes crested and wild hues o'erspread,
Girt him like feverish phantoms ; and pale stars
Looked through the branches as through dungeon bars,
Shedding no hope.—He knew, he felt his doom —
Oh ! what a tale to shadow with its gloom
That happy hall in England !—Idle fear !
Would the winds tell it ?—Who might dream or hear
Tho secret of the forests ?—To the stake
    They bound him ; and the proud young soldier strove
50

His father's spirit in his breast to wake,
  Trusting to die in silence !   He, the love
Of many hearts ! — the fondly reared, —the fair,
Gladdening all eyes to see ! — And fettered there
He stood beside his death-pyre, and the brand
Flamed up to light it, in the chieftain's hand.
He thought upon his God.—Hush ! hark ! — a cry
Breaks on the stern and dread solemnity, —
A step hath pierced the ring ! — Who dares intrude
On the dark hunters in their vengeful mood ? —
A girl — a young slight girl — a fawn-like child
Of green Savannas and the leafy wild,
Springing unmarked till then, as some lone flower,
Happy because the sunshine is its dower ;
Yet one that knew how early tears are shed, —
For *hers* had mourned a playmate brother dead.

She had sat gazing on the victim long,
Until the pity of her soul grew strong ;
And, by its passion's deepening fervour swayed,
Ev'n to the stake she rushed, and gently laid
His bright head on her bosom, and around
His form her slender arms to shield it wound
Like close Liannes ; then raised her glittering eye
And clear-toned voice that said, " He shall not die !"

" He shall not die !" — the gloomy forest thrilled
  To that sweet sound.   A sudden wonder fell
On the fierce throng ; and heart and hand were stilled,
  Struck down, as by the whisper of a spell.
They gazed, — their dark souls bowed before the maid,
She of the dancing step in wood and glade !
And, as her cheek flushed through its olive hue,
As her black tresses to the night-wind flew,
Something o'ermastered them from that young mien —
Something of heaven, in silence felt and seen ;
And seeming, to their child-like faith, a token
That the Great Spirit by her voice had spoken.

They loosed the bonds that held their captive's breath :
From his pale lips they took the cup of death ;
They quenched the brand beneath the cypress tree ;
" Away," they cried, " young stranger, thou art free !"

THE LANDING OF THE PILGRIM FATHERS.

The breaking waves dashed high
On a stern and rock-bound coast,
And the woods, against a stormy sky,
Their giant branches tost ;

And the heavy night hung dark
The hills and waters o'er,
When a band of exiles moored their bark
On the wild New England shore.

Not as the conqueror comes,
They, the true-hearted came,
Not with the roll of the stirring drums,
And the trumpet that sings of fame ;

Not as the flying come,
In silence and in fear, —
They shook the depths of the desert's gloom
With their hymns of lofty cheer.

Amidst the storm they sang,
And the stars heard and the sea !
And the sounding isles of the dim woods rang
To the anthem of the free !

The ocean-eagle soared
From his nest by the white wave's foam,

And the rocking pines of the forest roared —
This was their welcome home!

There were men with hoary hair,
   Amidst that pilgrim-band —
Why had they come to wither there
   Away from their childhood's land?

There was woman's fearless eye,
   Lit by her deep love's truth;
There was manhood's brow serenely high,
   And the fiery heart of youth.

What sought they thus afar?
   Bright jewels of the mine?
The wealth of seas, the spoils of war?
   — They sought a faith's pure shrine!

Ay, call it holy ground,
   The soil where first they trod!
They have left unstained what there they found —
   Freedom to worship God!

THE TRAVELLER AT THE SOURCE OF THE NILE.

In sunset's light o'er Afric thrown,
   A wanderer proudly stood
Beside the well-spring, deep and lone,
   Of Egypt's awful flood;
The cradle of that mighty birth,
So long a hidden thing to earth.

He heard its life's first murmuring sound,
   A low mysterious tone;
A music sought, but never found
   By kings and warriors gone;

He listened — and his heart beat high —
That was the song of victory!

The rapture of a conqueror's mood
    Rushed burning through his frame,
The depths of that green solitude
    Its torrents could not tame,
Though stillness lay, with eve's last smile,
Round those calm fountains of the Nile.

Night came with stars : — across his soul
    There swept a sudden change,
E'en at the pilgrim's glorious goal,
    A shadow dark and strange,
Breathed from the thought, so swift to fall
O'er triumph's hour — *And is this all?*

No more than this ! — what seemed it *now*
    First by that spring to stand ?
A thousand streams of lovelier flow
    Bathed his own mountain land !
Whence, far o'er waste and ocean track,
Their wild sweet voices called him back.

They called him back to many a glade,
    His childhood's haunt of play,
Where brightly through the beechen shade
    Their waters glanced away ;
They called him, with their sounding waves,
Back to his fathers' hills and graves.

But darkly mingling with the thought
    Of each familiar scene,
Rose up a fearful vision, fraught
    With all that lay between ;
The Arab's lance, the desert's gloom,
The whirling sands, the red simoom !

KK

Where was the glow of power and pride ?
    The spirit born to roam ?
His weary heart within him died
    With yearnings for his home ;
All vainly struggling to repress
That gush of painful tenderness.

He wept — the stars of Afric's heaven
    Beheld his bursting tears,
E'en on that spot where fate had given
    The meed of toiling years.
— Oh, happiness ! how far we flee
Thine own sweet paths in search of thee ! *

MOZART'S REQUIEM.

A short time before the death of Mozart, a stranger of remarkable appearance, and dressed in deep mourning, called at his house, and requested
him to prepare a requiem, in his best style, for the funeral of a distinguished
person. The sensitive imagination of the composer immediately seized
upon the circumstance as an omen of his own fate ; and the nervous anxie-
ty with which he laboured to fulfil the task, had the effect of realizing his
impression. He died within a few days after completing this magnificent
piece of music, which was performed at his interment.

These birds of Paradise but long to flee
Back to their native mansion.
                                    Prophecy of Dante.

A requiem ! —and for whom ?
For beauty in its bloom ?
For valour fallen — a broken rose or sword ?
    A dirge for king or chief,
    With pomp of stately grief,
Banner, and torch, and waving plume deplored ?

---

* The arrival of Bruce at what he considered to be the source of the Nile,
was followed almost immediately by feelings thus suddenly fluctuating from
triumph to despondence.—See his *Travels in Abyssinia.*

Not so, it is not so !
That warning voice I know,
From other worlds a strange mysterious tone ;
A solemn funeral air
It called me to prepare,
And my heart answered secretly — my own !

One more then, one more strain,
In links of joy and pain
Mighty the troubled spirit to inthral !
And let me breathe my dower
Of passion and of power
Full into that deep lay — the last of all !

The last ! — and I must go
From this bright world below,
This realm of sunshine, ringing with sweet sound !
Must leave its festal skies,
With all their melodies,
That ever in my breast glad echoes found.

Yet have I known it long
Too restless and too strong
Within this clay hath been th' o'ermastering flame ;
Swift thoughts, that came and went,
Like torrents o'er me sent,
Have shaken, as a reed, my thrilling frame.

Like perfumes on the wind,
Which none may stay or bind,
The beautiful comes floating through my soul ;
I strive with yearnings vain,
The spirit to detain
Of the deep harmonies that past me roll !

Therefore disturbing dreams
Trouble the secret streams
And founts of music that o'erflow my breast ;

Something far more divine
Than may on earth be mine,
Haunts my worn heart, and will not let me rest.

Shall I then *fear* the tone
That breathes from worlds unknown ? —
Surely these feverish aspirations *there*
Shall grasp their full desire,
And this unsettled fire
Burn calmly, brightly, in immortal air.

One more then, one more strain,
To earthly joy and pain
A rich, and deep, and passionate farewell !
I pour each fervent thought
With fear, hope, trembling fraught,
Into the notes that o'er my dust shall swell.

THE HOUR OF DEATH.

Leaves have their time to fall,
And flowers to wither at the north-wind's breath,
And stars to set — but all,
Thou hast all seasons for thine own, oh! Death.

Day is for mortal care,
Eve for glad meetings round the joyous hearth,
Night for the dreams of sleep, the voice of prayer —
But all for thee, thou Mightiest of the earth.

The banquet hath its hour,
Its feverish hour of mirth, and song, and wine ;
There comes a day for grief's o'erwhelming power,
A time for softer tears — but all are thine.

Youth and the opening rose
May look like things too glorious for decay,
    And smile at thee — but thou art not of those
That wait the ripened bloom to seize their prey.

    Leaves have their time to fall,
And flowers to wither at the north-wind's breath,
    And stars to set — but all,
Thou hast all seasons for thine own, oh ! Death.

    We know when moons shall wane,
When summer-birds from far shall cross the sea,
    When autumn's hue shall tinge the golden grain —
But who shall teach us when to look for thee ?

    Is it when Spring's first gale
Comes forth to whisper where the violets lie ?
    Is it when roses in our paths grow pale ? —
They have *one* season — *all* are ours to die !

    Thou art where billows foam,
Thou art where music melts upon the air ;
    Thou art around us in our peaceful home,
And the world calls us forth — and thou art there.

    Thou art where friend meets friend,
Beneath the shadow of the elm to rest —
    Thou art where foe meets foe and trumpets rend
The skies, and swords beat down the princely crest.

    Leaves have their time to fall,
And flowers to wither at the north-wind's breath,
    And stars to set — but all,
Thou hast all seasons for thine own, oh, Death !

51   KK*

THE ADOPTED CHILD.

" Why wouldst thou leave me, oh ! gentle child ?
Thy home on the mountain is bleak and wild,
A straw-roofed cabin with lowly wall —
Mine is a fair and pillared hall,
Where many an image of marble gleams,
And the sunshine of picture for ever streams."

" Oh ! green is the turf where my brothers play,
Through the long bright hours of the summer-day,
They find the red cup-moss where they climb,
And they chase the bee o'er the scented thyme ;
And the rocks where the heath-flower blooms they know —
Lady, kind lady, oh ! let me go."

" Content thee, boy ! in my bower to dwell,
Here are sweet sounds which thou lovest well ;
Flutes on the air in the stilly noon,
Harps which the wandering breezes tune ;
And the silvery wood-note of many a bird
Whose voice was ne'er in thy mountains heard."

" My mother sings, at the twilight's fall,
A song of the hills far more sweet than all ;
She sings it under our own green tree,
To the babe half slumbering on her knee ;
I dreamt last night of that music low —
Lady, kind lady, oh ! let me go."

" Thy mother is gone from her cares to rest,
She hath taken the babe on her quiet breast ;
Thou wouldst meet her footstep, my boy, no more,
Nor hear her song at the cabin door.
— Come thou with me to the vineyards nigh,
And we 'll pluck the grapes of the richest dye."

'Is my mother gone from her home away?
— But I know that my brothers are there at play.
I know they are gathering the fox-glove's bell,
Or the long fern-leaves by the sparkling well,
Or they launch their boats where the bright streams flow —
Lady, kind lady, oh! let me go."

"Fair child! thy brothers are wanderers now,
They sport no more on the mountain's brow,
They have left the fern by the spring's green side,
And the streams where the fairy barks were tried.
— Be thou at peace in thy brighter lot,
For thy cabin-home is a lonely spot."

"Are they gone, all gone from the sunny hill?
— But the bird and the blue-fly rove o'er it still,
And the red-deer bound in their gladness free,
And the turf is bent by the singing bee,
And the waters leap, and the fresh winds blow —
Lady, kind lady, oh! let me go."

CHARLOTTE ELIZABETH, (MRS. TONNA.)

THIS celebrated woman, who for the ability, variety, and extent of her literary labours may be classed with Hannah More, was the daughter of an Episcopal clergyman in Norwich, and at an early age was married to Captain Phelan, an officer of the British army, with whom she went to Nova Scotia, where she resided several years. She subsequently passed some time in Ireland, and her husband being again ordered abroad, she refused to accompany him, and turned her attention to literature as a means of support. Her principal Prose Works are *Derry, a Tale of the Revolution ; The Rockite ; Letters from Ireland ; Judah's Sion ; The Flower Garden ; Falsehood and Truth ; The Wrongs of Women ; The Deserter ; Combination ; Principalities and Powers in Heavenly Places ; Judæa Capta ; The Church Visible in all Ages ; Perseverance ;* and *Personal Recollections ;* giving, in the last, an account of her own history, down to the year 1840. Her longest Poem, containing about three thousand lines, is entitled *Osric, a Missionary Tale ;* besides which a volume of her *Miscellaneous Poems* has recently been published. Captain Phelan died in 1837 ; in 1841 she became the wife of Mr. Lucius H. J. Tonna, of London ; and she died on the 12th of July, 1846. She was for years afflicted with deafness, and those who conversed with her did so by signs, as with the deaf and dumb. .

TO A HORSE.

(Written in America.)

I know by the ardour thou canst not restrain,
By the curve of thy neck and the toss of thy mane,
By the foam of thy snorting which spangles my brow,
The fire of the Arab is hot in thee now.

'T were harsh to control thee, my frolicksome steed,
I give thee the rein — so away at thy speed ;
Thy rider will dare to be wilful as thee,
Laugh the future to scorn, and partake in thy glee.
Away to the mountain — what need we to fear ?
Pursuit cannot press on my Fairy's career,
Full light were the heel and well balanced the head
That ventured to follow the track of thy tread ;
Where roars the loud torrent, and starts the rude plank,
And thunders the rock-severed mass down the bank,
While mirror'd in chrystal the far-shooting glow,
With dazzling effulgence is sparkling below.
One start, and I die ; yet in peace I recline,
My bosom can rest on the fealty of thine ;
Thou lov'st me, my sweet one, and would'st not be free
From a yoke that has never borne rudely on thee.
Ah, pleasant the empire of those to confess,
Whose wrath is a whisper, their rule a caress.

Behold how thy playmate is stretching beside,
As loth to be vanquish'd in love or in pride,
While upward he glances his eye-ball of jet,
Half dreading thy fleetness may distance him yet.
Ah Marco, poor Marco — our pastime to-day
Were reft of one pleasure if he were away.

How precious these moments ? fair Freedom expands
Her pinions of light o'er the desolate lands :
The waters are flashing as bright as thine eye,
Unchain'd as thy motion the breezes swept by ;
Delicious they come, o'er the flower-scented earth,
Like whispers of love from the isle of my birth ;
While the white bosom'd Cistus her perfume exhales,
And sighs out a spicy farewell to the gales.
Unfeared and unfearing we 'll traverse the wood,
Where pours the rude torrent the turbulent flood :
The forest's red children will smile as we scour
By the log-fashion'd hut and the pine-woven bower ;

The feathery footsteps scarce bending the grass,
Or denting the dew-spangled moss where we pass.

What startles thee ?   'T was but the sentinel gun
Flashed a vesper salute to thy rival the sun :
He has closed his swift progress before thee, and sweeps
With fetlock of gold, the last verge of the steeps.
The fire-fly anon from his covert shall glide,
And dark fall the shadows of eve on the tide.
Tread softly — my spirit is joyous no more,
A northern aurora, it shone and is o'er ;
The tears will fall fast as I gather the rein,
And a long look reverts to yon shadowy plain.

A NIGHT STORM AT SEA.

From " Osric."

'T is eve : — ascending high, the ocean storm
Spreads in dark volume his portentous form ;
His hollow breezes, bursting from the clouds,
Distend the sail, and whistle through the shrouds.
Roused by the note of elemental strife,
The swelling waters tremble into life ;
Lo ! through the tumult of the dashing spray
The storm beat vessel labours on her way.
With bending mast, rent sail, and straining sides,
High on the foaming precipice she rides,
Then reeling onward with descending prow,
In giddy sweep, glides to the gulf below :
Her fragile form conflicting billows rock,
Her timbers echo to the frequent shock,
While bursting o'er the deck, each roaring wave
Bears some new victim to a hideous grave.
The voice of thunder rides upon the blast,
And the blue death-fire plays around the mast :

Beneath the pennon of a riven sail,
That vessel drives, abandoned to the gale.
Above, more darkly frowns the brow of night,
Beneath, the waters glow more fiercely bright ;
Ploughing a track of mingled foam and fire,
Fast flies the ship before the tempest's ire,
While reeling to and fro the hapless crew
Gaze on the wild abyss, and shudder at the view.

THE MILLENIUM.

When from scattered lands afar
Speeds the voice of rumoured war,
Nations in conflicting pride
Heaved like Ocean's stormy tide,
When the solar splendours fail,
And the crescent waxeth pale,
And the powers that star-like reign
Sink dishonoured to the plain,
World, do thou the signal dread,
We exalt the drooping head,
We uplift the expectant eye —
Our redemption draweth nigh.
When the fig-tree shoots appear,
Men proclaim their summer near ;
When the hearts of rebels fail,
We the coming Saviour hail ;
Bridegroom of the weeping spouse,
Listen to her longing vows —
Listen to her widow'd moan,
Listen to creation's groan !
Bid, oh bid, the trumpet sound,
Gather thine elect around ;
Gird with saints thy flaming car,
Gather them from climes afar,

Call them from life's cheerless gloom,
Call them from the marble tomb,
From the grass-grown village grave,
From the deep dissolving wave,
From the whirlwind and the flame,
Mighty Head ! thy members claim !

Where are those whose fierce disdain
Scorn'd Messiah's gentle reign ?
Lo, in seas of sulph'rous fire,
Now they taste his tardy ire,
Prison'd till th' appointed day
When this world shall pass away.

Quelled are all thy foes, O Lord,
Sheath again the victor sword.
Where thy cross of anguish stood,
Where thy life distilled in blood,
Where they mocked thy dying groan,
King of nations, plant thy throne.
Send the law from Zion forth,
Over all the willing earth :
Earth, whose Sabbath beauties rise
Crowned with more than paradise.

Sacred be the opposing veil !
Mortal sense and sight must fail.
Yet the day, the hour is nigh,
We shall see thee eye to eye.
Be our souls in peace possest
While we seek the promised rest.
And from every heart and home
Breathe the prayer, Lord Jesus come !
Haste to set thy people free ;
Come ; creation groans for thee !

THE HONOURABLE MRS. NORTON.

AMONGST the Poetesses of our land Mrs. Norton certainly claims a most distinguished place. Not a few critics, indeed, assign her the very first. And I think it would be difficult to disprove her right to a position with the loftiest. It is most assuredly not my intention to attempt such a demonstration ; for if I do not agree unreservedly with the assertion of her superiority over all, I at all events am prepared to maintain her equality with any of, her sister poets. I will go further, and avow my belief that, under other and more favourable circumstances, Mrs. Norton might have gained even greater fame than she has yet achieved. Just as some paintings give one the idea that the artist has power to produce works of higher merit, so do Mrs. Norton's poems suggest the possession of latent genius far transcending that which is displayed in them.

But we must speak of her as she is.

The Quarterly Review, in a criticism of Mrs. Norton's writings, says of her — that " she is *the Byron* of our modern poetesses. She has very much of that intense personal passion by which Byron's poetry is distinguished from the larger grasp and deeper communion with man and nature of Wordsworth. She has also Byron's beautiful intervals of tenderness, his strong practical thought, and his forceful expression. It is not an artificial imitation, but a natural parallel." I think we cannot safely adopt this opinion without some little qualification. That Mrs. Norton has a fervour, a tenderness, and a force of expression which greatly resemble Byron's, there cannot be a doubt : but there all similarity ceases. Byron is the personification of passionate selfishness : his range of sympathy is extremely small : Mrs. Norton, on the other hand, has a large and generous heart, essentially unselfish in its feelings, and universal in its sympathies. Byron has a sneering, mocking, disbelieving spirit : Mrs. Norton

52

a simple, beautiful, childlike implicitness of soul. Byron's strains resemble the vast, roaring, wilful Waterfall, rushing headlong over desolate rocks, with a sound like the wail of a lost spirit: Mrs. Norton's, the soft full-flowing River, margined with flowers, and uttering sweet music. What is there in Byron that resembles this : —

THE MOTHER'S HEART.

When first thou camest, gentle, shy, and fond,
　My eldest born, first hope, and dearest treasure,
My heart received thee with a joy beyond
　All that it yet had felt of earthly pleasure ;
Nor thought that any love again might be
So deep and strong as that I felt for thee.

Faithful and true, with sense beyond thy years,
　And natural piety that lean'd to heaven ;
Wrung by a harsh word suddenly to tears,
　Yet patient of rebuke when justly given —
Obedient, easy to be reconciled,
And meekly cheerful — such wert thou, my child !

Not willing to be left: still by my side
　Haunting my walks, while summer-day was dying ;
Nor leaving in thy turn ; but pleas'd to glide
　Through the dark room, where I was sadly lying ;
Or by the couch of pain, a sitter meek,
Watch the dim eye, and kiss the feverish cheek.

O boy ! of such as thou are oftenest made
　Earth's fragile idols ; like a tender flower,
No strength in all thy freshness — prone to fade —
　And bending weakly to the thunder-shower —
Still round the loved, thy heart found force to bind,
And clung like woodbine shaken in the wind.

Her passionate poems display a radical difference from those of Byron. Byron is, even in his purest moments, sensual and

earthly; Mrs. Norton is invariably serene and spiritual. Byron's
passion is like a lightning flash.   Mrs. Norton's like a sunbeam.
I would refer the reader to her exquisite poem of " Sappho," in
illustration.   I deeply regret that I am not permitted to present
the lines themselves.

Mrs. Norton has a truer moral vision than Byron had : no
where in Byron can be found a philosophical truth so calmly and
justly asserted as in the following beautiful comparison of *woman's* endurance with man's : —

Warriors and statesmen have their meed of praise,
    And what they do, or suffer, men record ;
But the long sacrifice of *woman's* days
    Passes without a thought, without a word ;
And many a lofty struggle for the sake
    Of duties sternly, faithfully fulfill'd —
For which the anxious mind must watch and wake,
And the strong feelings of the heart be still'd —
Goes by unheeded as the summer wind,
And leaves no memory and no trace behind !
Yet it may be, more lofty courage dwells
    In one meek heart which braves an adverse fate,
Than his whose ardent soul indignant swells
    Warm'd by the fight, or cheer'd through high debate :
The soldier dies surrounded : could he *live*
Alone to suffer, and *alone* to strive ?

A fine proof of Mrs. Norton's wide range of sympathy is to
be found in the poem descriptive of an Arab's farewell to his
Horse. The enthusiastic regard which it is well known the Arab
always entertains for his steed finds a most eloquent expositor in
our author. The feeling is a beautiful one, and it is beautifully
rendered.

THE ARAB'S FAREWELL TO HIS STEED.

My beautiful ! my beautiful ! that standest meekly by,
With thy proudly arch'd and glossy neck, thy dark and fiery eye —

Fret not to roam the desert now with all thy winged speed,
I may not mount on thee again, thou'rt sold, my Arab steed !
Fret not with that impatient hoof, snuff not the breezy wind,
The farther that thou fliest now, so far am I behind.
The stranger hath thy bridle-rein, thy master hath his gold,
Fleet limbed and beautiful, farewell! thou 'rt sold, my steed,
    thou 'rt sold!

Farewell! those free untired limbs full many a mile must roam,
To reach the chill and wintry sky which clouds the stranger's
    home ;
Some other hand, less fond, must now thy corn and bread prepare,
Thy silky mane, I braided once, must be another's care.
The morning sun shall dawn again, but never more with thee
Shall I gallop through the desert paths where we were wont to be.
Evening shall darken on the earth, and o'er the sandy plain
Some other steed, with slower step, shall bear me home again.

Yes! thou must go! the wild free breeze, the brilliant sun and sky,
Thy master's house, from all of these my exil'd one must fly.
Thy proud dark eye will grow less proud, thy step become less
    fleet,
And vainly shalt thou arch thy neck thy master's hand to meet.
Only in sleep shall I behold that dark eye glancing bright;
Only in sleep shall hear again that step so firm and light;
And when I raise my dreaming arm to check or cheer thy speed,
Then must I, starting, wake to feel thou 'rt sold, my Arab steed!

Ah, rudely then, unseen by me, some cruel hand may chide,
Till foam-wreaths lie, like crested waves, along thy panting side;
And the rich blood that 's in thee swells in thy indignant pain,
Till careless eyes which rest on thee, may count each starting
    vein.
Will they ill-use thee? If I thought — but no, it cannot be —
Thou art so swift, yet easy curb'd, so gentle yet so free.
And yet if haply when thou 'rt gone, my lonely heart should yearn,
Can the same hand which casts thee off command thee to return?

Return? Alas, my Arab steed, what shall thy master do,
When thou, who wert his all of joy, hast vanish'd from his view?
When the dim distance cheats mine eye, and through the
     gathering tears,
Thy bright form for a moment like the false mirage appears.
Slow and unmounted will I roam with weary foot alone,
Where with fleet step and joyous bound thou oft hast borne
     me on:
And sitting down by that green well, will pause and sadly
     think,
'T was here he bow'd his glossy neck, when last I saw him
     drink.

When last I saw him drink! Away! the fever'd dream is o'er;
I could not live a day, and know that we should meet no more;
They tempted me, my beautiful! for hunger's power is strong,
They tempted me, my beautiful! but I have lov'd too long;
Who said that I had given thee up? Who said that thou wert
     sold?
'T is false, 't is false! my Arab steed! I fling them back their
     gold.
Thus, thus, I leap upon thy back, and scour the distant plains,—
Away! — Who overtakes us now shall claim thee for his pains!

Of Mrs. Norton's impassioned verses none perhaps excel the
lines addressed by her *To the Duchess of Sutherland*, when that
noble lady remained steadfastly her friend under the most discouraging circumstances. Noble was the friendship, and noble
is the monument erected to it.

Once more, my harp! once more, although I thought
     Never to wake thy silent strings again;
A wandering dream thy gentle chords have wrought,
     And my sad heart, which long hath dwelt in pain,
Soars like a wild bird from a cypress bough,
Into the poet's heaven, and leaves dull grief below!

II*

And unto thee, the beautiful and pure,
  Whose lot is cast amid that busy world
Where only sluggish Dulness dwells secure,
  And Fancy's generous wing is faintly furl'd ;
To thee — whose friendship kept its equal truth
Through the most dreary hour of my embitter'd youth —

I dedicate the lay.   Ah ! never bard,
  In days when Poverty was twin with Song ;
Nor wandering harper, lonely and ill-starr'd,
  Cheer'd by some castle's chief, and harbour'd long ;
Nor Scott's Last Minstrel, in his trembling lays,
Woke with a warmer heart the earnest meed of praise !

For easy are the alms the rich man spares
  To sons of Genius, by misfortune bent ;
But thou gav'st me, what woman seldom dares,
  Belief — in spite of many a cold dissent —
When slander'd and malign'd, I stood apart
From those whose bounded power hath wrung, not crush'd, my
      heart.

Thou, then, when cowards lied away my name
  And scoff'd to see me feebly stem the tide ;
When some were kind on whom I had no claim,
  And some forsook on whom my love relied,
And some who might have battled for my sake,
Stood off in doubt to see what turn the world would take —

Thou gav'st me that the poor do give the poor,
  Kind words and holy wishes and true tears ;
The lov'd, the near of kin could do no more,
  Who chang'd not with the gloom of varying years,
But clung the closer when I stood forlorn,
And blunted Slander's dart with their indignant scorn.

For they who credit crime, are they who feel
  Their own hearts weak to unresisted sin ;

Memory, not judgment, prompts the thoughts which steal
  O'er minds like these, an easy faith to win ;
And tales of broken truth are still believed
Most readily by those who have themselves deceived.

But like a white swan down a troubled stream,
  Whose ruffling pinion hath the power to fling
Aside the turbid drops which darkly gleam
  And mar the freshness of her snowy wing,—
So thou, with queenly grace and gentle pride,
Along the world's dark waves in purity dost glide.

Thy pale and pearly cheek was never made
  To crimson with a faint false-hearted shame ;
Thou didst not shrink — of bitter tongues afraid,
  Who hunt in packs the object of their blame ;
To thee the sad denial still held true,
For from thine own good thoughts thy heart its mercy drew.

And though my faint and tributary rhymes
  Add nothing to the glory of thy day,
Yet every poet hopes that after-times
  Shall set some value on his votive lay ;
And I would fain one gentle deed record,
Among the many such with which thy life is stored.

In conclusion I would say of Mrs. Norton that with a considerable similarity to Byron in manner, she is essentially unlike him in spirit : that whereas *his* imagination is daring and vigorous, hers is timid and gentle : that whereas *his* passion is selfish and infatuating, hers is mild and tender and pervading : that whereas *he* scoffs and sneers at the best and happiest ties of life, she does her most to strengthen and extend their influence : and that while *he* with a proud scepticism flings from him the consolations and delights of religion, she clasps them closely to her heart, and finds in them a balm for the bitterest wounds of her spirit.

THE VISIONARY PORTRAIT.

I.

As by his lonely hearth he sate,
    The shadow of a welcome dream
Passed o'er his heart,— disconsolate
    His home did seem :
Comfort in vain was spread around,
For something still was wanting found.

II.

Therefore he thought of one who might
    For ever in his presence stay ;
Whose dream should be of him by night,
    Whose smile should be for him by day ;
And the sweet vision, vague and far,
Rose on his fancy like a star.

III.

" Let her be young, yet not a child,
    Whose light and inexperienced mirth
Is all too wingëd and too wild
    For sober earth, —
Too rainbow-like such mirth appears,
    And fades away in misty tears.

IV.

" Let youth's fresh rose still gently bloom
    Upon her smooth and downy cheek,
Yet let a shadow, not of gloom,
    But soft and meek,
Tell that *some* sorrow she hath known,
Though not a sorrow of her own.

V.

" And let her eyes be of the grey,
    The soft grey of the brooding dove,

Full of the sweet and tender ray
  Of modest love ;
For fonder shows that dreamy hue
Than lustrous black or heavenly blue.

VI.

" Let her be full of quiet grace,
  No sparkling wit with sudden glow
Bright'ning her purely chisell'd face
  And placid brow ;
Not radiant to the *stranger's* eye, —
A creature easily pass'd by :

VII.

" But who, once seen, with untold power
  For ever haunts the yearning heart,
Raised from the crowd that self-same hour
  To dwell apart,
All sainted and enshrined to be,
The idol of our memory !

VIII.

" And oh ! let Mary be her name —
  It hath a sweet and gentle sound,
At which no glories dear to fame
  Come crowding round,
But which the dreaming heart beguiles
With holy thoughts and household smiles.

IX.

" With peaceful meetings, welcomes kind,
  And love, the same in joy and tears,
And gushing intercourse of mind
  Through faithful years ;
Oh ! dream of something half divine,
Be real — be mortal — and be mine !"

53

TO THE LADY H. O.

Isle of Wight, September, 1839.

I.

Come o'er the green hills to the sunny sea!
The boundless sea that washeth many lands,
Where shells unknown to England, fair and free,
    Lie brightly scatter'd on the gleaming sands.
There, 'midst the hush of slumbering ocean's roar,
    We 'll sit and watch the silver-tissued waves
Creep languidly along the basking shore,
    And kiss thy gentle feet, like Eastern slaves.

II.

And we will take some volume of our choice,
    Full of quiet poetry and thought,
And thou shalt read me, with thy plaintive voice,
    Lines which some gifted mind hath sweetly wrought;
And I will listen, gazing on thy face,
    (Pale as some cameo on the Italian shell!)
Or looking out across the far blue space,
    Where glancing sails to gentle breezes swell.

III.

Come forth! The sun hath flung on Thetis' breast
    The glittering tresses of his golden hair;
All things are heavy with a noonday rest,
    And floating sea-birds leave the stirless air.
Against the sky, in outlines clear and rude,
    The cleft rocks stand, while sunbeams slant between;
And lulling winds are murmuring through the wood,
    Which skirts the bright bay with its fringe of green.

IV.

Come forth! All motion is so gentle now,
    It seems *thy* step alone should walk the earth,—

Thy voice alone, the " ever soft and low,"
Wake the far-haunting echoes into birth.
Too wild would be Love's passionate store of hope,
    Unmeet the influence of his changeful power—
Ours be companionship, whose gentle scope
    Hath charm enough for such a tranquil hour.

v.

And slowly, idly wandering, we will roam,
    Where the high cliffs shall give us ample shade ;
And watch the glassy waves, whose wrathful foam
    Hath power to make the seaman's heart afraid.
Seek thou no veil to shroud thy soft brown hair,—
    Wrap thou no mantle round thy graceful form ;
The cloudless sky smiles forth as still and fair
    As though earth ne'er could know another storm.

vi.

Come ! Let not listless sadness make delay,—
    Beneath Heaven's light that sadness will depart ;
And as we wander on our shoreward way,
    A strange, sweet peace shall enter in thine heart.
We will not weep, nor talk of vanish'd years,
    When, link by link, Hope's glittering chain was riven :
Those who are dead, shall claim from love no tears,—
    Those who have injured us, shall be forgiven.

vii.

Few have my summers been, and fewer thine ; —
    Youth blighted is the weary lot of both :
To both, all lonely shows our life's decline,
    Both with old friends and ties have waxëd wroth.
But yet we will not weep ! The breathless calm
    Which lulls the golden earth, and wide blue sea,
Shall pour into our souls mysterious balm,
    And fill us with its own tranquillity.

VIII.

We will not mar the scene — we will not look
    To the veil'd future, or the shadowy past ;
Seal'd up shall be sad Memory's open book,
    And childhood's idleness return at last !
Joy, with his restless, ever-fluttering wings,
    And Hope, his gentle brother, — all shall cease :
Like weary hinds that seek the desert springs,
    Our one sole feeling shall be peace — deep peace !

THE BLIND MAN'S BRIDE.

I.

When first, beloved, in vanish'd hours
    The blind man sought thy love to gain,
They said thy cheek was bright as flowers
    New freshen'd by the summer rain :
They said thy movements, swift yet soft,
    Were such as make the wingëd dove
Seem, as it gently soars aloft,
    The image of repose and love.

II.

They told me, too, an eager crowd
    Of wooers praised thy beauty rare,
But that thy heart was all too proud
    A common love to meet or share.
Ah ! thine was neither pride nor scorn,
    But in thy coy and virgin breast
Dwelt preference, not of PASSION born,
    The love that hath a holier rest !

III.

Days came and went — thy step I heard —
    Pause frequent as it pass'd me by : —

Days came and went ; — thy heart was stirr'd,
   And answer'd to my stifled sigh !
And thou didst make a humble choice,
   Content to be the blind man's bride.
Who loved thee for thy gentle voice,
   And own'd no joy on earth beside.

IV.

And well by that sweet voice I knew
   (Without the happiness of sight)
Thy years, as yet, were glad and few, —
   Thy smile, most innocently bright :
I knew how full of love's own grace
   The beauty of thy form must be ;
And fancy idolized the face
   Whose loveliness I might not see !

V.

Oh ! happy were those days, beloved !
   I almost ceased for light to pine
When through the summer vales we roved,
   Thy fond hand gently link'd in mine,
Thy soft " Good night" still sweetly cheer'd
   The unbroken darkness of my doom ;
And thy " Good morrow, love," endear'd
   Each sunrise that return'd in gloom !

VI.

At length, as years roll'd swiftly on,
   They spoke to me of Time's decay —
Of roses from thy smooth cheek gone,
   And ebon ringlets turn'd to grey.
Ah ! then I *bless'd* the sightless eyes
   Which could not feel the deepening shade,
Nor watch beneath succeeding skies
   Thy withering beauty faintly fade.

MM

VII.

I saw no paleness on thy cheek,
  No lines upon thy forehead smooth,—
But still the BLIND MAN heard thee speak
  In accents made to bless and soothe :
Still he could feel thy guiding hand
  As through the woodlands wild we ranged,—
Still in the summer light could stand,
  And know thy HEART and VOICE unchanged.

VIII.

And still, beloved, till life grows cold,
  We 'll wander 'neath a genial sky,
And only know that we are old
  By counting happy years gone by :
For thou to me art still as fair
  As when those happy years began,—
When first thou camest to soothe and share
  The sorrows of a sightless man !

IX.

Old Time, who changes all below,
  To wean men gently for the grave,
Hath brought us no increase of woe,
  And leaves us all he ever gave :
For I am still a helpless thing,
  Whose darken'd world is cheer'd by thee —
And thou art she whose beauty's spring
  The blind man vainly yearn'd to see !

WEEP NOT FOR HIM THAT DIETH.

"Weep ye not for the dead, neither bemoan him; but weep sore for him that goeth away, for he shall return no more, nor see his native country."—*Jeremiah* xxii. 10.

I.

Weep not for him that dieth —
  For he sleeps, and is at rest ;

And the couch whereon he lieth
  Is the green earth's quiet breast:
But weep for him who pineth
  On a far land's hateful shore,
Who wearily declineth
  Where you see his face no more !

II.

Weep not for him that dieth,
  For friends are round his bed,
And many a young lip sigheth
  When they name the early dead :
But weep for him that liveth
  Where none will know or care,
When the groan his faint heart giveth
  Is the last sigh of despair.

III.

Weep not for him that dieth,
  For his struggling soul is free,
And the world from which it flieth
  Is a world of misery ;
But weep for him that weareth
  The captive's galling chain :
To the agony *he* beareth,
  Death were but little pain.

IV.

Weep not for him that dieth,
  For *he* hath ceased from tears,
And a voice to his replieth
  Which he hath not heard for years ;
But weep for him who weepeth
  On that cold land's cruel shore —
Blest, blest is he that sleepeth,—
  Weep for the dead no more !

LÆTITIA ELIZABETH MACLEAN.

THIS remarkable writer, better known perhaps as Miss Landon, or L. E. L., may, I think, be considered the Byron of our poetesses. In character, history, and genius, there are not a few striking points of similitude between her and the great bard referred to : both acquired a world-wide fame in youth ; both were shamefully maligned and misrepresented; both became gloomy and misanthropical under the falsehoods asserted of them ; both died young, and abroad.

Mrs. Maclean's history is perhaps the more tragic of the two. Early deprived of parental care and assistance, she had almost from childhood to struggle with the worst difficulties of life ; and none but those who have experienced similar endurances can understand how much a young warm heart can be chilled by them, and changed for the worse. When her circumstances became ameliorated by her success in literature, she had to contend against the worst evils of over-praise, unjust censure, and infamous slander. Can we wonder that she acquired unhealthy views of life ? Ought we not rather to wonder that her sentiments are on the whole as sound as we find them ? Oh, the world is a hard task-master. It first spoils its pupil, and then complains of his deficiencies ! Finally, in the zenith of her fame, Mrs. Maclean, formed, more than most beings, for social intercourse, quits her country and her friends, for a solitary home on the coast of Africa : there to pine in loneliness for a month or two, and then to die. Yes ! it is a *very* mournful story.

Of Mrs. Maclean's genius there can be but one opinion. It is distinguished by very great intellectutal power, a highly sensitive and ardent imagination, an intense fervour of passionate emotion, and almost unequalled eloquence and fluency. Of mere art she displays but little. Her style is irregular and careless, and her painting sketchy and rough : but there is genius in every line she has written.

Mrs. Maclean has herself given us a just portraiture of her peculiar powers. In the concluding lines of her fine poem entitled *The Golden Violet*, she says

> " If that I know myself what keys
> Yield to my hand their sympathies,
> I should say 't is those whose tone
> Is *Woman's Love* and *Sorrow's own.*"

No writer certainly has written more of Love and Sorrow than Mrs. Maclean. She touches scarcely any other strings. I called her the female Byron : in this respect she is particularly so. Passion and Sadness are the idols of her pen. She herself says

> " Sad were my shades : methinks they had
> Almost a tone of prophecy —
> I ever had, from earliest youth,
> A feeling what my fate would be."

Her love-passages are certainly not inferior to Byron's. I would cite the following lines from *The Improvisatrice* in proof :

> I lov'd him as a young Genius loves,
> When its own mild and radiant heaven
> Of starry thought burns with the light,
> The love, the life, by passion given.
> I loved him, too, as woman loves —
> Reckless of sorrow, sin, or scorn :
> Life had no evil destiny
> That, with him, I could not have borne !
> I had been nurs'd in palaces ;
> Yet earth had not a spot so drear,
> That I should not have thought a home
> In paradise, had he been near !
> How sweet it would have been to dwell,
> Apart from all, in some green dell

54   MM*

Of sunny beauty, leaves and flowers :
And nestling birds to sing the hours !
Our home, beneath some chestnut's shade
But of the woven branches made :
Our vesper hymn, the low lone wail
The rose hears from the nightingale ;
And waked at morning by the call
Of music from a waterfall.
But not alone in dreams like this,
Breathed in the very hope of bliss,
I loved : my love had been the same
In hush'd despair, in open shame.
I would have rather been a slave,
   In tears, in bondage by his side,
Than shared in all, if wanting him,
   This world had power to give beside !
My heart was wither'd — and my heart
   Had ever been the world to me :
And love had been the first fond dream,
   Whose life was in reality.
I had sprung from my solitude,
   Like a young bird upon the wing,
To meet the arrow : so I met
   My poison'd shaft of suffering.
And as that bird with drooping crest
And broken wing, will seek his nest,
But seek in vain : so vain I sought
My pleasant home of song and thought.
There was one spell upon my brain,
Upon my pencil, on my strain ;
But one face to my colours came ;
My chords replied to but one name —
Lorenzo ! — all seem'd vow'd to thee,
To passion, and to misery !

That Mrs. Maclean could paint Sorrow as well as she could
delineate Love we have plenty of proof. Sorrow seems indeed
an essential part of her nature. Persons who knew her intimately

say that she was *not* naturally sad: that she was all gaiety and cheerfulness: but there is a mournfulness of soul which is never to be seen on the cheek or in the eye: and this I believe to have dwelt in Mrs. Maclean's breast more than in most people's. How otherwise are we to understand her poetry? We cannot believe her sadness to have been put on like a player's garb: to have been an affectation, an unreality: it is too earnest for that. We must suppose that she *felt* what she wrote: and if so, her written sadness was real sadness. Take the following lines from *The Golden Violet:* no one can believe that the sentiment they contain is unreal.

SONG.

My heart is like the failing hearth
   Now by my side;
One by one its bursts of flame
   Have burnt and died.
There are none to watch the sinking blaze,
   And none to care
Or if it kindle into strength,
   Or waste in air.
My fate is as yon faded wreath
   Of summer flowers:
They've spent their store of fragrant health
   On sunny hours,
Which reck'd them not, which heeded not
   When they were dead;
Other flowers, unwarn'd by them
   Will spring instead.
And my own heart is as the lute
   I now am waking:
Wound to too fine and high a pitch,
   They both are breaking.
And of their song what memory
   Will stay behind?
An echo, like a passing thought
   Upon the wind.

Silence, forgetfulness and rust,
    Lute, are for thee;
And such my lot; neglect, the grave,
    These are for me !

The same sad desolate tone pervades nearly all her compositions : but it invariably becomes intensest when she speaks of
herself. We always see a shadow on her heart. The following
lines beautifully illustrate this tendency :

Silent and dark is the source of yon river,
    Whose birth-place we know not, and seek not to know,
Though mild as the flight of the shaft from yon quiver,
    Is the course of its waves as in music they flow.

Oh, my heart, and my song, which is as my heart's flowing,
    Read thy fate in yon river, for such is thine own !
'Mid those the chief praise on thy music bestowing,
    Who cares for the lips from whence issue the tone ?

Dark as its birth-place, so dark is my spirit,
    Whence yet the sweet waters of melody come :
'T is the long after-course, not the source, will inherit
    The beauty and glory of sunshine and fame.

And nothing seems able to " make a sunshine in this shady
place." No burst of cheerfulness ever displays relief. Amidst
every kind of scenery and circumstance the darkness is the
same. Her pensiveness is her familiar spirit. She delights in it:

" Call it madness, call it folly,
    You cannot drive her gloom away,
There 's such a charm in melancholy,
    She would not if she could be gay."

Sorrow must have been at the core of her heart, or she never
could have written like this :

SONG.

Farewell, farewell ! I 'll dream no more,
　　'T is misery to be dreaming :
Farewell, farewell ; and I will be
　　At least like thee in seeming.
I will go forth to the green vale,
　　Where the sweet wild flowers are dwelling,
Where the leaves and the birds together sing,
　　And the woodland fount is welling.
Not there, not there, too much of bloom
　　Has Spring flung o'er each blossom ;
The tranquil place too much contrasts
　　The unrest of my bosom.
I will go to the lighted halls,
　　Where midnight passes fleetest ;
Oh, memory there too much recalls
　　Of saddest and of sweetest.
I 'll turn me to the gifted page,
　　Where the bard his soul is flinging ;
Too well it echoes mine own heart
　　Breaking e'en while singing.
I must have rest ! Oh, heart of mine,
　　When wilt thou lose thy sorrow ?
Never, till in the quiet grave :
　　— Would I slept there to-morrow !

This strong tendency towards melancholy frequently led Mrs.
Maclean into most erroneous views and sentiments ; which,
though we may make what excuses we will for them out of consideration for the author, should be heartily and honestly condemned for the sake of moral truth.   For instance, when we find
her saying —

Oh, when the grave shall open for me,—
(I care not how soon that time may be,—)
Never a rose shall grow on that tomb,
It breathes too much of hope and bloom ;

> But there be that flower's meek regret,
> The bending and dark blue *Violet* —

when we read such passages as this, it is our duty to speak in
terms of rebuke and repudiation.   There is an evil spirit in such
sentiments which should be bidden behind us.   Why should we
reject the blooming and beautiful, and cling after this poor fashion
to the sad and sorrowful ?   It is false philosophy, we may be sure.
Violets, indeed !   Why, what were roses made for ?   To be
slighted and contemned and despised, as it were, like this ?   Oh,
no, no !   Roses were made to gladden and delight us, and give
us ideas of beauty and hope : nay, more than this, to make us
grateful to the Giver of all good besides.

Here is another instance of our fair author's tendency to look
upon the dark side of life.   In a little poem entitled *Change* she
thus writes :

> And this is what is left of youth !
> There were two boys, who were bred up together,
> Shared the same bed, and fed at the same board.
> Each tried the other's sport, from their first chase,
> Young hunters of the butterfly and bee,
> To when they followed the fleet hare, and tried
> The swiftness of the bird.   They lay beside
> The silver trout stream, watching as the sun
> Play'd on the bubbles : Shared each in the store
> Of either's garden ; and together read
> Of *him*, the master of the desert isle,
> Till a low hut, a gun and a canoe
> Bounded their wishes.   Or if ever came
> A thought of future days, 't was but to say
> That they would share each other's lot, and do
> Wonders, no doubt.   But this was vain ; they parted
> With promises of long remembrance, words
> Whose kindness was the heart's, and those warm tears,
> Hidden like shame by the young eyes that shed them,
> But which are thought upon in after years
> As what we would give worlds to shed once more.

They met again,—but different from themselves,—
At least what each remembered of themselves :
The one proud as a soldier of his rank,
And of his many battles : and the other
Proud of his Indian wealth, and of the skill
And toil which gather'd it : each with a brow
And heart alike darken'd by years and care.

They met with cold words and yet colder looks ;
Each was chang'd in himself, and yet each thought
The other only chang'd, himself the same.
And coldness bred dislike ; and rivalry
Came like the pestilence o'er some sweet thoughts
That linger'd yet, healthy and beautiful,
Amid dark and unkindly ones.   And they
Whose boyhood had not known one jarring word,
Were strangers in their age : if their eyes met,
'T was but to look contempt, and when they spoke,
Their speech was wormwood !
—And this, this is life !

No ! with all due respect to our fair poetess, this is *not* life.
Doubtless there have been, and are, and long will be instances of
brethren who have loved each other in childhood becoming
strangers, almost haters, in manhood : but to assert that life is
composed of such cases is to libel Providence and to dishearten
man.   Let the melancholy say what they will, enduring affection
is not a fable, not a poet's dream : it is a high and a holy reality,
one of the least deniable truths existing in the world : and only
an erring or bewildered soul can doubt it.

Life ! — No !   Doubt and distrust, change and coldness, these
are not *Life* — they form but the merest fraction of life.   LIFE !
— a never-ending rush of varied, new-created, unsoiled moments,
every one of which bears its freight of happiness, every one of
which may be turned to our enjoyment if we please ; countless
bright fountains around us, from which pleasure never ceases to
flow ; friends to cheer, — kindred to bless, — flowers of beauty
and sounds of infinite music to soothe and to charm — high hopes

and glorious aspirations — the proud consciousness of Being and
Thinking — and above all, the irrepressible expectation of a still
brighter, more beautiful, more high and noble world ; — this,
though a poor and feeble picture, is at least more like life than the
other. O, a glorious heritage Life is ! To LIVE ! — what ineffable
meaning there is in that short expression ! — *to live !* To be
a part of never-ending Life ! To be more immortal than worlds,
— more eternal than the stars, — more indestructible than Nature, — more strong than Death : — to be a part of — to be joined
to — the one great Everlasting Principle of Being : — what power,
what glory, what majesty there is in the thought ! Pain, sorrow,
sin, evil, are *these* man's heritage and lot, then ? No ! Joy,
Friendship, Affection, Hope — " this, *this* is Life ; " — and that
soul is not a true poet's soul which would seek to persuade us to
the contrary.

Few writers are so picturesque as Mrs. Maclean. Her descriptions are perfect paintings, and often indeed give us a better idea
of a scene than an actual representation of it. Some of her
poetical illustrations of the pictures in *Fisher's Drawing-Room
Scrap-Book* are as superior in intelligence to the plates as a living
being is to a marble statue.

The following poem will give a good general idea of Mrs.
Maclean's picturesque manner.

THE SOLDIER'S FUNERAL.

And the muffled drum roll'd on the air,
Warriors with stately step were there ;
On every arm was the black crape bound,
Every carbine was turn'd to the ground :
Solemn the sound of their measur'd tread,
As silent and slow they follow'd the dead.
The riderless horse was led in the rear,
There were white plumes waving over the bier,
Helmet and sword were laid on the pall,
For it was a Soldier's Funeral.

That soldier hath stood on the battle plain,
Where every step was over the slain;
But the brand and the ball had pass'd him by,
And he came to his native land to die.
'T was hard to come to that native land
And not clasp one familiar hand!
'T was hard to be number'd amid the dead,
Or ere he could hear his welcome said!
But 't was something to see its cliffs once more,
And to lay his bones on his own lov'd shore;
To think that the friends of his youth might weep
O'er the green grass turf of the soldier's sleep.
The bugles ceased their wailing sound
As the coffin was lower'd into the ground:
A volley was fired, a blessing said,
One moment's pause — and they left the dead!
— I saw a poor and an aged man,
His step was feeble, his lip was wan;
He knelt him down on the new rais'd mound,
His face was bow'd on the cold damp ground,
He rais'd his head, his tears were done,
The Father had pray'd o'er his only Son!

As a further specimen of Mrs. Maclean's descriptive power I present the following truly fine poem. Campbell would hardly have written better.

THE GRASP OF THE DEAD.

'T was in the battle-field, and the cold pale moon
  Look'd down on the dead and dying;
And the wind passed o'er with a dirge and a wail
  Where the young and brave were lying.

With his father's sword in his red right hand,
  And the hostile dead around him,
Lay a youthful chief: but his bed was the ground,
  And the grave's icy sleep had bound him.

55   NN

A reckless rover, 'mid death and doom,
　Pass'd a soldier, his plunder seeking;
Careless he stept, where friend and foe
　Lay alike in their life-blood reeking.

Drawn by the shine of the warrior's sword,
　The soldier paus'd beside it;
He wrench'd the hand with a giant's strength,
　— But the grasp of the dead defied it.

He loos'd his hold, and his English heart
　Took part with the dead before him;
And he honour'd the brave who died sword in hand,
　As with soften'd brow he leant o'er him.

" A soldier's death thou hast boldly died,
　A soldier's grave won by it:
Before I would take that sword from thine hand,
　My own life's blood should dye it.

" Thou shalt not be left for the carrion crow,
　Or the wolf to batten o'er thee;
Or the coward insult the gallant dead,
　Who in life had trembled before thee."

Then dug he a grave in the crimson earth,
　Where his warrior foe was sleeping;
And he laid him there in honour and rest,
　With his sword in his own brave keeping!

　There is far down in woman's heart a beautiful tendency and
love towards the heroic, which does more to cultivate and extend
that sentiment than the much fiercer but less pure passion for it
which nerves the arm and fires the words of man. A noble deed
always receives its best response of approbation from woman.
Woman sees the signs of true greatness far more readily than
man. Mark how Mrs. Maclean celebrates a hero!

CRESCENTIUS.

I look'd upon his brow — no sign
  Of guilt or fear was there ;
He stood as proud by that death-shrine
  As even o'er despair
He had a power ; in his eye
There was a quenchless energy,
  A spirit that could dare
The deadliest form that death could take,
And dare it for the daring's sake.

He stood — the fetters on his hand :
  He raised them haughtily ;
And had that grasp been on the brand,
  It could not wave on high
With freer pride than it waved now ;
Around he look'd with changeless brow
  On many a torture nigh :
The rack, the chain, the axe, the wheel,
And, worst of all, his own red steel.

I saw him once before ; he rode
  Upon a coal-black steed ;
And tens of thousands throng'd the road,
  And bade their warrior speed ;
His helm, his breastplate, were of gold,
And graved with many a dent, that told
  Of many a soldier's deed ;
The sun shone on his sparkling mail,
And danced his snow-plume on the gale.

But now he stood chain'd and alone,
  The headsman by his side,
The plume, the helm, the charger gone ;
  The sword which had defied
The mightiest lay broken near ;
And yet no sign or sound of fear
  Came from that lip of pride ;

And never king or conqueror's brow
Wore higher look than his did now.

He bent beneath the headsman's stroke
  With an uncover'd eye ;
A wild shout from the numbers broke
  Who throng'd to see him die.
It was a people's loud acclaim,
  The voice of anger and of shame,
    A nation's funeral cry ;
Rome's wail above her only son,
Her patriot and her latest one.

With one more extract I conclude.   It is a Ballad called

SIR WALTER MANNY AT HIS FATHER'S TOMB.

"Oh, show me the grave where my father is laid,
  Show his lowly grave to me ;
A hundred pieces of broad red gold,
  Old man, shall thy guerdon be."

With torch in hand, and barëd head,
  The old man led the way :
And cold and shrill pass'd the midnight wind
  Through his hair of silvery grey.

A stately knight follow'd his steps,
  And his form was tall and proud ;
And his step fell soft, and his helm was off,
  And his head on his bosom bow'd.

They pass'd through the cathedral aisles,
  Whose sculptur'd walls declare
The deeds of many a noble knight,
  De Manny's name was not there.

They pass'd next a low and humble church,
   Scarce seen amid the gloom ;
There was many a grave, yet not even there
   Had his father found a tomb.

They travers'd a bleak and barren heath,
   Till they came to a gloomy wood ;
Where the dark trees droop'd, and the dark grass grew,
   As curs'd with the sight of blood.

There stood a lorn and blasted tree,
   As heaven and earth were its foes,
And beneath was a piled-up mound of stones,
   Where a rude grey cross arose.

" And lo !" said the ancient servitor,
   " It is here thy father is laid ;
No mass has bless'd the lowly grave,
   Which his humblest follower made.

" I would have wander'd through every land
   Where his gallant name was known,
To have pray'd a mass for the soul of the dead,
   And a monumental stone.

" But I knew thy father had a son,
   To whom the task would be dear ;
Young knight, I kept the warrior's grave
   For thee, and thou art here."

Sir Walter grasped the old man's hand,
   But spoke he never a word ; —
So still it was that the fall of tears
   On his mailëd vest was heard.

Oh, the heart has all too many tears :
   But none are like those that wait
On the blighted love, the loneliness
   Of the young orphan's fate.

         NN*

He call'd to mind when for knighthood's badge
    He knelt at Edward's throne,
How many stood by a parent's side,
    But he stood there alone!

He thought how often his heart had pined,
    When his was the victor's name,
Thrice desolate, strangers might give,
    But could not share his fame.

Down he knelt in silent prayer
    On the grave where his father slept;
And many the tears, and bitter the thoughts
    As the warrior his vigil kept.

And he built a little chapel there,
    And bade the deathbell toll,
And prayers be said, and mass he sung,
    For the weal of the warrior's soul.

Years pass'd, and ever Sir Walter was first
    Where warlike deeds were done;
But who would not look for the gallant knight
    In the leal and loyal son?

THE AWAKENING OF ENDYMION.

Lone upon the mountain, the pine-trees wailing round him,
    Lone upon a mountain the Grecian youth is laid;
Sleep, mystic sleep, for many a year has bound him,
    Yet his beauty, like a statue's pale and fair, is undecay'd.
            When will he awaken?
When will he awaken? a loud voice hath been crying
    Night after night, and the cry has been in vain;

Winds, woods, and waves, found echoes for replying,
  But the tones of the beloved one were never heard again.
      When will he awaken?
      Ask'd the midnight's silver queen.

Never mortal eye has looked upon his sleeping;
  Parents, kindred, comrades, have mourned for him as dead;
By day the gathered clouds have had him in their keeping,
  And at night the solemn shadows round his rest are shed.
      When will he awaken?
Long has been the cry of faithful Love's imploring,
  Long has Hope been watching with soft eyes fixed above;
When will the Fates, the life of life restoring,
  Own themselves vanquished by mnch-enduring love?
      When will he awaken?
      Asks the midnight's weary queen.

Beautiful the sleep that she has watch'd untiring,
  Lighted up with visions from yonder radiant sky,
Full of an immortal's glorious inspiring,
  Softened by the woman's meek and loving sigh,
      When will he awaken?
He has been dreaming of old heroic stories,
  The poet's passionate world has entered in his soul;
He has grown conscious of life's ancestral glories,
  When sages and when Kings first upheld the mind's control.
      When will he awaken?
      Ask'd the midnight's stately queen.

Lo! the appointed midnight! the present hour is fated;
  It is Endymion's planet that rises on the air;
How long, how tenderly his goddess love has waited,
  Waited with a love too mighty for despair.
      Soon he will awaken!
Soft amid the pines is a sound as if of singing,
  Tones that seem the lute's from the breathing flowers depart;
Not a wind that wanders o'er Mount Latmos, but is bringing
  Music that is murmur'd from nature's inmost heart.
      Soon he will awaken,
      To his and midnight's queen!

Lovely is the green earth — she knows the hour is holy ;
   Starry are the heavens, lit with eternal joy ;
Light like their own is dawning sweet and slowly
   O'er the fair and sculptured forehead of that yet dreaming boy.
       Soon he will awaken !
Red as the red rose towards the morning turning,
   Warms the youth's lip to the watcher's near his own,
While the dark eyes open, bright, intense, and burning
   With a life more glorious than ere they closed was known.
       Yes, he has awakened
       For the midnight's happy queen !

What is this old history but a lesson given,
   How true love still conquers by the deep strength of truth,
How all the impulses, whose native home is heaven,
   Sanctify the visions of hope, faith, and youth.
       'T is for such they waken !
When every worldly thought is utterly forsaken,
   Comes the starry midnight, felt by life's gifted few ;
Then will the spirit from its earthly sleep awaken
   To a being more intense, more spiritual and true.
       So doth the soul awaken,
       Like that youth to night's fair queen !.

WE MIGHT HAVE BEEN !

We might have been ! — these are but common words,
   And yet they make the sum of life's bewailing ;
They are the echo of those finer chords,
   Whose music life deplores when unavailing.
       We might have been !

We might have been so happy ! says the child,
   Pent in the weary school-room during summer,
When the green rushes 'mid the marshes wild,
   And rosy fruits, attend the radiant comer.
       We might have been !

It is the thought that darkens on our youth,
    When first experience — sad experience — teaches
What fallacies we have believed for truth,
    And what few truths endeavour ever reaches.
           We might have been !

Alas ! how different from what we are
    Had we but known the bitter path before us;
But feelings, hopes, and fancies left afar,
    What in the wide bleak world can e'er restore us ?
           We might have been !

It is the motto of all human things,
    The end of all that waits on mortal seeking ;
The weary weight upon Hope's flagging wings,
    It is the cry of the worn heart while breaking —
           We might have been !

And when, warm with the heaven that gave it birth,
    Dawns on our world-worn way Love's hour Elysian,
The last fair angel lingering on our earth,
    The shadow of what thought obscures the vision ?
           We might have been !

A cold fatality attends on love,
    Too soon or else too late the heart-beat quickens ;
The star which is our fate springs up above,
    And we but say — while round the vapour thickens —
           We might have been !

Life knoweth no like misery; the rest
    Are single sorrows,— but in this are blended
All sweet emotions that disturb the breast;
    The light that was our loveliest is ended.
           We might have been !

Henceforth, how much of the full heart must be
    A sealed book at whose contents we tremble ?
56

A still voice mutters 'mid our misery,
 The worst to hear, because it must dissemble —
  We might have been!

Life is made up of miserable hours,
 And all of which we craved a brief possessing,
For which we wasted wishes, hopes, and powers,
 Comes with some fatal drawback on the blessing.
  We might have been!

The future never renders to the past
 The young beliefs intrusted to its keeping;
Inscribe one sentence — life's first truth and last —
 On the pale marble where our dust is sleeping —
  We might have been.

STANZAS ON THE DEATH OF MRS. HEMANS.

" The rose — the glorious rose is gone."—*Lays of Many Lands*

Bring flowers to crown the cup and lute,—
 Bring flowers,— the bride is near;
Bring flowers to soothe the captive's cell,
 Bring flowers to strew the bier!
Bring flowers! thus said the lovely song;
 And shall they not be brought
To her who linked the offering
 With feeling and with thought?

Bring flowers, — the perfumed and the pure, —
 Those with the morning dew,
A sigh in every fragrant leaf,
 A tear on every hue.
So pure, so sweet thy life has been,
 So filling earth and air
With odours and with loveliness,
 Till common scenes grew fair

Thy song around our daily path
　Flung beauty born of dreams,
And scattered o'er the actual world
　The spirit's sunny gleams.
Mysterious influence, that to earth
　Brings down the heaven above,
And fills the universal heart
　With universal love.

Such gifts were thine, — as from the block
　The unformed and the cold,
The sculptor calls to breathing life
　Some shape of perfect mould,
So thou from common thoughts and things
　Didst call a charmed song,
Which on a sweet and swelling tide
　Bore the full soul along.

And thou from far and foreign lands
　Didst bring back many a tone,
And giving such new music still,
　A music of thine own.
A lofty strain of generous thoughts,
　And yet subdued and sweet, —
An angel's song, who sings of earth,
　Whose cares are at his feet.

And yet thy song is sorrowful,
　Its beauty is not bloom ;
The hopes of which it breathes, are hopes
　That look beyond the tomb.
Thy song is sorrowful as winds
　That wander o'er the plain,
And ask for summer's vanish'd flowers,
　And ask for them in vain.

Ah ! dearly purchased is the gift,
　The gift of song like thine ;

A fated doom is her's who stands
   The priestess of the shrine.
The crowd — they only see the crown,
   They only hear the hymn ;
They mark not that the cheek is pale,
   And that the eye is dim.

Wound to a pitch too exquisite,
   The soul's fine chords are wrung ;
With misery and melody
   They are too highly strung.
The heart is made too sensitive
   Life's daily pain to bear;
It beats in music, but it beats
   Beneath a deep despair.

It never meets the love it paints,
   The love for which it pines ;
Too much of Heaven is in the faith
   That such a heart enshrines.
The meteor-wreath the poet wears
   Must make a lonely lot;
It dazzles, only to divide
   From those who wear it not.

Didst thou not tremble at thy fame,
   And loathe its bitter prize,
While what to others triumph seemed,
   To thee was sacrifice ?
Oh, Flower brought from Paradise,
   To this cold world of ours,
Shadows of beauty such as thine
   Recall thy native bowers.

Let others thank thee —'t was for them
   Thy soft leaves thou didst wreathe ;
The red rose wastes itself in sighs
   Whose sweetness others breathe !

And they have thanked thee — many a lip
 Has asked of thine for words,
When thoughts, life's finer thoughts, have touched
 The spirit's inmost chords.

How many loved and honoured thee
 Who only knew thy name ;
Which o'er the weary working world
 Like starry music came !
With what still hours of calm delight
 Thy songs and image blend ;
I cannot choose but think thou wert
 An old familiar friend.

The charm that dwelt in songs of thine
 My inmost spirit moved ;
And yet I feel as thou hadst been
 Not half enough beloved.
They say that thou wert faint, and worn
 With suffering and with care ;
What music must have filled the soul
 That had so much to spare !

Oh, weary One ! since thou art laid
 Within thy mother's breast —
The green, the quiet mother-earth —
 Thrice blessed be thy rest !
Thy heart is left within our hearts,
 Although life's pang is o'er ;
But the quick tears are in my eyes,
 And I can write no more.

oo

MRS. ABDY

Is a well-known and very able contributor to many of our Annuals and Magazines. She has published a Volume of Poems, for private circulation, many of the pieces in which are distinguished by a purity of diction and loftiness of sentiment, which leave her little, if at all, behind the best writers among her sex. Mrs. Abdy is one of the many female poets who, like Mrs. Hemans, have consecrated their spiritual gifts to the service of religion. Her piety is fervent, without a tinge of bigotry : and her verse is full of that serenity and cheerfulness which only a warm faith can inspire.

THE DESTINY OF GENIUS.

"How often I have exclaimed, — 'I am not beloved as I love!' "
Miss Landon.

Daughter of song ! how truly hast thou spoken !
  Yet deem not that to thee alone belong
Sad memories of idols crush'd and broken,
  Of wounding falsehood, and of bitter wrong :
Oh ! in thy cares, thy trials, I can trace
The lot appointed for thy gifted race.

Genius is all too lavish of its feelings,
  It gives its tenderness of heavenly birth,
To waste its bright and beautiful revealings
  On the dull common natures of the earth,
Casting the flowers of a celestial land,
To droop and wither upon barren sand.

And earth's cold children cherish not the treasure,
  The pure and blessed offering they repel,
Busied in worldly toil, or worldly pleasure,
  Their souls respond not to the hidden spell

Touch'd by a hand whose skilful power was given
As the peculiar boon of favouring Heaven.

And must it then be so? — must cold rejection
　　Still mock the heart where Genius warmly glows?
No! there is One on whom its deep affection
　　In fearless trusting ardour may repose;
Exhausting all the riches of its store,
Yet ever in return receiving more.

Yes: let it safely guard its true devotion
　　From the low commerce of the worthless sod,
Laying each fond and rapturous emotion
　　A tribute at the holy shrine of God:
Oh! where can gifted spirits wisely love,
Save when they fix their hopes on One above?

THE CHILD IN A GARDEN.

Child of the flaxen locks, and laughing eye,
　　Culling with hasty glee the flowerets gay,
Or chasing with light foot the butterfly,
　　I love to mark thee at thy frolic play.

Near thee I see thy tender father stand,
　　His anxious eye pursues thy roving track;
And oft with warning voice and beckoning hand,
　　He checks thy speed, and gently draws thee back.

Why dost thou meekly yield to his decree?
　　Fair boy, his fond regard to thee is known;
He does not check thy joys from tyranny —
　　Thou art his lov'd, his cherish'd, and his own.

When worldly lures, in manhood's coming hours,
　　Tempt thee to wander from discretion's way;
Oh! grasp not eagerly the offer'd flowers,
　　Pause if thy *Heavenly* Father bid thee stay.

Pause, and in Him revere a friend and guide,
Who does not willingly thy faults reprove,
But ever, when thou rovest from his side,
Watches to win thee back with pitying love

WHERE SHALL I DIE?

Where shall I die? — Shall Death's cold hand
Arrest my breath while dear ones stand
In silent watchful love, to shed
Their tears around my quiet bed?
Or, shall I meet my final doom
Far from my country and my home?
Lord, to Thy will I bend the knee;
Thou evermore hast cared for me.

How shall I die? — Shall Death's harsh yoke
Subdue me by a single stroke?
Or shall my fainting frame sustain
The tedious languishing of pain,
Sinking in weariness away,
Slowly and sadly, day by day?
Lord, I repose my cares on Thee;
Thou evermore hast cared for me.

When shall I die? — Shall Death's stern call
Soon come, my spirit to appal?
Or shall I live through circling years,
A pilgrim in this vale of tears;
Surviving those I loved the best,
Who in the peaceful church-yard rest?
Lord! I await Thy wise decree;
Thou evermore hast cared for me.

Yet, oh, sustain me by Thy power!
Be with me in Life's parting hour:

Tell me of peace and pardon won
Through the dear mercies of Thy Son :
Then shall I feel resign'd to go
From Life's brief joy and fleeting woe,
If I in death the Saviour see,
Who evermore hath cared for me.

The subjoined lines on the death of Mrs. Hemans contain so fine an appreciation of that gifted lady's genius, and furnish so noble a lesson to our Poetesses from one of their own number, that I am sure I shall be cheerfully pardoned for transcribing it.

LINES WRITTEN ON THE DEATH OF MRS. HEMANS.

Yes, she has left us. She, whose gifted lays
So nobly earned a nation's love and praise,
Entranced the high and lofty ones of earth, —
And shed a radiance o'er the peasant's hearth,
She from the world is taken. Her sweet lute
Hangs on the willow desolate and mute ;
And while we half unconsciously repeat
Strains we have learned as household words to greet,
How mournful is the thought, that she can pour
Songs of such touching melody no more !

Oh ! what a range of mind was hers, how bright
Her pages seemed with Inspiration's light ;
And yet, though skilled to dazzle and o'erwhelm,
Queen of Imagination's fairy realm,
Her highest excellence appeared to be
In the calm region of reality.
In Nature's wondrous workings lay her art,
From that exhaustless mine, the human heart,
She brought her gems. 'T was hers, with gentle skill
The slumbering feelings to arouse and thrill ;

With colours not more beautiful than true
The modest virtues of her sex she drew.
" Records of Woman."   At that name arise
Fair shapes of truth and goodness to our eyes:
Not the gay phantoms seen in Fancy's trance,
Not the bright paragons of old romance,
Nor yet the wonders of a later age,
The heroines of Reason's formal page,
Full of cold, calculating, worldly sense,
And self-elate in moral excellence !
No — at Religion's pure and sacred flame
Her torch she kindled — 't was her wish and aim
That in her female portraits we should see
The blest effects of humble piety,
Proving that, in this world of sin and strife,
None could fulfil the charities of life,
Or bear its trials, save the path they trod
Were hallowed by the guiding grace of God.

And well her spirit in her life was shown,
No character more lovely than her own
Fell from her gifted pen — though numbers breathed
Her name, though laurel bands her brow enwreathed,
She sought not in the world's vain scenes to roam,
Her duties were her joys, her sphere her home :
And Memory still a pensive pleasure blends
With the affliction of her weeping friends,
When they recall the meek calm lowliness
With which she bore the blaze of her success :
But trials soon as well as triumphs came,
Sickness subdued her weak and languid frame,
Then was she patient, tranquil, and resigned,
Religion soothed and fortified her mind ;
She knew that for the blessed Saviour's sake,
In whom she trusted, she should sleep to wake
In glory, and she yielded up her breath,
Feeling she won eternity by death.

Oh ! may her holy principles impress
The soul of each surviving poetess ;
No trivial charge is to her care consigned,
Who gives to public view her stores of mind :
Even though her sum of treasures may be small,
Good can be worked, if Heaven permit, by all :
She who a single talent holds in store,
By patient zeal may make that little more ;
And though but few, alas ! can boast the powers
Of her now lost, the gift may still be ours
Humbly to imitate her better part ;
And strive to elevate each reader's heart
To themes of purer and of holier birth
Than the low pleasures and vain pomps of earth.
Never may Woman's lays their service lend
Vice to encourage, soften, or defend,
Nor may we in our own conceit be wise,
Weaving frail webs of mere moralities :
No, may we ever on His grace reflect,
To whom we owe our cherished intellect,
Deem that such powers in trust to us were given
To serve and glorify our Lord in heaven,
And place, amid the highest joys of fame,
Our best distinction in a Christian's name.

Mrs. Abdy's verses have invariably this great merit — that they
are written with a purpose. She never fails to urge a truth, or
enforce a duty, in her writings. The subjoined poems are good
illustrations of this assertion.

THE BUILDERS OF THE ARK.

The ark is on the waters, and one family alone,
Amid a lost and guilty race, its saving succour own ;
Why are so few a number to the sacred shelter brought ?
Where are the many builders who the wondrous structure wrought?

Alas ! they laboured at their task with cold mechanic skill ;
They had no hope of future grace, no fear of future ill;
Vainly the holy ark they view, vainly its refuge crave —
Others are by their efforts saved, themselves they cannot save.

May not the record of their fate a warning truth convey,
To some who in religion's cause unwearied zeal display ?
Our anxious cares extend to all, our active works abound,
But say, within our secret hearts is true devotion found ?

We send the blessed Book of Life to cheer the heathen's night,
But do we duly read and prize its words of hope and light ?
Where bands of pious Christians meet we eagerly repair,
Do we with equal fervour breathe our solitary prayer ?

The sinful we reclaim and warn, the ignorant we teach,
We place them in the narrow road, a land of joy to reach ;
How dire the thought, that, while they bless their firm and friendly
         guide,
They may attain the gates of heaven, and miss us from their side !

Our prompt and ready labours may the praise of man demand ;
Man judges of the spirit by the workings of the hand :
But God's unfailing wisdom seeks religion's hidden part,
And marks if true and vital faith be cherished in the heart.

Yet let us not unmindful of our erring brethren prove ;
No, let increasing energy inspire our deeds of love,
But while to save another's soul our ardent zeal is shown,
O, let us watch with ceaseless care the welfare of our own !

THE DARKNESS OF EGYPT.

" But all the children of Israel had light in their dwellings." (*Exodus*, x. 23.)

Lo ! Moses stretcheth forth at God's command
    His hand to heaven, and at the mystic sign
Thick darkness gathers over Egypt's land ;
    The glorious lights above no longer shine ;

None knows another — each one rooted stays
By his sad hearth through these appalling days.

And do their captives share their mournful doom?
    Must Israel's wretched children gaze in fear
On the dark horrors of surrounding gloom,
    Making imprisonment's long hours more drear?
The judgment to redress their wrongs was sent,
And must they then partake the punishment?

They do not share it: favoured is the race
    Of injured Israel, and the mists of night
Invade them not; each sees his dwelling-place
    Cheered and illumed by its accustomed light:
Dim shadows the oppressor's home molest,
Yet reach not the abode of the opprest.

And thus, when darkness wraps the worldly crowd,
    Sad aliens from the brightness of the word
Its sullen influence shall never shroud
    The true and faithful servants of the Lord;
Without them is the dreary gloom of sin,
But rays from heaven shall comfort them within.

False accusation, poverty, reproach,
    Loss of loved friends, oppression, slavery, pain,
These darkening clouds their dwellings may approach,
    Yet strive to quench its holy light in vain:
The flame shall brightly and securely shine,
Kindled and cherished by a hand divine.

And when, amid the gloomy vale of death,
    Conscience the sinner's terrors shall enhance,
The firm believer shall, in steadfast faith,
    Walk in the light of God's own countenance,
Cast off his bondage, and amid the blest,
Enjoy eternal light — eternal rest!

THE WHITE POPPY.

Thou hast no power to charm our eye,
    Or aid us in our need,
Disdainfully we pass thee by,
    Thou pale and worthless weed !
Bright flowers are near thy dwelling-place,
    And corn is waving round,
Thou dost but sadden and deface
    This gay and fertile ground.

Yet hold — my censure I repress —
    Thy wondrous juice contains
A spell to soothe in drowsiness,
    The weary sufferer's pains ;
He sighs for sleep — in thought he shrinks
    From night's long train of woes,
Till of thy lulling draught he drinks,
    And sinks to soft repose.

What were to him the fragrant flowers
    That lavish Nature yields,
What the rich vineyard's purple stores,
    The harvest of the fields ?
Scarce fruits improved by careful art,
    Fair buds of varied dyes,
How would they mock his throbbing heart,
    How cheat his aching eyes !

Let me no more with erring sense
    God's mystic works arraign,
The mighty hand of Providence
    Hath nothing made in vain ;
Nor need I quit this lonely mead
    His gracious love to scan,
Since even in a simple weed
    I trace his care for man.

THE LANGUAGE OF FLOWERS.

The mystic science is not mine
    That Eastern records teach ;
I cannot to each bud assign
    A sentiment and speech ;
Yet, when in yonder blossom'd dell
    I pass my lonely hours,
Methinks my heart interprets well
    The eloquence of flowers.

Of life's first thoughtless years they tell,
    When half my joy and grief
Dwelt in a lily's opening bell,
    A rosebud's drooping leaf —
I watched for them the sun's bright rays,
    And feared the driving showers,
Types of my girlhood's radiant days
    Were ye, sweet transient flowers.

And sadder scenes ye bring to mind,
    The moments ye renew
When first the woodbine's wreaths I twined,
    A loved one's grave to strew ;
On the cold turf I weeping spread
    My offering from the bowers,
Ye seemed meet tribute to the dead,
    Pale, perishable flowers.

Yet speak ye not alone, fair band,
    Of changefulness and gloom,
Ye tell me of God's gracious hand,
    That clothes you thus in bloom,
And sends to soften and to calm
    A sinful world like ours,
Gifts of such purity and balm
    As ye, fresh dewy flowers.

And while your smiling ranks I view,
    In vivid colours drest,
My heart, with faith confirmed and true,
    Learns on the Lord to rest :
If He the lilies of the field
    With lavish glory dowers,
Will he not greater bounties yield
    To me, than to the flowers ?

Still, still they speak — around my track
    Some faded blossoms lie,
Another spring shall bring them back,
    Yet bring them, but to die :
But we forsake this world of strife,
    To rise to nobler powers,
And share those gifts of endless life,
    Withheld from earth's frail flowers.

O may I bear your lessons hence,
    Fair children of the sod,
Yours is the calm mute eloquence,
    That leads the thoughts to God :
And oft amid the great and wise,
    My heart shall seek these bowers,
And turn from man's proud colloquies,
    To commune with the flowers.

MRS. SARAH ELLIS.

Miss Sarah Stickney, now Mrs. Ellis, is best known as a
writer of prose, though entitled to no mean reputation as a Poet.
Her *Pictures of Private Life, Hints to make Home Happy,
Women of England, Sons of the Soil, Poetry of Life*, &c., have
been extremely popular. The only volume of her Poems that
has fallen under our notice, is *The Wild Irish Girl, and other
Poems*, published in London and in New York, in 1844. Mrs.
Ellis resides at Pentonville.

THE PILGRIM'S REST.

Pilgrim, why thy course prolong?
Here are birds of ceaseless song,
Here are flowers of fadeless bloom,
Here are woods of deepest gloom,
Cooling waters for thy feet:
Pilgrim, rest; repose is sweet.

Tempt me not with thoughts of rest.
Woods in richest verdure dressed,
Scented flowers and murmuring streams,
Lull the soul to fruitless dreams.
I would seek some holy fane,
Pure and free from earthly stain.

Based upon the eternal rock,
Braving time and tempest's shock;
Seest thou not yon temple grey?
There thy weary steps may stay,
There thy lowly knees may bend,
There thy fervent tears descend.

Has that temple stood the storm ?
Could no touch of time deform ?
Was the altar there so pure,
That its worship must endure ?
Whence those noble ruins then ?
Why the wondering gaze of men ?

No.　The Sybil's power is gone.
Hushed is each mysterious tone.
Closed the eye, whose upward gaze
Read the length of human days ;
Blindly darkened to her own,
Shrine and goddess both are gone.

Onward, then, my feet must roam ;
Not for me the marble dome,
Not the sculptured column high,
Pointing to yon azure sky.
Let the Heathen worship there,
Not for me that place of prayer.

Pilgrim, enter.　Awe profound
Waits thee on this hallowed ground.
Here no mouldering columns fall,
Here no ruin marks the wall ;
Marble pure, and gilding gay,
Woo thy sight, and win thy stay.

Here the priest, in sacred stole
Welcomes every weary soul.
Here what suppliant knees are bending !
Here what holy incense lending
Perfume to the ambient air !
Ecstacy to praise and prayer !

Pilgrim, pause ; and view this pile.
Leave not yet the vaulted aisle.
See what sculptured forms are here !
See what gorgeous groups appear !

Tints that glow, and shapes that live,
All that art or power can give !

Hark, the solemn organ sounds !
How each echoing note rebounds !
Now along the arches high,
Far away it seems to die.
Now it thunders, deep and low,
Surely thou mayst worship now.

Tempt me not. The scene is fair,
Music floats upon the air,
Clouds of perfume round me roll;
Thoughts of rapture fill my soul.
Tempt me not, I must away,
Here I may not—dare not stay.

Here amazed — entranced I stand,
Human power on every hand
Charms my senses — meets my gaze,
Wraps me in a wildering maze.
But the place of prayer for me,
Purer still than this must be.

From the light of southern skies,
Where the stately columns rise —
Wanderer from the valleys green,
Wherefore seek this wintry scene ?
Here no stranger steps may stay,
Turn thee, pilgrim — haste away.

Here, what horrors meet thy sight !
Mountain-wastes, of trackless height ;
Where the eternal snows are sleeping,
Where the wolf his watch is keeping,
While in sunless depths below,
See the abodes of want and wo !

Here what comfort for thy soul!
Storm and tempest o'er thee roll,
Spectral forms around thee rise,
In thy pathway famine lies;
All is darkness, doubt, and fear,
Man is scarce thy brother here.

Tempter — cease.   Thy words are vain.
'T is no dream of worldly gain,
'T is no hope in luxury dressed,
'T is no thought of earthly rest,
Earthly comfort, or repose,
Lures me to these Alpine snows.

I would seek, amid this wild,
Fervent faith's devoted child.
Holy light is on his brow,
From his lips are words that glow,
In his bosom depths of love
Filled from heaven's pure fount above.

I would follow, where his feet
Mountain-rocks and dangers meet.
I would join his simple band,
Linked together, heart and hand;
There I fain would bend my knee,
'T is the place of prayer for me!

LOVE'S EARLY DREAM.

Love's early dream has music
In the tale it loves to tell;
Love's early dream has roses
Where it delights to dwell;

It has beauty in its landscape,
   And verdure in its trees,
Unshadowed by a passing cloud,
   Unruffled by a breeze.

Love's early dream has moonlight
   Upon its crystal lake,
Where stormy tempest never blows
   Nor angry billows break ;
It has splendour in its sunshine,
   And freshness in its dew,
And all its scenes of happiness
   Are beautiful, and — *true ?*

Love's early dream has kindness
   In every look and tone ;
Love's early dream has tenderness
   For one, and one alone.
It has melody of language,
   And harmony of thought,
And knows no sound of dissonance
   By ruder science taught.

Oh ! early dream of happiness,
   Where is thy waking bliss ?
What brings thy golden promises
   To such a world as this ?
Perchance thou art some shadow
   Of that which is to come —
The fluttering of an angel's wings,
   To lead the wanderer home.

PP *

MARIA JANE JEWSBURY.—(MRS. FLETCHER.)

THE late Mrs. Fletcher, better known by her maiden name of Maria Jane Jewsbury, was born in Warwickshire, and wrote at an early age, *Phantasmagoria, or Essays of Life and Literature*, which was followed by *Letters to the Young, Lays for Leisure Hours*, and *Her Three Histories*. She died in Bombay, in 1833, having left England for that country soon after her marriage, with her husband, who was an officer of the East India Company.

THE LOST SPIRIT.

"No man cared for my soul."—*Psalm* cxlii. 4.

Weep, Sire, with shame and ruin,
Weep for thy child's undoing !
For the days when I was young,
And no prayer was taught my tongue;
Nor the record from on high,
Of the life that cannot die:
Wiles of the world and men —
Of their threescore years and ten;
Earthly profit — human praise,
Thou didst set before my gaze,
As the guiding stars of life,
As the meed of toil and strife;
　　I ran the world's race well,
　　And find my guerdon — HELL !

Weep, Mother, weep — yet know
'T will not shorten endless wo,
Nor thy prayer unbind my chain,
Thy repentance soften pain,

Nor the life-blood of thy frame,
For one moment quench this flame!
Weep not beside my tomb,
That is gentle, painless gloom;
Let the worm and darkness prey
On my senseless slumbering clay;
Weep for the priceless gem
That may not hide with them;
Weep the lost spirit's fate,
Yet know thy tears too late:—
    Had they sooner fallen — well,
    I had not wept in HELL!

Physician, canst thou weep?
Then let tears thy pillow steep:
Couldst thou view Time's nearing wave,
Doomed to whelm me in its grave;
The last and lessening space,
My life's brief hour of grace,
Yet with gay, unfaltering tongue,
Promise health and sojourn long?
On the brink of that profound
Without measure, depth, or bound,
View me busied with the toys
Of a world of shadowy joys?
Oh, had look, or sign, or breath,
Then whispered aught of death;
Though nature in the strife,
Had loosed her hold on life,
And the worm received its prey
Perchance an earlier day —
    This — this — and who can tell
    That I had dwelt in HELL!

False Prophet, faltering Priest,
Full fraught with mirth and feast!
Thy weeping should not fail
But with life's dark-ended tale!

For the living — for the dead —
There is guilt upon thy head !
Thou didst make the " narrow way,"
As the broad one, smooth and gay ;
So speak in accents bland
Of the bright and better land,
That the soul unchanged within,
The sinner in his sin,
Of God and Christ unshriven,
Lay down with dreams of heaven !
  False Priest, thy labours tell,
  I dreamed — and woke in HELL !

THE DYING GIRL TO HER MOTHER.

My mother ! look not on me now
 With that sad earnest eye ;
Blame me not, mother, blame not thou
 My heart's last wish — to die !
I cannot wrestle with the strife
 I once had heart to bear ;
And if I yield a youthful life,
 Full hath it been of care.

Nay, weep not ! on my brow is set
 The age of grief — not years ;
Its furrows thou may'st wildly wet,
 But ne'er wash out with tears.
And couldst thou see my weary heart,
 Too weary e'en to sigh,
Oh ! mother, mother ! thou wouldst start,
 And say, " 'T were best to die !"

I know 't is summer on the earth —
 I hear a pleasant tune

Of waters in their chiming mirth —
I feel the breath of June :
The roses through my lattice look,
The bee goes singing by,
The peasant takes his harvest-hook,—
Yet, mother, let me die !

There's nothing in this time of flowers
That hath a voice for me :
The whispering leaves, the sunny hours,
The bright, the glad, the free !
There's nothing but thy own deep love,
And *that* will live on high !
Then, mother, when my heart's above,
Kind mother, let me die !

A DREAM OF THE FUTURE.

A new age expands
Its white and holy wings, above the peaceful lands. — *Bryant.*

It was not in a curtained bed,
When winter storms were howling dread,
This pleasant dream I knew ;—
But in the golden month of June,
Beneath the bright and placid moon,
In slumber soft as dew

Alone, in a green and woody dell,
Where the lovely light of the moonbeams fell,
With soft sheen on the grass ;
Still, except when a wandering breeze
Stirring the boughs of the beechen trees,
Made shadows come and pass.

59

Silent — but for the midnight bird
That makes the spot where'er 't is heard
　　With spell and sorcery fraught ;
Filling the mind with imaged things
Of dreams, and melodies, and wings,
　　The faery-land of thought.

The flowers had folded up their hues,
But their odours mixed with air and dews
　　Made it a bliss to breathe ;
How could I choose but dream that night,
With a bower above of bloom and light,
　　A mossy couch beneath ?

I dreamt — and of this world of woe,
This very world of gloom and show,
　　Where love and beauty cease ;
This world wherein all fair is frail,
And but wrong and sorrow never fail,
　　Changed to a world of peace.

And yet remained it as of old,
Peopled by men of human mould,
　　To human feelings wed ;
Yet, was their traffic in the town,
Yet, wore the king his glittering crown,
　　And peasants earned their bread.

And day and night were then as now,
And the stars on heaven's mighty brow,
　　Twinkled their sleepless eyes ;
Like watchers sent by the absent sun,
To look on all things said and done,
　　'Till he again arise.

Spring with its promise went and came,
And Summer with its breath of flame,
　　Flushing the earth with flowers ;

And Autumn like a sorcerer bold,
Transmuting by his touch to gold,
   The fruitage of the bowers.

Earth still but knew an earthly lot;
Yet 't was a changed and charmed spot,
   Where'er the free foot trod ;
For now no longer crime and sin,
Like cratered fires its breast within,
   Flamed forth against its God.

The curse that chained its strength was gone,
And pleasantly in order shone
   The seasons into life,
With only Winter plucked away,
And heat and cold in tempered sway,
   Nature no more at strife.

The pole had Eden-wealth of flowers,
The tropic — noons of breezy hours,
   The seamen feared no storm ;
The traveller far from haunts of men,
Slept dreadless near the lion's den ;
   Nor did the serpent's form

With its splendid coat of many dyes,
Bid hate and fear alternate rise,
   For in the peace prepared,—
The holy peace that upward ran,
From man to God, from beast to man,
   Even the serpent shared.

No clarion stirred the quiet air,
No banner with its meteor-glare
   The playful breezes saw ;
Unknown the warrior's battle-blade,
And judge in gloomy pomp arrayed,
   For love alone was law.

There might be tears on childhood's cheek,
But few, and passionless, and meek,
   For strife of soul was dead ;
And every smile with love was fraught,
And glance of eye, spoke glance of thought,
   Far off deceit and dread.

Shrined in the bosom of the seas
Like gardens of Hesperides,
   Lay each beloved land,
Inhabited by peaceful men,
Each happy in his calling then,
   In city, vale, or strand.

For poverty and greatness knew
Their brotherhood — and service true
   Each from the other won ;
The slave looked on his broken chain,
And with a spirit freed from pain,
   Smiled upward on the sun.

It was a holy, holy time !
The soul like nature reached its prime,
   And grew an angel-thing ;
A paradise of blissful thought —
A fountain never-fearing drought,
   A palace — God its King.

It was a holy time ; no sight
But wore an aspect of delight,
   Peace was in every sound ;
Peace in the song for the blissful wed,
Peace in the chaunt for the tranquil dead,
   The buried and the crowned.

And ever rose on the swelling breeze,
From hamlets poor and palaces,
   Cities and lonely ways,

Pealing through all earth's pulses strong,
Like the roar of ocean turned to song,
  A hymn of lofty praise.

And Death, with light and loving hand,
Marshalled with smiles his radiant band
  Into a higher sphere,
Even as a shepherd kind and old
Calleth at night his flock to fold,
  With strains of music clear.

Thus dreamt I through the live-long night,
Till the freshened breeze of morning bright,
  Sleep from my eyelids shook;
And then with thoughts where joy held sway,
And longings bright — my musing way
  Back to the world I took.

QQ

LADY FLORA HASTINGS.

T<small>HIS</small> accomplished woman was the eldest daughter of Francis, Marquis of Hastings, and was born in February, 1806. Her learning and abilities made her a favourite in the most intellectual society of Great Britain and the continent, and, with the advantages of her birth, secured for her the appointment of Lady of the Bed-chamber to the Duchess of Kent. While she was in this position, a disease, (enlargement of the liver,) caused her death, on the 5th of July, 1839. A collection of her Poems was published soon after, by her sister.

THE CROSS OF VASCO DA GAMA.

We have breasted the surge, we have furrow'd the wave,
We have spread the white sail to the favouring breeze ;
We have sped from the land of the fair and the brave,
Widely to wander o'er untried seas.
There is hope in our hearts, there is joy on our brow,
For the bright cross is beaming before us now !

Sadly we swept through the sounding deep,
Sadly we thought of our distant home —
Of the land where our fathers' ashes sleep,
Of the land where our fairy children roam.
Brothers ! our sad tears must cease to flow,
For the bright cross is beaming before us now !

Spread we the sail to the winged wind —
Hail to the waves of the southern sea !
Deep is the furrow we leave behind,
As we dash through the waters merrily ;

And snowy the spray round our lofty prow,
For the bright cross is beaming before us now !

Cross of the south, in the deep blue heaven —
Herald of mercy, thy form hath shone !
Gladly we welcome the presage given —
The land, the fair land of the south is our own ;
And mildly the light of true faith shall glow,
For the bright cross is beaming before us now !

THE SWAN SONG.

Grieve not that I die young. — Is it not well
To pass away ere life hath lost its brightness ?
Bind me no longer, sisters, with the spell
Of love and your kind words.   List ye to me :
Here I am bless'd — but I would be *more free ;*
I would go forth in all my spirit's lightness.
Let me depart !

Ah ! who would linger till bright eyes grow dim,
Kind voices mute, and faithful bosoms cold ?
Till carking care, and coil, and anguish grim,
Cast their dark shadows o' er this faëry world;
Till fancy's many-colour'd wings are furl'd,
And all, save the proud spirit, waxeth old ?
I would depart !

Thus would I pass away — yielding my soul
A joyous thank-offering to *Him* who gave
That soul to be, those starry orbs to roll.
Thus — thus exultingly would I depart,
Song on my lips, ecstacy in my heart.
Sisters — sweet sisters, bear me to my grave —
Let me depart !

MARY ANNE BROWNE, (MRS. GRAY.)

MARY ANNE BROWNE was born in Maiden Head, Berkshire, in 1812. In 1827 she published *Mont Blanc;* in 1828 *Ada;* in 1829 *Repentance;* in 1834 *The Coronal;* in 1836 *The Birth Day Gift;* and in 1839 *Ignatia;* and she was a frequent contributor to the *Dublin University Magazine,* and other British Periodicals, and to *The Lady's Companion,* and *The Knickerbocker Magazine* in the United States. From 1830 to 1842 she resided most of her time in Liverpool, to which city her father removed in the former year. In 1842 she was married to Mr. James Gray, a Scottish gentleman, and she died in Cork in 1844. Her poems are distinguished for grace and tenderness, a ready command of poetical imagery, and a taste delicately skilled in the harmonies of language.

THE EMBROIDERESS AT MIDNIGHT.

She plies her needle till the lamp
　　Is waxing pale and dim;
She hears the watchman's heavy tramp,
　　And she must watch like him: —
Her hands are dry, her forehead damp,
　　Her dark eyes faintly swim.

Look on her work! — here blossom flowers,
　　The lily and the rose,
Bright as the gems of summer hours,
　　But not to die like those;
Here, fadeless as in Eden's bowers,
　　For ever they repose.

Once, maiden, thou wast fresh and fair
  As those sweet flowers of thine ;
Now, shut from sunny light and air,
  How canst thou choose but pine ?
Neglected flows thy raven hair,
  Like the uncultured vine.

Look on her work !—no common mind
  Arranged that glowing group —
Wild wreaths the stately roses bind,
  Sweet bells above them droop —
Ye almost *see* the sportive wind
  Parting the graceful troop !

Look on her work ! — but look the more
  On her unwearied heart,
And put aside the chamber-door
  That doth the daughter part
From that dear mother, who before
  Taught her this cunning art.

She sleeps — that mother, sick and pale —
  She sleeps — and little deems
That she, who doth her features veil,
  All day, in flitting gleams
Of anxious hope, this hour doth hail,
  But not for happy dreams.

God bless her in her lone employ,
  And fill those earnest eyes
With visions of the coming joy,
  Waiting her sacrifice,
When they, who give her this employ,
  Pay her its stinted price !

Think how her trembling hand will clasp
  The treasure it will hold,

60   QQ*

With that which seems a greedy grasp —
  Yet not for love of gold :
That look — that sigh's relieving gasp,
  Its deeper springs unfold.

Think how her hasty feet will roam
  The market and the street,
To purchase for her humble home
  The food and clothing meet,
And with what gladness she will come
  Back to this poor retreat !

Poor maiden ! if the fair ones who
  Thy graceful 'broidery buy,
Only *one-half* thy struggles knew,
  And filial piety,
Methinks some drop of pity's dew
  Would gem the proudest eye !

It is not *here* its full reward
  Thy gentle heart will prove ;
Here ever must thy lot be hard,
  But there is ONE above
Who sees, and will not disregard,
  Thy consecrated love.

THE BRIDEGROOM TO HIS BRIDE.

Four years ago, dear love,
And we were strangers; in a distant land
Long had it been my lonely lot to rove ;
And I had never touched that gentle hand,
Or looked into the lustre of those eyes,
Or heard that voice of lovely melodies,

Winning its way unto the listener's heart,
And gladdening it, as a fresh stream doth part
The grass and flowers, and beautifies its road
With fresher hues, by its sweet tides bestowed.
Then I had never heard that name of thine,
Which in this blessed day hath merged in mine!

Three years ago, mine own!
And we had met — 'twas but acquaintanceship;
There was no tremour in the courteous tone
Which, greeting thee, flowed freely to my lip
At each new interview. Thy beauty seemed
Indeed the very vision I had dreamed
Of woman's loveliest form, but that it shrined
So bright a gem, so true and pure a mind,
I did not early learn; for thou art one
Whose gentle, kindly actions ever shun
The glare of day. I knew not *then* the power
That seems thy richest gift at this blest hour.

Another year went by,
And we were *friends!* — "dear friends" we called each other —
We said our bosoms throbbed in sympathy,
That we were like a sister and a brother.
Ah! but do brothers' hearts thrill through each chord,
At a dear sister's smile or gracious word?
Do sisters blush, and strive the blush to hide,
When a fond brother lingers at their side?
Do friends, and nothing more, shrink from surmise,
And dread to meet the keen world's scrutinies,
And tremble with a vague and groundless shame,
And start when each doth hear the other's name?

One little year ago,
And we were lovers — lovers pledged and vowed —
The unsealed fountains of our hearts might flow:
Our summer happiness had scarce a cloud.

We smiled to think upon the dubious past,
How could so long our self-delusion last?
We laughed at our own fears, whose dim array
One spoken word of love had put away.
In love's full-blessed confidence we talked,
We heeded not who watched us as we walked;
And day by day hath that affection grown,
Until this happy morn that makes us one.

    Beloved! 'tis the day,
The summer day, to which our hearts have turned,
  As to a haven that before them lay —
A haven dim and distantly discerned.
  Now we have reached it, and our onward gaze
  Must henceforth be beyond earth's fleeting days,
Unto a better home, when having loved
One more than e'en each other — having proved
Faithful to Him, and faithful to the vow
That in our hearts is echoing even now,
We two shall dwell His glorious throne before,
With souls, not bound, but blended evermore.

MRS. SARA COLERIDGE.

In the beautiful story of *Phantasmion*, which is all poetry though partly in the form of prose, Mrs. Coleridge has vindicated her right to a high rank among the female poets of England.

SONG.

Many a fountain cool and shady
May the traveller's eye invite ;
One among them all, sweet Lady,
Seems to flow for his delight ;
In many a tree the wilding bee
Might safely hide her honey'd store ;
One hive alone the bee will own,
She may not trust her sweets to more.

Say'st thou, " Can that maid be fairer ?
Shows her lip a livelier dye ?
Hath she treasures richer, rarer ?
Can she better love than I ?" —
What form'd the spell I ne'er could tell,
But subtle must its working be,
Since, from the hour I felt its pow'r,
No fairer face I wish to see.
Light-wing'd Zephyr, ere he settles
On the loveliest flower that blows,
Never stays to count thy petals,
Dear, delicious, fragrant Rose !
Her features bright elude my sight,
I know not how her tresses lie ;
In fancy's maze my spirit plays,
When she with all her charms is nigh.

FALSE LOVE.

False Love, too long thou hast delay'd,
Too late I make my choice;
Yet win for me that precious maid,
And bid my heart rejoice —
Then shall mine eyes shoot youthful fire,
My cheek with triumph glow,
And other maids that glance desire
Which I on one bestow.

Make her with smile divinely bland
Beam sunshine o'er my face,
And Time shall touch with gentlest hand
What she hath deign'd to grace ;
O'er scanty locks full wreaths I 'll wear,
No wrinkled brow to shade,
Her joy will smooth the furrows there
Which earlier griefs have made.

Though sports of youth be tedious toil
When youth has pass'd away,
I 'll cast aside the martial spoil
With her light locks to play :
Yea, turn, sweet Maid, from tented fields
To rove where dewdrops shine,
Nor care what hand the sceptre wields,
So thou wilt grant me thine !

One face alone, one face alone,
    These eyes require ;
But when that long'd-for sight is shown,
    What fatal fire
Shoots thro' my veins a keen and liquid flame,
That melts each fibre of my wasting frame !

One voice alone, one voice alone,
   I pine to hear ;
But when its meek, mellifluous tone
   Usurps mine ear,
Those slavish chains about my soul are wound,
Which ne'er, till death itself, can be unbound.

One gentle hand, one gentle hand,
   I fain would hold ;
But when it seems at my command,
   My own grows cold ;
Then low to earth I bend in sickly swoon,
Like lilies drooping mid the blaze of noon.

MISS ELIZA COOK.

It is scarcely necessary to say that this lady is a living writer of great celebrity. By the simple force of genius, and without any aid from adventitious circumstances, Miss Cook has pushed her way into the front rank of female talent, and stands acknowledged as one of the most attractive writers of song in our literature.

If I may venture to express somewhat plainly my estimate of Miss Cook's powers, I would say of her that hers is one of those strong, true-seeing, fearless souls, which, disdaining the aids of artificial refinement, and careless alike of censure and applause, present their thoughts in their first shape to the world, and give free, bold utterance to every sentiment and feeling that they experience. There is no bowing to established opinion, no deprecation of criticism, no respect for conventionalism, in Miss Cook ; and I for one highly admire and honour so frank and fearless and honest a writer.

Miss Cook has, I think, the boldest spirit of any Poetess in our language. Her single example goes far to prove that there is no sexuality in soul. I do not know a more unsexual style than hers. And the remark applies as much to the sentiment, too. The subjects of her verse, the thoughts it embodies, and the language in which she expresses herself, are all of the same free, sinewy, large, and massive nature. There is no timidity, no reserve, no rounding-off in her poetry ; but it is plain, and terse, and energetic, and muscular. It might all have been written by a man ; and not better written either. She has a man's sense of freedom ; a man's self-reliance ; a man's sceptical spirit ; a man's wide, grasping, general, original vision ; and to these qualities she adds the quick instinctive perceptions, the pure love of Beauty, and the ardent, sensitive affectionateness which so eminently distinguish woman.

As a sample of her sense of freedom, I quote

THE GIPSY'S TENT.

Our fire on the turf, and our tent 'neath the tree,
Carousing by moonlight, how merry are we!
Let the lord boast his castle, the baron his hall,
But the house of the gipsy is widest of all:
We may shout o'er our cups, and laugh loud as we will,
Till echo rings back from wood, welkin, and hill;
No joy seems to us like the joys that are lent
To the wanderer's life, and the gipsy's tent.

Some crime and much folly may fall to our lot,
We have sins, and pray where is the one who has not?
We are rogues, arrant rogues; yet remember! 't is rare
We take but from those who can very well spare;
You may tell us of deeds justly branded with shame,
But if great ones heard truth you would tell them the same.
And there 's many a king would have less to repent,
If his throne were as pure as the gipsy's tent.

Pant ye for beauty? Oh, where would ye seek
Such bloom as is found on the tawny one's cheek?
Our limbs that go bounding in freedom and health,
Are worth *all* your pale faces and coffers of wealth:
There are none to control us: we rest or we roam;
Our will is our law, and the world is our home:
Even Jove would repine at *his* lot if he spent
A night of wild glee in the gipsy's tent.

I have more than once heard it said that the essential, somewhat scornful, freedom of thought and verse which is apparent in our author's works, is scarcely what we have been taught to look for in a female writer. It is pleasing, such critics say, from its piquancy: but that it is consistent with the common idea of the female character, they exceedingly doubt. It seems to be generally, and I think justly, held, that the female mind is intrinsically less

61 RR

radical, less revolutionary, than the male mind : and that it is far more disposed to acquiesce in the customs and conventions of society. But while I grant that we often find our fair author chanting the praises of gipsy lawlessness, and often unfashionably democratic, I perceive on the other hand no lack of that beautiful conservatism which so gracefully distinguishes woman, and which acts as so important a curb upon the levelling, destroying tendency of the rougher sex.

For myself, I highly admire Miss Cook's free spirit. I see in it a true originality, and an evidence of conscious strength. I look upon her as one of the best and most powerful of all our female poets, and one who is greatly raising and purifying our estimate of woman's mind. She has by her example disproved the long prevalent dogma, that the female soul cannot rise above the trifling, minute, and evanescent affairs of life ; and has clearly shown that when the mind of woman is emancipated from its petty restraints, and lifted above life's conventionalisms, it is at least as strong in essence, and as striking in its developments, as the mind of the male.

Amongst the prominent characteristics of Miss Cook's genius, the sound, healthy, cheerful nature of her philosophy, stands with the first. Female writers too frequently indulge in pensive, melancholy, morbid views of life, and thus tend rather to lower than to raise our estimate of humanity and nature. But Miss Cook is for making us happy. The bright side of our destiny is what she loves to dwell on, and she often urges her cheerful views with the happiest effect. I do not know where to find a better instance of this than in her Poem called

THE WORLD.

Talk who will of the world as a desert of thrall,
    Yet, yet there is bloom on the waste ;
Though the chalice of Life hath its acid and gall,
    There are honey-drops, too, for the taste.

We murmur and droop should a sorrow-cloud stay,
    And note all the *shades* of our lot ;

But the rich rays of *sunshine* that brighten our way,
　Are bask'd in, enjoy'd and forgot.

Those who look on Mortality's ocean aright,
　Will not mourn o'er each billow that rolls ;
But dwell on the beauties, the glories, the might,
　As much as the shipwrecks and shoals.

How thankless is he who remembers alone
　All the bitter, the drear and the dark ;
Though the *raven* may scare with its woe-boding tone,
　Do we ne'er hear the song of the *lark?*

We may utter farewell when 't is torture to part,
　But in meeting the dear one again
Have we never rejoic'd with that wildness of heart
　Which outbalances ages of pain ?

Who hath not had moments so laden with bliss,
　When the soul in its fulness of love,
Would waver if bidden to choose between this
　And the paradise promised above ?

Though the eye may be dimmed with its grief-drop awhile,
　And the whiten'd lip sigh forth its fear,—
Yet pensive indeed is that face where the smile
　Is not oftener seen than the tear !

There are times when the storm-gust may rattle around,
　There are spots where the poison-shrub grows,
Yet are there not homes where nought else can be found
　But the southwind, the sunshine, and rose ?

O haplessly rare is the portion that 's ours,
　And strange is the path that we take,—
If there spring not beside us a few precious flowers,
　To soften the thorn and the brake.

The wail of regret, the rude clashing of strife,
  The soul's harmony often may mar,—
But I think we must own, in the discord of Life,
  'T is ourselves that oft waken the jar.

Earth is not *all* fair, yet it is not all gloom ;
  And the voice of the grateful will tell
That HE who allotted Pain, Death, and the Tomb,
  Gave Hope, Health, and the Bridal, as well.

Should Fate do its worst, and my spirit oppress'd,
  O'er its own shatter'd happiness pine,—
Let me witness the joy in another's glad breast,
  And some pleasure *must* kindle in mine !

Then say not the world is a desert of thrall,
  There is bloom, there is light, on the waste ;
Though the chalice of Life hath its acid and gall,
  There are honey-drops, too, for the taste.

If further evidence of Miss Cook's cheerful spirit be needed,
we may find it in the following fine Song.

WE 'LL SING ANOTHER CHRISTMAS SONG.

We 'll sing another Christmas song, for who shall ever tire
To hear the olden ballad theme around a Christmas fire ?
We 'll sing another Christmas song, and pass the wassail cup,
For fountains that refresh the heart should never be dried up.
Ne'er tell us that each Yule tide brings more silver to our hair :
Time seldom scatters half the snow that quickly gathers there.
The goading of ambition's thorns — the toiling heed of gold —
'T is these do more than rolling years in making us grow old :
Then shake old Christmas by the hand — in kindness let him dwell,
For he 's king of right good company, and we should treat him well.

Why should we let pale Discontent fling canker on the hours —
Unjust regrets lurk round the soul like snakes in leafy bowers;
And though the flood of Plenty's tide upon our lot may pour,
How oft the lip will murmur still the horse-leech cry for " more."
We sigh for wealth — we pant for place — and getting what we
    crave,
We often find it only coils fresh chains about the slave.
Year after year may gently help to turn the dark locks white,
But Time ne'er fades a flower so soon as cold and worldly blight:
Then shake Old Christmas by the hand — in kindness let him dwell,
For he's king of right good company, and we should treat him well.

Be glad — be glad — stir up the blaze, and let our spirits yield
The incense that is grateful as the lilies of the field;
" Good will to all " — 't is sweet and rich, and helps to keep away
The wrinkled pest of frowning brows — and mildew shades of grey.
Be glad — be glad — and though we have some cypress in our
    wreath,
Forget not there are rosebuds too, that ever peep beneath.
And though long years may line the cheek, and wither up the
    heart,
It is not Time, but selfish Care, that does the saddest part:
Then shake Old Christmas by the hand — in kindness let him dwell,
For he's king of right good company, and we should treat him well.

    Miss Cook excels greatly in pathos. No pathos can be finer.
There is nothing maudlin or whining in it; but it is always true,
deep and unaffected. The following poem has always appeared
to me very beautiful and touching.

THE MOURNERS.

    King Death sped forth in his dreaded power,
    To make the most of his silent hour;
    And the first he took was a white rob'd girl,
    With the orange bloom twin'd in each glossy curl;
    The fond betroth'd hung o'er her bier,
    Bathing her shroud with the gushing tear;
        RR*

He madly raved, he shriek'd his pain,
With frantic speech and burning brain;
"There 's no joy," said he, "now my dearest is gone;
Take, take me, Death! for I cannot live on!"

The *Sire* was robb'd of his eldest born,
And he bitterly bled while the branch was torn;
Other scions were 'round, as good and fair,
But none seem'd so bright as the deathless heir.
"My hopes are crush'd," was the father's cry;
"Since my darling is lost, I, too, would die!"
The valued *Friend* was snatch'd away,
Bound to another from childhood's day;
And the one that was left exclaimed in despair,
"Oh, he sleeps in the tomb, let me follow him there!"

A *Mother* was taken, whose constant love
Had nestled her child like a fair young dove;
And the heart of that child to the mother had grown,
Like the ivy to oak, or the moss to the stone;
Nor loud nor wild was the burst of woe,
But the tide of anguish was strong below;
And the reft one turn'd from all that was light,
From the flowers of day, and the stars of night,—
Breathing where none might hear or see,
"Where thou art, my mother! thy child would be!"

Death smil'd as he heard each earnest word —
"Nay, nay," said he, "be this work deferr'd;
I 'll see thee again in a fleeting year,
And if grief and devotion live on sincere,
I promise thee then thou shalt share in the rest
Of the being pluck'd from thy doting breast;
Then if thou cravest the coffin and pall,
As thou dost this moment, my spear *shall* fall!"
—And Death fled: — till Time on his rapid wing,
Gave the hour that brought back the skeleton king.

But the Lover was ardently wooing again,
Kneeling in serfdom and proud of his chain ;
He had found an idol to adore,
Rarer than that he had worshipp'd before ;
His step was gay, his laugh was loud,
As he led the way for the bridal crowd ;
And his brow own'd not a moment's shade,
Though he pass'd o'er the grave where his lost love laid :
" Ha, ha !" cried Death, " 't is passing clear
That I am a guest not wanted here !"

The *Father* was seen in his children's games
Kissing their flush'd brows, and blessing their names ;
And his eye grew bright as he mark'd the charms
Of the boy at his knee and the girl in his arms ;
His voice rang out in the merry noise,
He was first in all their hopes and joys ;
He ruled their sports in the setting sun,
Nor gave a thought to the missing one !
" Are ye ready ?" cried Death, as he raised his dart,—
" Nay, nay," shrieked the father, " in mercy depart !"

The *Friend* again was quaffing the bowl,
Warmly pledging his faith and soul ;
His bosom cherish'd with glowing pride,
A stranger form that sat by his side ;
His hand the hand of that stranger press'd,
He prais'd his song, he echoed his jest ;
And the mirth and wit of that new found mate,
Made a blank of the name so priz'd of late :
" See, see !" cried Death, as he hurried past,
" How bravely the bonds of friendship last !"

But the *Orphan-Child*, — oh, where was she?
With clasping hands, and bending knee,
All alone on the churchyard sod,
Mingling the names of " Mother " and " God ; "

Her dark and sunken eye was hid,
Fast weeping beneath the swollen lid ;
Her sigh was heavy, her forehead was chill,
Betraying the wound was unhealëd still ;
And her smother'd prayer was heard to crave
A speedy home in the self-same grave.

Hers was the love all holy and strong,
Hers was the sorrow fervent and long ;
Hers was the spirit whose light was shed
As an incense fire above the dead.
Death linger'd there, — and paus'd awhile,
But she beckon'd him on with a welcoming smile ;
" There 's a solace," cried he, " for all others to find,
But a mother leaves no equal behind ! "
— And the kindest blow Death ever gave,
Laid the mourning child in its parent's grave.

I think that none of our female writers surpass Miss Cook in strength and force of style. Miss Landon's verse may be as showy, — nay it is more so ; but it has none of the sustained power that characterizes Miss Cook's : Mrs. Howitt's resembles it, but it has a soft garb which quite marks the sex of the writer, and which scarcely ever distinguishes Miss Cook's. There is in Miss Cook that fine eloquence which grows as it advances. There is a gradual deepening in the following powerful lines, that reminds one of a widening river, rolling broader and deeper towards the sea :

" He that is without sin among you, let him first cast a stone." — (*St. John*, Chap. 8, verse 7th.)

Beautiful eloquence, thou speakest low,
    But the world's clashing cannot still thy tones ;
Thou livest, as the stream with gentle flow
    Runs through the battle-field of strife and groans.

Thine is the language of a simple creed,
  Whose saving might has no priest-guarded bound,
If soundly learn'd, say would the martyr bleed?
  Or such dense shadows fall on " hallowed ground? "
Oh, how we boast our knowledge of " the Right,"
But blast the Christian grain with Conduct's blight.

'T is well to ask our Maker to " forgive
  Our trespasses ; " but 't is as we may bear
The trespasses of those who breathe and live
  Amid the same Temptation, Doubt and Care.
Oh ! ye, who point so often to the herd
  Whose dark and evil works are all uncloaked,
Is there no other than condemning word,
  For minds untaught and spirits sorely yoked?
Are ye quite sure no hidden leper taint
Blurs your own skin if we look through the paint.

Ye throw from ambush ! — let Truth's noontide light
  Flash on the strength that nerves such eager aims,
Bring pigmy greatness from its giant height,
  Where would be then the splendour of your names?
Ye harsh denouncers, 't is an easy thing
  To wrap yourselves in Cunning's specious robes,
And sharpen all the polished blades ye fling,
  As though ye held diploma for the probes :
But if the charlatan and knave were dropp'd,
Some spreading trees would be most closely lopp'd.

Ye, that so fiercely show your warring teeth
  At every other being on your way,
Is your own sword so stainless in its sheath,
  That ye can justify the braggart fray?
The tricks of policy — the hold of place —
  The dulcet jargon of a courtly rote —
The sleek and smiling mask upon the face —
  The eye that sparkled but to hide its mote :
Tell me, ye worms, could ye well bear the rub,
That tore these silken windings from the grub?
  62

Ye lips, that gloat upon a brother's sin,
    With moral mouthing in the whisper'd speech,
Methinks I 've seen the poison fang within,
    Betray the viper rather than the leech.
I 've marked the frailties of some gifted one,
    Blazon'd with prudent doubt and virtuous sigh,
But through the whining cant of saintly tone,
    Heard Joy give Pity the exulting lie,
As if it were a pleasant thing to find,
The racer stumbling and the gaze-hound blind.

Too proud — too ignorant, — too mighty Man —
    Why dost thou so forget the lesson taught ?
Why not let Mercy cheer our human span ?
    Ye say ye serve Christ — heed him as ye ought :
He did not goad the weeping child of clay,
    He heaped no coals upon the erring head,
Fixed no despair upon the sinner's way,
    And dropp'd no gall upon the sinner's bread :
He heard Man's cry for Vengeance, but he flung
Man's Conscience at the yell, and hushed the tongue.

Great teaching from a greater teacher — fit
    To breathe alike to Infancy and Age :
No garbled mystery o'ershadows it,
    And noblest hearts have deepest read the page.
Carve it upon the mart and temple arch,
    Let our fierce judges read it as they go,
Make it the key-note of Life's pompous march,
    And trampling steps will be more soft and slow.
For God's own voice says from the Eternal throne,
    " Let him that is without sin cast the stone."

One more passage, and I conclude my extracts from Miss Cook's writings. The lines are noble ones, and full of the true poet's fire.

LOVE.

Love, beautiful and boundless Love — oh! who shall hymn thy
    praise?
Who shall exalt thy hallow'd name with fitting anthem lays?
When shall thy workings all be seen — thy power all revealed?
Oh! who shall count thy fairy steps upon Earth's rugged field?

There are few things of gloom that meet our Sorrow or our Hate,
Where Love and Beauty have not once been portion of their state;
Few things are seen in charmless guise that shutteth out all trace
Of God's infinitude of Joy, of Purity, and Grace.

There's not a palsied ruin bows its patriarchal head
That has not rung with Triumph shouts while Revel banquets
    spread:
There's not a desolated hearth but where the cheerful pile
Of blazing logs has sparkled and the cricket sung the while.

The broken mandolin that lies in silent, slow decay,
Has quicken'd many a gentle pulse that heard its measures play;
The stagnant pool that taints and kills the mallow and the rush,
Has filtered through the silver clouds and cool'd the rainbow's
    flush.

There's not a dark, dull coffin-board but what has stood to bear
A swarm of summer warblers in the mellow greenwood air;
There's not a thread of cere-cloth but has held its blossom bells,
And swung the morning pearls about within the fragrant wells.

Love lurketh round us everywhere — it fills the great design,
It gives the soul its chosen mate — it loads the autumn vine;
It dyes the orchard branches red — it folds the worm in silk,
It rears the daisy where we tread, and bringeth corn and milk.

Love stirreth in our beings all unbidden and unknown,
With aspirations leaping up like fountains from the stone;
It prompts the great and noble deeds that nations hail with pride,
It moveth when we grieve to miss an old dog from our side.

It bids us plant the sapling to be green when we are grey,
It pointeth to the Future, and yet blesses while we stay ;
It opens the Almighty page where — though 't is held afar,
We read enough to lure us on still higher than we are.

The child at play upon the sward who runs to snatch a flower,
With earnest passion in his glee that glorifies the hour —
The doting student — pale and meek — who looks into the night
Dreaming of all that helps the soul to gauge Eternal might ; —

The rude, bold savage, pouring forth his homage to the sun,
Asking for other " hunting fields," when life's long chase is run —
The poet boy who sitteth down upon the upland grass,
Whose eagle thoughts are nestled by the Zephyr wings that pass ;—

The weak old man that creepeth out once more before he dies,
With longing wish to see and feel the sunlight in his eyes —
Oh ! these are the unerring types that Nature setteth up,
To tell that an Elixir drop yet sanctifies our cup.

Love, beautiful and boundless Love, thou dwellest here below,
Teaching the human lip to smile — the violet to blow ;
Thine is the breath ethereal that yet exhales and burns
In sinful breasts as incense steals from dim unsightly urns.

Thou art the holy record seal that Time can ne'er annul,
The dove amid the vulture tribe — the lamp within the skull —
Thou art the one bright Spirit Thing that is not bought and sold,
The cherub elve that laugheth in the giant face of Gold.

Love — exquisite, undying Love — runs through Creation's span,
Gushing from countless springs to fill the ocean heart of Man ;
And there it broadly rolleth on in deep unfathomed flood,
Swelling with the Immortal Hope that craveth more of " Good."

It is the rich magnetic spark yet shining in the dust,
The fair salvation ray of Faith that wins our joyful trust,
The watchword of the Infinite, left here to lead above,
That 's ever seen and ever heard, and tells us " God is Love."

THE OLD ARM CHAIR.

I love it, I love it; and who shall dare
To chide me for loving that old arm-chair?
I 've treasured it long as a sainted prize,
I 've bedewed it with tears, and embalmed it with sighs;
'T is bound by a thousand bands to my heart;
Not a tie will break, not a link will start.
Would ye learn the spell? a mother sat there,
And a sacred thing is that old arm-chair.

In childhood's hour I lingered near
The hallowed seat with listening ear;
And gentle words that mother would give,
To fit me to die and teach me to live.
She told me shame would never betide,
With truth for my creed and God for my guide;
She taught me to lisp my earliest prayer,
As I knelt beside that old arm-chair.

I sat and watch'd her many a day,
When her eye grew dim, and her locks were gray;
And I almost worshipp'd her when she smiled
And turn'd from her Bible to bless her child.
Years roll'd on, but the last one sped —
My idol was shatter'd, my earth-star fled;
I learnt how much the heart can bear,
When I saw her die in that old arm-chair.

'T is past! 't is past! but I gaze on it now
With quivering breath and throbbing brow:
'T was there she nursed me, 't was there she died;
And memory flows with lava tide.
Say it is folly, and deem me weak,
While the scalding drops start down my cheek;
But I love it, I love it, and cannot tear
My soul from a mother's old arm-chair.

WASHINGTON.

Land of the west! though passing brief the record of thine age,
Thou hast a name that darkens all on history's wide page!
Let all the blasts of fame ring out — thine shall be loudest far:
Let others boast their satellites — thou hast the planet star.
Thou hast a name whose characters of light shall ne'er depart;
'T is stamped upon the dullest brain, and warms the coldest heart;
A war-cry fit for any land where freedom 's to be won.
Land of the west! it stands alone — it is thy Washington!

Rome had its Cæsar, great and brave; but stain was on his
    wreath;
He lived the heartless conquerer, and died the tyrant's death.
France had its Eagle; but his wings, though lofty they might soar,
Were spread in false ambition's flight, and dipped in murder's
    gore.
Those hero-gods, whose mighty sway would fain have chained
    the waves —
Who fleshed their blades with tiger zeal, to make a world of
    slaves —
Who, though their kindred barred the path, still fiercely
    waded on —
Oh, where shall be *their* "glory" by the side of Washington?

He fought, but not with love of strife; he struck but to defend;
And ere he turned a people's foe, he sought to be a friend.
He strove to keep his country's right by reason's gentle word,
And sighed when fell injustice threw the challenge·— sword to
    sword.
He stood the firm, the calm, the wise, the patriot and the sage;
He showed no deep, avenging hate — no burst of despot rage.
He stood for liberty and truth, and dauntlessly led on,
Till shouts of victory gave forth the name of Washington.

No car of triumph bore him through a city filled with grief;
No groaning captives at the wheels proclaimed him victor chief:

He broke the gyves of slavery with strong and high disdain,
And cast no sceptre from the links when he had crushed the chain.
He saved his land, but did not lay his soldier trappings down
To change them for the regal vest, and don a kingly crown.
Fame was too earnest in her joy — too proud of such a son —
To let a robe and title mask a noble Washington.

England, my heart is truly thine — my loved, my native earth !—
The land that holds a mother's grave, and gave that mother birth !
Oh, keenly sad would be the fate that thrust me from thy shore,
And faltering my breath, that sighed, "Farewell for evermore !"
But did I meet such adverse lot, I would not seek to dwell
Where olden Heroes wrought the deeds for Homer's song to tell.
Away, thou gallant ship ! I 'd cry, and bear me swiftly on :
But bear me from my own fair land to that of Washington !

THE LOVED ONE WAS NOT THERE.

We gathered round the festive board,
　The crackling faggot blazed,
But few would taste the wine that poured,
　Or join the song we raised.
For there was now a glass unfilled —
　A favoured place to spare ;
All eyes were dull, all hearts were chilled —
　The loved one was not there.

No happy laugh was heard to ring,
　No form would lead the dance ;
A smothered sorrow seemed to fling
　A gloom in every glance.
The grave had closed upon a brow,
　The honest, bright, and fair ;
We missed our mate, we mourned the blow —
　The loved one was not there.

FRANCES ANNE BUTLER.

IT is scarcely necessary to say that Mrs. Butler is the late Miss Fanny Kemble. Her literary abilities have been variously manifested. Prose, Verse, and Drama, have alike engaged her; and in all she has attracted a large share of public attention and applause: with her *poetical* genius, however, we have alone to do on the present occasion.

I venture to say that Mrs. Butler's poetry may safely challenge comparison with the verse of most female writers in our literature. I do not say that it has the softness of Mrs. Hemans's, the delightful simplicity of Mary Howitt's, or the sweet gracefulness of Miss Mitford's, — " one star *differeth* from another star in glory," — but it has character and individualism : it displays immense intellectual power; sympathies of a pure, high, unaffected order ; and what, in these days (as in all), is one of the greatest possible excellencies, a thorough hatred and avoidance of all hypocrisy, pretence, and cant. I never met with a more natural writer; and, surely, where there is honesty of soul, a few sins against taste may be pardoned. Mrs. Butler's faults proceed not from a deficiency, but from a redundancy, of power ; which is a very excusable, inasmuch as it is a very uncommon, failing. I believe that in the course of a few years, when time shall have sobered down the perhaps too-vividly painted lines of her mental character, and shall have corrected her hasty estimates of the world and of humanity, Mrs. Butler will rank with the foremost poets of our land.

The following verses will fairly represent Mrs. Butler's energetic, thoughtful, picturesque style. Byron has no grander impersonations.

I.

AUTUMN.

I hear a voice low in the sunset woods :
    Listen ; it says " Decay, decay, decay :"

I hear it in the murmuring of the floods,
  And the wind sighs it as it flies away.
Autumn is come ; seest thou not in the skies
The stormy light of his fierce lurid eyes ?
Autumn is come; his brazen feet have trod,
Withering and scorching, o'er the mossy sod.
The fainting year sees her fresh flowery wreath
Shrivel in his hot grasp; his burning breath
Dries the sweet water-springs that in the shade
Wandering along, delicious music made.
A flood of glory hangs upon the world,
Summer's bright wings shining ere they are furl'd.

II.

WINTER.

I saw him on his throne, far in the North,
Him ye call Winter, picturing him ever
An aged man, whose frame, with palsied shiver
Bends o'er the fiery element, his foe.
But him I saw was a young god whose brow
Was crown'd with jagged icicles, and forth
From his keen spirit-like eyes there shone a light
Broad, glaring, and intensely cold and bright.
His breath, like sharp-edged arrows, pierced the air ;
The naked earth crouched shuddering at his feet ;
His finger on all murmuring waters sweet
Lay icily, — motion nor sound was there ;
Nature seem'd frozen — dead ; and still and slow
A winding sheet fell o'er her features fair,
Flaky and white from his wide wings of snow.

Mrs. Butler's plays scarcely come within the scope of the present work, for there is not much that is poetical in them.   They
exhibit a quick, discerning eye, a bold fancy, and a firm, determined, wide-grasping intellect: but they want the compression
and cohesion which only practice can give.

That our fair Authoress has however an eminently dramatic
mind cannot I think be doubted for a moment.   Her poems are
essentially dramatical: terse, vigorous, graphic, and impersona-
tive.   The following Ballad is a perfect drama.

BALLAD.

The Lord's son stood at the clear spring head,
  The May on the other side ;
" And stretch me your lily hand," he said,
  " For I must mount and ride.

" And waft me a kiss across the brook,
  And a curl of your yellow hair ;
Come summer or winter, I never shall look
  Again on your eyes so fair.

" Bring me my coal-black steed, my squire,
  Bring Fleet-foot forth," he cried ;
" For three-score miles he must not tire
  To bear me to my bride.

" His foot must be swift though my heart be slow,
  He carries me towards my sorrow ;
To the Earl's proud daughter I made my vow,
  And I must wed her to-morrow."

The Lord's son stood at the altar-stone,
  The Earl's proud daughter near :
" And what is that ring you have gotten on,
  That you kiss so oft and so dear ?

" Is it a ring of the yellow gold,
  Or something more precious and bright ?
Give me that ring in my hand to hold,
  Or I plight ye no troth to-night !"

" It is not a ring of the yellow gold,
  But something more precious and bright ;

But never shall hand, save my hand, hold
  This ring by day or night."

" And now I am your wedded wife,
  Give me the ring I pray."—
" You may take my lands, you may take my life,
  But never this ring away."

They sat at the board, and the lady bride
  Red wine in a goblet pour'd ;
" And pledge me a health, sweet sir," she cried,
  " My husband and my lord."

The cup to his lips he had scarcely press'd,
  When he gasping drew his breath ;
His head sank down on his heaving breast,
  And he said " It is death ! it is death !

" Oh, bury me under the gay green shaw,
  By the brook, 'neath the heathery sod,
Where last her blessed eyes I saw,
  Where her blessed feet last trod !"

TO ——.

Oh ! turn those eyes away from me !
  Though sweet, yet fearful are their rays ;
And though they beam so tenderly,
  I feel I tremble 'neath their gaze.
Oh, urn those eyes away ! for though
  To meet their glance I may not dare,
I know their light is on my brow
  By the warm blood that mantles there.

ELIZABETH BARRETT BROWNING.

A VERY considerable number of our Female Poets have distinguished themselves by their *learning*. From the time of Lady Berners down to the present day, scholastic acquirements have attracted many of our female writers. Lady Berners herself, Lady Jane Grey, Queen Elizabeth, Lady Carew, the Countess of Pembroke, the Duchess of Newcastle, Lady Mary Wortley Montagu, Miss Carter, and other lady authors, may be instanced.

Our own day has its examples of the same fact. Mrs. Hemans, Mrs. Howitt, and Miss Mitford all display great classical knowledge and lingual proficiency. And the distinguished lady whose name heads this Chapter, Mrs. Robert Browning, formerly Miss Elizabeth Barrett Barrett, is a fresh illustration of the assertion. I think it may be said that she is chief amongst the learned poetesses of our land : at least, I know of no British female writer who exhibits so intimate an acquaintance with the *spirit* of both antique and modern philosophy, or so refined a perception of intellectual purity and beauty. Her poetry is the poetry of pure reason.

It may be a question, however, whether an intense devotion to scholastic learning is not rather injurious than beneficial to the female mind. It cannot be pretended, of course, that school-craft, and the philosophy of art, science, and reason, ought to be altogether overlooked and unstudied by woman : — the proposition would be monstrous. But it may perhaps be fairly argued that, as woman's faculties are rather perceptive than investigative, and as her knowledge of truth is rather intuitive than acquired, there is a possibility of her understanding being injured by over-cultivation. Just as some flowers lose their native beauty when forced by horticultural art, may the female mind be spoiled by excess of intellectual culture.

Far as we should carry female education, we should, I think, take especial care not to found it on the same studies as appear necessary to man's. The acquirements of the sexes must be kept *unlike*, or man will find in woman, not a help meet, but a rival. Harmony results not from similarity, but from difference; and the law applies as much to the mental as to the physical world. Two minds exactly alike would soon grow tired of each other; for each would see in the other only the continual reflection of its own image, and would be like a person condemned to behold no human face but that which he saw in his mirror.

Further, the spheres of the sexes are different and require different faculties, and different education. The man — " for contemplation formed " — should learn by study, and reflection, and comparison, and investigation; the woman — " for softness formed and sweet attractive grace " — should acquire knowledge mainly through her rapid instincts, her wide-spreading sympathies, and her quick instantaneous perceptions.

The male and female minds arrive at truth by different roads. Man reaches it by proof; woman, by faith. Man knows it; woman feels it. Man demonstrates it; woman believes it. Mary recognised the risen Christ when He spake to her; Thomas would not believe until he had thrust his finger into the Saviour's side.

Science, then, and learning, the logical *signs* of knowledge, are means comparatively of but little value to the female mind in its acquisition of truth, and in excess tend rather to cloud and confuse than to enlighten and inform it.

In proof of these remarks I think I can fairly say that learned poetesses, however great their genius, have rarely been so effective and popular as less cultivated writers, possessed of even smaller natural powess. How charmingly, for instance, Katherine Philips shines out from the thick cluster of learned ladies who surround her. Her *Ode Against Pleasure* is worth all that her more showy sisters produced altogether. Hers is moral knowledge; theirs intellectual: hers feeling; theirs logic. Mrs. Opie, again, contrasts sweetly with Miss Carter, Mrs. More, and other erudite ladies of that era. Her poem, *The Orphan Boy*, will outweigh all the learned odes produced by the female minds of her generation.

To come however (at last) to the lady whose poetical works
this Chapter proposes to consider, I scruple not to say that she
is certainly most effective in her least laboured compositions.
Her genius, it is impossible not to see, is of the highest order —
strong, deep-seeing, enthusiastic and loving ; but although all her
compositions prove this, I find the greatest evidences of her powers in her most unpretending works. Where there is effort, there
is often obscurity ; but where she gives her soul free unconscious
vent, she writes with a truth and force of touch which none of
the poetic sisterhood surpass.

In justification of the opinion which I have here expressed, I
would particularly instance the poem called *A Drama of Exile*.
The intellect displayed in this noble production is stupendous.
The conception is massive : the treatment of the prominent idea
truly consistent and powerful : the pathos such as only a woman
could have written : and the moral tone of the work most lofty
and pure. But, in spite of all these excellencies, the poem often
fatigues us. It keeps the mind too much on the stretch ; requires
an unceasing exercise of our deepest thoughts ; and while we
never fail at last to see the extreme beauty of the writer's ideas,
we grow tired in studying them. The following *Chorus of Eden
Spirits*, highly poetical as it is, may be cited as an illustration of
my argument. It will be seen how far the meaning often lies
beneath the surface : —

> Hearken, oh hearken ! let your souls, behind you,
>   Lean, gently moved !
> Our voices feel along the Dread to find you,
>   O lost, beloved !
> Through the thick-shielded and strong-marshall'd angels,
>   They press and pierce :
> Our requiems follow fast on our evangels, —
>   Voice throbs in verse !
> We are but orphan'd Spirits left in Eden,
>   A time ago —
> God gave us golden cups ; and we were bidden
>   To feed you so !
> But now our right hand hath no cup remaining,
>   No work to do ;

The mystic hydromel is spilt, and staining
    The whole earth through ;
And all those stains lie clearly round for showing
    (Not interfused !)
That brighter colours were the world's foregoing,
    Than shall be used.
Hearken, oh hearken ! ye shall hearken surely,
    For years and years,
The noise beside you, dripping coldly, purely,
    Of spirit's tears !
The yearning to a beautiful, denied you,
    Shall strain your powers : —
Ideal sweetnesses shall over-glide you,
    Resumed from ours !
In all your music, our pathetic minor
    Your ears shall cross ;
And all fair sights shall mind you of diviner,
    With sense of loss !
We shall be near, in all your poet-languors
    And wild extremes ;
What time ye vex the desert with vain angers,
    Or light with dreams !
And when upon you, weary after roaming,
    Death's seal is put,
By the foregone ye shall discern the coming,
    Through eyelids shut.

But in justice to Mrs. Browning we must confess that her lofty ideality is far oftener an excellence than a blemish. It is only from such a mind as hers that we can get a conception like that contained in Gabriel's reply to the taunt of Lucifer regarding "the vacant thrones in heaven."

  " Angel, there are no vacant thrones in Heaven
  To suit thy bitter words.   Glory and life
  Fulfil their own depletions : *and if God*
  Sigh'd you far from Him, His next breath drew in

> *A compensative splendour up the skies,*
> *Flushing the starry arteries.*"

To the same refining faculty we owe such passages as this
which follows: —

> The essence of all beauty I call love.
> The attribute, the evidence, and end,
> The consummation to the inward sense,
> Of beauty apprehended from without,
> I still call love. As form, when colourless,
> Is nothing to the eye : that pine-tree there,
> Without its black and green, being all a blank ;
> So, without love, is beauty undiscern'd,
> In man or angel.

Mrs. Browning proves the genuineness of her poetic fire in
nothing more clearly than in her high estimate of poetry, and in
her just appreciation of other poets. Poetry is quite other than
a plaything to her : it is the earnest serious business of her life.
She has Milton's high sense of the nobility of song ; and, by the
way, much of Milton's lofty imaginative power and daring. Her
estimate of the chief poets of the world is singularly just and
discriminating: in her *Vision of Poets* some of the portraits are
painted as with a lightning-flash. One of the stanzas speaks of —

> —— " Shelley, in his white ideal,
> All statue blind."

I think that portrait perfect. In another she points —

> " To Shakspere ! on whose forehead climb
> The crowns of the world ! O eyes sublime !
> With tears and laughters for all time ! "

Schlegel and Hazlitt together have not said more than that.
One of the chief characteristics of Mrs. Browning's poetry is
the unvarying elevation of its thought and sentiment. There is

never a grovelling or earthy idea in it : it all tends upward : and sometimes, in its pure unwavering morality, approaches the sacred words of inspiration. The following is very loftily conceived : —

THE MEASURE.

"He comprehendeth the dust of the earth in a measure."—*Isaiah,* xl.
"Thou givest them tears to drink in a measure."—*Psalm,* lxxx.

God, the Creator, with a pulseless hand
Of unoriginated power, hath weigh'd
The dust of earth and tears of man, in one
    Measure, and by one weight ; —
    So saith His Holy Book.

Shall we, then, who have issued from the dust
And there return ; shall *we*, who toil for dust,
And wrap our winnings in this dusty life,
    Say "No more tears, Lord God !
    The measure runneth o'er ? "

O holder of the balance, laughest Thou ?
Nay, Lord ! be gentler to our foolishness,
For His sake who assumed our dust, and turns
    On Thee pathetic eyes,
    Still moisten'd with our tears !

And teach us, O our Father, while we weep,
To look all patiently on earth, and learn —
Waiting in that meek gesture, till at last
    These tearful eyes be fill'd
    With the dry dust of death !

Mrs. Browning is never more successful than when reflecting on some calm sweet promise of Scripture. Her womanly faith and trust then rise superior to all earthly thoughts, and inspire her with most pure and holy utterances. I know scarcely any poem that has a more soothing and sustaining influence than that which she calls —

THE SLEEP.

He giveth His beloved, sleep.—*Psalm,* cxxvii. 2.

Of all the thoughts of God that are
Borne inward unto souls afar
Along the Psalmist's music deep —
Now tell me if that any is
For gift or grace, surpassing this —
" He giveth His belovëd, sleep " ?

What would we give to our belov'd ?
The hero's heart, to be unmov'd —
The poet's star-tuned harp to sweep —
The senate's shout to patriot vows —
The monarch's crown to light the brows ?
" He giveth *His* belovëd, sleep."

What do we give to our belov'd ?
A little faith, all undisprov'd —
A little dust, to over weep —
And bitter memories to make
The whole earth blasted for our sake ?
" He giveth *His* belovëd, sleep."

" Sleep soft, belov'd !" we sometimes say,
But have no tune to charm away
Sad dust that through the eyelids creep :
But never doleful dream again
Shall break the happy slumber when
" He giveth *His* belovëd, sleep."

O Earth, so full of dreary noises !
O men, with wailing in your voices !

O delvëd gold! the wailer's heap!
O strife, O curse, that o'er it fall!
God makes a silence through you all,
"And giveth His belovëd, sleep!"

His dews drop mutely on the hill:
His cloud above it resteth still,
Though on its slope men toil and reap!
More softly than the dew is shed,
Or cloud is floated overhead,
"He giveth His belovëd, sleep!"

Yea! men may wonder when they scan
A living, thinking, feeling man,
In such a rest his heart to keep:
But angels say — and through the word
I ween their blessed smile is *heard* —
"He giveth His belovëd, sleep!"

For me, my heart, that erst did go
Most like a tired child at a show,
That sees through tears the juggler's leap,
Would now its wearied vision close,
Would childlike on *His* love repose,
"Who giveth His belovëd, sleep!"

And friends! dear friends! when it shall be
That this low breath is gone from me,
And round my bier ye come to weep,—
Let one, most loving of you all,
Say, "Not a tear must o'er her fall—
He giveth His belovëd, sleep!"

One of Mrs. Browning's most effective poems, and the next I shall quote, is founded upon a touching incident in the history of her present majesty.

When Queen Victoria was informed of her accession to the throne on the death of her uncle, she was so affected with the consciousness of the heavy responsibilities which had in a moment fallen upon her, that she wept.

Only a woman could have versified that incident as Mrs. Browning has done.

VICTORIA'S TEARS.

O maiden! heir of kings!
A king has left his place;
The majesty of Death has swept
All other from his face!
And thou, upon thy mother's breast,
No longer lean adown,
But take the Glory for the Rest,
And rule the land that loves thee best.
She heard and wept —
She wept to wear a crown!

They deck'd her courtly halls;
They rein'd her hundred steeds;
They shouted at her palace gate
"A noble Queen succeeds!"
Her name has stirr'd the mountain's sleep,
Her praise has fill'd the town,
And mourners God had stricken deep,
Look'd hearkening up, and did not weep.
Alone she wept,
Who wept, to wear a crown!

She saw no purples shine,
For tears had dimm'd her eyes;
She only knew her childhood's flowers
Were happier pageantries!
And while her heralds play'd their part,
Those million shouts to drown —
"God save the Queen" from hill to mart,
She heard through all her beating heart,
And turn'd and wept —
She wept to wear a crown!

God save thee, weeping Queen!
Thou shalt be well beloved!
The tyrant's sceptre cannot move
As those pure tears have moved !
The nature in thine eyes we see
That tyrants cannot own —
The love that guardeth liberties !
Strange blessing on the nation lies,
Whose sovereign wept —
Yea, wept to wear a crown!

God bless thee! weeping Queen!
With blessing more divine !
And fill with happier love than earth's
That tender heart of thine !
That when the thrones of earth shall be
As low as graves brought down,—
A piercëd hand may give to thee
The crown which angels shout to see !
Thou wilt *not* weep
To wear that heavenly crown!

CATARINA TO CAMOËNS.

Dying in his absence abroad, and referring to the Poem in which he recorded the sweetness of her eyes.

On the door you will not enter,
I have gazed too long — adieu !
Hope withdraws her peradventure —
Death is near me,— and not *you!*
Come, O lover !
Close and cover
These poor eyes, you called, I ween,
" Sweetest eyes, were ever seen."

TT*

When I heard you sing that burden
   In my vernal days and bowers,
Other praises disregarding,
   I but hearkened that of yours,—
      Only saying
      In heart-playing,
" Blessed eyes mine eyes have been,
If the sweetest, HIS have seen !''

But all changeth !   At this vesper,
   Cold the sun shines down the door !
If you stood there, would you whisper
   " Love, I love you," as before,—
      Death pervading
      Now, and shading
Eyes you sang of, that yestreen,
As the sweetest, ever seen ?

Yes ! I think, were you beside them,
   Near the bed I die upon,—
Though their beauty you denied them,
   As you stood there, looking down,
      You would truly
      Call them duly,
For the love's sake found therein,—
" Sweetest eyes, were ever seen."

And if *you* looked down upon them,
   And if *they* looked up to *you*,
All the light which has foregone them
   Would be gathered back anew !
      They would truly
      Be as duly
Love-transformed to Beauty's sheen,—
" Sweetest eyes, were ever seen. "

But, ah, me ! you only see me
   In your thoughts of loving man,

Smiling soft perhaps and dreamy,
  Through the wavings of my fan,—
    And unweeting
    Go repeating,
In your reverie serene,
" Sweetest eyes, were ever seen."

While my spirit leans and reaches
  From my body still and pale,
Fain to hear what tender speech is
  In your love, to help my bale —
    O my poet,
    Come and show it!
Come, of latest love, to glean
" Sweetest eyes, were ever seen."

O my poet, O my prophet,
  When you praised their sweetness so,
Did you think, in singing of it,
  That it might be near to go?
    Had you fancies
    From their glances,
That the grave would quickly screen
" Sweetest eyes, were ever seen?"

No reply! The fountains warble
  In the court-yard sounds alone!
As the water to the marble
  So my heart falls with a moan,
    From love-sighing
    To this dying!
Death forerunneth Love, to win
" Sweetest eyes, were ever seen."

Will you come? when I'm departed
  Where all sweetnesses are hid —
When thy voice, my tender-hearted,
  Will not lift up either lid.

Cry, O lover,
Love is over !
Cry beneath the cypress green —
" Sweetest eyes, were ever seen."

When the angelus is ringing,
  Near the convent will you walk,
And recall the choral singing
  Which brought angels down our talk ?
    Spirit-shriven
    I viewed Heaven,
Till you smiled— " Is earth unclean,
Sweetest eyes, were ever seen ?"

When beneath the palace-lattice,
  You ride slow as you have done,
And you see a face there — *that* is
  Not the old familiar one.—
    Will you oftly
    Murmur softly,
" Here, ye watched me morn and e'en,
Sweetest eyes, were ever seen !"

When the palace ladies sitting
  Round your gittern, shall have said,
" Poet, sing those verses written
  For the lady who is dead,"—
    Will you tremble,
    Yet dissemble,—
Or sing hoarse, with tears between,
" Sweetest eyes, were ever seen ?"

Sweetest eyes !   How sweet in flowings,
  The repeated cadence is !
Though you sang a hundred poems,
  Still the best one would be this.
    I can hear it
    'Twixt my spirit

And the earth-noise, intervene —
" Sweetest eyes, were ever seen !"

But the priest waits for the praying,
  And the choir are on their knees,—
And the soul must pass away in
  Strains more solemn high than these !
    Miserere
    For the weary —
Oh, no longer for Catrine,
" Sweetest eyes, were ever seen !"

Keep my riband ! take and keep it,—
  I have loosed it from my hair ;*
Feeling, while you overweep it,
Not alone in your despair,—
    Since with saintly,
    Watch, unfaintly,
Out of Heaven shall o'er you lean
" Sweetest eyes, were ever seen."

But — but *now* — yet unremoved
  Up to Heaven, they glisten fast —
You may cast away, Beloved,
  In your future, all my past ;
    Such old phrases
    May be praises
For some fairer bosom-queen —
" Sweetest eyes, were ever seen !"

Eyes of mine, what are ye doing?
  Faithless, faithless,— praised amiss,
If a tear be of your showing,
  Drop for any hope of HIS !
    Death hath boldness
    Besides coldness,
If unworthy tears demean
" Sweetest eyes, were ever seen."

* She left him the riband from her hair.

65

I will look out to his future —
　I will bless it till it shine !
Should he ever be a suitor
　Unto sweeter eyes than mine,
　　Sunshine gild them,
　　Angels shield them,
Whatsoever eyes terrene
Be the sweetest HIS have seen !

THE CRY OF THE HUMAN.

" There is no God," the foolish saith,—
　But none, " There is no sorrow ;"
And nature oft, the cry of faith,
　In bitter need will borrow ;
Eyes which the preacher could not school,
　By wayside graves are raised ;
And lips say, " God be pitiful,"
　Who ne'er said, " God be praised."
　　　　　　　　Be pitiful, O God !

The tempest stretches from the steep
　The shadow of its coming —
The beasts grow tame, and near us creep,
　As help were in the human —
Yet, while the cloud-wheels roll and grind
　We spirits tremble under ! —
The hills have echoes ; but we find
　No answer for the thunder.
　　　　　　　　Be pitiful, O God !

The battle hurtles on the plains —
　Earth feels new scythes upon her :
We reap our brothers for the wains,
　And call the harvest . . honour,—

Draw face to face, front line to line,
 One image all inherit,—
Then kill, curse on, by that same sign,
 Clay, clay,— and spirit, spirit.
      Be pitiful, O God!

The plague runs festering through the town,—
 And never a bell is tolling ;
And corpses, jostled 'neath the moon,
 Nod to the dead-cart's rolling !
The young child calleth for the cup —
 The strong man brings it weeping ;
The mother from her babe looks up,
 And shrieks away its sleeping.
      Be pitiful, O God !

The plague of gold strikes far and near,—
 And deep and strong it enters :
This purple chimar which we wear,
 Makes madder than the centaur's.
Our thoughts grow blank, our words grow strange ;
 We cheer the pale gold-diggers —
Each soul is worth so much on 'Change,
 And marked, like sheep, with figures.
      Be pitiful, O God !

The curse of gold upon the land,
 The lack of bread enforces —
The rail-cars snort from strand to strand,
 Like more of Death's White Horses !
The rich preach "rights" and future days,
 And hear no angel scoffing :
The poor die mute — with starving gaze
 On corn-ships in the offing.
      Be pitiful, O God !

We meet together at the feast—
 To private mirth betake us —

We stare down in the winecup, lest
　　Some vacant chair should shake us !
We name delight, and pledge it round —
　　"It shall be ours to-morrow !"
God's seraphs ! do your voices sound
　　As sad in naming sorrow ?
　　　　　　　　Be pitiful, O God !

We sit together, with the skies,
　　The steadfast skies, above us :
We look into each other's eyes,—
　　" And how long will you love us ?"—
The eyes grew dim with prophecy,
　　The voices, low and breathless —
" 'Till death us part !"— O words, to be
　　Our *best* for love the deathless!
　　　　　　　　Be pitiful, dear God !

We tremble by the harmless bed
　　Of one loved and departed —
Our tears drop on the lips that said
　　Last night, " Be stronger hearted !"
O God,— to clasp those fingers close,
　　And yet to feel so lonely ! —
To see a light on dearest brows,
　　Which is the daylight only !
　　　　　　　　Be pitiful, O God !

The happy children come to us,
　　And look up in our faces :
They ask us — Was it thus, and thus,
　　When we were in their places ?
We cannot speak : — we see anew
　　The hills we used to live in ;
And feel our mother's smile press through
　　The kisses she is giving.
　　　　　　　　Be pitiful, O God !

We pray together at the kirk,
  For mercy, mercy, solely —
Hands weary with the evil work,
  We lift them to the Holy!
The corpse is calm below our knee —
  Its spirit, bright before Thee —
Between them, worse than either, **we**
  Without the rest or glory!
             Be pitiful, O God!

We leave the communing of men,
  The murmur of the passions;
And live alone, to live again
  With endless generations.
Are we so brave? — The sea and sky
  In silence lift their mirrors;
And, glassed therein, our spirits high
  Recoil from their own terrors.
             Be pitiful, O God!

We sit on hills our childhood wist,
  Woods, hamlets, streams, beholding!
The sun strikes, through the farthest mist,
  The city's spire to golden.
The city's golden spire it was,
  When hope and health were strongest,
But now it is the churchyard grass,
  We look upon the longest.
             Be pitiful. O God!

And soon all vision waxeth dull —
  Men whisper, " He is dying :''
We cry no more, " Be pitiful!" —
  We have no strength for crying! —
No strength, no need! Then, Soul of mine,
  Look up and triumph rather —
Lo! in the depth of God's Divine,
  The Son adjures the Father —
          BE PITIFUL, O GOD!
            VV

COWPER'S GRAVE.

I will invite thee, from thy envious herse
To rise, and 'bout the world thy beams to spread,
That we may see there 's brightness in the dead.
                                        HABINGTON.

It is a place where poets crown'd
    May feel the heart's decaying - -
It is a place where happy saints
    May weep amid their praying —
Yet let the grief and humbleness
    As low as silence languish ;
Earth surely now may give her calm
    To whom she gave her anguish.

O poets ! from a maniac's tongue
    Was pour'd the deathless singing !
O Christians ! at your cross of hope
    A hopeless hand was clinging !
O men, this man in brotherhood,
    Your weary paths beguiling,
Groan'd inly while he taught you peace,
    And died while ye were smiling !

And now, what time ye all may read
    Through dimming tears his story
How discord on the music fell,
    And darkness on the glory —
And how, when, one by one, sweet sounds
    And wandering lights departed,
He wore no less a loving face,
    Because so broken-hearted.

He shall be strong to sanctify
    The poet's high vocation,
And bow the meekest Christian down
    In meeker adoration :

Nor ever shall he be in praise
    By wise or good forsaken;
Named softly, as the household name
    Of one whom God hath taken !

With sadness that is calm, not gloom,
    I learn to think upon him ;
With meekness that is gratefulness,
    On God, whose heaven hath won him —
Who suffer'd once the madness-cloud
    Towards His love to blind him ;
But gently led the blind along,
    Where breath and bird could find him ;

And wrought within his shatter'd brain
    Such quick poetic senses,
As hills have language for, and stars
    Harmonious influences !
The pulse of dew upon the grass
    His own did calmly number ;
And silent shadow from the trees
    Fell o'er him like a slumber.

The very world, by God's constraint,
    From falsehood's chill removing,
Its women and its men became
    Beside him true and loving ! —
And timid hares were drawn from woods
    To share his home-caresses,
Uplooking to his human eyes,
    With sylvan tendernesses.

But while in blindness he remain'd,
    Unconscious of the guiding,
And things provided came without
    The sweet sense of providing,
He testified this solemn truth,
    Though frenzy desolated,—

Nor man nor nature satisfy
Whom only God created!

Like a sick child, that knoweth not
   His mother while she blesses,
And droppeth on his burning brow
   The coolness of her kisses ;
That turns his fever'd eyes around —
   " My mother ! where 's my mother ? "
As if such tender words and looks
   Could come from any other . —

The fever gone, with leaps of heart
   He sees her bending o'er him ;
Her face all pale from watchful love,
   Th' unweary love she bore him —
Thus, woke the poet from the dream
   His life's long fever gave him,
Beneath those deep pathetic eyes
   Which closed in death to save him !

Thus ! oh, not *thus !* no type of earth
   Could image that awaking,
Wherein he scarcely heard the chaunt
   Of seraphs round him breaking
Or felt the new immortal throb
   Of soul from body parted ;
But felt *those eyes alone,* and knew
   " *My* Saviour ! *not* deserted ! "

Deserted ! who hath dreamt that when
   The cross in darkness rested,
Upon the Victim's hidden face
   No love was manifested ?
What frantic hands outstretched have e'er
   Th' atoning drops averted —
What tears have washed them from the soul —
   That *one* should be deserted ?

Deserted ! God could separate
  From His own essence rather :
And Adam's sins *have* swept between
  The righteous Son and Father —
Yea ! once, Immanuel's orphan'd cry
  His universe hath shaken —
It went up single, echoless,
  " My God, I am forsaken ! "

It went up from the Holy's lips
  Amid his lost creation,
That of the lost, no son should use
  Those words of desolation ;
That earth's worst frenzies, marring hope,
  Should mar not hope's fruition :
And I, on Cowper's grave, should see
  His rapture, in a vision !

66   vv*

MISS LOWE.

This accomplished lady is a daughter of the Dean of Exeter, and is the author of a volume entitled *Poems, chiefly Dramatic, edited by Thomas Bell Lowe,* and published in London in 1840. She has a fine command of language, and has succeeded admirably in catching the style of Milton.

We extract the following from " *Cephalus and Procris.*" —

HAMADRYAD.

Sweet Zephyr, stay !
Thy breath has caught the ocean freshness ;
  On my parched brow let it play.
Tell me whence thou wanderest hither,
And thy course directed whither.

ZEPHYR

Far on the confines of the west,
Beyond the Broad Atlantic's breast,
In silence and eternal gloom
Doth ancient darkness spread his dome.
There in slumbers soft I lay,
Till wafted to the realms of day,
On the Islands Blest descending,
  O what joyous life was mine !
Mid bright bowers and sweet vales blending
  All delights divine.
No churlish winds had license there ;
  Only my gentle race might waken
The odorous flowers, and perfumes rare
  From groves of spice and incense shaken ;

And from their shades the music bear
  Of harpings and entrancing song ;
Pure spirits breathe that golden air,
  And godlike forms are seen among,
Wanderers from their star-paved dwelling ;
  But severed from that happy throng,
By stern Æolus' compelling,
Once more I skimmed the briny main,
And paused on wide Iberia's plain.
Thence unheeding, still proceeding
Towards the rising of the sun ;
Forests deep and hills of frost,
And smiling valleys I have cross'd,
And whate'er I breathed upon
Straight with livelier gladness shone ;
But weary now I fain would close
My filmy pinions in repose.

HOUR OF NIGHT DEPARTING.

Soft pacing down the western sky,
  Sad-suited Night in silence goes ;
Her dragons slow, with sleepless eye,
  She guideth to repose.
And following still the noiseless wain,
I must not loiter from her train ;
Nor ever gaze on light's gay throng,
Nor join my sisters' dance and song,
  When glows the orient main.
Her cypress veil, far-floating spread,
In darkness shrouds my drooping head,
And solemn is our gliding tread
  Towards Erebus' domain.

MISS CHARLOTTE YOUNG.

THIS lady, who has very recently published her first volume of poetry "*The World's Complaint, and other Poems*," bids fair to display, indeed may be said to display already, poetical powers of the highest order; and to take a very distinguished place among the poetesses of the present generation. She has a large share of Eliza Cook's spirit; she possesses much of Mrs. Hemans's grace, with more force; and all Miss Landon's eloquent facility, with greater purity of sentiment.

I do not know where, in all the writings of our Female Poets, to find a more melodious, simple-hearted and instructive little poem than this : —

THE BIRD AND THE FOUNTAIN.

There was once a little fountain,
　That flow'd away unseen,
In the bosom of a mountain,
　Where man had never been ;
Yet on it wander'd brightly,
　With a pretty bubbling sound,
Whilst its waters sprinkled lightly
　The plants that grew around.

But one evening, at the " gloaming,"
　A Swallow, pert and vain,
From far distant countries roaming,
　Came soaring o'er·the plain ;
And staying by the mountain,
　To rest his weary wing,
To that pretty little fountain
　He thus began to sing : —

" Poor humble thing, and lowly,
  Confined to one lone spot,
Condemn'd to suffer slowly
  Thy solitary lot!
Oh! had you seen the bowers
  O'er which I 've lately flown,
How poor you 'd think the flowers
  That blossom here alone!

"For there, 'midst scenes of splendour,
  A fountain's life should run,
And all its sweetness render
  Beneath an Eastern sun;
There should your cooling waters,
  In fragrance and perfume,
Descend to bless the daughters
  Of Oriental bloom."

The little fountain listen'd,
  And, for a moment's space,
Perhaps less brightly glisten'd
  In her lonely hiding-place:
Perchance the swallow's measure
  A passing shadow threw
On every simple pleasure
  Her humble spirit knew.

And soon that pretty Fountain,
  Once happy and content,
Perchance had scorn'd the mountain
  Where all her life was spent,
Had not a thirsty flower
  Just caught her sparkling eye,
Who, but for her sweet shower,
  Must pine away and die.

Oh, then she said, " Pert stranger,
  I do not envy thee,

Though o'er those scenes a ranger,
 Which I may never see ;
Since in my quiet flowing
 I 've joys to thee unknown,
The bliss of bliss bestowing, —
 The sweetest ever known !"

She said, and soft reclining
 Within her crystal bed,
She kissed that flow'ret pining,
 And raised its drooping head.
The Swallow and his story
 Were soon forgotten quite,
For *his* was fading glory,
 And *hers* enduring light !

There is something perfectly feminine in the foregoing passage.
A man could not have written it. The sweet placidity of the sentiment is such as a woman only could indite : and nothing can be
more charming than the effect produced by it.

The following lines contain, I think, a noble burst of womanly
philosophy : —

EVERY-DAY HEROES.

We speak and we read of the hero's deeds,
 And envy perchance his fame ;
We would tread, like him, some path that leads
 To gaining a deathless name ;
And we sigh as our time is vainly spent,
" Oh, 't was not for *this* that I was meant !"

We feel, with a touch of deep regret,
 What nothings, alas ! we 've been ;
How like a stagnant pool, as yet,
 Has been to us Life's stream.
There seem'd to our souls a warning sent,—
" Mortal ! for this thou wert not meant."

Yet we sit and we dream of a better day,
    And idly its coming wait,
When, like the hero of poet's lay,
    We too may be something great ;
And still through the mist our spirits grope,
For the distant gleam of this better hope.

For alas ! while we dream these airy dreams,
    And sigh for the better afar,
We are dwelling on that which only seems,
    While we slight the truths that are.
We are looking for flowers more fair and sweet,
While we trample the fairest 'neath our feet.

The wearisome, lone, and monotonous lot,
    Where To-day 's as the day that is gone ;
Where To-morrow brings nothing To-day has not,
    Nor evening the hopes of the morn ;
Oh ! even here, in the loneliest hours,
Are there lying some fair but neglected flowers.

Some being we gaze on from day to day,
    And tend with a holy care,
Lightening the woes in each other's way,
    Each breathing a mutual prayer.
Oh ! here, in the homeliest act or speech,
May we to the fame of a hero reach.

For when selfish thoughts are for others subdued,
    And smiles conquer the rising frown,
When we love our own in another's good,
    Oh ! we weave us a deathless crown,
That many a hero's, present or past,
With all its glory, has never surpass'd.

Oh ! did we but see how in smallest things
    Are beginnings of all that 's great,

Life's soil would be water'd by countless springs,
   That now 'neath the surface wait.
We should feel that when earthward kindly sent,
   For heroes and heroines all were meant.

One of the chief attributes of Miss Young's muse is its *cheer-fulness*. There is no discontent, no peevishness, no fretfulness in her philosophy. Her very melancholy is healthy. The opening verses of *The World's Complaint* are very excellent in this respect : —

Through all the changes of unnumber'd years,
   I 've roll'd around the life-bestowing Sun ;
Yet still each season fresh and bright appears
   As when my onward course was first begun.
Spring with its new-born beauty does not shun,
   Awakening as of old the sleepy earth ;
And Summer in its brightness loseth none
   Of all its early loveliness and worth.
Still blooms the flower, and glows the ripen'd fruit,
And through the ground the tender leaflets shoot.

And yet, alas ! I long have been misnamed
   A desert wilderness, — a worthless clod ;
And man, vain man, is not a whit ashamed
   Thus to abuse the bounty of his God :
And say that, till he rests beneath the sod,
   There 's nothing worthy of his noble thought ;
But day by day he still must toil and plod ;
   And seek, but never find the object sought.
And me he calls a waste, a fleeting show, —
A dismal charnal-house for man below.

Ungrateful mortal ! canst thou look around,
   Upon the waving trees and meadows green ?
Canst listen to the universal sound
   Of joy and gladness filling every scene ?

Canst see the stars benignant shine at e'en ?
   Canst feel the breeze refresh thy sullen brow,
And cherish still thy bosom's inward spleen ?
   Oh ! haste at once thy stubborn will to bow.
Think ! would such beauty be bestow'd on me,
If I were made to nourish misery ?

Come, now, and look upon my laughing face ;
   View the bright colours of the simplest flower ;
The merry rivulet's meanderings trace
   In the glad sunlight of the morning hour ;
And, yielding to the soul-pervading power
   That 's deep enshrined in all created things,
See if thy gloomy visions dare to lower
   Where e'en the insect in his gladness sings.
Look forth, and tell me where the spot appears
That should be called by man " the vale of tears."

There is great truth of thought in the following finely expressed
lines : —

OH ! EVER THUS DO SUN AND SHADE.

Oh ! did you list at morning to the merry bridal bell,
That stealing through the fields and woods, so soft and cheery
    fell ?
And hear you now so mournfully the knell of parting life,
That minds you of some sever'd tie, — of husband, son, or wife ?
       Oh ! ever thus do sun and shade
       By turns this mortal life pervade.

And did you see the passing gloom upon the maiden's brow,
The silent tear upon her cheek ? — And do you see her now,—
Her face lit up with sunny smiles, all radiant with delight,
Her eyes that beam with innocence, in Love's own beauty bright ?
       Oh ! ever thus do sun and shade
       By turns this mortal life pervade.

Night follows day, and day the night; the sun succeeds the shower;
And deepest gloom may hover near, to chase the sportive hour.
But though it darken for a time, sweet Hope will soon prevail,
As grateful calms will come to soothe where blew the boisterous
      gale.
              For ever thus do sun and shade
              By turns this mortal life pervade.

I know no writer who can employ familiar and homely images
with more success and effect than Miss Young. The lines which
I mark in italics in the following poem, afford a fine proof of her
power in this respect : —

EVENING.

How like *a tender mother*,
   With loving thoughts beguiled,
Fond Nature seems to lull to rest
   Each faint and weary child !
Drawing the curtain tenderly,
   Affectionate and mild.

Hark ! to the gentle lullaby
   That through the trees is creeping,—
Those *sleepy trees* that nod their heads
   Ere the moon as yet comes peeping,
Like a tender nurse, to see if all
   Her little ones are sleeping.

One little fluttering bird,
   Like a child in a dream of pain,
Has chirp'd and started up,
   Then nestled down again.
Oh! a child and a bird, as they sink to rest,
   Are as like as any twain.

The chief charm, however, in Miss Young's poetry is its
strong, earnest, hearty, human sympathies. She can feel for the

meanest of her species: and that most honestly and nobly. There is a world of true charity and fine philanthropy in these verses entitled —

THE POOR MAN'S FLOWER.

Wandering along his weary way,
    In dirty tatters meanly dress'd,
A beggar-man one summer day,
    Seem'd hastening to some place of rest.
No smile was on his wither'd face,
    It nought but anxious care exprest;
Grim Poverty had left its trace,
    And inly rankled at his breast;
Yet in his coat that weary hour
The poor man nursed a cherished flower.

'T was no choice plant in hothouse bred,
    And guarded with a tender care;
No hand had propp'd its drooping head,
    Or shielded it from midnight air;
Yet choicest flowers might fail to bring
    To their rich owners thoughts as fair,
As did that simple, lowly thing,
    To that unhappy man of care,
Who from the hedge-side, free to all,
Had pluck'd himself that blossom small.

No flow'ret in a lady's dress,
    Where all beside is meet and bright,
And she, in her own loveliness,
    Seems but another flower of light,
Has aught so sacred or so dear,
    So touching to the gazer's sight,
As that bright spot amongst the drear,
    That star amidst the gloom of night; —
The flow'ret pluck'd by fingers rude,
To cheer the beggar's solitude.

On, on he pass'd, that human flower,
   Whom men set foot on like a weed ;
Yet, waiting for a kinder hour,
   Within was many a precious seed.
The beggar's spirit, like his dress,
   Might not be wholly fair, indeed ;
Yet some bright bud of loveliness,
   The germ of many a noble deed,
Did we but take the pains to find,
Blooms fresh in each neglected mind.

The simple plucking of that flower
   Betray'd a tenderness of thought,
Ready to find in every hour
   The kindred sweetness that it sought :
A sense of beauty seldom found
   Where all within is darkly fraught,
But often trampled to the ground,
   And mercilessly set at nought,
By those who in their selfish power
Treat as the weed what is the flower.

Yet brighter days begin to dawn ;
   The weeds of prejudice and pride,
Though slowly, yet are surely drawn,
   From bosoms where they used to hide :
And, thou, poor scorn'd and wither'd flower,
   With wealth and grandeur unallied,
Shalt see, ere long, the happy hour,
   When men, from falseness purified,
Shall learn to estimate the worth
Of all the toiling sons of earth.

Miss Young's muse bears a strong resemblance to Mrs. Howitt's. It seems like a younger sister. It cannot, of course, be
said that Miss Young as yet displays that calm consciousness of
strength, and that exquisite perfection of style which so remarka-

bly distinguish the poetry of Mrs. Howitt; but still the likeness is great. Both writers exhibit a pure simplicity of thought and feeling; both have a strong and refined sense of natural and moral beauty; both earnest, truthful, loving hearts; both fervently dedicate their powers to the service and welfare of humanity. And I venture to predict that in the course of a few years, when practice shall have matured, and experience ripened her genius, Miss Young will take a place in the estimation of the world, not very far below the great poetess to whom I have here compared her. She could not copy from a better model, or desire a prouder glory.

THE END.

SELECTED BIBLIOGRAPHY

BACKGROUND WORKS

The following books and articles provide a background for the study and understanding of the work of English women poets, and their lives. Many of these studies relate to the social setting out of which the poets represented in *Female Poets of Great Britain* wrote; others supply a background to Rowton's ideas. Studies of American authors have also been listed where particularly germane to the English setting or authors.

Adburgham, Alison. *Women in Print: Writing Women and Women's Magazines from the Restoration to the Accession of Victoria.* London: Allen and Unwin, 1972.

Altick, Richard D. *Victorian People and Ideas.* New York; W. W. Norton, 1973.

Balfour, Clara Lucas. *Working Women of this Century: The Lesson of Their Lives.* London: Cassell, Petter, and Galpin, 1868.

Ballard, George. *Memoirs of Several Ladies of Great Britain.* Oxford: W. Jackson, 1752.

Basch, Francoise. *Relative Creatures: Victorian Women in Society and the Novel.* New York: Schocken Books, 1974.

Bax, Clifford and Stewart, Meum, eds. *The Distaff Muse: An Anthology of Poetry Written by Women.* London: Hollis and Carter, 1949.

Bernikow, Louise, ed. *The World Split Open: Four Centuries of Women Poets in England and America, 1552–1950.* New York: Random House, 1974.

Blease, W. Lyon. *The Emancipation of English Women.* London: Constable, 1910.

Bloch, Ruth H. "Untangling the Roots of Modern Sex Roles: A Survey of Four Centuries of Change." *Signs* 4 (1978):237-52.

Bouten, Jacob. *Mary Wollstonecraft and the Beginnings of Female Emancipation in France and England.* Amsterdam: H. J. Paris, 1923.

Branca, Patricia. *Silent Sisterhood: Middle-Class Women in the Victorian Home.* Pittsburgh, Pa.: Carnegie Mellon University Press, 1975.

Butturff, Douglas and Epstein, Edmund L., eds. *Women's Language and Style.* University of Akron Studies in Contemporary Language no. 1. Akron, Ohio: L and S Books, 1978.

Chester, Laura and Barba, Sharon, eds. *Rising Tides: Twentieth-Century American Women Poets.* New York: Washington Square Press, 1973.

Clinton, Katherine. "Femme et Philosophe." *Eighteenth-Century Studies* 8 (1975):283-99.

Colby, Vineta. *Yesterday's Woman: Domestic Realism in the English Novel.* Princeton: Princeton University Press, 1974.

Cosman, Carol; Keefe, Joan; Weaver, Kathleen, eds. *The Penguin Book of Women Poets.* New York: Penguin Books, 1978.

Cott, Nancy F. "Passionlessness: An Interpretation of Victorian Sexual Ideology, 1790–1850." *Signs* 4 (1978):219-36.

————, ed. *Root of Bitterness: Documents of the Social History of American Women.* New York: E. P. Dutton, 1972.

Courtney, Janet E. *The Adventurous Thirties: A Chapter in the Women's Movement.* Oxford: Oxford University Press, 1933.

Crow, Duncan. *The Victorian Woman.* London: Allen and Unwin, 1971.

Douglas, Ann. *The Feminization of American Culture.* New York: McGraw-Hill, Avon Books, 1977.

Dunbar, Janet. *The Early Victorian Woman: Some Aspects of Her Life, 1837–57.* London: George Harrap, 1953.

Duncombe, John. *The Feminaed or Female Genius.* 2d ed. London: R. and J. Dodsley, 1757.

Een, Jo Ann Delores and Rosenberg-Dishman, Marie B., eds. *Women and Society: An Annotated Bibliography.* Beverly Hills and London: Sage Publications, 1978.

Ehrenpreis, Irvin. "Letters of Advice to Young Spinsters." Halsband, Robert. "Ladies of Letters in the Eighteenth Century." *The Lady of Letters in the Eighteenth Century.* Los Angeles: William Andrews Clark Memorial Library of UCLA, 1969.

Ellmann, Mary. *Thinking About Women.* New York: Harcourt Brace Jovanovich, 1968.

Ewbank, Inga-Stina. *Their Proper Sphere: A Study of the Brontë Sisters as Early-Victorian Female Novelists.* Cambridge, Mass.: Harvard University Press, 1966.

Fritz, Paul and Morton, Richard, eds. *Women in the Eighteenth Century and Other Essays.* Toronto: Hakkert, 1976.

Gilbert, Sandra M. and Gubar, Susan, eds. *Shakespeare's Sisters: Feminist Essays on Women Poets.* Bloomington and London: Indiana University Press, 1979.

Gornick, Vivian and Moran, Barbara K., eds. *Women in Sexist Society: Studies in Power and Powerlessness.* New York: Mentor, New American Library, 1971.

Goulianos, Joan, ed. *By a Woman Writt: Literature from Six Centuries by and about Women.* Baltimore: Penguin Books, 1974.

Hale, Sarah Josepha. *Woman's Record.* 1855. Reprint. New York: Source Book Press, 1970.

Hall, Samuel Carter. *A Book of Memories of Great Men and Women of the Age.* London: Virtue and Co., 1876.

Harrison, Brian. "Underneath the Victorians." *Victorian Studies* 10 (1967):239-62.

Harrison, J. F. C. *The Early Victorians, 1832–1851.* New York: Praeger, 1971.

Hays, Mary. *Female Biography; or Memoirs of Illustrious and Celebrated Women.* Philadelphia: Byrch and Small, 1807.

Hill, Georgiana. *Women in English Life from Medieval to Modern Times.* 2 vols. London: Richard Bentley, 1896.

Houghton, Walter E. *The Victorian Frame of Mind, 1830–1870*. New Haven: Yale University Press, 1957.

Howe, Florence and Bass, Ellen, ed. *No More Masks! An Anthology of Poems by Women*. New York: Doubleday Anchor, 1973.

Jerrold, Walter C. *Five Queer Women*. New York: Brentano's, 1929. Aphra Behn, Mary de la Rivière Manley, Susanna Centlivre, Eliza Haywood, Laetitia Pilkington.

Juhasz, Suzanne, *Naked and Fiery Forms: Modern American Poetry by Women, A New Tradition*. New York: Harper and Row, 1976.

Kamm, Josephine. *Rapiers and Battleaxes: The Women's Movement and Its Aftermath*. London: Allen and Unwin, 1966.

Kelley, Mary. "The Sentimentalists: Promise and Betrayal in the Home." *Signs* 4 (1979):434-46.

Kraditor, Aileen S., ed. *Up from the Pedestal: Selected Writings in the History of American Feminism*. Chicago: Quadrangle Books, 1966.

Laslett, Peter. *The World We Have Lost*. New York: Scribners, 1965.

Le Gates, Marlene. "The Cult of Womanhood in Eighteenth-Century Thought." *Eighteenth-Century Studies* 10 (1977):21-39.

MacCarthy, Bridget G. *Women Writers: Their Contribution to the English Novel, 1621–1744*. Cork: Cork University Press, 1944.

———. *The Later Women Novelists, 1744–1818*. Cork: Cork University Press, 1947.

Mahl, Mary R. and Koon, Helene, eds. *The Female Spectator: English Women Writers before 1800*. Bloomington: Indiana University Press, and Old Westbury, N.Y.: Feminist Press, 1977.

Mitchell, Sally. "Sentiment and Suffering: Women's Recreational Reading in the 1860s." *Victorian Studies* 21 (1977):29-45.

Moers, Ellen. *Literary Women: The Great Writers*. New York: Doubleday, 1976.

Moore, Katherine. *Victorian Wives*. New York: St. Martin's Press, 1974.

Myers, Carol F. *Women in Literature: Criticism of the Seventies*. Metuchen, N.J.: Scarecrow Press, 1976.

Oakley, Ann. *Woman's Work: The Housewife, Past and Present*. New York: Random House, 1974.

O'Faolain, Julia and Martines, Lauro, eds. *Not in God's Image*. London: Temple Smith, 1973.

O'Malley, I. B. *Women in Subjection: A Study of the Lives of English Women before 1832*. London: Duckworth, 1933.

Ossioli, Margaret Fuller. *Woman in the Nineteenth Century*. Edited by Bernard Rosenthal. New York, W. W. Norton, 1971.

Phillips, Margaret and Tomkinson, W. S. *English Women in Life and Letters*. Oxford: Oxford University Press, 1927.

Reynolds, Myra. *The Learned Lady in England, 1650–1760*. Boston: Houghton Mifflin, 1920.

Robertson, Eric S. *English Poetesses: A Series of Critical Biographies with Illustrative Extracts.* London: Cassell, 1883.

Robinson, Lillian S. *Sex, Class, and Culture.* Bloomington and London: Indiana University Press, 1978.

Rothman, Sheila M. *Woman's Proper Place: A History of Changing Ideals and Practices, 1870 to the Present.* New York: Basic Books, 1978.

Rowbotham, Sheila. *Hidden from History: Rediscovering Women in History, from the Seventeenth Century to the Present.* New York: Random House, 1974.

Sackville-West, Vita; Dobrée, Bonamy; Brown, Beatrice; Armstrong, Martin; Willis, Irene Cooper; and West, Geoffrey. *Six Brilliant Englishwomen.* London: G. Howe, 1930. Aphra Behn, Sarah Churchill, Elizabeth Chudleigh, Lady Hester Stanhope, Elizabeth Barrett Browning, and Annie Besant.

Schneir, Miriam, ed. *Feminism: The Essential Historical Writings.* New York: Random House, 1972.

Segnitz, Barbara and Rainey, Carol, eds. *Psyche: The Feminine Poetic Consciousness.* New York: Dial Press, 1973.

Showalter, Elaine. *A Literature of Their Own: British Women Novelists from Brontë to Lessing.* Princeton: Princeton University Press, 1977.

———, ed. *Women's Liberation and Literature.* New York: Harcourt Brace Jovanovich, 1971.

Smith, Lewis W. and Weitz, A.C., eds. *Women's Poetry Today.* New York: George Sully, 1929.

Spacks, Patricia Meyer. *The Female Imagination.* New York: McGraw-Hill, Avon Books, 1972.

Standford, Ann, ed. *The Women Poets in English.* New York: McGraw-Hill, 1972.

Stenton, Doris Mary. *The English Woman in History.* London: Allen and Unwin, 1957. Reprint. New York: Schocken Books, 1977.

Stone, Donald. "Victorian Feminism and the Nineteenth Century Novel." *Women's Studies* 1 (1972):65-91.

Stone, Lawrence. *The Family, Sex, and Marriage in England, 1500–1800.* New York: Harper and Row, 1977.

Tanner, Leslie B., ed. *Voices from Women's Liberation.* New York: Harcourt Brace, New American Library, 1970.

Thompson, Roger. *Women in Stuart England and America: A Comparative Study.* London: Routledge and Kegan Paul, 1974.

Tytler, Sarah and Watson, J. L., eds. *The Songstresses of Scotland.* London: Strahan, 1871. Alicia Cockburn, Jane Elliott, Susan Blamire, Anne Barnard, Joanna Baillie.

Vicinus, Martha, ed. *Suffer and Be Still: Women in the Victorian Age.* Bloomington: Indiana University Press, 1972.

———, ed. *A Widening Sphere: Changing Roles of Victorian Women.* Bloomington: Indiana University Press, 1977.

Wallas, Ada. *Before the Bluestockings.* London: Allen and Unwin, 1929.

Women and Literature: An Annotated Bibliography of Women Writers. Cambridge, Mass.: Women and Literature Collective, 1977.

INDIVIDUAL AUTHORS

Listed here are selected works by poets represented in *Female Poets of Great Britain,* as well as critical and biographical commentary about them. The order of names is Rowton's. The poetical works cited below are available, except in the rare cases indicated, in American libraries. If a poet's work is not available, her name is omitted from the list; when she has written in other genres that fact is recorded, but in the interests of space, I have in most cases restricted entries to poetical works and commentary on the author's life and poetry.

Book-length critical studies from all periods are included, though the selection favors modern scholarship. Journal articles are predominantly from the last decade. At the end of each entry I have noted when a poet's work may be found in three recent anthologies: Bernikow's *The World Split Open,* Stanford's *The Women Poets in English,* and Mahl and Koon's *The Female Spectator;* the latter contains comprehensive bibliographies for the authors listed here. I have also indicated when information about a poet is available in the *Dictionary of National Biography* (DNB) and in historical studies (especially the inclusive biographical dictionaries that were popular in the nineteenth century) cited in Background Works.

Married authors' maiden names, if known, are in parentheses; alternate spellings and pseudonyms are in brackets.

LADY JULIANA BERNERS [BARNES]

The Book of Hawking, Hunting and Blastings of Arms. St. Albans, 1486.

The Booke of Haulkyng Huntyng and Fysshyng with all the Properties and Medecynes . . . to be kept. London: for R. Tottel, 1561.

Hawking, Hunting, and Fishing, with the True Measures of Blowing. London: Edward Allde, 1586.

Represented in *DNB,* Hays, Stanford.

ANNE ASKEW[E]

The first Examinaciō of Anne Askewe . . . , wyth the elucydacyon of John Bale. 1546–47.

"I am a woman poor and blind." . . . "True is, O man in desparation." London, 1635.

The lattre Examinacion of Anne Askewe and the Ballade . . . in Newgate. n.d.

Writing of Edward the Sixth, William Hugh, Queen Catherine Parr, Anne Askew, Lady Jane Grey, Hamilton and Balnaves. Philadelphia: Presbyterian Board of Publication, 1842. First American edition.

Represented in *DNB,* Hale, Stanford.

ELIZABETH I

The Poems of Queen Elizabeth I. Edited by Leicester Bradner. Providence: Brown University Press, 1964.

Represented in Bernikow, Mahl and Koon, Stanford.

MARY (SIDNEY) HERBERT, countess of Pembroke

The Countess of Pembroke's Antonie. Edited by Alice Luce. Weimar: E. Felber, 1897.

The Countess of Pembroke's Emanuell, together with certaine Psalms. Edited by Abraham Fraunce. London: Posonby, 1591.

The Psalms of Sir Philip Sidney and the Countess of Pembroke. Edited by J. C. A. Rathmell. New York: New York University Press, 1963. Bibliography.

The Triumph of Death and Other Unpublished and Uncollected Poems. Edited by G. F. Waller. Salzburg: Institut für Englishe Sprache und Literatur, Universität Salzburg, 1977. Bibliography.

Commentary

Young, Frances C. *Mary Sidney, Countess of Pembroke.* London: D. Nutt, 1912.

Represented in *DNB*, Hale, Hays, Mahl and Koon, Stanford.

ELIZABETH MELVILLE [COLVILLE], called Lady Culross

A Godlie Dreame. Edinburgh: R. Chartens, 1606.

Represented in *DNB*, Stanford.

LADY ELIZABETH CAREW [CAREY]

Rowton confused Elizabeth Carew with her sister-in-law Elizabeth (Tanfield) Cary, viscountess Falkland, who wrote *The Tragedy of Mariam* and dedicated it to Elizabeth Carew. The biographical facts Rowton cites apply to the viscountess, a distinguished person, and the first woman to write a play in English.

The Tragedie of Mariam, the Faire Queene of Iewry. London: T. Creede, 1613. Reprint. Edited by A. C. Dunstan and W. W. Greg. Oxford: Oxford University Press, 1914.

Commentary

Murdock, Kenneth B. *The Sun at Noon.* New York: Macmillan, 1939.

Pearse, Nancy Cotton. "Elizabeth Carey, Renaissance Playwright." *Texas Studies in Language and Literature* 18 (1977):601-8.

Represented in *DNB*, Hale, Hays, Mahl and Koon, Stanford.

LADY MARY WROTH

The Countess of Mountgomeries Urania. London: I. Marriott and I. Grismond, 1621. *Pamphilia to Amphilanthus* appended.

Pamphilia to Amphilanthus. Edited by G. F. Waller. Salzburg: Institut für Englishe Sprache und Literatur, Universität Salzburg, 1977. Bibliography.

Commentary

Parry, Graham. "Lady Mary Wroth's *Urania.*" *Proceedings of the Leeds Philosophical and Literary Society* 16 (1975):51-60.

Roberts, Josephine A. "An Unpublished Literary Quarrel Concerning the Suppression of Mary Wroth's *Urania* (1621)." *Notes and Queries* 24 (1977):532-35.

Represented in *DNB*, Mahl and Koon, Reynolds, Stanford.

DIANA PRIMROSE

A Chaine of Pearle. Or, A Memoriall . . . of Queene Elizabeth, of Glorious Memory.
London: T. Paine, 1630.

Represented in Reynolds, Stanford.

MARY FAGE

*Fames Rovle: or, The Names of Our Dread Soveraigne Lord King Charles, His Royall
Queen Mary, and His Most Hopefull Posterity. . . . anagrammatiz'd and expressed
by acrosticke lines on their names.* London: R. Oulton, 1637.

Represented in Reynolds.

ANN COLLINS

Divine Songs and Meditacions. 1653. Facsimile reprint. Edited by Stanley N. Stewart.
Los Angeles: UCLA for the Augustan Reprint Society, 1961. Bibliography.

Represented in Bernikow, *DNB*, Stanford.

KATHERINE PHILIPS

The Orinda Booklets. Edited by J. R. Tutin. Cottingham near Hull, 1903.

Poems. Unauthorized ed. London: R. Marriot, 1664.

Poems. 1678. Edited by George Saintsbury. In *Minor Poets of the Caroline Age*, 1:405-
662. Oxford: Clarendon Press, 1905.

*Poems by Mrs. Katherine Philips, the Matchless Orinda. . . . With several other trans-
lations out of the French.* Edited by Sir Charles Cotterell. London: Henry Herringman, 1667. London: Henry Herringman, 1678.

Selected Poems. Edited by L. I. Guiney. 2 vols. Cottingham near Hull, 1904-5.

Commentary

Elmen, Paul. "Some Manuscript Poems by the Matchless Orinda." *Philological Quarterly* 30 (1951):53-57.

Mambretti, Catherine Cole. "'Fugitive Papers': A New Orinda Poem and Problems in
Her Canon." *Papers of the Bibliographical Society of America* 71 (1977):443-52.

Souers, Philip W. *The Matchless Orinda.* Cambridge, Mass.: Harvard University Press,
1931.

Thomas, Patrick. "Orinda, Vaughn and Watkyns: Anglo-Welsh Literary Relationships
during the Interregnum." *Anglo-Welsh Review* 26 (1976):96-102.

Represented in Bernikow, *DNB*, Hale, Hays, Mahl and Koon, Reynolds, Stanford,
Stenton.

FRANCES BOOTHBY

Marcelia: or the Treacherous Friend. A Tragicomedy. London: William Cademan, 1670.

MARGARET (LUCAS) CAVENDISH, duchess of Newcastle

In addition to poetry, Cavendish wrote natural philosophy, plays, essays, and a biography of her husband.

Poems and Fancies. London: J. Martin and J. Allestrye, 1653. Facsimile reprint. New York: Scholar Press, 1972.

Commentary

Grant, Douglas. *Margaret the First: A Biography of Margaret Cavendish, Duchess of Newcastle,* London: Hart-Davis, 1957. Checklist of works.

Longueville, Thomas. *The First Duke and Duchess of Newcastle-upon-Tyne.* London: Longman, 1910.

Perry, Henry T. E. *The First Duchess of Newcastle and Her Husband as Figures in Literary History.* Boston: Ginn, 1918. Bibliography.

Represented in *DNB*, Hale, Mahl and Koon, Reynolds, Stanford, Stenton.

ANNE KILLIGREW

Poems. London: S. Lowndes, 1686. Facsimile reprint. Edited by Richard Morton. Gainesville, Fla.: Scholars Facsimiles and Reprints, 1967. Dryden's *Ode* prefixed.

Commentary

Sigworth, Oliver F. "A New Way of Looking at Some Baroque Poems." In *Studies in Eighteenth-Century Culture.* Edited by H. E. Pagliaro. Madison: University of Wisconsin Press, 1975.

Represented in Bernikow, *DNB*, Hale, Hays, Reynolds, Stanford.

ANNE (LEE) WHARTON, erroneously called Marchioness

Whartoniana: or Miscellanies, in Verse and Prose. Vols. 3 and 4. London: Curll, 1727. *Whartoniana* includes writings by the Wharton family and several others; includes *Lamentations of Jeremiah Paraphrased* by Anne Wharton.

Represented in *DNB*, Hale, Hays.

APHRA [APHARA] BEHN

Behn also wrote plays, histories, and novels.

Poems upon Several Occasions: with a Voyage to the Island of Love. London: Tonson, 1684.

The Works of Aphra Behn. Edited by Montague Summers. 6 vols. London: W. Heineman, 1915. Reprint. New York: Blom, 1967; New York: Phaeton Press, 1967.

Commentary

Day, Robert H. "Aphra Behn's First Biography." *Studies in Bibliography* 22 (1969): 227-40.

Duchovnay, Gerald. "Aphra Behn's Religion." *Notes and Queries* 23 (1976):235-37.

Duffy, Maureen. *The Passionate Shepherdess: Aphra Behn.* London: J. Cape, 1977. Bibliography.

Gardiner, Judith K. "Aphra Behn: Sexuality and Self-Respect." *Women's Studies,* in press.

Link, Frederick. *Aphra Behn.* New York: Twayne, 1968. Bibliography.

O'Neill, John H. "An Unpublished 'Imperfect Enjoyment' Poem." *Papers in Language and Literature* 13 (1977):197-202.

Sackville-West, Victoria Mary. *Aphra Behn, the Incomparable Astrea.* London: G. Howe, 1927.

Shea, Peter K. "Alexander Pope and Aphra Behn on Wit." *Notes and Queries* 22 (1974):12.

Woodcock, George. *The Incomparable Aphra.* London: T. V. Boardman, 1948.

Represented in Adburgham, Bernikow, *DNB,* Hale, Hays, Jerrold, Mahl and Koon, Reynolds, Stanford, Stenton.

LADY MARY (LEE) CHUDLEIGH

Poems on Several Occasions. Together with the Song of the Three Children Paraphras'd. London: Bernard Lintot[t], 1703.

Poems on Several Occasions. 4th ed. corrected. London: J. Wren, 1750. Contains *Songs of Three Children* and *The Ladies Defence.*

Commentary

Coleman, Antony. "'The Provok'd Wife' and 'The Ladies Defence.'" *Notes and Queries* 17 (1970):88-91.

Represented in *DNB,* Hale, Hays, Reynolds, Stanford, Stenton.

MARY MONK

Marinda: Poems and Translations upon Several Occasions. London: Tonson, 1716.

Represented in *DNB,* Hale, Hays.

ANNE (KINGSMILL) FINCH, countess of Winchelsea

The Poems of Anne, Countess of Winchelsea. Edited by Myra Reynolds. Chicago: University of Chicago Press, 1903. From the original edition (1713) and unpublished manuscripts.

Poems. Edited by John Middleton Murry. London: J. Cape, 1928.

Commentary

Dowden, Edward. *Essays Modern and Elizabethan.* London: J. M. Dent, 1910.

Sena, John F. "Melancholy in Anne Finch and Elizabeth Carter: The Ambivalence of an Idea." *Yearbook of English Studies* 1 (1971):108-19.

Represented in Bernikow, *DNB,* Hale, Hays, Reynolds, Stanford.

ESTHER VANHOMRIGH

Known as Swift's "Vanessa."

Vanessa and Her Correspondence with Jonathan Swift. Edited by A. M. Freeman. London: Selwyn and Blount, 1921.

Commentary

Ehrenpreis, Irvin. "Letters of Advice to Young Spinsters." In *The Lady of Letters in the Eighteenth Century.* Los Angeles: William Andrews Clark Memorial Library of UCLA, 1969.

Hardy, Evelyn. *The Conjured Spirit, Swift: A Study in the Relationship of Swift, Stella, and Vanessa.* London: Hogarth Press, 1949.

LeBrocquy, Sybil. *Cademus: A Reassessment in Light of New Evidence of the Relationships between Swift, Stella, and Vanessa.* Dublin: Dolmen Press, 1962.

Represented in *DNB*, Hale.

SUSANNA CENTLIVRE

The Works of the Celebrated Mrs. Centlivre. 3 vols. London: J. Knapton, 1761. Reprint. London: J. Pearson, 1872; New York: AMS Press, 1968.

Commentary

Bowyer, John Wilson. *The Celebrated Mrs. Centlivre.* Durham, N.C.: Duke University Press, 1952.

Lock, F. P. *Susanna Centlivre.* Boston: Twayne, 1979.

Represented in Adburgham, *DNB*, Hale, Hays, Jerrold, Mahl and Koon, Reynolds.

CATHERINE (TROTTER) COCKBURN

The Female Wits. 1704. Facsimile reprint. Edited by Lucyle Hook. Los Angeles: UCLA for the Augustan Reprint Society, 1967.

The Works of Mrs. Catherine Cockburn. Edited by Thomas Birch. London: J. and P. Knapton, 1751.

Represented in Adburgham, *DNB*, Hale, Hays, Reynolds, Stenton.

ELIZABETH THOMAS

The Metamorphoses of the Town: or, A View of Present Fashions. 5th ed. London: J. Wilford, 1774. Contains two poems by Swift.

Miscellany Poems on Several Subjects. London: T. Combes, 1722.

Poems on Several Occasions. London: T. Combes, 1726.

Poems on Several Occasions . . . Written by a Lady. London, 1727.

Represented in *DNB*, Hale, Hays, Reynolds.

MARY BARBER

A Tale, Being an Addition to Mr. Gay's Fables. Dublin: George Ewing, 1728.

Poems on Several Occasions. London: C. Rivington, 1734.

Poems on Several Occasions . . . to which is prefix'd a recommendatory letter from the Rev'd Dr. Swift, London: Printed for the author, 1736.

Represented in *DNB*, Reynolds.

ELIZABETH ROWE

Devout Exercises of the Heart in Meditation and Soliloquy. Edited by Isaac Watts. London: R. Hett, 1738.

An Expostulatory Epistle to Sir Richard Steele upon the Death of Mr. Addison. London: W. Hinchliffe, 1720.

Friendship in Death: Twenty Letters from the Dead to the Living. London: Lintot[t], 1740.

The Hermit: a Poem. Philadelphia, 1753.

The History of Joseph: a Poem. London: T. Worral, 1736.

Poems on Several Occasions. Written by Philomela. London: John Dunton, 1696.

The Works. 4 vols. Edinburgh, 1770.

The Works. Edited by Theophilus Rowe. 4 vols. London: J. and A. Arch, 1796.

Represented in *DNB*, Hale, Hays, Reynolds.

JANE BRERETON

Merlin: a Poem . . . To which is added, The Royal Hermitage: a Poem. London: E. Cave, 1735.

Poems on Several Occasions. London, 1744.

Represented in Stanford.

MARY CHANDLER

A Description of Bath: a Poem. London: J. Leake, 1773. Poems were added to the 1736 edition, and *A True Tale* was added to the 1755 edition.

Represented in *DNB*, Hale, Hays, Reynolds.

ELIZA (FOWLER) HAYWOOD [HEYWOOD]

Wrote novels, letters, plays, journalism.

Epistles for Ladies. By the Authors of the Female Spectator. London: T. Gardner, 1749.

The Female Spectator. London: T. Gardner, 1745.

The Works. 4 vols. London: Dan Browne, 1724.

Commentary

Spacks, Patricia Meyer. "Ev'ry Woman Is at Heart a Rake." *Eighteenth-Century Studies* 8 (1974):27-64.

Whicher, G. F. *The Life and Romances of Mrs. Eliza Haywood.* New York: Columbia University Press, 1915.

Represented in Adburgham, *DNB*, Hale, Hays, Jerrold, Mahl and Koon, Reynolds.

ELIZABETH TOLLET

Poems on Several Occasions. With Anne Boleyn to King Henry VIII, an Epistle. London: J. Clarke, 1755.

Represented in *DNB*, Hale, Hays.

LAETITIA PILKINGTON

An Answer to Seasonable Advice to the Publick Concerning a Book of Memoirs Lately Published. London, 1748.

Memoirs of Mrs. Laetitia Pilkington. . . . Wherein are occasionally interspersed, all her poems. Dublin: Printed for the author, n.d. London: G. Woodfall, 1748. Reprint. Edited by Iris Barry. London: G. Routledge, 1928.

The Celebrated Mrs. Pilkington's Jests . . . To Which is Now First Added, a Great Variety of Bon Mots . . . of the Inimitable Dr. Swift. London: W. Nicoll, 1764.

Represented in Adburgham, DNB, Hale, Hays, Jerrold, Stanford.

MARY LEAPOR

Poems upon Several Occasions. Edited by I. H. Browne. London: J. Roberts, 1751.

Represented in DNB, Hale, Hays, Reynolds.

MARY MASTERS

Familiar Letters and Poems on Several Occasions. London: D. Henry and R. Cave, 1755.

Poems on Several Occasions. London: T. Browne, 1733.

Represented in DNB, Reynolds.

JUDITH (COWPER) MADAN

The Progress of Poetry. London: Dodsley, 1783.

Represented in Reynolds.

LADY MARY (PIERREPONT) WORTLEY MONTAGU

The Complete Letters. Edited by Robert Halsband. 3 vols. Oxford: Clarendon Press, 1965.

Essays and Poems and "Simplicity," a Comedy. Edited by Robert Halsband and Isobel Grundy. Oxford: Clarendon Press, 1977.

The Nonsense of Common-Sense, 1737– 38. Edited by Robert Halsband. Evanston: Northwestern University Press, 1947.

Commentary

Benkovitz, Miriam J. "Some Observations on Woman's Concept of Self in the Eighteenth Century." In Woman in the Eighteenth Century and Other Essays. Edited by Paul Fritz and Richard Morton. Toronto: Hakkert, 1976.

Grundy, Isobel. "'The Entire Works of Clarinda': Unpublished Juvenile Verse by Lady Mary Wortley Montagu." Yearbook of English Studies 7 (1977):91-107.

————. "A Moon of Literature: Verse by Lady Mary Wortley Montagu." *New Rambler* 112 (197 .):6-22.

————. "Ovid and Eighteenth-Century Divorce: An Unpublished Poem by Lady Mary Wortley Montagu." *Review of English Studies* 23 (197 .):417-28.

————. " 'Verses Address'd to the Imitator of Horace': A Skirmish between Pope and Some Persons of Rank and Fortune." *Studies in Bibliography* 30 (1977):96-119.

Halsband, Robert. " 'The Lady's Dressing Room' Explicated by a Contemporary." In *The Augustan Milieu: Essays Presented to Louis Landa.* Oxford: Clarendon Press, 1970.

————. "Ladies of Letters in the Eighteenth Century." *The Lady of Letters in the Eighteenth Century.* Los Angeles: William Andrews Clark Memorial Library of UCLA, 1969.

————. *The Life of Lady Mary Wortley Montagu.* Oxford: Clarendon Press, 1957.

Rawson, C. J. "Seeing Sappho Plain." *Books and Bookmen* 22 (1977):37-38.

Spacks, Patricia M. *The Female Imagination.* New York: McGraw-Hill, Avon Books, 1972.

Represented in Adburgham, Bernikow, *DNB,* Hale, Hays, Reynolds, Stanford, Stenton.

FRANCES (CHAMBERLAINE) SHERIDAN

Wrote fiction and drama.

The Discovery, A Comedy. London: T. Davies, 1763.

The Dupe, A Comedy. London: A. Millar, 1764.

This History of Nourjahad. Oxford: Dodsley, 1767. Reprint. Edited by H. V. Marrott. London: Mathews and Marrott, 1927.

Represented in Hale and Hays.

MARY JONES

Miscellanies in Prose and Verse. Oxford: Dodsley, 1750; Oxford: R. Griffiths, 1760.

Represented in Reynolds, Stenton.

ANNE STEELE

Hymns, Psalms and Poems. With a Memoir by John Sheppard. London: D. Sedgwick, 1863.

Poems on Subjects Chiefly Devotional. 2 vols. London: J. Buchland, 1760.

Poems on Subjects Chiefly Devotional . . . A New Edition. 3 vols. Bristol: W. Pine, 1780.

Represented in *DNB,* Hale.

FRANCES (MOORE) BROOKE

Primarily wrote novels.

Marian: A Comic Opera. London: Longman, 1800.

Rosina, A Comic Opera. London: T. Cadell, 1783.

The Siege of Sinope, a Tragedy. London: T. Cadell, 1781.

Represented in *DNB*, Hale.

FANNY (M'CARTNEY) GREVILLE

Hale lists *Maxims and Characters* (1756), but no poems are extant except "Prayer for Indifference."

CONSTANTIA GRIERSON

Wrote history and Sunday school stories and translated classics. Her only extant poem is printed in Mary Barber's *Poems on Several Occasions (1734).*

Represented in *DNB*, Hale, Hays, Stanford.

HENRIETTA O'NEIL

Two poems preserved in the work of Charlotte Smith.

Represented in Stanford.

MARY (DARBY) ROBINSON

Memoirs of the Late Mrs. Robinson, Written by Herself. With some Posthumous Pieces. Edited by Mary Elizabeth Robinson. 4 vols. London: R. Phillips, 1801.

The Poetical Works. Edited by Mary Elizabeth Robinson. 3 vols. London: R. Phillips, 1806.

Posthumous Pieces. Edited by Mary Elizabeth Robinson. 4 vols. London: R. Phillips, 1801.

Commentary

Bass, Robert Duncan. *The Green Dragoon: The Lives of Banastre Tarleton and Mary Robinson.* New York: Holt, 1957.

Makower, S. V. *Perdita: A Romance in Biography.* London: Hutchinson, 1908. Bibliography.

Represented in *DNB*,

HESTER (MULSO) CHAPONE

The Works . . . To Which is Prefixed an Account of Her Life and Character, Drawn Up by Her Own Family. 4 vols. London: J. Murray, n.d. Edinburgh: A. Constable, 1807-8.

Represented in *DNB*, Hale, Hays, Reynolds, Stenton.

GEORGIANA (SPENCER) CAVENDISH, duchess of Devonshire

Georgiana: Extracts from the Correspondence of Georgiana, Duchess of Devonshire. Edited by the Earl of Bessborough. London: Murray, 1955.

The Sylph: A Novel. 2 vols. London: T. Lowndes, 1779.

Commentary

Calder-Marshall, Arthur. *The Two Duchesses.* London: Hutchinson, 1978. Bibliography.

Palmer, Iris Irma. *The Face Without a Frown: Georgiana, Duchess of Devonshire.* London: F. Muller, 1944.

Represented in *DNB*, Hale.

ELIZABETH CARTER

Wrote essays, translated Epictetus.

Memoirs of the Life of Mrs. Elizabeth Carter with a New Edition of her Poems. Edited by Montagu Pennington. London: F. C. and J. Rivington, 1807.

Poems on Several Occasions. London: J. Rivington, 1762.

Commentary

Gaussen, Alice C. *A Woman of Wit and Wisdom: A Memoir of Elizabeth Carter.* London: Smith, Elder, 1906.

Hampshire, G. "Johnson, Elizabeth Carter and Pope's Garden." *Notes and Queries* 19 (1972):221-22.

Represented in Adburgham, *DNB*, Hale, Reynolds, Stenton.

ANN YEARSLEY

Poems on Several Occasions. London: T. Cadell, 1785.

Represented in *DNB*, Hale.

CHARLOTTE SMITH

Wrote novels, books for children, essays, plays.

Beachy Head, with Other Poems. London: Printed for the author, 1807.

Elegaic Sonnets, and Other Essays. London: Dodsley, 1784. Third edition (1786) has twenty additional sonnets. 5th ed. 2 vols. T. Cadell and T. Davies, 1797.

The Emigrants, a Poem in Two Books. London: T. Cadell, 1793.

Represented in *DNB*, Hale, Stanford.

ANNA SEWARD

Elegy on Captain Cook. London: Dodsley, 1780.

Llangollen Vale with Other Poems. London: G. Sael, 1796.

Monody on Major Andre. Lichfield: J. Jackson, 1781.

One on General Eliott's Return from Gibraltar. London: T. Cadell, 1787.

Original Sonnets on Various Subjects; and Odes Paraphrased from Horace. London: G. Sael, 1799.

Poem to the Memory of Lady Miller. London: G. Robinson, 1782.

The Poetical Works . . . with Extracts from her Literary Correspondence. Edited by Sir Walter Scott. 3 vols. Edinburgh: J. Ballantyne, 1810. Reprint. New York: AMS Press, 1974.

Commentary

Ashmun, Margaret. *The Singing Swan.* New Haven: Yale University Press, 1931.

Lucas, E. V. *A Swan and Her Friends.* London: Methuen, 1907.

Monk, Samuel H. "Anna Seward and the Romantic Poets: A Study in Taste." In *Wordsworth and Coleridge: Studies in Honor of G. L. Harper.* Edited by E. L. Griggs. New York: Russell and Russell, 1939.

Myers, Robert M. *Anna Seward. An Eighteenth-Century Handelian.* Williamsburg, Va.: Manson Park Press, 1947.

Pearson, Hesketh. *The Swan of Lichfield.* London: Hamish and Hamilton, 1936.

Wooley, James D. "Johnson as Despot: Anna Seward's Rejected Contribution to Boswell's Life." *Modern Philology* 70 (1972):140-45.

Represented in *DNB*, Hale, Mahl and Koon.

MARY (BLACHFORD) TIGHE

Psyche: or the Legend of Love. London: J. Carpenter, 1805.

Psyche, with Other Poems. London: Longman, 1811.

Commentary

Weller, Earle V., ed. *Keats and Mary Tighe: The Poems of Mary Tighe with Parallel Passages from the Work of John Keats.* New York: Modern Language Association of America, 1928. Bibliography.

Represented in *DNB*, Hale.

MARIA AND HARRIET FALCONAR

Poems, by Maria and Harriet Falconar. London: Johnson and Egerton, 1788.

Poems on Slavery. London: Egerton, 1788.

ELIZABETH TREFUSIS

Poems and Tales. 2 vols. London: S. Tipper, 1808.

JANE ELLIOT[T]

Only known work is "The Flowers of the Forest," published in *Songstresses of Scotland.* Edited by Sarah Tytler and J. L. Watson. London: Strahan, 1871.

Also in *DNB*, Stanford.

ALISON [ALICIA] (RUTHERFORD) COCKBURN

Letter and Memoir of Her Own Life . . . and Various Songs. Edited by T. Craig-Brown. Edinburgh: D. Douglas, 1900.

Represented in *DNB, Songstresses of Scotland.*

HANNAH COWLEY

Best known for her plays, especially *The Belle's Strategem.*

Works: Dramas and Poems. 3 vols. London: Wilkie and Robinson, 1813.

Represented in DNB, Hale, Reynolds.

ISABELLA (BYRON) HOWARD, countess of Carlisle

Rudiments of Taste . . . to Which are added, Maxims Addressed to Young Ladies. Philadelphia, 1790.

Thoughts in the Form of Maxims, Addressed to Young Ladies, on Their First Establishment in the World. London: T. Cornell, 1789.

HANNAH MORE

Most famous as author of cheap repository tracts, *Coelebs in Search of a Wife,* and essays.

The Complete Works of Hannah More. New York: J. C. Derby, 1856.

Florio and Bas Bleu. London, 1786.

Slavery, a Poem. London: T. Cadell, 1788.

The Works of Hannah More. 11 vols. London: T. Cadell, 1830.

The Works of Hannah More. 2 vols. New York: Harpers, 1843.

The Works of Hannah More in Prose and Verse. Cork, 1778.

Commentary

Balfour, C. L. *Working Women of this Century: The Lesson of Their Lives.* London and New York: Cassell, Petter and Galpin, 1868.

Courtney, L. W. *Hannah More's Interest in Education and Government.* Waco, Tex.: Baylor University Press, 1929.

Shaw, William. *The Life of Hannah More.* London: T. Hurst, 1802.

Represented in Adburgham, *DNB,* Hale, Mahl and Koon, Stenton.

HELEN MARIA WILLIAMS

Famous for her *Letters from France* (1794), about the French Revolution.

An Ode to the Peace. London: T. Cadell, 1783.

Peru, a Poem. London: T. Cadell, 1784.

Poems, moral, elegant and pathetic: viz. Essay on Man, by Pope . . . And Original Sonnets by Helen Maria Williams. London: E. Newberry, 1796.

Commentary

Adams, M. R. "Helen Maria Williams and the French Revolution." In *Wordsworth and Coleridge: Studies in Honor of G. L. Harper.* Edited by E. L. Griggs. New York: Russell and Russell, 1939.

Woodward, Lionel D. *Une Anglaise amie de la revolution française, Helene-Maria Williams, et ses amis.* Paris: H. Champion, 1930. Bibliography.

Represented in *DNB,* Hale.

ELEANOR ANNE (PORDEN) FRANKLIN

The Arctic Expeditions, a Poem by Miss Porden. London: J. Murray, 1818.

Coeur de Lion. London, 1822.

Ode Addressed to . . . Viscount Belgrave on his Marriage. London: Cox and Baylis, 1819.

The Veils: or the Triumph of Constancy. London: J. Murray, 1815.

Represented in *DNB*, Hale.

SUSANNA BLAMIRE

The Poetical Works of Miss Susanna Blamire. Edited by Henry Lonsdale and Patrick Maxwell. Edinburgh: J. Menzies, 1842.

Represented in *DNB*, Hale, *Songstresses of Scotland.*

MARY (BALFOUR) BRUNTON

Primarily a novelist.

The Works of Mary Balfour Brunton. 7 vols. Edinburgh: Manners and Miller, 1820.

Represented in *DNB*, Hale.

ANNA LAETITIA (AIKIN) BARBAULD

Memoir, Letters and a Selection from the Poems and Prose Writings of Mrs. Barbauld. Edited by Grace A. Ellis. 2 vols. Boston: J. R. Osgood, 1874.

Poems. London: J. Johnson, 1773.

Poems, New Edition with Epistle to William Wilberforce. London: J. Johnson, 1792.

The Works . . . with a Memoir by Lucy Aikin. 2 vols. London: Longman, 1825.

Commentary

Le Breton, A. L. *Memoir of Mrs. Barbauld.* London, 1874.

Murch, Jerom. *Mrs. Barbauld and Her Contemporaries.* London: Longman, 1877.

Pickering, Samuel F. "Mrs. Barbauld's Hymns in Prose: An Air-Blown Particle of Romanticism?" *Southern Humanities Review* 9 (1975):259-68.

Rodgers, Betsy. *Georgian Chronicle: Mrs. Barbauld and her Family.* London: Methuen, 1958. Bibliography.

Zall, P.M. "The Cool World of Samuel Taylor Coleridge: Mrs. Barbauld's Crew and the Building of a Mass Reading Class." *Wordsworth Circle* 2 (1971):74-79.

———. "Wordsworth's 'Ode' and Mrs. Barbauld's *Hymns.*" *Wordsworth Circle* 1 (1970):177-79.

Represented in Balfour, *DNB*, Hale, Mahl and Koon, Stenton.

LADY ANNE (LINDSAY) BARNARD

Known for her prose newsletters, *South Africa a Century Ago,* 1797-1801.

Auld Robin Gray: a Ballad. Edited by Sir Walter Scott. Edinburgh: Ballantyne, 1825.

Lays of the Lindsays: Being Poems by the Ladies of the House of Balcarres. Edinburgh: Ballantyne, 1824.

Poems of Love and Death. London: K. Paul, Trench, Trübner, 1907.

Represented in Hale, *Songstresses of Scotland,* Stanford.

ANNE (MAC VICAR) GRANT

Blue Bells of Scotland. New York and London: White and Allen, 1889.

Dear Old Songs. New York and London: White and Allen, 1889.

Eighteen Hundred and Thirteen: a Poem in Two Parts. Edinburgh: Ballantyne, 1814.

The Highlanders and Other Poems. Edinburgh, 1803.

Poems on Various Subjects. Edinburgh: J. Moir, 1803.

Represented in *DNB,* Hale.

ANNE (HOME) HUNTER

Poems by Mrs. John Hunter. London: T. Payne, 1802.

The Sports of the Genii. London: T. Payne, 1804.

Represented in *DNB,* Hale.

HESTER LYNCH (SALUSBURY) THRALE PIOZZI

Best known for her friendship with Dr. Johnson.

Autobiography, Letters and Literary Remains. Edited by A. Hayward. Boston: Ticknor and Fields, 1861.

Commentary

Clifford, James L. *Hester Lynch Piozzi.* Oxford: Clarendon Press, 1968.

Hyde, Mary. *The Impossible Friendship: Boswell and Mrs. Thrale.* Cambridge, Mass.: Harvard University Press, 1972.

Riley, J. C. and Ribiero, Alvaro. " 'Mrs. Thrale' on the Tour: A Boswellian Puzzle." *Papers of the Bibliographical Society of America* 69 (1975):151-63.

Spacks, Patricia Meyer. *The Female Imagination.* New York: Avon, 1972.

———. "Reflecting Women." *Yale Review* 63 (1973):26-42.

———. "Scrapbook of the Self: Mrs. Piozzi's Late Journals." *Harvard Library Bulletin* 18 (1970):221-47.

Represented in *DNB,* Hale.

ANN (WARD) RADCLIFFE

Most famous for her novels, which incorporate poetry.

The Mysteries of Udolpho . . . Interspersed with Some Pieces of Poetry. Edited by Bonamy Dobrée. London: Oxford University Press, 1966.

The Posthumous Works. London: H. Colburn, 1833.

The Romance of the Forest: Interspersed with Some Pieces of Poetry. 3 vols. London: T. Hookham and J. Carpenter, 1792. Reprint. New York: Arno, 1976.

Commentary

Grant, Aline. *Ann Radcliffe, a Biography.* Denver: A. Swallow, 1951. Bibliography.

Murray, E. B. *Ann Radcliffe.* New York: Twayne, 1972.

Ware, Malcolm. "The Telescope Reversed: Ann Radcliffe and Natural Scenery." In *A Provision of Human Nature.* Edited by Donald Kay. University. Ala.: University of Alabama Press, 1977.

Represented in *DNB*, Hale, Stanford.

MRS. HENRY ROLLS

Legends of the North: or, the Feudal Christmas; a Poem. London: W. Simpkin and R. Marshall, 1825.

A Poetical Address to Lord Byron. London: W. Hone, 1816.

Sacred Sketches from Scripture History. London, 1815.

LADY SOPHIA (RAYMOND) BURRELL

Poems. London: J. Cooper, 1793.

Poems; contains Comala, a Dramatic Poem in three acts. London, 1793.

Represented in *DNB*.

LUCY AIKIN

Primarily a writer of memoirs and collector of others' poetry.

Epistles on Women . . . in Various Ages and Nations. With Miscellaneous poems. London: J. Johnson, 1810.

Represented in *DNB*, Hale.

AMELIA (ALDERSON) OPIE

New Tales. 4 vols. London: Longman, 1818.

Poems. London: Longman, 1803.

The Warrior's Return, and Other Poems. London: Longman, 1808.

Commentary

Brightwell, C. L. *Memorials of the Life of Amelia Opie.* Norwich: Fletcher and Alexander, 1854.

Macgregor, Margaret E. *Amelia Alderson Opie: Worldling and Friend.* Northhampton, Mass.: Smith Studies in Modern Languages, 1933.

Represented in *DNB*, Hale, Hall.

JOANNA BAILLIE

Chiefly a dramatist.

The Dramatic and Poetical Works. Complete in One Volume. London: Longman, 1851.

The Family Legend. Edinburgh: John Ballantyne, 1810. Facsimile reprint with *Metrical Legends.* Edited by Donald H. Reiman. New York: Garland, 1976.

Fugitive Verses. London: E. Moxon, 1840.

Metrical Legends of Exalted Characters. London: Longman, 1821. Fascimile reprint with *The Family Legend.* Edited by Donald H. Reiman. New York: Garland, 1976.

Commentary

Carswell, Donald. *Scott and His Circle.* Garden City, N.J.: Doubleday, 1930.

Garhart, Margaret S. *The Life and Work of Joanna Baillie.* New Haven: Yale University Press, 1923.

Represented in *DNB*, Hale, Stanford.

MARGARET (HOLFORD) HODSON

Margaret of Anjou: A Poem in Ten Cantos. London: J. Murray, 1816.

Poems. London: Longman, 1811.

Wallace; or The Fight at Falkirk; a Metrical Romance. London: T. Cadell and W. Davies, 1809.

Represented in *DNB*, Hale, Hall.

MARY RUSSELL MITFORD

Known primarily for *Village Sketches* and dramas.

Poems. London: Longman, 1810.

The Works of Mary Russell Mitford. Philadelphia: Crissy and Markley, 1846.

Commentary

Watson, Vera. *Mary Russell Mitford.* London: Evans, 1949.

Represented in *DNB*, Hale, Hall.

MARY (BOTHAM) HOWITT

Ballads and Other Poems. London: Longman, 1847.

Birds and Flowers; or, Lays and Lyrics of Rural Life. London and New York: T. Nelson, 1873.

The Poems, With a Memoir. New York: G. A. Leavitt, 1844.

The Poetical Works of Howitt, Milman and Keats. Philadelphia: Crissy and Markley, 1853.

Commentary

Butler, James A. "Wordsworth's Funeral: A Contemporary Report." *English Language Notes* 13 (1975):27-29.

Kienesberger, Konrad F. "Mary Howitt und ihre Stifter-Übersetzungen: Zur Rezeption des Dichters im viktorianischen England." *Adalbert Stifter Institut des Landes Oberosterreich: Vieteljahrschrift*, 25 (1976):13-55.

Woodring, Carl Ray. *Victorian Samplers: William and Mary Howitt*. Lawrence, Kan.: University of Kansas Press, 1952.

Represented in *DNB*, Hale.

CAROLINE (BOWLES) SOUTHEY

Autumn Flowers and Other Poems. Boston: Saxton, Pierce, 1844.

The Birthday; a Poem, in Three Parts: to Which Have Been Added Occasional Verses. Edinburgh: Blackwood, 1836.

Ellen Fitzarthur: a Metrical Tale, in Five Cantos. London: Longman, 1820.

Poetical Works of Caroline Bowles Southey. Collected Edition. Edinburgh and London: Blackwood, 1867.

Solitary Hours. Edinburgh: Blackwood, 1826.

Tales of the Factories. Edinburgh: Blackwood, 1833.

The Widow's Tale, and Other Poems. London: Longman, 1822.

Commentary

Fairbanks, A. Harris. "'Dear Native Brook': Coleridge, Bowles, and Thomas Wharton, the Younger." *Wordsworth Circle* 6 (1975):313-15.

Represented in *DNB*, Hale, Hall.

FELICIA DOROTHEA (BROWNE) HEMANS

The Complete Works. Edited by Mrs. Hughes. 2 vols. New York: D. Appleton, 1853.

Poems: England and Spain, Modern Greece. 1808. Facsimile reprint; includes *Poems* (1808), *England and Spain* (1808), and *Modern Greece* (1817). Edited by Donald H. Reiman. New York: Garland, 1978.

Records of Woman: with Other Poems. Edinburgh: Blackwood, 1828.

The Works . . . with a Memoir of Her Life by Her Sister, Mrs. Hughes. 7 vols. Edinburgh and London: Blackwood, 1844-57.

Commentary

Chorley, H. F. *Memorials of Mrs. Hemans*. 2 vols. New York and London: Saunders and Otley, 1836.

Represented in *DNB*, Hale, Stanford.

CHARLOTTE ELIZABETH (BROWNE) TONNA

Wrote fiction, moral tales, history for children, protest works.

The Works of Charlotte Elizabeth. Edited by Harriet Beecher Stowe. 2 vols. New York: M. W. Dodd, 1852.

Posthumous and Other Poems. London: Seeley, Burnside, and Seeley, 1846.

Commentary

Wallins, Roger P. "Victorian Periodicals and the Emerging Social Conscience." *Victorian Periodicals Newsletter* 8 (1975):47-59.

Represented in Balfour, *DNB*, Hale, Hall, Moers.

LADY CAROLINE (SHERIDAN) NORTON

The Child of the Islands: a Poem. London: Chapman and Hall, 1845.

The Coquette, and Other Tales and Sketches, in Prose and Verse. London: E. Churton, 1835.

The Dream and Other Poems. London: H. Colborn, 1840.

The Lady of La Garaye. London: Macmillan, 1862.

Poems. Edited by Rufus Griswold. New York: World Publishing House, 1875.

Tales and Sketches in Prose and Verse. London: E. Churton, 1850.

The Undying One, and Other Poems. London: H. Colburn and R. Bentley, 1830.

A Voice from the Factories. London: J. Murray, 1836; Boston: Putnam, 1847.

Commentary

Acland, Alice. *Caroline Norton:* London: Constable, 1948.

Moore, Katherine. *Victorian Wives.* New York: St. Martin's Press, 1974.

Represented in *DNB*, Hale, Stenton.

LAETITIA ELIZABETH (LANDON) MACLEAN [L.E.L.]

Complete Works. Boston: Philips, Sampson, 1853. Boston: Crosby, Nicols and Lee, 1860.

The Fate of Adelaide, a Swiss Romantic Tale; and Other Poems. London: J. Warren, 1821.

Flowers of Loveliness. London: Ackerman, 1838.

The Golden Violet, with its Tales of Romance and Chivalry. London: Longman, 1827.

The Improvisatrice, and Other Poems. London: Hurst, Robinson, 1824.

The Venetian Bracelet, the Lost Pleiad, a History of the Lyre, and Other Poems. London: Longman, 1829.

The Vow of the Peacock, and Other Poems. London: Saunders and Otley, 1836.

The Works. Philadelphia: Carey and Hart, 1838. Philadelphia: J. Harding, 1847.

Represented in Adburgham, *DNB*, Hale, Hall.

MARIA (SMITH) ABDY

Poetry. London: J. Robins, 1834.

Represented in *DNB*, Hale.

SARAH (STICKNEY) ELLIS

Known primarily as the author of such books of advice to women as *Women of England* (1838) and *Daughters of England* (1842).

Irish Girl: and Other Poems. New York: J. Langely, 1844.

The Poetry of Life. London: Saunders and Otley, 1835.

The Sons of the Soil, a Poem. London: Fisher, [1840?].

Represented in *DNB*, Hale.

MARIA JANE (JEWSBURY) FLETCHER

Lays of Leisure Hours. London: J. Hatchard, 1829.

Phantasmagoria; or Sketches of Life and Literature. London: Hurst, Robinson, 1825.

Represented in *DNB*, Hale, Hall.

LADY FLORA ELIZABETH HASTINGS

Poems. Edited by Sophia Hastings Crichton-Stuart. Edinburgh and London: Blackwood, 1841; 1842.

Represented in *DNB*, Hale.

MARY ANNE (BROWNE) GRAY

Felicia Hemans' sister.

Ada, and Other Poems. London: Longman, 1828.

The Birthday. London: Hamilton, Adams, 1834.

Mont Blanc, and Other Poems. London; Hatchard, 1827.

Repentance; and Other Poems. London: Longman; 1829.

Represented in Hale.

SARA (COLERIDGE) COLERIDGE

The editor of the works of Samuel Taylor Coleridge; most of her poetry was fugitive.

Phantasmion. London: Pickering, 1837.

Represented in *DNB*, Hale.

ELIZA COOK

Edited *Eliza Cook's Journal*, which dealt seriously with contemporary issues such as slavery.

Complete Poetical Works. New York: T. Y. Crowell, 1912.

Diamond Dust. London: F. Pitman, 1865.

The Glass of Gin. New York: Brogard, 1851.

Lays of a Wild Harp. London: J. Bennett, 1835.

Melaia, and Other Poems. London: R. J. Wood, 1838.

New Echoes and Other Poems. London: Routledge, Warne and Routledge, 1864.

Represented in Hale.

FRANCES ANNE (KEMBLE) BUTLER

Primarily known for dramas and journal.

Poems, by Frances Anne Butler (Late Fanny Kemble). London: H. Washbourne; Edinburgh; Oliver and Boyd; Dublin: Machen, 1844. Philadelphia: Pennington, 1844.

Commentary

Marshall, Dorothy. *Fanny Kemble.* London: Weidenfeld and Nicholson, 1977.

Represented in *DNB*, Hale, Stanford.

ELIZABETH (BARRETT) BROWNING

Aurora Leigh. London: Chapman and Hall, 1857. Facsimile Reprint of 1864 edition. Introduction by Gardner B. Taplin. Chicago: Academy Chicago, 1979.

Casa Guidi Windows. Edited by Julia Markus. New York: Browning Institute, 1977.

Complete Poetical Works. Edited by H. W. Preston. Boston and New York: Houghton Mifflin, 1900.

Complete Works. Edited by Charlotte Porter and Helen A. Clarke. New York: T. Y. Crowell, 1900. Reprint. New York: AMS, 1973.

Sonnets from the Portuguese. Facsimile reprint. Edited by William Peterson. Barre, Mass.: Barre, 1977. British Library manuscript.

Commentary

Secondary works listed are bibliographies and books only.

Barnes, Warner. *A Bibliography of Elizabeth Barrett Browning.* Austin: University of Texas Press, 1967.

Hayter, Alethea. *Mrs. Browning: A Poet's Work and Its Setting.* London: Faber and Faber, 1962.

Hewlett, Dorothy. *Elizabeth Barrett Browning: A Life.* New York: Knopf, 1952. Reprint. New York: Octagon, 1972. Bibliography.

Lupton, Mary J. *Elizabeth Barrett Browning.* Long Island, New York: Feminist Press, 1972.

Peterson, William S. *Robert and Elizabeth Barrett Browning: An Annotated Bibliography, 1951-1970.* New York: Browning Institute, 1974.

——, and Kenan, Richard C. "Robert and Elizabeth Barrett Browning: An Annotated Bibliography." Annually in *Browning Institute Studies,* 1973–.

Radley, Virginia L. *Elizabeth Barrett Browning.* New York: Twayne, 1972. Bibliography.

Taplin, Gardner B. *The Life of Elizabeth Barrett Browning.* New Haven: Yale University Press, 1957.

————. "Elizabeth Barrett Browning." *Victorian Poetry* 12 (1974): 241-44; 14 (1976): 211-12. Bibliographical review articles.

HELEN LOWE

Poems, Chiefly Dramatic. Edited by Thomas Hill-Lowe, London: W. Pickering, 1840.

The Prophecy of Balaam, the Queen's Choice, and Other Poems. London: J. Murray, 1841.

Taormina, and Other Poems. London: T. C. Newby, 1864.

Zareefa, a Tale, and Other Poems. London: W. Pickering, 1844.

Represented in Hale.

CHARLOTTE YOUNG

The World's Complaint and Other Poems. London, 1847. Available in British Museum.

Represented in Hale.

SOURCES

Listed here are the various editions and printings of *Female Poets of Great Britain*, as well as Alexander Dyce's *Specimens of British Poetesses* and George Bethune's *British Female Poets*, with the libraries that hold copies of each.

FREDERIC ROWTON

1. *The female poets of Great Britain, chronologically arranged: with copious selections and critical remarks.* By Frederic Rowton. London: Longman, Brown, Green, and Longmans, 1848. xxviii, 508 p.

   University of British Columbia, Vancouver
   University of Delaware, Newark

   185? printing:

   Boston Public Library
   Library Company of Philadelphia
   Library of Congress

2. *The female poets of Great Britain, chronologically arranged: with copious selections and critical remarks.* By Frederic Rowton. With additions of an American editor, and elegantly engraved illustrations by celebrated artists. Philadelphia: Carey and Hart, 1849. xviii, 25-533 p.

   Boston Public Library
   Library of Congress
   Pack Memorial Public Library, Asheville, N.C.
   Smith College, Northhampton, Mass.
   University of Mississippi, Union, Miss.
   Vassar College, Poughkeepsie, N.Y.
   Wistar Institute of Anatomy and Biology, Philadelphia, Pa.

3. ———. Philadelphia: H. C. Baird, 1854.

Boston Public Library
Catholic University of America, Washington, D.C.
Cleveland Public Library
Florida State University, Tallahassee
Indiana University, Bloomington
Yale University, New Haven, Conn.

1856 printing:

Boston Public Library

4. *Cyclopaedia of female poets; chronologically arranged with copious selections and critical remarks, with additions by an American editor.* Philadelphia: J. B. Lippincott, [185?]. 533 p.

Indiana University
New York Public Library
University of North Carolina, Chapel Hill
University of Pennsylvania, Philadelphia
Wagner Free Institute of Science, Philadelphia, Pa.

[1874] printing:

Brown University, Providence, R.I.
Harvard University, Cambridge, Mass.

Printing with no date:

Florida Technological University, Orlando

5. *Cyclopedia of female poets, chronologically arranged with copious selections and critical remarks. With additions by an American editor. Complete in one large royal octávo volume. Illustrated with numerous steel engravings.* Dayton, Ohio: Alvin Peabody, 1883. xviii, 25-533 p.

Dayton and Montgomery County Public Library, Dayton, O.

ALEXANDER DYCE

Specimens of British poetesses; selected and chronologically arranged by the Rev. Alexander Dyce. London: T. Rodd, 1825. xvi, 446 p.

Boston Public Library
Case Western Reserve University, Cleveland, O.
Enoch Pratt Free Library, Baltimore, Md.
Harvard University, Cambridge, Mass.
Kent State University, Kent, O.
Princeton University, Princeton, N.J.
University of Oregon, Eugene

University of Pennsylvania, Philadelphia
University of Texas, Austin
University of Virginia, Charlottesville
Yale University, New Haven, Conn.

1827 printing:

Boston Public Library
Buffalo and Erie County Public Library, Buffalo, N.Y.
Case Western Reserve University, Cleveland, O.
Cleveland Public Library
Cornell University, Ithaca, N.Y.
Folger Shakespeare Library, Washington, D.C.
Huntington Library, San Marino, Calif.
Library of Congress
Massachusetts Historical Society, Boston
Ohio State University, Columbus
University of Cincinnati, Cincinnati, O.
University of Michigan, Ann Arbor
University of South Carolina, Columbia

1828 printing:

University of Pennsylvania, Philadelphia

GEORGE W. BETHUNE

1. *The British female poets: with biographical and critical notices by George W. Bethune.* Philadelphia: Lindsay & Blakiston, 1848. xi, 490 p.

Alfred University, Alfred, N.Y.
Athenaeum of Philadelphia
Case Western Reserve University, Cleveland, O.
Cleveland Public Library
John Crerar Library, Chicago, Ill.
Detroit Public Library, Detroit, Mich.
Dickinson College, Carlisle, Pa.
Florida Technological University, Orlando
Free Library of Philadelphia
Jacksonville Public Library, Jacksonville, Fla.
Library Company of Philadelphia
Montana State University, Bozeman
New Brunswick Theological Seminary, New Brunswick, N.J.
New York Public Library
Oberlin College, Oberlin, O.
Ohio State University, Columbus
Public Library of Cincinnati and Hamilton County, Cincinnati, O.
Seattle Public Library, Seattle, Wash.
State University of New York, Geneseo
Toledo-Lucas County Public Library, Toledo, O.

United States Military Academy, West Point, N.Y.
University of Denver, Denver, Colo.
University of Pennsylvania, Philadelphia
University of South Carolina, Columbia
University of South Florida, Tampa
University of Texas, Austin
University of Virginia, Charlottesville
Willamette University, Salem, Ore.

1849 printing:

Boston Public Library
Duke University, Durham, N.C.
Library of Congress
University of Oregon, Eugene
Villanova University, Villanova, Pa.

1853 printing:

Buffalo and Erie County Public Library, Buffalo, N.Y.
Haverford College, Haverford, Pa.

1854 printing:

University of Virginia, Charlottesville

1856 printing:

Pack Memorial Public Library, Asheville, N.C.
University of Cincinnati, Cincinnati, O.

1858 printing:

Cleveland Public Library

1865 printing:

University of Illinois, Urbana

2. *The British Female poets: with biographical and critical notices by George W. Bethune.* New York: Butler Brothers [1849?]. xv, 13-490 p.

Rochester University, Rochester, N.Y.
Southern Illinois University, Carbondale

3. ———. New York: Crowell, n.d.

Case Western Reserve University, Cleveland, O.

4. ———. New York, Hurst, n.d.

Amherst College, Amherst, Mass.
Cleveland Public Library
Michigan State University, East Lansing
University of North Carolina, Chapel Hill

5. ———. New York: Hurst, [1860?].

    University of Michigan, Ann Arbor

6. ———. New York: Allen Brothers, 1869.

    California State Library, Sacramento
    Harvard University, Cambridge, Mass.
    Pack Memorial Public Library, Asheville, N.C.
    University of North Carolina, Greensboro
    University of South Carolina, Columbia
    Yale University, New Haven, Conn.

7. ———. New York: Worthington, [189?].

    University of Illinois, Urbana

8. *Pearls from the British female poets.* New York: Leavitt and Allen, 1869. 490 p. (This is the same book with a different title.)

    Detroit Public Library, Detroit, Mich.
    Oberlin College, Oberlin, O.

9. ———. New York: World Publishing House, 1875.

    Harvard University, Cambridge, Mass.
    Walsh College, Canton, O.
    Youngstown State University, Youngstown, Pa.

10. ———. New York: Chapman Publishing House, 1876.

    Cleveland Public Library
    Library of Congress

The Female Poets of Great Britain was edited by Frederic Rowton (1818–1854), a young Victorian gentleman involved in humanitarian causes and a "lecturer in general literature." His anthology, first published in 1848, contains selections of three centuries of poetry written by English women, as well as commentary on the poets and their literary works.

Marilyn L. Williamson is professor of English at Wayne State University and a former fellow of the Bunting Institute of Radcliffe College.

The manuscript was prepared for publication by Wendy Lyon Wienner. The book was designed by Mary Primeau. The typeface for the new text is VIP Caledonia, designed by W. A. Dwiggins about 1938.

The test is printed on 60 lb. S. D. Warren's 1854 Text and the book is bound in Holliston Mills' Kingston Finish cloth over binder's boards. Manufactured in the United States of America.